Raspberry Pi®
Projects

FOR DUMMIES®

A Wiley Brand

Raspberry Pi® Projects

FOR DUMMIES®

A Wiley Brand

by Mike Cook, Jonathan Evans,
and Brock Craft

Raspberry Pi® Projects For Dummies®

Published by: **John Wiley & Sons, Inc.,** 111 River Street, Hoboken, NJ 07030-5774, www.wiley.com

Copyright © 2015 by John Wiley & Sons, Inc., Hoboken, New Jersey

Published simultaneously in Canada

For general information on our other products and services, please contact our Customer Care Department within the U.S. at 877-762-2974, outside the U.S. at 317-572-3993, or fax 317-572-4002. For technical support, please visit www.wiley.com/techsupport.

Wiley publishes in a variety of print and electronic formats and by print-on-demand. Some material included with standard print versions of this book may not be included in e-books or in print-on-demand. If this book refers to media such as a CD or DVD that is not included in the version you purchased, you may download this material at http://booksupport.wiley.com. For more information about Wiley products, visit www.wiley.com.

Library of Congress Control Number: 2015942453

ISBN 978-1-118-76669-9 (pbk); ISBN 978-1-118-76672-9 (ebk); ISBN 978-1-118-76671-2 (ebk)

Manufactured in the United States of America

10 9 8 7 6 5 4 3 2 1

Contents at a Glance

Table of Contents

Introduction

●●

Raspberry Pi Projects For Dummies is designed for people who are looking
for something exciting to do with the Raspberry Pi. This book contains
projects to amaze and inspire you! It takes you into a world of switches,
lights, motors, home automation, and computer vision. It not only covers the
theory behind what you're doing, but also gives you examples of putting that
theory into practice, so you can learn to work on your own projects and not
just blindly follow a list of instructions.

Sure, we could just give you a list of steps to follow. But we believe that you
should try to understand what you're doing and why you're doing it, and
that's what this book is all about. With this book as a resource, we encourage
you to put your own stamp on projects, which is why many projects in this
book aren't just cut-and-dried lists of things to do, but suggestions about how
you can customize the projects and make them your own.

About This Book

The projects in this book all make use of the computer language Python 2.
This book shows you how to use a wide variety of input and output devices,
from a simple switch to a webcam. You can explore LEDs and multicolored
LEDs, learn about a keypad matrix and see how they can be integrated to
become part of your code so you can make these devices do what you want.
Reach out with your Raspberry Pi and become part of the cloud or build your
own web server. This book shows you how.

The Raspberry Pi can interface with other electronic devices, and in this
book we show you how to interact with LEGO's latest robotic MINDSTORMS
set, the EV3. You can send messages into the LEGO system or do your
own thing and control the MINDSTORMS peripherals directly from the
Raspberry Pi. Not only do we show you how these two systems interact, but
we also show you some projects you can make using the Raspberry Pi and
MINDSTORMS set together.

Linux is the staple operating system used in the Raspberry Pi world.
However, there is a major alternative operating system you can run for
just the price of another very small SD card, RISC OS. RISC OS is a mature,
well-honed operating system, designed from the ground up to run on ARM

chips, and as such, it's fast and compact. This book shows you how you can explore the RISC OS and gives you a glimpse of another world.

A few final notes about the book: Sidebars (text in gray boxes) and Technical Stuff paragraphs are skippable. Finally, within this book, you may note that some web addresses break across two lines of text. If you're reading this book in print and want to visit one of these web pages, simply key in the web address exactly as it's noted in the text, pretending as though the line break doesn't exist. If you're reading this as an e-book, you've got it easy — just click the web address to be taken directly to the web page.

Foolish Assumptions

In writing this book, we made a few assumptions about you:

- ✔ **You have a Raspberry Pi.** You could certainly read this book without a Raspberry Pi, but you won't get much out of it unless you have a Raspberry Pi to play with.

- ✔ **You have a computer other than the Raspberry Pi.** You need a computer to set up the Raspberry Pi. *Note:* We provide instructions on how to set up your Pi, but this information isn't the main thrust of the book. If you need more information on setting up your Raspberry Pi, a good companion book to this one is *Raspberry Pi For Dummies,* by Sean McManus and Mike Cook (Wiley), which covers in much more detail your first steps with this remarkable machine.

- ✔ **Your Raspberry Pi has some connection to the Internet.** It may not be connected all the time, but you're at least able to connect it for setting up the libraries you need to install.

- ✔ **You don't mind voyaging into less charted waters and you have an open mind on what constitutes computing and operating systems.**

- ✔ **You're eager to begin exploring the world of physical computing.** Physical computing takes a fresh look at inputs and outputs to a computer. The computer produces physical outputs — signals that make lights flash, sounds play, or robots move. Inputs are more than just typing — they include everything from simple push buttons to color sensors to webcams.

- ✔ **You have access to some basic hand tools, like a small saw and drill along with a soldering iron.** If you don't have these tools on hand, we assume you have the money to buy them — or you have a friend or family member whose toolkit you can raid!

- ✔ **You don't mind spending some money on the components you need to make your projects.** Most of these components aren't very expensive, but you'll need to buy them (and we recommend sources in this book).

Icons Used in This Book

In this book, we use a handful of *icons* (little pictures in the margins) to draw your attention to key pieces of information. Here's what those icons mean:

When we give you an especially useful bit of information — something that can make your life with the Raspberry Pi easier or help you do something faster — we mark it with the Tip icon.

You don't need to commit this book to memory — it's a resource for you to turn to whenever you need it. But every once in a while, we tell you something so important that you'll want to remember it. When we do, we mark it with the Remember icon.

What can we say? We're geeks. And as such, we sometimes get a little technical, telling you more than you really need to know to get the job done. When we veer into the technical, we mark that text with the Technical Stuff icon. If you're short on time, you can skip anything marked with this icon without missing anything critical to the task at hand.

You're bound to come across some pitfalls on your journey with the Raspberry Pi. We've walked this road before, so think of the Warning icon as orange cones in the road, helping you steer clear of those tire-destroying potholes or open manhole covers.

Beyond the Book

In addition to the material in the print or e-book you're reading right now, this product also comes with some access-anywhere goodies on the web. Check out the free Cheat Sheet at `www.dummies.com/cheatsheet/raspberrypiprojects` for information on connecting the Arduino and the Raspberry Pi, GPIO pin alternate functions, and powering other devices from the Raspberry Pi.

Also, at `www.dummies.com/extras/raspberrypiprojects`, you can find free bonus articles on topics like contact bounce and facial recognition.

Finally, throughout the book, we mention files that you can download from the book's companion website, `www.dummies.com/go/raspberrypiprojects`.

Where to Go from Here

If you're a beginner, you can't do better than starting at Chapter 1 and making sure you have your Raspberry Pi and your workspace set up. Even if you're experienced, it's worth reading the early chapters to pick up hints we've gathered from our extensive experience. If you're champing at the bit to start playing with your Pi, feel free to dive into the parts of the book that interest you most!

Part I

Getting Started with Raspberry Pi Projects

In this part . . .

- Learn about your Raspberry Pi.
- Set up the hardware and operating system and your project-building workspace.
- Learn construction techniques.
- Understand the basics of programming.
- Install language extensions.
- Discover the Raspberry Pi family of computers.

Chapter 1

Getting to Know the Raspberry Pi

*Y*ou probably wouldn't have picked up this book if you hadn't already heard about the amazing, low-cost computer for everyone, the Raspberry Pi. Besides being inexpensive, what's made the Raspberry Pi so appealing is that it's pretty easy to use. You can even change it to do things its designers never dreamed of. Unlike most consumer electronics, tablets, and desktop computers, the Raspberry Pi is designed to let you investigate how it works and change how it operates by writing your own software programs.

This is all possible because the Raspberry Pi uses an inexpensive but powerful processor and a free operating system, which is based upon the popular Linux platform. In this chapter, we take a look at what you need to get going and show you how to set it up.

We also tell you where to get a Raspberry Pi and the accessories you need to run it. We explain how to set up the operating system, how to connect the hardware, and what to do if you run into any problems along the way. Before long, you'll be able to make your Raspberry Pi say, "Hello, world!"

Getting a Raspberry Pi

If you're interested in building projects with a Raspberry Pi, you probably already have one. But if you don't yet have your own Raspberry Pi, this is the section for you! You'll be glad to know that there are a few places you can pick one up quickly and cheaply.

The Raspberry Pi comes in several versions: Model A is shown in Figure 1-1, and Model B is shown in Figure 1-2. There are other versions of the Raspberry Pi, though — Chapter 4 has a full rundown. The Model A and Model B use the same kind of processor, but the Model A is cheaper and uses less power; it has a single USB port and connections for your screen and audio. Model B has everything Model A has, plus an additional USB port and an Ethernet port for connecting to a network, so it costs a little more. For the projects in this book, you'll want to get a Model B.

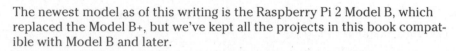

The newest model as of this writing is the Raspberry Pi 2 Model B, which replaced the Model B+, but we've kept all the projects in this book compatible with Model B and later.

The Raspberry Pi Foundation (which is technically a UK charity, not a business) created the Raspberry Pi. The Raspberry Pi Foundation licenses the manufacture of the Raspberry Pi to the biggest names in electronics in the UK, RS Components (www.rs-components.com) and Farnell, which supports Raspberry Pi under the brand name element14 (www.element14.com/community/community/raspberry-pi). If you're buying a Raspberry Pi for personal or home use, Farnell's outlet is CPC (order from http://cpc.farnell.com). In the United States, you can also buy

Figure 1-1:
Raspberry
Pi Model A.

Photograph courtesy of the Raspberry Pi Foundation

Figure 1-2:
Raspberry
Pi Model B.

from Newark (www.newark.com), which is a part of Farnell, and Adafruit (www.adafruit.com). These suppliers can provide you with everything you need to get your Raspberry Pi up and going, but you can only buy from them online.

If you simply can't wait to get your hands on a Raspberry Pi, and you live in the UK, you can also walk in to any Maplin electronics shop, where they're usually kept in stock. You'll pay a bit more for the convenience of shopping in a store, but you can get personal advice from the salespeople, which can be pretty useful if you have questions. At the time of this writing, you can walk into a Radio Shack in the United States and buy a Raspberry Pi starter kit, but this may change because the company is restructuring.

You can also find the Raspberry Pi for sale on eBay. There are usually plenty of listings for just a Raspberry Pi or for bundles that include all the accessories you need in order to hook it up.

If you decide to buy a Raspberry Pi on eBay, be sure to purchase from a reputable seller with plenty of good feedback. There are knock-offs out there, and they can't be guaranteed to be manufactured to the same standards as the real thing. We tend to think the cost savings isn't worth the risk of buying from eBay.

Discovering What You Can and Can't Do with a Raspberry Pi

This book shows you how to get going with Raspberry Pi projects. After you've done some, you'll have a pretty good idea of what's possible. But when you want to go a bit further with your ideas, it's good to know what you can realistically expect to achieve.

The first thing you see when you get up and running is a text-based prompt on the screen. You can do a lot of things just with text, but most people prefer to launch the familiar graphical user interface (GUI), the desktop environment you're used to on any other computer. The operating system supports all the things you'd want to do in a desktop system, including playing games, browsing the web, word processing, using spreadsheets, editing photos, and playing audio and video.

But that's not where the Raspberry Pi really shines. The great things you can do with the Pi come into play when you write your own programs and hook it up to electronics or other objects in the real world using the general-purpose input/output (GPIO) connector. Your Pi is well suited for this because these kinds of things don't usually require the beefy processor in your desktop or laptop. Using your Pi for things you may not do with your usual computer is what makes it really fun — and that's what this book is all about!

The Raspberry Pi uses a Broadcom BCM2835 central processing unit (CPU) and a VideoCore IV graphics processing unit (GPU) and shares the onboard memory between them. Either 256MB or 512MB of onboard memory is available. The CPU is an impressive piece of technology that enables fairly complex computing power at an extremely low price. The trade-off is that the Pi is not nearly as powerful as the full-fledged CPU in desktop and laptop computers — it's a bit slower, roughly comparable to the capabilities of mainstream computers in the '90s. You shouldn't plan to do high-performance computing or run heavily graphics-intensive applications like gams or 3D modeling software — the Pi will run these, but they may be unusably slow.

You probably won't be replacing your main computer with a Pi, but you can do a lot of experimentation with it that you may not try with your desktop or laptop, and you can easily connect your Raspberry Pi to sensors and motors in the real world, which we show you how to do in the projects in this book. And if you make any big mistakes that damage your Pi, it doesn't cost a lot to get another one and start experimenting again!

Getting Familiar with Your Raspberry Pi

The Raspberry Pi is about the size of a credit card and has all the components that you need onboard so that you can connect it to a TV or display and start using it. These connections are shown in Figure 1-3.

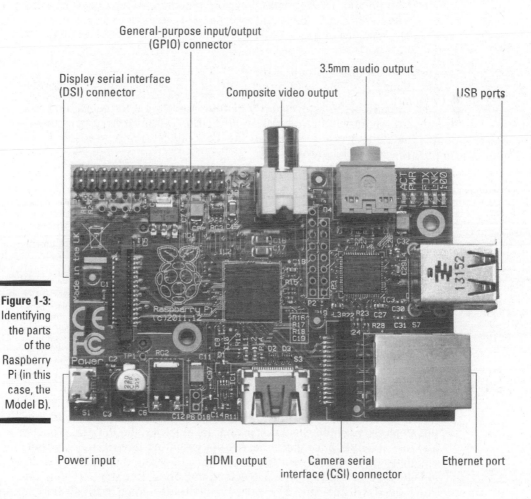

General-purpose input/output (GPIO) connector

Display serial interface (DSI) connector

3.5mm audio output

Composite video output

USB ports

Figure 1-3: Identifying the parts of the Raspberry Pi (in this case, the Model B).

Power input

HDMI output

Camera serial interface (CSI) connector

Ethernet port

Going clockwise around the board from the top left, you'll find the following connections:

✒ **General-purpose input/output (GPIO) connector:** This is a port for getting electrical signals into and out of your Raspberry Pi, such as for reading sensors and controlling motors. It's composed of two parallel rows of pins and is labeled P1 (for "Plug 1"). Different models of Raspberry Pi use these pins slightly differently due to the way the pins are routed on the board.

- ✔ **Composite video output:** This jack is used for connecting your Raspberry Pi to a composite video (standard TV) connection using an RCA cable.

- ✔ **Audio output:** This is a black 3.5mm jack on the upper right of the board.

- ✔ **USB port(s):** These ports allow you to connect USB accessories (such as a keyboard and mouse and external storage devices) to your board. The Model A has only one USB port to reduce costs. The Model B has two USB ports.

- ✔ **Ethernet port (Model B only):** This port is for connecting your Raspberry Pi to an Ethernet network and for accessing the Internet.

- ✔ **Camera serial interface (CSI) connector:** This slim black connector between the Ethernet jack and the HDMI output is for connecting a small camera such as a webcam. CSI connectors are available from the Raspberry Pi store.

- ✔ **HDMI output:** This port is used for sending digital video to a computer monitor. The HDMI output also can route your audio, so you may not need to use the audio output port.

- ✔ **Power input:** On the lower-left side is the micro USB power socket. The power is provided via a micro USB power supply that plugs into this port.

- ✔ **Display serial interface (DSI) connector:** In the middle of the left side of the board is a slim connector for connecting high-speed displays. It's used for connecting a small LCD panel directly to your Raspberry Pi. You can use it for touch-based input as well!

Selecting Your Accessories

You probably have some of the important accessories lying around the house already, which was exactly what its creators had in mind. You can just use old stuff that's gathering dust — you don't have to buy anything, which keeps the cost down. You don't have to get all the accessories shown in Figure 1-4 to complete the projects in this book. But at a bare minimum, you'll need a display and a keyboard to get things going. Here's what you see in Figure 1-4:

- ✔ **Monitor:** The Raspberry Pi's onboard HDMI output allows you to connect a high-definition feed to just about any modern computer display. If your display has an HDMI input, all you need is a cable between the two.

  If your monitor doesn't have an HDMI input, it probably supports DVI, which has a larger, wider connector. You can buy adapters that convert

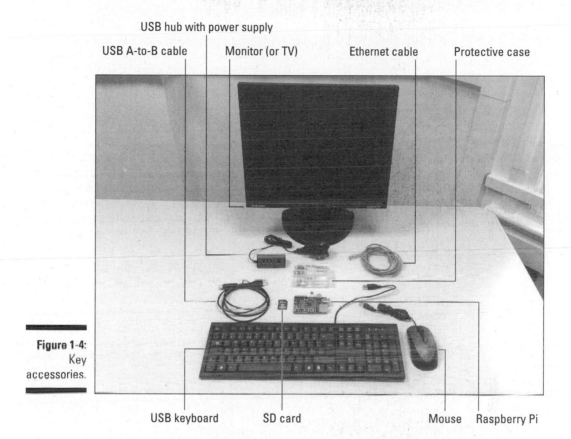

USB hub with power supply

USB A-to-B cable Monitor (or TV) Ethernet cable Protective case

Figure 1-4:
Key
accessories.

USB keyboard SD card Mouse Raspberry Pi

from HDMI to DVI that will allow you to use your DVI monitor. You can also use a VGA monitor (the VGA input contains three rows of holes), though these aren't officially supported. If you want to use VGA, make sure to get an adapter that is specifically meant to work with a Raspberry Pi.

If you don't want to use a computer display and you have an old TV, you can use it as a display. Your Raspberry Pi has an RCA connection, which allows you to use a composite video signal to a TV with a composite video input. The picture won't be as sharp as with a display, and text can be hard to read, so we recommend using a monitor if you can.

✔ **Ethernet cable:** Some of the projects in this book require connecting your Raspberry Pi to a network. For these projects, you'll need an Ethernet cable.

✔ **Case:** You can use your Raspberry Pi as is, right out of the box. It's pretty durable, but accidents happen, so lots of people have fun making cool cases to protect the circuit board from spills and dust. Some cases are even enhanced with glowing LEDs. The designer of the Raspberry Pi logo, Paul Beech, has designed some cool cases — check out `http://shop.pimoroni.com` to find them.

- **Mouse:** Any USB mouse will work fine. The Model A only has one USB port, so if you're using a Model A, you'll need to use a USB hub so that you can plug in both your mouse and your keyboard. You can also plug your mouse into your keyboard, if the keyboard has an extra USB port on it.

- **Keyboard:** There is a USB port on the Raspberry Pi circuit board, so you can plug in a USB keyboard. If you have an older keyboard with a round (PS/2) connector, you can use it, but you'll need a small adapter plug to convert between PS/2 and USB.

- **SD card:** Your Raspberry Pi doesn't have a hard drive, so you'll need to use some kind of external storage. An onboard SD card slot is provided for this purpose. When you plug in an SD card, your Raspberry Pi treats it just like a hard drive. SD cards are pretty cheap, so go for one with at least 8GB or 16GB of storage. SD cards have class numbers to indicate how fast they can read and write data. We recommend you get a Class 6 SD card or better.

- **USB hub:** If you're using a Model A Raspberry Pi, you may need a USB hub to connect your keyboard and mouse (see the preceding bullet). If you're using a Model B, you don't need a USB hub, but you'll probably want extra USB inputs into your Pi, because your keyboard and mouse will take up the two USB ports. Make sure to get a USB hub that has its own power source — the Raspberry Pi can provide only limited power output via USB.

- **USB memory stick (not shown):** Memory sticks (also called *memory keys* or *flash drives*) can provide a great deal of extra storage that is fast and reliable. They're also handy for moving files from another computer or laptop to your Raspberry Pi.

- **SD card writer (not shown):** The Linux operating system for your Raspberry Pi is stored on an SD card. You can buy SD cards with the operating system already loaded, but you'll probably want to write your own at some point, so you need to make sure your computer has an SD card slot. Most desktops and laptops have one these days, but if yours doesn't, you should get an SD card writer. It plugs into your USB port and allows your computer to see what's on the card and write files to it.

- **Speakers (not shown):** Your Raspberry Pi has a 3.5mm audio jack so you can plug in headphones or external speakers. If you're using the HDMI connection and HDMI monitor as a display, the audio is sent over that cable to your screen.

- **Micro USB power supply (not shown):** Your Raspberry Pi gets its power via the micro USB connector on the side. You can use just about any power charger that fits this port, but it needs to supply 700 milliamperes (mA) of current (check the specifications printed on the side of the charger). Most good mobile phone chargers will work fine, as long as they supply 5V 700mA (3.5 watts). We recommend a Raspberry Pi–compatible power adapter, which should be available from the supplier of your Raspberry Pi.

Setting Up Your Operating System

To do anything useful with your Raspberry Pi, you need to have an operating system. The operating system provides the basic functions like the GUI, which most people know as the "desktop environment." It also supports reading and writing files, runs general-purpose applications like your word processor and web browser, and runs the programs you write for your Raspberry Pi projects. Your Raspberry Pi uses the Linux operating system to do this.

Your operating system is stored on an SD card, not on a hard drive like most computers. When you turn on your Raspberry Pi, it reads the operating system that's on the SD card. If your card isn't inserted, the Raspberry Pi won't be able to start up, so you need to get the operating system onto an SD card before you can do anything else.

Selecting your Linux distribution

Because it's an open project, many different versions of Linux are out there in the wild. These are referred to as Linux *distributions* (or *distros*), and you can download them for free. The different distributions are specialized for a variety of purposes. Some are made to be as bare bones as possible; others are optimized for performance.

The Raspberry Pi Foundation has endorsed a special distribution for beginners called Raspbian Wheezy, which is a version of the Debian Linux distribution. It includes a GUI called the Lightweight X11 Desktop Environment (LXDE). It also supports the programming languages that you use to write code for the projects in this book. Most of the projects use a scripting language called Python; some use a programming language called C. We assume you're using Raspbian Wheezy for the projects in this book. (*Tip:* Your operating system is on your SD card, so if you ever want to use something other than Wheezy, you can load it onto an SD card and pop it into the SD card slot.)

You need to download Raspbian Wheezy so you can copy it to your card. The best place to get it is from the Raspberry Pi website at www.raspberrypi.org/downloads. Click the Download ZIP button next to Raspbian Debian Wheezy and save the file on your system in a place that you can easily find it. After you download Wheezy, you'll need to unzip the compressed file by clicking it. (*Note:* If you have a Mac, you don't need to unzip the file before you create the SD card. Just follow the instructions for Mac later in this chapter.)

There is also a download file called NOOBS (which stands for "new out of the box software") on the Raspberry Pi website, which you can use to automate the process of creating an SD card. It's designed to be really easy to use. You just download NOOBS, unzip it, and put it on your SD card. NOOBS then manages the setup of your Raspberry Pi automatically. Even though NOOBS is supposed to be easy, problems sometimes occur, requiring you to get another program to format your SD card. We think it's simpler just to download the Raspbian Debian Wheezy and create your SD card yourself in a few easy steps.

Linux is a free operating system, unlike the ones used on Windows and Mac. It's an open-source project, which means anyone can contribute to it — and thousands of people do. The Linux Foundation (www.linuxfoundation. org) coordinates these efforts and manages the standard Linux *kernel* (the core code that makes it work). All you have to do is download a copy of the operating system (see the nearby sidebar) and put it on your SD card.

You also can buy premade SD cards that already have the operating system written onto them. With one of these cards, all you have to do is insert your card and power up your Raspberry Pi. You can buy them from RS, element14, Amazon, eBay, or other online outlets. If you already have one, skip to the section on setting up your hardware, later in this chapter.

Flashing Your SD Card

Your operating system is made up of a bunch of files that are run from the SD card itself. However, when you write the operating system's files to the SD card, they're written in a special format that Linux can read. You can't just copy them over as you would with other kinds of files. The Linux distribution you downloaded is in a special format called a *disk image*. And you *flash* the disk image to the SD card using a special little program. The program you need depends on whether you're using Windows, Mac, or Linux.

Flashing an SD card in Windows

To create the image file in Windows, you use a special program called Image Writer for Windows. It's free and pretty easy to use. Just follow these steps:

1. **Insert your SD card into your computer's SD card slot or, if you don't have one, into your SD card reader.**

   Take note of which drive letter is assigned to your SD card.

2. **Download the files at www.sourceforge.net/projects/win32 diskimager/files/latest/download.**

   If you want more information about Image Writer for Windows, go to www.launchpad.net/win32-image-writer.

3. **Double-click the file to extract it, click Extract All Files to unzip the archive into a folder, and then open the folder.**

   Note: If the filename of the file you downloaded ends with .exe, when you double-click the file, an installation wizard may run.

   You should see the list of extracted files. Make sure that you aren't looking at the zipped files.

4. Click the file `Win32DiskImager.exe` to open it.

5. Click the folder icon to the right of the long white box and navigate to the Linux `.img` file you just unzipped; double-click to select it.

   This will put the file path into the long white box for you.

6. From the Device menu, select the drive letter that your SD card has been assigned.

   Be absolutely sure you've got the correct drive selected — the one that contains your SD card. Whatever drive you've chosen in the device menu will be completely erased!

7. After you've double-checked that you've selected the right drive, click the Write button to create the image file on your SD card.

Flashing an SD card on a Mac

On a Mac, you can use a simple script called RasPiWrite to do the work of flashing your image file to your SD card. First, you create a folder that RasPiWrite can use while it's flashing your SD card. Then you use the script to create your image file. You do some of this by typing commands on the command line, using the Terminal program, which is found in your `Applications/Utilities` folder.

You need your system password to be able to flash the SD card. Just follow these steps:

1. In your `Documents` folder, create a folder called `SD Card Prep`; in the `SD Card Prep` folder, create a folder called `RasPiWrite`.

2. Go to `https://github.com/exaviorn/RasPiWrite` to download the zip file of RasPiWrite.

3. Double-click the file you downloaded and open the resulting folder.

4. Drag the files in this folder to the `RasPiWrite` folder you created in Step 1.

5. Drag the zip file of your Linux distribution into your `RasPiWrite` folder.

6. Open the Terminal application, located in `Applications/Utilities`, and type `cd` and then a space.

7. Use the Finder to locate the `SD Card Prep` folder you created in Step 1; make sure you can see both the Finder window and the Terminal window, and then drag the RasPiWrite folder into the Terminal window.

   This places that path name of that folder into the command line for you. (It's easier than typing it all out.)

8. **Press Return.**

   This switches you to the folder containing RasPiWrite.

9. **Type** ls **and press Return.**

   The list command produces a list of files in the RasPiWrite folder. You use it later to tell RasPiWrite where to get the source files for your disk image.

10. **Remove any external memory cards, USB sticks, or other pluggable storage device from your system so that you don't accidentally erase them.**

11. **Type** sudo python raspiwrite.py **to run RasPiWrite.**

12. **Enter your system password.**

    You see a progress report as your script creates the disk image. If all goes well, you should see a raspberry made of text characters.

13. **Insert your SD card into your Mac's SD card slot or to an external SD card writer and press Return.**

14. **Follow the prompts to select the disk that corresponds to your SD card.**

    You can double-check to make sure you've selected the correct one by ensuring that the disk's size (listed in the size column) corresponds to the size of your SD card. You don't want to erase all the data on your main hard drive!

15. **You'll be asked if you want to download a distribution; because you already did that, type** N.

    The program asks you to locate the disk image file.

16. **Scroll back up to where you used the** ls **command and copy the file-name of the distribution; then scroll back down and paste this file-name at the prompt and press Return.**

    The program extracts the image file and prepares it to upload onto your SD card. It then asks you to confirm that you're about to erase your SD card. Be sure you've got the right SD card.

17. **Type accept to continue installing the image, and press Return.**

The flash process can take a long time. You'll see some dots on your screen as the process continues. Depending on your system, it can take 30 minutes or even up to an hour. You can use your computer for other things during this process, but if you lose power or restart, you'll have to start all over again.

If you're presented with a message immediately after typing **accept**, there's a problem. Even though the message may say `Transfer Complete`, the immediate response means that the transfer hasn't been accomplished. This sometimes happens if the image file isn't located where you indicated it was or if the distribution contains just an image file rather than an image file within a folder of the same name. If it happens, create a folder with the same name as the image file, drag the image file into it, and try again.

Flashing an SD card in Linux

If you're using Linux, the process of flashing an SD card for your Raspberry Pi is pretty straightforward. We assume you're using Ubuntu, one of the most popular Linux distributions. If you're using another distribution, the following steps will be very similar.

When you download the Raspbian Wheezy distribution, make sure you save it where you can find it, such as in the `Documents` directory. Then follow these steps to flash your SD card.

1. **Remove any external drives, USB keys, or other SD cards from your system and insert the SD card you would like to flash for your Raspberry Pi.**

2. **Open a Terminal window.**

   This is located in the Applications menu under Accessories.

3. **Type** sudo fdisk –l **(the last character of this command is the letter l, not the number 1).**

   This starts the fixed disk program, a tool you can use to manage, erase, and separate disk drives into different logical partitions. It also shows you which drives are available on your system.

4. **Locate your SD card in the device list.**

   The list gives details about each of the drives on your system, including the size of each device in bytes and other details such as the number of heads, sectors, cylinders, and so on. Find the device that most closely matches the size of your SD card in bytes. For example, an 8GB SD card will be listed as about 8,068MB. Take note of the name of that disk's directory. For example, on our system, the SD card is located in the directory: `/dev/sdg`.

5. **Use the** cd **command ("change directory") to navigate to the directory where you saved your Raspbian Wheezy distribution.**

   For example, if it's in the `Documents` directory, type **cd Documents** and press Enter.

6. **Display the name of your Raspbian Wheezy image file by typing** ls *.img.

7. **To write the Raspbian Wheezy image to the SD card, use the dd command.**

   Here's what we would type on our system:

   ```
   sudo dd if=mydistribution.img of=/dev/sdc bs=2M
   ```

   You need to substitute the name of your distribution file where it says mydistribution.img. Substitute the directory where your SD card is located where it says /dev/sdc.

   The sudo command stands for "super user do" and tells Linux that you're issuing the dd command as the administrator of the system. The operating system assumes you know exactly what you're doing, and there are no protections for making any grave mistakes. The dd command is short for "data description," but some people have joked that it stands for "destroy disk" or "delete data," because if you aren't careful, it can erase your system's hard drive. When these two commands are combined, you can imagine the consequences of making a mistake. So, be sure you've typed everything precisely!

8. **Press Enter to start flashing the image file your SD card.**

   It should take about two or three minutes to do this operation. You won't see a progress update, but you may see the light next to your SD card slot flickering. When it's finished, you'll be advised how much data was copied and how long the operation took to complete. Pat yourself on the back. You're ready to fire up your Raspberry Pi!

Connecting Your Hardware

When you've got the essential accessories and the operating system, you can set up your hardware. This is simply a matter of connecting the right bits together. Figure 1-5 shows you how things are connected using a Raspberry Pi Model B.

Follow these steps to set up your hardware:

1. **Locate the SD card slot on the bottom of your Raspberry Pi and insert the newly flashed SD card snugly, with the label facing down.**

   The card will stick out from the side of the circuit board a little bit.

2. **Connect your computer monitor or TV to your Raspberry Pi.**

   If you're using a monitor or TV with an HDMI connection, just connect the two with an HDMI cable. If your monitor has a DVI connection instead, insert the HDMI cable into an HDMI-to-DVI adapter and then plug it into your monitor. If you're using a TV without an HDMI connection, connect a yellow RCA connector cable to the round RCA jack on the top of your Raspberry Pi and plug the other end into your TV's composite video input.

You may need to manually select which input your monitor or TV is using. Check the manual if you aren't sure how to do this. Also, make sure the power to your display is switched on.

3. **Connect your USB hub into one of the two USB sockets on the right side of your Raspberry Pi.**

   If you're using a Raspberry Pi Model A, there will be only one socket. Your hub should have a power adapter — plug it into an electrical socket.

4. **Plug your keyboard and mouse into the USB hub.**

   If you're using a keyboard or a mouse with an older PS/2-style connector, you'll need a PS/2-to-USB adapter. You can also connect them directly to your Raspberry Pi's remaining USB socket, but it's a good idea to use the hub, which has more available power.

To USB hub power adapter   To mouse

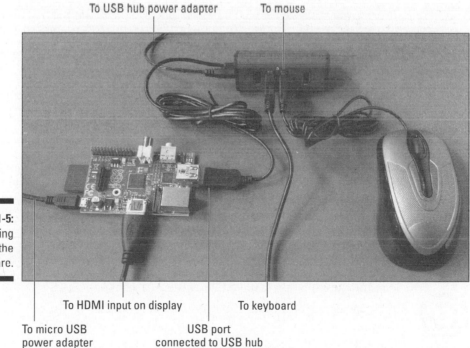

Figure 1-5:
Hooking
up all the
hardware.

To HDMI input on display   To keyboard

To micro USB   USB port
power adapter   connected to USB hub

5. **Connect your audio.**

   If you're using an HDMI monitor with audio, the audio will go through your HDMI cable. If you're using external speakers or a TV, your audio output is the black 3.5mm socket on the top-right edge of your Raspberry Pi. Connect your speaker cable there.

6. **Connect to your network.**

   If you're using a Model A, you can skip this step. There is no network connection available for it.

   If you're using a Model B, connect an Ethernet cable to your Ethernet socket on the right side of the board. When your operating systems starts up, it will automatically connect to your home router, as long as it supports Dynamic Host Configuration Protocol (DHCP). (Most home routers do.) If you have trouble connecting to the network, see your Internet service provider's instructions for setting up new devices using DHCP on your home router. In rare cases, DHCP may be switched off.

7. **Connect your micro USB power supply to your power socket on the bottom-left corner of your board.**

   Some power supplies have standard-size USB ports. You connect a USB–to–micro USB adapter cable from the standard USB output on these power adaptors to the micro USB input on your Raspberry Pi. There is no power switch. To cycle the power, you remove the adapter plug and put it back in, which is a little awkward. If you have an extension lead with a switch, you can connect your power adapter and use the switch on the lead to cycle to turn the power on and off more easily.

   Don't connect your Raspberry Pi to your computer's USB port via a USB–to–micro USB adapter cable. Your computer's USB port isn't designed to deliver enough power for your Raspberry Pi, via the USB port.

When you power up your Raspberry Pi you should briefly see a rainbow-colored screen, which confirms that the hardware itself is working. Then the Linux operating system on your SD card will start to run and you'll see an avalanche of text on your screen as all the various parts of the system are started. It can be pretty fun to watch. This will take a little time to complete. When it's finished, you'll be able to move on to setting up the system in the next section.

You'll also see a little status light on the board next to the audio jack. The PWR light should be on. When your Raspberry Pi accesses the SD card to load the operating system, you'll see the ACT light activated.

If you're using an earlier Revision 1.0 board, the ACT light is labeled OK.

The FDX light indicates that you have a good Ethernet connection. The LNK light will flash whenever there is network traffic on the wire. The 100 light indicates a high-speed (100 Mbit) Ethernet connection.

Setting Up with Raspi-config

Raspi-config is a little program that automatically loads to help you to get your Raspberry Pi ready to run, the first time you start up. It gives you a list of the basic system options in case you want to change them. After it's set up the first time, it won't run again unless you launch it manually. You use the keyboard arrows to move up and down the menu of options and the left and right arrows to select options. Pressing Enter confirms your selection.

The options in the menu change from time to time. You may encounter an older version of the software with different menu items, but here's a rundown of what they are and what they do (as of this writing):

- **Expand Filesystem:** When you flash your SD card with your operating system, it makes an exact copy (an "image") of the Linux distribution files, and the formatting of the disk itself is likely to be smaller than the actual available space on your card. The image files don't take up much space, and if you have a large SD card, it will look like your SD card has much less capacity than it actually does.

  To overcome this problem, it's very important to use this option to expand your root file system to use all the available space on the card. Otherwise, you could run out of room! When you press Enter with this option, it runs immediately. The next time you start your Raspberry Pi, the command will resize your file system to use all the available room. This can take a few minutes; the screen won't respond until it's done. After it's finished, all the space will be available to you.

- **Change User Password:** Lets you set the password for the default user of your Raspberry Pi, which is the user *pi*. You don't need to change this. If you do, make sure not to forget it because there's no way to get it back from the system!

- **Enable Boot to Desktop/Scratch:** You can use this option to make your Raspberry Pi go straight into the graphical operating system at startup. Otherwise, you have to start it manually (see the next section).

- **Internationalization Options:** This option takes you to a submenu where you can configure several options depending on where you're located:

  - *Change locale:* Allows you to change your language and character set. Leave this option alone if you want to use your Raspberry Pi in English.

  - *Change timezone:* Tells your Raspberry Pi where you're located. Afterward, it detects the time from your Internet connection.

- *Configure_keyboard:* Allows you to select your keyboard model and layout. When you press Enter, a long list of keyboards will be displayed. If nothing seems to be happening, be patient. It can take a few seconds for the list of keyboards to show up. Choose the one you want to use and then select the keyboard layout you want to use (for example, UK).

✓ **Enable Camera:** If you've purchased an optional Camera Module, this menu allows you to set it up to work with your Raspberry Pi.

✓ **Add to Rastrack:** Racktrack allows you to add your Raspberry Pi to the global map of users around the world. You can see all the other tracked Raspberry Pis on their website at `http://rastrack.co.uk`.

✓ **Overclock:** *Overclocking* is a way of speeding up the CPU to perform calculations faster than the manufacturer intended. The clock speed is the heartbeat that determines how many instructions your CPU processes per second. Manufacturers build in a bit of leeway to ensure that they can guarantee the speed that your CPU is rated to. If you overclock your CPU, your Raspberry Pi will run faster, but its lifespan may be reduced, and it's likely to run a bit hotter. If you change this setting and your Raspberry Pi no longer works, hold down the Shift key when you power up to return your Raspberry Pi to disable overclocking.

✓ **Advanced Options:** Advanced Options contains several settings that are a bit more involved, so we don't use them in this book. But they are good to know. The options are as follows:

- *Overscan:* Allows you to ensure that the picture is centered on your monitor and uses the available room correctly. If you have a black border around your image that you don't want, disable this option. Otherwise, you can leave it alone.

- *Hostname:* Allows you to set the name of your Raspberry Pi network. You probably won't need to modify this.

- *Memory Split:* Your onboard memory is shared between the CPU and the GPU. Depending on what you're doing with your Raspberry Pi, your programs may use one or the other more intensively. For example graphics and gaming programs make more intensive demands on the GPU, so you can increase your Raspberry Pi's performance by giving more memory to the GPU. Raspbian Wheezy uses 64MB to the GPU by default, and for most purposes this will be fine. You can experiment with this setting to see what setting works best for you.

- *SSH:* Secure Shell (SSH) is a secure way of communicating between computers using an encrypted connection, so that you can control one computer from another one. Unless you're familiar with this feature, you can ignore this option.

- *I2C:* A communication protocol used by some external devices and sensors. This option allows you to enable or disable the I2C module so you can use these devices.

- *Serial:* Allows you to enable or disable messages from the system on the serial interface. You most likely won't need to change this unless you're doing some kind of debugging.

- *Audio:* Allows you to select whether audio is sent via the onboard 3.5mm audio jack or via the HDMI port. It's set to auto by default, which means your audio will be routed via HDMI only when an HDMI screen is connected.

- *Update:* From time to time, you may have to update Raspi-config. You'll need an Internet connection to do this, but if you're using a recently download distribution, you should be up to date.

 ✔ **About raspi-config:** This just describes what the Raspi-config tool does.

When you're finished making your selections, press the right arrow key twice to get to the Finish option and press Enter. You may have to reboot your Raspberry Pi, depending on the options you've selected.

If you want to use Raspi-config later, you can start it by typing **sudo raspi-config**.

Starting Up the Desktop Environment

When you've finished configuring your Raspberry Pi with Raspi-config, you're ready to start up. After you switch on your power, you may have to enter your username and password, depending on your settings. For Raspbian Wheezy, the username is pi and the password is raspberry. Make sure you type these in lowercase.

After you log in, you'll see the command prompt:

```
pi@raspberrypi ~ $
```

This means you're up and running and you've logged into the operating system. Give yourself a cheer!

It doesn't like the graphical operating system you're used to with a desktop computer, but the command line is the direct connection to your Raspberry Pi's capabilities. You can execute all the main system commands and even do programming using only the command line interface. In a sense, the graphical environment is just a way of prettying up the command line and make it easier to use.

To get pretty, you launch the GUI, LXDE, by entering its startup command on the command line. To fire it up, type **startx**. It will take a moment or two to start up, and the screen will go blank for a bit. After startup, you should see the LXDE and a lovely red raspberry logo on the desktop wallpaper, as shown in Figure 1-6.

Figure 1-6: Starting up the desktop environment.

When you've got the desktop working, you can move on to learning about the programming tools in Chapter 3 or dive straight into the projects, if you're familiar with programming.

We recommend you peruse through Chapter 2 to make sure your workbench is set up for building the projects in this book. You'll need a few tools to get going on many of them, and it's a good idea to set up your workspace before you begin.

Troubleshooting Your Raspberry Pi

Things don't always go according to plan. Here are some common problems and how you can try to solve them:

- ✔ **No lights on your Raspberry Pi:** This can happen if you forgot to connect the micro USB power connector or if the power supply isn't capable of supplying your Raspberry Pi with enough power. Check that it's rated to at least 5V 700mA (3.5 watts).

- ✔ **Only the red light comes on:** Your Raspberry Pi has power, but it can't read the operating system on your SD card. First, make sure your SD card is firmly inserted. Then check that you've correctly created the disk image. If that doesn't work, you can try testing your SD card on another Raspberry Pi to see if you get the same problem. If all else fails, try using a pre-imaged SD card.

- ✔ **No output on the monitor:** Check your monitor connection and your monitor's power connection. Make sure that your monitor is turned on. (Sounds silly, but we've all done this at least once!) Then check that your monitor is using the correct input source. Use a button on the front of the monitor to cycle through them or use the monitor's remote control.

- ✔ **Inconsistent behavior or hang-ups:** Your Raspberry Pi uses power at different amounts depending on what it's doing. Make sure you have a good power supply and that it isn't overtaxed.

If you have a lot of peripherals connected to your Raspberry Pi, they may be demanding power as well. If your power supply is right at the limit of its capabilities and your processor needs extra power for computing-intensive tasks, it could exceed what's available and cause your Raspberry Pi to hang. This is particularly common if you try to power your Raspberry Pi from a USB socket.

If these tips don't fix the problems you're experiencing, your next port of call should be the user forums at the Raspberry Pi Foundation (www. raspberrypi.org/forums). The user community there is extremely knowledgeable and very helpful, particularly for beginners. Your problem may already have been solved in the discussions there. If not, post your problem, describing exactly the trouble you're having. More often than not, you'll get an answer within a few hours. Making it easy to experiment with your Raspberry Pi is what the user community is all about!

Chapter 2

Setting Up Your Tools and Workbench

. . . .

In This Chapter

▶ Setting up a project-building workspace

▶ Choosing the right tools for the job

▶ Selecting your accessories

▶ Using breadboards and soldering

▶ Finding out about Raspberry Pi LEGO projects

. . . .

The first thing you need to do to get started with Raspberry Pi projects is to get your workspace ready. You need a dedicated work area and the right tools so that you can build the projects quickly and easily. In this chapter, we explain how to create a good workspace with the right set of tools for the projects in this book.

The project chapters assume that you have the basic workspace and tools ready to go. After you dive into a project, it can be a drag to interrupt your work to get some basic tool that you've overlooked. But if you have most (or all) of the basics of your workspace covered, you won't have to stop what you're doing to go get a hand tool or run to the hardware store.

Getting Ready to Build Your Projects

You can start working on Raspberry Pi projects almost anywhere, but it's best to have a dedicated spot in which to build them. Completing the projects will take some time, so you want to choose a place where you can work comfortably and see what you're doing. Generally, setting up and taking down unfinished projects is a hassle — it takes more time and can introduce errors if your connections come loose. You can avoid this problem by setting aside a dedicated workspace.

Setting up your workspace

You need a dedicated area where you can build and test your projects — especially the advanced ones in this book, which can take a few hours or more. You have to connect all the components together, provide power, keep the cables and connection wires organized, and do some light fabrication. So, find a spot in your house, apartment, shed, garage, studio, or wherever, where you and your work will be undisturbed and where you can make a bit of a mess. The workspace in Figure 2-1 has all these things covered.

You don't want to get interrupted by distractions hunting for parts, or not having the right tools, so it's important to get the work area ready. In our experience, a good Raspberry Pi workspace has the following:

- ✔ A solid workbench or desk
- ✔ A comfortable chair
- ✔ Dry air and good ventilation (especially for evacuating soldering fumes)

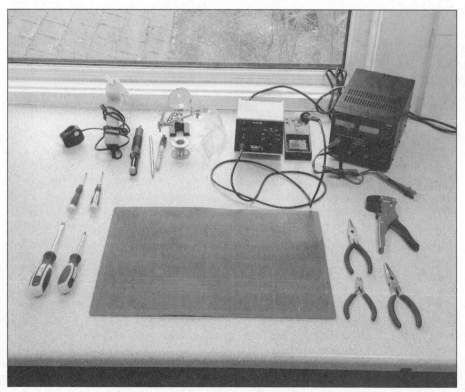

Figure 2-1:
A good
working
environment
and some
basic tools.

✔ Plenty of power outlets, ideally at desk height

✔ Enough room for the screen, keyboard, and mouse, and some extra workbench space for assembly and fabrication

✔ A nearby network connection or Wi-Fi router

✔ Shelving and storage for projects you're working on

✔ Small boxes and drawers for organizing parts and tools

The environment needs to be comfortable to work in for a long stretch. If it's too cold or too hot, too noisy, or filled with distractions, it'll take you longer to complete the work. Make yourself a sort of hideaway where you can stay focused.

Your Raspberry Pi is a fine computer in its own right, but an extra computer is sometimes useful during the project-building process, so it's good to have room for a desktop or laptop computer on the workbench. Plus, you'll want to be able to hunt for references online, look up datasheets, and post questions to forums, so a reliable Internet connection is vital.

Keeping an eye on safety

A few of the projects in this book deal with low-voltage electronics. Safety is always a factor when working with electrical circuits. None of these projects works with wall power, but you should always treat electronic projects as if they could have potentially dangerous voltages. If children may roam around your work area, take special precautions to keep them away. Little kids love pulling on cords and cables and could easily drag everything off your desk with one quick tug. A hot soldering iron left unattended could cause severe burns, besides being a fire hazard.

It's probably best to keep food and drink separate from your workbench. Empty pizza boxes or soda cans may hide critical parts, and you can waste time hunting for things. Accidentally spilled drinks don't do good things for live circuits.

Assembling Your Tools

You need some basic tools to build several of the projects in this book. The tools basically fall into two categories: electronics tools and physical building and fabrication tools. You can get most or all of these components from electronics retailers such as Radio Shack (in the United States) or Maplin (in the

UK). Specialty electronics suppliers on the Internet also stock them and are often cheaper, so hunt around at places like Farnell (www.farnell.com), Newark (www.newark.com), Rapid Electronics (www.rapidonline.com), and RS (www.rs-components.com). Sometimes you can find good deals on Amazon (www.amazon.com) and eBay (www.ebay.com), too.

Electronics tools

Here are the basic electronics tools you'll want on your shopping list:

- **A multimeter:** A multimeter is an essential tool for most electronic projects. You use it to perform basic tests to make sure that you have good connections in your electrical circuits. With a multimeter, you can measure the characteristics of an electrical circuit and trouble-shoot why something may not be working. A multimeter is also handy for testing and measuring individual electronic components. You should have one on hand for testing and troubleshooting your projects. (See the following section, "Selecting a multimeter," for more information.)

- **A breadboard and jumper wires:** Some of the projects in this book involve wiring up electrical components, LEDs, sensors, or actuators to your Raspberry Pi. This can be as simple as one or two wires, but some of the projects have many connections. A breadboard is a simple tool to help you easily make all these electrical connections. You need jumper wires to make connections when you're using a breadboard. Wires come in solid core and stranded versions (which contain many fine wires). You need solid core jumper wires for working with breadboards.

- **A soldering iron:** A breadboard is ideal for temporary connections and prototyping, but for some connections you'll want something more permanent. This is where a soldering iron comes in. You use a soldering iron to make strong, permanent connections between electronic components. If you want to mount buttons onto an enclosure for your project, you'll probably want to solder wires to the buttons and connect these to your Raspberry Pi. You can even build part of your circuit on a breadboard and use soldered connections for switches or sensors that are located some distance away. (See the upcoming section, "Selecting a soldering iron and accessories," for more information on what to look for.)

- **A power supply:** None of the projects in this book requires a desktop power supply, so this is optional. But for general electronics experimenting, you'll probably want to have a power supply on hand.

Selecting a multimeter

A multimeter is an essential tool for testing, measuring, and diagnosing problems in electronic circuits. You use a multimeter to measure several basic attributes of your circuit, including:

- ✔ **Continuity:** Whether there is a good connection between two points

- ✔ **Voltage:** The measure of potential electromotive force in a circuit

- ✔ **Current:** The measure of the continuous, uniform flow of electrons through an unbroken pathway in an electrical circuit

- ✔ **Resistance:** Opposition to the flow of current within a circuit

With a multimeter, you can also measure the voltage provided by batteries and power supplies, and the characteristics of discrete electronic components, such as resistors, capacitors, diodes, and transistors.

Different models have different features, and the more expensive ones have advanced features you may not need. That said, there are two important features to look for:

- ✔ **Continuity with audio signal:** Checking continuity — making sure that the things you think are connected really are connected — is the task you'll use your multimeter for most often. You touch the two probes to part of a circuit to see if they're connected, and the multimeter screen displays a confirmation. With cheap multimeters, you need to hold the probes in place while looking at the screen, which can be annoying if the probes slip off. It's a pain to check continuity by holding leads on a circuit while you're also looking at the display. It's much easier to just poke around and listen for an audio signal. Meters with audio output will beep when you test for good continuity so you don't have to take your attention away from the circuit. If you can, spend a little more for a multimeter that has this feature.

- ✔ **Auto-ranging:** Inexpensive multimeters require you to estimate the range of measurement and set the dial accordingly. On auto-ranging multimeters, you don't have to set the dial to select the range of measurement that you're reading. Auto-ranging is particularly handy and can be worth paying slightly more for.

Older multimeters used a needle and graduated scales for the display, but modern ones use a digital readout. If you don't already have a multimeter, we recommend getting a digital one, like the one shown in Figure 2-2.

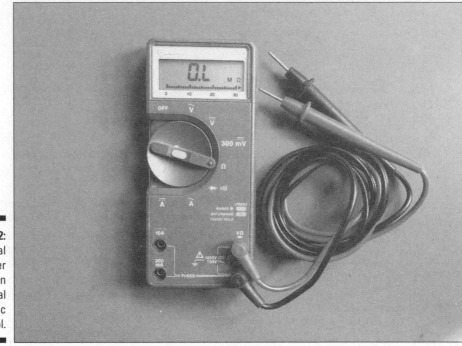

Figure 2-2:
A digital
multimeter
is an
essential
diagnostic
tool.

Selecting a soldering iron and accessories

Many of the projects in this book can be built without soldering anything at all, but you'll need to do a little bit of soldering for some of the projects, so it's good to have a soldering iron on hand.

Soldering involves melting *solder* (a metal alloy that melts at about 700°F) and allowing it to cool, creating a strong, conductive joint. You can solder wires to each other and join wires to components. You can bond wires to circuit prototyping boards such as perfboards and stripboards. Soldering secures components in place, while creating a good electrical connection for a more permanent, longer-lasting project. You can also simply solder certain components (like switches and displays) to wires that lead to your breadboard. That way, you can mount them in a project box. On some projects, you may want to move buttons or switches from the breadboard to the project enclosure, which means you'll need to solder extension wires on them.

Your soldering iron provides the heat for creating a soldered joint. Many people have the impression that you melt solder onto the parts that you want to connect, but this is actually backward. When soldering, you use a soldering iron to heat up both the solder and the components that are being joined together. When the components are hot enough, the solder will flow onto them, at which point, you remove the tip of the soldering iron and, thus, the heat supply. The solder cools rapidly and, if done correctly, forms a reliable bond.

Figure 2-3 shows a basic array of soldering tools. The key soldering tools you need at your workbench are as follows:

✔ **Soldering iron:** Your main soldering tool. Irons can be very inexpensive, but the professional ones can set you back hundreds. If you want to save money, avoid the cheapest ones and aim for a soldering iron that's at the top end of the low-range options. You'll need one that supplies at least 30 watts. A soldering iron with an adjustable temperature setting can be useful if you need extra heat for large joints, but it's not essential.

✔ **Solder:** A metal alloy you use to create soldered joints. There are both leaded and lead-free varieties. Some purists prefer leaded 60/40 solder (60 percent tin, 40 percent lead), but lead is toxic, so unless you have a particular need for it, we recommend you opt for the lead-free variety, with a rosin core. The rosin core melts and helps to clean the surfaces you're joining. Solder comes in a variety of diameters measured in standard wire gauge (SWG). For most electronics soldering needs, 18 SWG or 20 SWG diameter is ideal. You can use 22 SWG for detailed work.

Somewhat counterintuitively, as the wire gauge number goes higher, the diameter of the wire gets smaller.

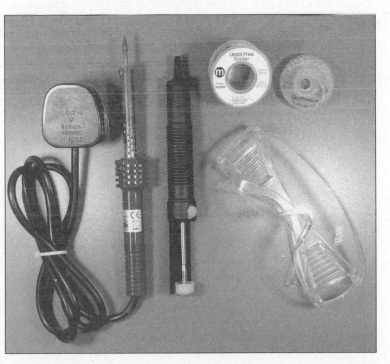

Figure 2-3:
An entry-level soldering iron and essential accessories.

✔ **Extra soldering tips:** Tips do the main work of the iron, directing the heat in the right place. Tips come in a variety of shapes and sizes. For most electronics work, you'll need a cone-shaped tip rather than a chisel tip. Because they come into contact with molten metal and impurities, tips can degrade over time, so it's a good idea to get spares.

Different manufacturers have different tip-mounting systems, so buy a couple extra tips when you buy your iron to avoid having to hunt for the right product later.

✔ **Soldering stand:** A device that holds the wand safely while it's hot. It may have a sponge for cleaning the tip. Soldering stands are often included with soldering iron kits.

✔ **Cellulose sponge and brass wire sponge:** You use these to clean the tip of your iron, which you do while the iron is hot. You can use either a cellulose sponge or a brass wire sponge, depending on your preference. The cellulose sponge can be any garden-variety kitchen sponge from the supermarket dipped in a bit of water and wrung out. Using a moist sponge cools down the tip of the iron, which is something to avoid because your iron will have to work harder to keep the tip at a constant temperature, and contaminants can build up on the tip. The brass wire sponge costs a little more, but it doesn't cool down the tip of the iron when you're cleaning it and it doesn't contaminate the tip. Using brass wire also means that your tip will last longer.

✔ **Desoldering tools:** You use these tools to remove unwanted blobs of solder from your work or disconnect wires, traces, or components that you may have soldered together by accident. You can find both desoldering wick and soldering suckers. A soldering sucker is a spring-loaded pen that you can use to suck liquefied solder away from your work piece. Desoldering wick is simply braided flat copper ribbon, which you press against your work while heating it. Capillary action draws the liquefied solder onto the braid and away from your work. We tend to prefer wick, which is cheaper and usually more effective.

✔ **Tip-cleaning paste:** Even with careful use, your tip may develop an oxidation coating, especially if you don't clean it regularly. This makes it very difficult to coat the tip and control the way your solder flows. Cleaning paste can help to remove oxidation and debris.

Physical building and fabrication tools

You also need some basic tools for light fabrication. Not all these tools are essential, but often the one tool you *don't* have is the one you need so you may want to stock up. Figure 2-4 shows some of the essential tools. We've listed these roughly in order of importance, from most to least:

- ✓ **A selection of precision screwdrivers:** Both flathead and Phillips-head screwdrivers are essential.

- ✓ **Helping hands:** This is a small clamp with two alligator clips to hold your work piece; it often comes with an integrated magnifying glass. This tool is essential for gripping objects you're working on — unless you have three arms.

- ✓ **Wire strippers:** You use these for cutting and stripping the insulation off of wires. They come in several different styles. Splurge a little here — if they're too cheap, they'll produce poor results and be frustrating to use.

- ✓ **Angled side cutters:** You use these for clipping component leads and cutting wires.

- ✓ **Needle-nose pliers:** Use these for holding fine objects. You should have both small and large ones on hand.

- ✓ **A task light with magnifier:** Use these to provide direct illumination and to make it easier to see fine work. Get one with a spring arm so that you can place it right over your work, if necessary.

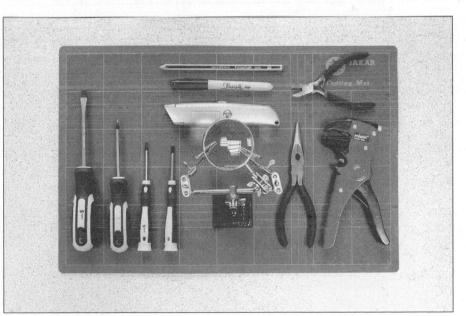

Figure 2-4:
Some essential light fabrication tools.

- ✔ **A box cutter/carpet knife with replaceable blades:** Use this for cutting sturdier materials.

- ✔ **A cutting mat:** You need this to protect your work surface.

- ✔ **A Sharpie and a pencil:** Use these for making cutting marks and permanent marks. No workbench is complete without a Sharpie!

- ✔ **Hand drill and small hand saw (not shown):** For small projects, you can probably use inexpensive hand tools, which you should be able to get at your local hardware store. Power tools will also work, but they're generally more expensive.

Using Your Tools Safely and Effectively

When you've assembled all the tools and set up your workspace, you'll probably be eager to dive right in! But before you do, take a few minutes to read the information in this section so you don't hurt yourself or those around you.

Working with electricity

In working with electronics, safety is critical. You should take basic precautions to protect yourself. None of the projects in this book involves connecting directly to the wall power, but you should use precautions anyway and develop good safety habits. Even though you may only be working with low DC voltages, it's a good idea to follow some basic safety rules when working with all electronic projects:

- ✔ **Don't touch metal contacts or leads in a live circuit.**

- ✔ **Don't alter a live circuit.** Always disconnect power before removing or adding components to your Raspberry Pi or breadboard.

- ✔ **Always test with one hand tied behind you back.** Well, at least one hand not on the work piece. If enough stray current flows between both your hands, and across your heart, it can cause arrhythmia. That's not likely at the low DC voltages we're working with here, but it's best to be safe and get into the habit.

- ✔ **Sounds crazy, but don't work barefoot.** Maximize the resistance between you and the floor by wearing good, rubber-soled shoes. A puddle of water is a great conductor, and you don't want to be in one, if something goes wrong.

✔ **Wear an antistatic wrist strap.** Your Raspberry Pi is a tough little computer, and if it's in an enclosure it should be well protected. However, it and other components are sensitive to wayward voltages, including static electricity. Several thousand volts of static electricity can build up on you, and you may not even know it, especially on carpeted floors. If it does and you touch your hardware, you can fry it in an instant. An inexpensive antistatic wrist strap will guard against unexpected sparks by connecting you at all times to ground, which diverts any electrical charge from building up on your body.

✔ **When fabricating or soldering, wear light, comfortable safety glasses.** Wire offcuts can fly around the room when they're clipped, and hot solder can sometimes spit and splutter. You don't want any molten metal heading for your eyes.

Laying the foundation for your electronics work

To quickly and easily connect your project circuits, start out by using a breadboard. All the projects involving electronic circuits in this book can be built on a breadboard. After testing on a breadboard, you can either put your Raspberry Pi and your breadboard inside an enclosure or build your circuit permanently on a stripboard or perfboard, which requires a bit of soldering.

Breadboards

A *breadboard* is a small block of plastic with lots of rows of holes into which you can insert jumper wires and electronic components. Underneath the holes are tiny metal strips forming springs, which grasp wires and the legs of components that are inserted into the holes. Because the springs are metal, if you connect wires or components to the same springs, they're electrically connected together.

Because breadboards use springs to hold the wires, you should always use solid core wire on them. Stranded wire (which is composed of multiple tiny wires) will get scrunched by the springs when you try to push them into the holes on the breadboard. It's a big pain to use stranded wire, so save yourself the trouble.

In the main work area on the breadboard, the holes are typically organized into rows of five and grouped into two columns. There is usually a trough between the two columns of holes, which allows you to insert an integrated circuit (IC) into the breadboard so that each of its legs is served by four adjacent holes.

Many breadboards have columns of holes running the full length of either side of the board. These holes aren't electrically connected to the main work area, and they're often labeled + (positive) and – (negative or "ground") and may be color coded. You use these as "rails" for power and ground. You'll often want to connect components to power or ground, so you usually need lots of connections to them.

Breadboards come in various sizes, from small (with 400 contact points) to large (with 830 points or more). You'll want to have at least a small one on hand for testing. If you run out of room, you can connect two breadboards using the notches and fingers on the sides of the boards. But be warned: There's no standard for these, so they usually need to be from the same manufacturer in order for you to connect them.

Stripboards and perfboards

Stripboards and perfboards are similar to breadboards — they have lots of holes to connect things together — but they're designed for permanent connections that are soldered in place. Stripboards are coated with adhesive strips of conductive copper that run underneath the holes. Electronic components are soldered to the strips of copper, providing an electrical connection and a strong physical bond. Perfboards have metallic pads that surround each individual hole, into which you can solder parts and which you can solder together to create electrical circuits.

Stripboards and perfboards come in a huge range of shapes and sizes (see Figure 2-5), so if and when you're ready to go for a more permanent solution, shop around for the size and type you need.

Prototyping boards

A number of manufacturers offer a printed circuit board that has a prototyping area for soldering electrical components, plus a multi-pin jack that you connect to the GPIO socket on your Raspberry Pi. This makes it easy to build circuits and experiment. Our favorite is the Humble Pi prototyping board, available from Ciseco (`http://shop.ciseco.co.uk`). If you're outside the UK, you should be able to find it from other online retailers, like Amazon (`www.amazon.com`).

This board stacks right on top of your Raspberry Pi to make a little sandwich, as shown in Figure 2-6. It comes in a kit form and is easy to put together. You simply solder the GPIO socket to the board. If you aren't confident with your soldering skills, this is a good kit to practice with, because it's difficult to damage it by making soldering mistakes.

Mini breadboard   Stripboard

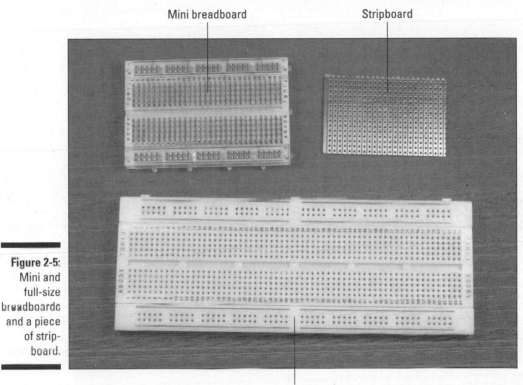

Figure 2-5:
Mini and
full-size
breadboards
and a piece
of strip-
board.

Full-size breadboard

Project boxes and housings

Many of the projects in this book are built on a breadboard because it's a fast and easy way to get going. If you want to protect the project, you can transfer it to a dedicated enclosure.

Potential project housings are everywhere, and almost anything that can be used as a small box will do. Electronics suppliers usually stock a range of generic enclosures, in both metal and plastic. When selecting one of these, make sure that you have the correct tools to fabricate your housing. If you're going to mount switches, buttons, or a display on the project box, you'll need to be able to cut through the material cleanly. It's really difficult to drill a hole into thick materials and metals without the right saws, drills, and bits, so make sure to select a housing that you can work with.

Another source of project enclosures is one of the new and popular laser cutting or 3D printing services, such as Pololu Robotics & Electronics (www.pololu.com), Ponoko (www.ponoko.com), and Thingiverse (www.thingiverse.com). You send off your design to them, and they'll ship you your finished custom laser-cut design. Many of these companies also have templates you can download for boxes and enclosures.

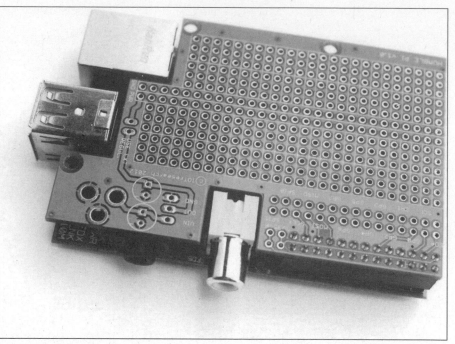

Photograph courtesy of Humble Pi

Figure 2-6:
A Humble Pi
prototyping
board
stacked
on top of a
Raspberry
Pi.

Soldering safely

When you're first trying your hand at soldering, it's a good idea to practice on some throwaway stuff that you won't mind messing up. It takes a while to get the hang of soldering — how long it takes to heat up the solder, how to flow it onto components, and how to make a good solder joint. You can use a piece of stripboard to do a few test connections, without worrying about damaging things on your project.

When soldering, follow these basic steps:

1. **Secure the main piece of the work (your stripboard, circuit board, or other components) to your worktable, or use a pair of helping hands to hold the piece.**

2. **Unwind a bit of solder from your spool.**

3. **Hold the iron as you would a pencil and place it in contact with the elements that you'll be soldering.**

4. **After a moment, press the end of the unwound bit of solder against the surfaces that you want to join.**

   This should be right near where the tip of the iron is heating up the components. The solder should begin to melt and coat the components.

5. **After the surfaces are well coated, remove the solder you're feeding into the joint.**

6. **Remove the iron and wait until the surfaces are cool.**

7. **Examine the joint.**

   The joint should be shiny. On a stripboard or perfboard, the joint should form a volcano shape around the wire that you're soldering and should be mechanically secure. It shouldn't wiggle around if you press against it.

WARNING! Try not to take a long time to solder the joint — ideally, only a few seconds. Excessive heat can damage the components, especially with sensitive components such as transistors and ICs. You may not even know they're damaged until you realize that your project isn't working and you have to track down the problem!

TIP Practice soldering on extra bits of wire or on resistors, because they're cheap and easy to work with and it doesn't matter if you overheat them — you can just throw them away after you're finished practicing. If you have any electronics board lying around, you can practice your desoldering skills, too, using a desoldering wick (see "Selecting a soldering iron and accessories," earlier in this chapter). Try to remove parts from the boards. You'll quickly see why it's a good idea to get your soldering skills up to speed — taking things off a circuit board is a lot harder than soldering things on!

Figure 2-7 shows an example of soldering components to a perfboard. When you're soldering, you apply the iron to the components and then flow the solder into the heated area. You need to ensure that the components are hot enough for the solder to adhere to them. You don't heat the solder and drip it onto the parts. The solder will liquefy around the components and coat them. When they're coated, remove the solder and the iron, and allow the parts to cool. The result should be a strong connection that you can't pull apart.

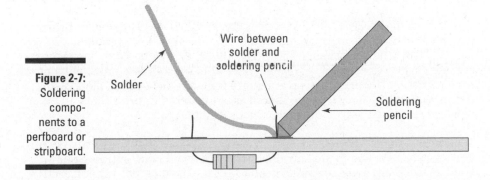

Figure 2-7: Soldering components to a perfboard or stripboard.

Solder

Wire between solder and soldering pencil

Soldering pencil

Here are some soldering tips to keep in mind:

- **Make sure your parts and surfaces are clean.** In particular, make sure you clean your soldering iron tip using a damp sponge.

- **When you first use your soldering iron, and periodically thereafter, coat the tip of your iron with a little solder — just enough to make it shiny.** This is called *tinning* and will make it easier to solder your connections.

- **Don't overheat parts.** You should heat the components just long enough to make a good connection. If you apply too much heat, some sensitive components could be damaged.

- **Safety first.** Make sure you aren't soldering over your hands or another part of your body. If the solder drops off your work, you could be burned. *Remember:* Make sure to wear safety goggles — burning solder can sometimes spit and fly in unexpected directions.

- **Be careful not to breathe in the soldering fumes.** Work in a well-ventilated area.

Getting Ready to Build Raspberry Pi LEGO Projects

Chapters 13 through 15 use the LEGO MINDSTORMS system. LEGO has been a popular toy for decades. Since the 1980s, it has produced a series of products that can interface with a computer and be programmatically controlled. Recently, the company has produced products geared toward robotics experimentation called MINDSTORMS. You can connect your Raspberry Pi to this latest range of products. We use the MINDSTORMS system to quickly and easily build complex projects. The modular building system makes the physical work of rigging up a robot or computer-controlled object very easy.

The core of the MINDSTORMS system is the MINDSTORMS Intelligent Brick, which contains the processor and memory required to do programmatic control. You send programs to the Intelligent Brick, which can then execute complex instructions, such as reading data from sensors or controlling motor drive systems. The brick has several ports for input and output, along with a display that you can program, as well as a number of buttons that can be used for input that you can read with your Raspberry Pi.

Several kinds of MINDSTORMS systems have been developed over the years, and the latest version is the MINDSTORMS EV3. If you plan on trying out some of the LEGO projects, you'll need to get the most recent version. You can buy the LEGO MINDSTORMS EV3 kit, which contains both the control brick and a bunch of extras to build several projects. This kit is pretty expensive (around $350), so if you want to save a little, you can just buy the control brick, which is about half the cost of the full kit. You can sometimes find the brick for sale on eBay at a lower price.

In Chapter 13, we provide more information on the EV3 system and using it with your Raspberry Pi.

Chapter 3

Focusing on Technique

*T*he easiest way to get know your Raspberry Pi is to play around with the Raspbian Wheezy operating system and familiarize yourself with what it can do. As soon as your Raspberry Pi finishes starting up, you can interact with the operating system in two ways:

✔ From the command-line interface, often referred to as the "shell"

✔ With the graphical user interface (GUI), the "desktop environment" people are most familiar with, called Lightweight X11 Desktop Environment (LXDE)

Raspberry Pi also has software to support writing your own software. The two software programming environments we use in this book are Python and C.

In this chapter, we cover the basics you need to know to use the Raspberry Pi operating system using the command line and LXDE and show what you need to know to get started writing programs in Python and C. We also show you how to download and install new software to use when you're writing code.

Getting Around Your Raspberry Pi

If you haven't yet set up your Raspberry Pi operating system, head back to Chapter 1, which covers the details.

After you turn on your Raspberry Pi, you see a number of messages on the screen as various parts of the operating system start up. When your operating system has finished starting up, you need to log in. The username is pi and the password is raspberry. (Make sure you type both of these in lowercase.)

If you've set up Raspi-config to bypass logging in with the command line, you start up into the LXDE. But you can access the command-line environment running "underneath" LXDE at any time by double-clicking the LXTerminal icon.

After you log in, you see the command-line interface prompt:

```
pi@raspberrypi ~ $
```

The prompt is your Raspberry Pi's way of telling you that it's ready to accept your commands. Anything you type after the $ is accepted as an instruction to do something. Later in this chapter, we discuss using the command-line interface to interact with the operating system. For now, type **startx** and press Enter to launch LXDE.

Using the desktop environment

The Raspberry Pi desktop environment, LXDE (refer to Figure 1-6 in Chapter 1), is an application that allows you to easily do all the things that you can do with the command-line shell. But because it's a GUI, it's easier to interact with for many tasks. Like a regular desktop computer or laptop, your Raspberry Pi comes with graphical applications that support common computing tasks, like word processing, creating presentations, using spreadsheets, browsing the web, and playing games.

Just as you see on the desktop of a Windows or Mac, you see several icons on top of the background wallpaper (most likely, a giant red raspberry icon) that provide quick access to the most commonly used programs. To launch one of these programs, you double-click the icon. The programs include the following:

- **Scratch:** A programming language that can be used to create simple programs, animations, and games.
- **LXTerminal:** A program that gives you access to the command-line interface. This tool is very handy — you'll use it often when you're building the projects in this book.
- **PI Store:** An online store for finding and downloading software for your Raspberry Pi.

✔ **IDLE and IDLE3:** Programs for creating software in Python. You use these to write to applications in Chapters 5 through 15.

✔ **Midori:** A web browser.

✔ **Debian Reference:** A collection of web pages stored on your SD card that gives you a quick reference to the Raspbian version of Linux. It's essentially a handbook for your Raspberry Pi.

✔ **Wi-Fi Config:** A tool for setting up your Raspberry Pi to use a Wi-Fi network. It requires an external wireless dongle that you connect to a USB port. We assume you're using either a Wi-Fi connection or an Ethernet connection for the projects that connect to the Internet. If you want to use a wireless connection, you need to set it up first with this configuration tool.

✔ **Python Games:** A collection of fun games that demonstrate the capabilities of the Python programming language.

Along the bottom of the LXDE is the taskbar, shown in Figure 3-1, which is very much like the taskbar in Windows. You can usually access the taskbar no matter what programs you're running. It's different from the taskbar at the top of the Mac desktop, which is located at the top of the screen and changes, depending on what program you're running.

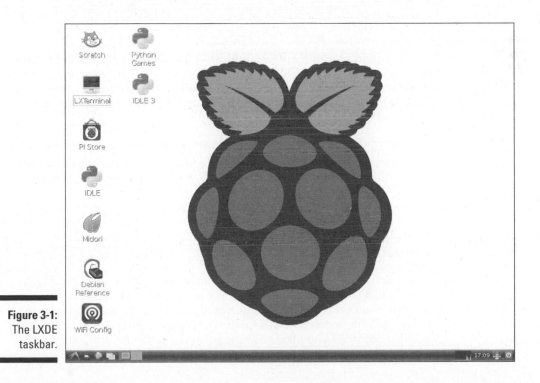

Figure 3-1:
The LXDE
taskbar.

The taskbar gives you quick access to the Programs menu, where you can access other applications you may already be running. The leftmost icon in the taskbar opens a menu containing a number of programs arranged in categories; it works like the Windows Start menu. You move your mouse over the categories of programs you want to use, and submenus reveal the available applications.

In LXDE, you can have several different desktops, all running at the same time. You can have many programs running on the different desktops, and you can quickly switch between them using the window icons on the taskbar. In practice, you probably won't be using multiple desktops very much because your Raspberry Pi just isn't up to the job of running lots of program simultaneously. However, to keep things consistent with beefier computers that are the cousins of your Raspberry Pi, you still have the capability of using multiple desktops, just like other Linux-based systems.

Using the File Manager

You manage files on your Raspberry Pi and any connected storage devices using the File Manager. The most common operations you need to do involve opening, closing, saving, moving, copying, and deleting files. You open the File Manager by clicking the File Manager icon, which is the second icon in the taskbar, shown in Figure 3-2.

The menu items at the top of the window — File, Edit, Go, Bookmarks, View, Tools, and Help — contain all the operations that you can perform on files on your system. If you get lost while you're working with your files or you can't figure out how to do something, these menus list all the functions you may need to perform.

Like the Windows File Manager or the Mac Finder, you see a view of the files and directories on your system (refer to Figure 3-2). You double-click a folder to open it and double-click files to open them with their default programs.

The left side of the File Manager window contains a list of special types of files and directories called Places. If you click one of these, the right pane displays the directories and items that are in that Place. The standard Places you see are as follows:

✔ **pi folder:** The pi folder is where you should store most of your files, including files that you create for the projects in this book. If you try to store files outside this folder, you'll encounter problems, because normal user accounts can save files only in this folder. You can create any directories you need to in the pi folder to keep your projects organized.

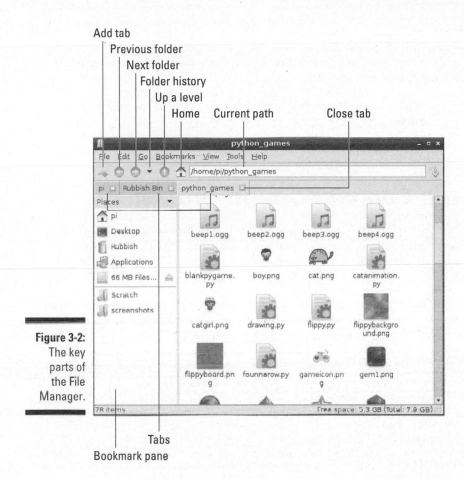

Add tab
Previous folder
Next folder
Folder history
Up a level
Home   Current path   Close tab

Figure 3-2:
The key
parts of
the File
Manager.

Tabs
Bookmark pane

✔ **Desktop folder:** The Desktop folder contains anything you can see on your desktop. Any file or folder you place on the desktop appears here.

✔ **Rubbish Bin:** The Rubbish Bin is a temporary holding area for directories and files you want to delete. You can highlight any file or folder and press the Delete key to send that file or folder to the Rubbish Bin. If you need the file or folder later, you can open the Rubbish Bin to get that file (assuming you haven't emptied the Rubbish Bin yet). After you've emptied the Rubbish Bin, any files that you placed there will be permanently deleted and you won't be able to recover them.

✔ **Applications folder:** The Applications folder contains the same items that are listed in the Programs menu.

Any connected external drives will also appear in Places. Click the triangular Eject button to safely remove a drive from your system before you physically disconnect the device.

Beneath the external drives is the Bookmarks pane, which contains a column of frequently used directories and files. If you have any directories that you use often, you can drag them into the pane. You can also add a bookmark using the Bookmarks menu.

You may also notice other items in the Bookmarks pane, depending on how your Raspberry Pi is configured and whether any additional drives are connected.

Using the Command-Line Interface

Underlying the LXDE is the command-line interface. Unless you configured your Raspberry Pi to automatically start up in LXDE, you were in the interface, also called the *shell,* right after you turned on your system and logged in.

When you're in LXDE, you can access the shell by clicking the LXTerminal icon. This opens a *console* in which you type your commands. You can even have multiple shell consoles open at the same time.

If you exit the LXDE, you find yourself at the command line, but with no desktop, no icons, and no use of the mouse. So, most people access the shell from within the LXDE and use a console to do things using the command line.

In the shell, you type text instructions at the command-line prompt. Your Raspberry Pi faithfully executes your commands, such as running programs, managing files, sending emails, and browsing the web. But like the commands you type, all the interaction is strictly text based.

You can change the color and size of the text in the console and even adjust the background color to suit your preferences. Just choose Edit ➪ Preferences.

The easiest way to get familiar with the shell is to do a few things in the shell and learn some basic commands. That's what this section is all about.

The command prompt

The shell shows you it's ready to do something by displaying the command-line prompt:

```
pi@raspberrypi ~ $
```

The prompt shows you your username followed by an at symbol (@), the system name, a tilde (~), and the dollar sign ($), which means the system is ready for input. The tilde means you're in the "home" directory of the user you're currently logged in as, which by default is the user pi.

The default directory for each user account is often referred to as the user's "home directory" or "user directory," which is the directory you see when you open the File Manager. This can be a bit confusing because there also is a system directory called "home," which contains all the default directories for the user accounts on your system. The home directory for each user account is labeled with that person's username and every one is stored in the system home directory.

If you were in another directory, it would be shown here. The dollar sign means you're logged in as an ordinary user and not a superuser; If you were a superuser, you would see a hash symbol (#).

The directory tree

Like your operating system, all the files and directories are stored on your SD card. Linux users talk about organizing files into "directories," rather than "folders," but they mean the same thing. They're just containers to put your files and other directories into. Just about any directory or file can be put into other directories or files. But there are thousands of files on your Raspberry Pi, so as with any Linux system, they're organized in a sensible way.

Linux file systems are organized as a hierarchy. This hierarchy is often thought of metaphorically as a tree, because a tree starts with a trunk from which everything else branches off. Part of this directory tree is shown in Figure 3-3.

At the top level is a single root directory (indicated by /), under which everything else is organized. Within the root directory are 20 subdirectories in which all your Raspberry Pi's files are organized. The most important among these subdirectories is your user folder, where all your files are stored. Your user folder is called pi by default; when you open a console in LXTerminal, you can look at all the files in your pi folder.

You do this with one of the most handy shell commands: list (ls). To show the files in any directory, type the ls command at the command prompt (what you need to type is shown in bold):

```
pi@raspberrypi ~ $ ls
```

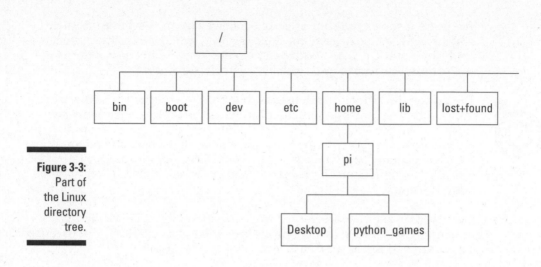

Figure 3-3:
Part of
the Linux
directory
tree.

Then press Enter.

A listing of the directories in your home folder is displayed:

```
Desktop ocr_pi.png python_games
pi@raspberrypi ~ $
```

The shell prompt shows the default username before the at symbol, which is why the prompt says pi@raspberrypi. If you change your user or log in with a different username, it will show that name before the at symbol.

You see the command prompt again, indicating that the system is ready for your next request. The names of directories are color-coded in blue. If you have any files in your home folder, they're shown in purple.

You can take a look at one of the other directories using the ls command, as well. Try listing the files in your python_games directory:

```
pi@raspberrypi ~ $ ls python_games
```

You see a long list of all the files and directories within the python_games directory. Because it's below the pi folder in the directory tree (refer to Figure 3-3), it's referred to as a subdirectory of your pi directory.

To see the full list of 20 Raspberry Pi directories stored in your root directory (represented by a forward slash /), type the following:

```
pi@raspberrypi ~ $ ls /
```

A full list of the directories is displayed, along with the subdirectories that are immediate subdirectories of the root.

 Any Linux command can also be issued with a number of options. Options are indicated by a dash and a letter or letters. For example, you can get further details about a file listing with the long listing option (-1), which formats the output as a single list and provides further detailed information about each file. Try it:

```
pi@raspberrypi ~ $ ls -l python_games
```

The resulting output shows each file or directory on a separate line and gives details about who can access it, how large it is, and when it was last modified. There are dozens of options you can use with the ls command.

 You can get more information about any of the Linux commands and their options by using the Unix Programmer's Manual, which is always available at the command line by typing **man** and the name of the command. Try getting information about the options available with the ls command:

```
pi@raspberrypi ~ $ man ls
```

A description of the ls command is provided, along with all its options. The information is very detailed and is presented as several pages of text. You use the up and down arrows to scroll through the text; you can skip forward or backward a page by pressing the Page Up and Page Down keys on your keyboard (the spacebar also works to skip forward). Type **h** to get help; to quit the manual at any time, simply type **q**.

Just as with the File Manager in LXDE, you can manipulate files and folders in the shell. Generally, using the File Manager to do these operations is easier, but sometimes examining and working with the files in the shell is useful.

 You'll notice that above your pi directory is a directory called home. This is a bit strange, because the pi directory *is* your home directory. That's because the default username is pi, and you are in the home directory for the user pi. But along with your pi directory, the home directories of any other user accounts are also located within the /home directory.

The commands you issue at the command prompt are executed from the directory you're located in. ***Remember:*** Your home directory is represented with a tilde (~) in front of the dollar sign ($) prompt. You can move to another directory with the change directory (cd) command. Try it:

```
pi@raspberrypi ~ $ cd python_games
pi@raspberrypi ~/python_games $
```

You're now within the `python_games` directory, and the prompt has changed to show the directory you're currently in: ~/python_games $. Type **ls**, and you get the same listing of files and folders as shown earlier.

The `pi` directory is above `python_games` in the directory tree and is referred to as its *parent directory*. To go back to the parent directory, type **cd** with a space and then two dots after it:

```
pi@raspberrypi ~/python_games $ cd ..
pi@raspberrypi ~ $
```

The prompt now shows that you're in your home directory (`pi`) with a tilde (~). The two dots (. .) are a sort of shorthand to tell the system to go up a level without your having to type out the full name of the parent directory. Keep going up the hierarchy, and you can go right up to the root directory that everything branches off from.

The file path

To tell the system to do something with a file or directory, you either need to be in the same directory as the file or folder you're working with, or you need to specify the file path of the file that you want to work with. The *file path* is the full location of the file within the directory tree, separated by forward slashes (/). For example, the file path of your `python_games` directory from the root directory is

```
/home/pi/python_games
```

You can use the file path to work with files in any part of the system, no matter where you're currently located. For example, from your home directory, you can get information about a file in another directory with the file (`file`) command.

To try this, change to your home directory. (If you aren't in your home directory, you can get back to your home directory from anywhere, by typing **cd** ~.) From your home directory, you only need to specify the file path as you would reach it, from home. Try it, by looking up the details about the `cat.png` image file that is located in the subdirectory `python_games`:

```
pi@raspberrypi ~ $ file python_games/cat.png
python_games/cat.png PNG image data, 125 x 79, 8 bit color RGBA, non-interlaced
```

The system responds with details about the `cat.png` image file that is located below your current home directory.

Just about any command can be used in this way. In fact, you already used this with the `ls` command earlier.

Directories

You'll want to organize your stuff into directories so you can find and use it. Creating new directories is easy. Try creating a directory in your home directory called `stuff` with the make directory (`mkdir`) command:

```
pi@raspberrypi ~ $ mkdir stuff
```

If you do a directory listing, you see a new folder:

```
Desktop python_games stuff
pi@raspberrypi ~ $
```

You can easily make multiple directories by separating their names with a space.

Because you're currently in your home directory (`pi`), the `stuff` directory was created in it. If you wanted to create a new directory in `python_games`, you would need to move to that directory, or specify its file path when you used the `mkdir` command. For example, you could create a `stuff` directory in `python_games` even if you're currently in your home directory by typing the following:

```
pi@raspberrypi ~ $ mkdir python_games/stuff
```

To make sure it worked, you type:

```
pi@raspberrypi ~ $ ls python_games
```

Your new `stuff` folder will be listed (highlighted in blue) among the other files and directories.

Getting rid of directories you don't need is also important, and easy. Use the remove directory (`rmdir`) command to delete the folder you just created in `python_games`. Type the following:

```
pi@raspberrypi ~ $ rmdir python_games/stuff
```

A directory listing of the directory will confirm that `stuff` is gone.

Be careful when using the `rmdir` command. After you've deleted a directory, there's no way to easily recover it. To prevent a disaster, `rmdir` won't delete a directory unless it's empty. You have to remove the contents of a directory before deleting it (although there is a way around this: using the `--ignore-if-non-empty` option).

Files

The `file` command shows you information about files in your directories. You can also move and remove files from the system. To try it out, create a dummy text file to play around with.

It's easy to create new files from the command line. This is something you may do when you're writing short bit of text or you want to try out a quick snippet of code. To create a new text file, you use a text editor.

There are legendary arguments in the Linux community about which is the best command-line text editor. One of the simplest and easiest editors is nano (which is a version of its ancestor, pico). Create a new dummy file using the nano editor by typing the following:

```
pi@raspberrypi ~ $ nano dummy.txt
```

The nano editor is a full-screen text editor that takes up the entire LXTerminal window while you're using it, as shown in Figure 3-4.

Figure 3-4:
Creating a
dummy file
in the nano
editor.

Type in some text for your new file; it appears on the first line of the editor:

```
This is a dummy text file.
```

Along the bottom of the screen are the commands available to you. The ^ character means to use the Ctrl key on your keyboard, so to exit the editor you press Ctrl+X. When you do so, you're asked if you want to save the file. In the status bar along the bottom of the screen, nano asks the following:

```
Save modified buffer (ANSWERING "No" WILL DESTROY CHANGES)
```

Because you want to save your changes, type **y** and press Enter to confirm. Now, if you do a directory listing you'll see your new dummy.txt file.

One of the most popular commands for reading files is the concatenate (cat) command. You can use it to display the contents of any file on the screen. Take a look at your dummy file by typing the following:

```
pi@raspberrypi ~ $ cat dummy.txt
This is a dummy text file.
pi@raspberrypi ~ $
```

You can use the cat command to display the contents of any file, but unless it's a text file, you'll probably see gibberish on the screen.

Now you can move your shiny new dummy text file to the stuff folder. To do so, use the move (mv) command. You follow the command by the name of the file you want to move, a space, and the location where you want to put the file. Move it to your stuff folder by typing the following:

```
pi@raspberrypi ~ $ mv dummy.txt stuff
```

Do a directory listing of stuff to confirm it's there:

```
pi@raspberrypi ~ $ ls stuff
dummy.txt
pi@raspberrypi ~ $
```

Removing a file is just as easy as moving it. You use the remove (rm) command. Deleting files can be risky business, so one way to ensure you're removing the right file is to use the confirmation option (-i) and set output to verbose mode (-v). You don't have to use the - sign before each option:

```
pi@raspberrypi ~ $ rm -iv stuff/dummy.txt
rm: remove regular file 'stuff/dummy.txt'?y
removed 'stuff/dummy.txt'
pi@raspberrypi ~ $
```

Type **y** to confirm the deletion. Your file has now been deleted, and you've received confirmation. Safe and easy!

Be careful when using the rm command. After you've deleted a file, there's no way to easily recover it. This is a good reason to make the confirmation option a habit.

Programming Like a Pro

To get the most power and flexibility out of your Raspberry Pi, you'll want to write your own programs, which is what this book is all about! We use two programming languages — Python and C — as a way to get you started with your own Raspberry Pi projects. We cover these languages in this section, and provide some basic tips on how to use text editors to write and update your code.

Python

Python (named after the popular *Monty Python* comedy series) is a powerful programming language that is relatively easy to learn and is widely used by big companies like Google and Amazon. It's easy to use and, unlike many programming languages, easy to read. We use Python for several of the projects in this book, so you need to know the basics, even if you're only going to copy the code we provide for you.

Python is an *interpreted language,* meaning that the code is written in a manner that is easy for humans to read rather than in native *machine code.* When the program is in the process of being executed, the Python command interpreter translates it into machine code for your operating system. By contrast, C is a *compiled language* and uses a compiler to prepare your code in advance for the operating system

To write programs in Python, you can simply create a text file using the commands that Python understands and save the file with the filename suffix .py. You don't have to have the .py suffix, but it's a good reminder that the file is a Python program. You can run the program within the Linux shell at the command prompt by sending your file to Python's interpreter. The command interpreter (which is, itself, an application) reads through the code and executes the instructions you've programmed. You do this by simply typing **python** and then the filename.

Your Raspbian Wheezy distribution comes with a couple versions of Python: versions 2.7 and 3. Python 3 contains a number of modifications of the syntax and capabilities of Python 2.7, and programs written for it may not by entirely compatible with Python 2.7. All the programs in this book are compatible with Python 2.7.

You can figure out which versions of Python you have from the command line by typing **python –V**.

The classic way to start learning a programming language is to create a simple program to print the phrase "Hello world!" The code to do this would be the following:

```
print("Hello world!")
```

If you were to save this instruction in a text file called hello.py, you could run it with Python's command interpreter.

Refer to the "Files" section earlier in this chapter to review how to create a text file from the command line.

To run the program with Python's command interpreter, you would type the following on the command line:

```
pi@raspberrypi ~ $ python hello.py
Hello world!
pi@raspberrypi ~ $
```

This statement tells your operating system to use the Python interpreter to read through the file and follow the instructions. The result is printed on the screen.

You can also use the interpreter (sometimes referred to as the shell) in interactive mode. Just as you can use the system shell to issue commands for the system to act on, you also can use the Python shell to issue commands for the Python interpreter. This can be a bit confusing, because both the system shell and the Python shell are text based. When you're using the desktop, they're in different windows.

To avoid confusion between the system shell and the Python shell, pay attention to the command prompt. If the prompt is pi@raspberrypi ~ $ (or any other username before the @ symbol), you're in the system shell. If the prompt is >>>, you're in the Python shell.

You open the Python shell by typing the following:

```
pi@raspberrypi ~ $ python3
```

You see version information followed by the interpreter's prompt (>>>):

```
Python 3.2.3 (default, Mar 1 2014, 11:53:50)
[GCC 4.6.3] on linux2
Type "help", "copyright", "credits" or "license" for more information.
>>>
```

Type the same command above and observe the output. Note that the commands you type are case sensitive:

```
>>> print("Hello world!")
Hello world!
>>>
```

The shell executes your command. Then the prompt returns and is ready for your next instruction. To leave the interpreter, press Ctrl+D.

IDLE

Writing programs as text files is very easy, but when your programs start to get more complicated, it's helpful to have a tool to support the code-writing process. In this book, we use a special programming application called IDLE (short for Integrated DeveLopment Environment), which provides a sort of sandbox where you can write code and test it to see if it works correctly. IDLE is an interactive graphical editor, so you have all the benefits of using your keyboard and mouse in LXDE.

There are two versions of IDLE on your Raspberry Pi. (IDLE3 is for Python 3, which is what you use for programs in this book.) Their icons are on the desktop. Start the IDLE Python shell by clicking the IDLE icon. The display looks much the same as the interactive shell (see the preceding section), as shown in Figure 3-5.

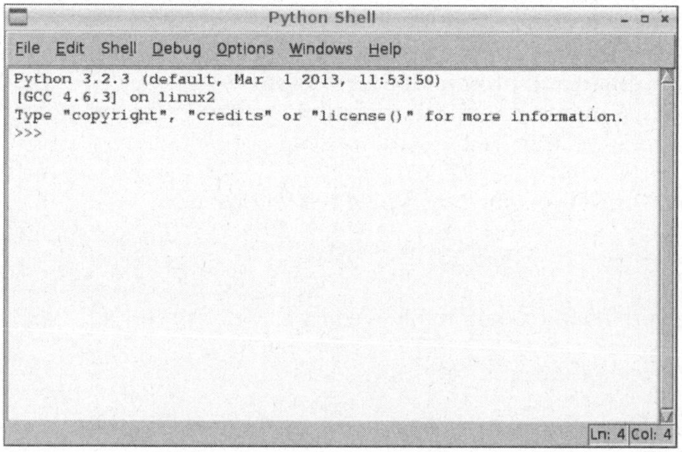

Figure 3-5: Using IDLE as an interactive Python shell.

IDLE offers several benefits over a text editor:

- ✔ It checks that your code is correctly formatted.
- ✔ It highlights key commands.
- ✔ It checks your syntax.

By design, Python is picky about the position of text in your code and IDLE checks this, too.

Try out the "Hello world!" program again, this time using the IDLE editor. Type the following:

```
>>>print("Hello world!")
```

Then press Enter. Notice that as you type the program, key instructions are highlighted in orange, and the text between quotes is made green. This is handy if you forget to type commands in the correct case. For example, if you type **Print** with a capital *P*, the command won't turn orange, and you'll know you have a problem. Functions (such as print) are in purple; other known terms (such as for) are in orange.

To create a runnable Python program in the shell, you change from interactive mode to script mode. Change to script mode by choosing File➪New Window. A blank window opens and is ready for your code, as shown in Figure 3-6.

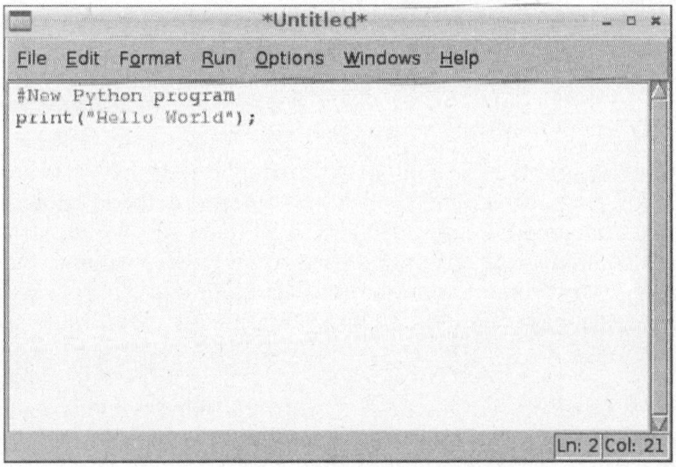

Figure 3-6:
Using IDLE to write Python programs.

Finding out more about Python

You know the basics you need for creating the projects that use Python. Chapter 4 covers important programming concepts for both C and Python, but this book isn't remotely big enough to comprehensively cover how to learn Python. For that, you can take a look at *Python For Dummies,* by Stef Maruch and Aahz Maruch (Wiley), which is an excellent, in-depth guide. The ultimate resource for anything to do with learning and using Python is the project's website (www.python.org). If you want to get started exploring what you can do with Python, there are a number of online learning tutorials at Codeacademy (www.codeacademy.com) that provide exercises and interactive help.

Start your program with a description of what it is. You enter this as a comment on the first line, using a hash symbol (#). Anything after the hash symbol is ignored by the interpreter, so it's used for making remarks about your code.

```
# New Python program
print("Hello world!")
```

Save your new program by choosing File➪Save As. Use the name `hello-world.py` and save it in your home directory. You can run the program by choosing Run➪Run Module. Alternatively, you can press F5.

You can also run this in a shell console by typing the following:

```
pi@raspberrypi ~ $ python helloworld.py
```

C

Some of the programs in this book are written in C. Unlike Python, C is a compiled language, which means that the human-readable code is converted to machine code in advance and saved as a binary file. As with Python, you can create code in a text editor and then run it from the command line. Alternatively, you can use an integrated development environment (IDE) to write your code; many people use one called Geany (see "Using apt-get," later in this chapter).

Compiling C programs entails working with four kinds of files, each with a different filename suffix. The suffix helps you determine what a file is without having to open it. The file types are as follows:

✔ **Source code:** The files you work with to write your code. Source code filenames end in .c.

✔ **Header files:** Files that contain declarations of functions and references to functions that may be outside the source code, and information for the C compiler's pre-processor. Header filenames end with .h.

✔ **Object files:** The output of the compiler; they contain function definitions in binary form, but they aren't executable. Object filenames end in in .o.

✔ **Binary files:** Also called executables, these contain the runnable code that is ready to be used. They don't usually have a suffix. These are the same .exe files on Windows systems.

When you finish writing the source code, you compile it, which generates a binary file. You can then run this file from the command line.

Try using nano to write a quick "Hello world!" C program called (not so creatively) hello.c, as shown in Figure 3-7. Create it in your /stuff directory so that it isn't jumbled with your other directories and files. Type the following:

```
cd stuff
pi@raspberrypi /stuff $ nano hello.c
```

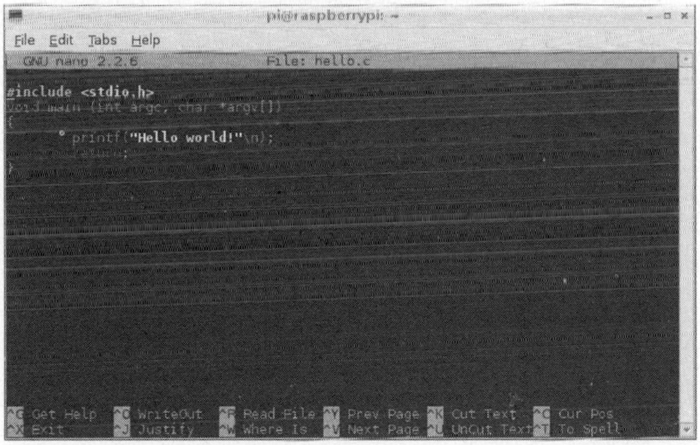

Figure 3-7:
Writing a
C program
using nano.

The nano editor launches and is ready for your program. Type the following:

```
#include <stdio.h>
void main(int argc, char *argv[])
{
printf("Hello world!\n");
return;
}
```

The first thing you notice is that nano understands when you're typing C commands and highlights them in different colors for you.

In the first line, you instruct the compiler to use a header file called Standard IO (stdio.h). Unlike Python, the hash symbol (#) is an instruction for the compiler's pre-processor to use the standard external header file that handles input and output.

The stdio.h header file is one of many built-in header files that contain common and useful functions. It has all the code needed to send your output to the screen — that way you don't have to write this! The pre-compiler knows where to find the built-in set of header files on your system. It locates them automatically when you compile your program. If you need to include other header files when you compile your code, you usually need to place these files in the same folder as your source-code file.

The next section of your source code creates a function called main that does the work of printing "Hello world!" It's not important to understand exactly how this works for now, because we're focused on compiling the code. Save the code by pressing Ctrl+X and typing **y** to save the changes.

Compiling and running your C code

On the command line, you can compile the code. Type the following:

```
gcc hello.c -o hello
```

After a very short delay, you see your command prompt again, and your file is compiled. Do a directory listing to confirm it's there:

```
pi@raspberrypi /stuff $ ls
hello hello.c
pi@raspberrypi /stuff $
```

Notice that the executable binary file is highlighted in green and the source code is not. The gcc command launches a program called the GNU C compiler. (GNU is the open-source software project that eventually led to the creation of Linux.) The -o hello option indicates that the binary executable file is to be called hello.

Now you can run your program. To do so, type the following:

```
pi@raspberrypi /stuff $ ./hello
Hello world!
pi@raspberrypi /stuff $
```

Congratulations! You've just written, compiled, and run your first C program!

You usually need to use the dot-slash (./) to execute your programs.

You don't need to know more about C to get the projects in this book running. C is one of the granddaddy programming languages, and learning it is a huge topic. *C For Dummies,* by Dan Gookin (Wiley), is a great starting point.

You may want to use an IDE to write your C programs, just as you can with Python, using IDLE. Geany is an IDE included with your Raspbian Wheezy distribution that many people use. To use it, you need to use a program called apt-get (see the following section).

Using apt-get

Sometimes you need to install other libraries of code (also called *packages*) or add new programs to your system. There's an easy way to do this from the command line using a tool called apt-get. Apt-get is a simple command line interface tool for managing, downloading, and installing packages and updating source code for packages from their repositories on the Internet. To use apt-get to update source files, you must have your Raspberry Pi connected to your network and have a connection to the Internet.

To install the Geany IDE, type the following:

```
pi@raspberrypi ~ $ sudo apt-get install geany
```

The superuser do (sudo) command is required for certain operations that need special privileges — in this case, accessing files in a directory that's only accessible to administrators. The next instruction launches apt-get and instructs it to install the Geany package on your system.

You see various status messages as apt-get prepares for the installation, checks the Internet for updates to the source files, downloads them, and installs the program.

When it's finished, you can find Geany in the Programming folder, as shown in Figure 3-8. Installing other packages and code libraries is done in a similar way. Geany is a very powerful IDE, and there is a lot to learn — too much to explain here. You can find more information on the Raspberry Pi website.

Figure 3-8: The Geany IDE is installed in your Pro-gramming folder.

Accessories	>
Other	>
Programming	> Geany
Sound & Video	>
System Tools	>
Preferences	>
Run	
Logout	

A fast and lightweight IDE using GTK2

When apt-get is needed for the projects in later chapters, we provide instructions on which packages you need to download and how to install them.

Troubleshooting

You'll be writing and copying a lot of code in the process of building these projects. As you do, there's always a chance that something can go wrong. In the case of the projects that involve building something, the problem could be with your software or your hardware. Here are a few things you should check:

- ✔ **Your code:** Make sure you type the code correctly. The color coding in your IDE can help you make sure you haven't introduced any errors. If you cut and pasted or downloaded the code from this book's companion website, make sure there weren't any typos introduced in the process.

- ✔ **Your connections:** If you aren't able to download a file or can't get apt-get to work, check your network connection. You may think you're online, but there could be a problem.

- ✔ For the projects that require physically building something, there is likely to be a lot of wiring or soldering. Make sure none of your connections came loose while you were working.

- ✔ **The Raspberry Pi forums** (www.raspberrypi.org/forums)**:** The Raspberry Pi forums are where the whole Raspberry Pi community shares their knowledge, experience, problems, and solutions. Here, you should be able to find the answer to your problem. Because Raspberry Pi is aimed at newcomers to programming, people are very friendly on the forums and no question is too basic. Newbies are welcome.

- ✔ **Stack Overflow** (www.stackoverflow.com)**:** One of the best resources you can find online. Here, thousands of experienced programmers who have trouble with their code post their questions to the community. People vote on the quality of answers, and the better answers rise to the top of the list. You can search the forums for postings related to your problem or post a new question about it. People within the community will likely answer your question quickly.

Chapter 4

The Raspberry Family

*I*n the beginning was the Raspberry Pi, and all was good. Then the Pi begat the revision 2 with more memory, which begat the Model A, which begat . . . well, you get the idea. With all this begating, we want to introduce you to what the Raspberry family looks like and how what you have may affect the projects you want to do. In this chapter, we show you how to understand the differences in the versions of Raspberry Pi that have been produced. By looking at the memory, GPIO, and video and processor variations that have been produced, you can see how the Raspberry Pi has improved over the years.

In the Beginning: Looking at the Evolution of the Raspberry Pi

The original Raspberry Pi, like so many firsts, did not need a qualifier to its name, but it had one. It was known as the Raspberry Pi Model B. The second version was known as the Model A. It's impossible for end-users to complete their own upgrades, so the two versions are separate models.

The Model A has no Ethernet socket, only one USB connector, and typically less memory; as a consequence, it's about $10 cheaper than the Model B. Also, the Model A consumes about one-third less power than the Model B, which can be important for battery-powered standalone applications.

Model B was first?

It might sound odd that the first Raspberry Pi was the Model B (not the Model A), but here's the story behind that name: Most of the people who made up the driving force behind the Raspberry Pi grew up in the UK, where another Cambridge-designed computer — the BBC computer, designed by Acorn Computers — was ubiquitous in education. Originally, there were two versions of the BBC computer: the Model B, and a cut-down version called the Model A.

From the start, the makers of the Raspberry Pi wanted to produce two models. They figured that most people would want the Model B version, as they did with the old BBC computer, so that's the one they produced first.

The Raspberry Pi Foundation, the creator of the Raspberry Pi, is a registered charity with the aim of promoting computer literacy. They worked for many years developing prototypes before they released anything. The original Raspberry Pi 1 Model B set the benchmark for what a Raspberry Pi was, and it's great credit to the developers that each new variant on the Raspberry Pi had improvements but did not break the compatibility with the previous models.

One confusing aspect of the Raspberry Pi is that changes and improvements to the Pi were not always accompanied by a change in name, so users are never quite sure what they're buying. We want to try to clear that confusion: There have only been three basic named versions of the Raspberry Pi to date — the original (or 1), the plus (+), and the 2. Given that there is a Model A and a Model B variant for each model, that means there are six named types of Raspberry Pi (see Table 4-1).

Table 4-1	Named Types of Raspberry Pi		
Name	*Release Date*	*Memory*	*Notes*
Raspberry Pi 1 Model B	February 19, 2012	256MB	The original Raspberry Pi.
Raspberry Pi 1 Model B Revision 2	September 5, 2012	512MB	Changes in the thermal fuses on the USB. Addition of unpopulated connector P5 for accessing more GPIO pins. Three changes to the GPIO pins on connector P1.

Name	Release Date	Memory	Notes
Raspberry Pi 1 Model A	February 4, 2013	256MB	The first cut-down version of the Raspberry Pi.
Raspberry Pi 1 Model B+	July 14, 2014	512MB	More I/O pins than previous models and a micro SD card.
Raspberry Pi 1 Model A+	November 10, 2014	256MB	Same number of I/O pins as the B+.
Raspberry Pi 2 Model B+	February 2, 2015	1GB	The first version with a quad-core processor.
Raspberry Pi 2 Model A+	Not expected until sometime in 2016	Not known as of this writing	Cut-down quad-core Raspberry Pi.

Deciding Which Raspberry Pi to Buy

Only immediately after the launch of a new version of the Raspberry Pi do you have any choice in what to buy. With backward compatibility and no change in price, there is little demand for older models. So your only real choice is whether to get a Model A or a Model B. In most cases, this is a no-brainer — the Model B is the obvious choice. You should only buy a Model A if you have some specific reason for doing so (for example, the cost, smaller form factor, or lower power consumption).

Memory

The memory chip used on every Raspberry Pi 1 was in an unusual form factor in the field of computers. It was the so-called *chip-on-chip system* — the processor chip had contacts on both sides (one set on the base to connect to the printed circuit board, and another set on the top for the memory chip). The memory chip was then soldered directly onto the processor chip to give a very compact design, only 1mm thick. This technique is more usually found in smartphones where space is at a premium. With the Raspberry Pi, it had the unfortunate effect of limiting the amount of memory that could be fitted, because this sort of memory chip was only available in a few memory sizes, with 512MB being the biggest.

The latest Raspberry Pi 2 versions have discontinued that trend and allowed a larger memory chip to be fitted. The Raspberry Pi 1 Model B+ and the Raspberry Pi 2 Model B+ look almost identical from the top, but on the underside you can clearly see the separate memory (the large black block), as shown in Figure 4-1 and Figure 4-2.

Figure 4-1:
Raspberry
Pi 1 Model
B+ (left) and
Raspberry
Pi 2 Model
B+ (right),
top view.

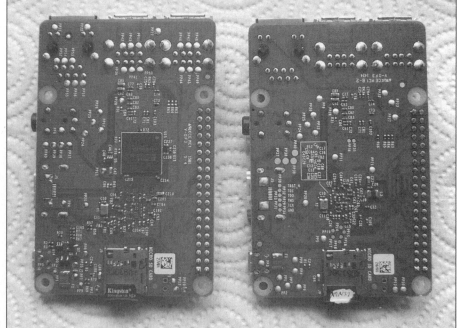

Figure 4-2:
Raspberry
Pi 1 Model
B+ (left) and
Raspberry
Pi 2 Model
B+ (right),
bottom
view.

General-purpose input/output (GPIO)

The plus models have 40-pin dual-row header pins to allow access to the general-purpose input/output (GPIO) port pins. Some of these pins are needed to turn the processor into a computer system by accessing the SD card and Ethernet and USB peripherals; others of the spare pins are brought out for the user. The GPIO pins carry logic signals that the computer can control or read and are how you can get the Raspberry Pi to switch outputs and sense inputs. Not all these pins are GPIO pins; there are several instances of 5V, 3V3, and ground. The pre-plus models had only a 26-pin connector and fewer pins were brought out. Figure 4-3 shows the pin out of this connector.

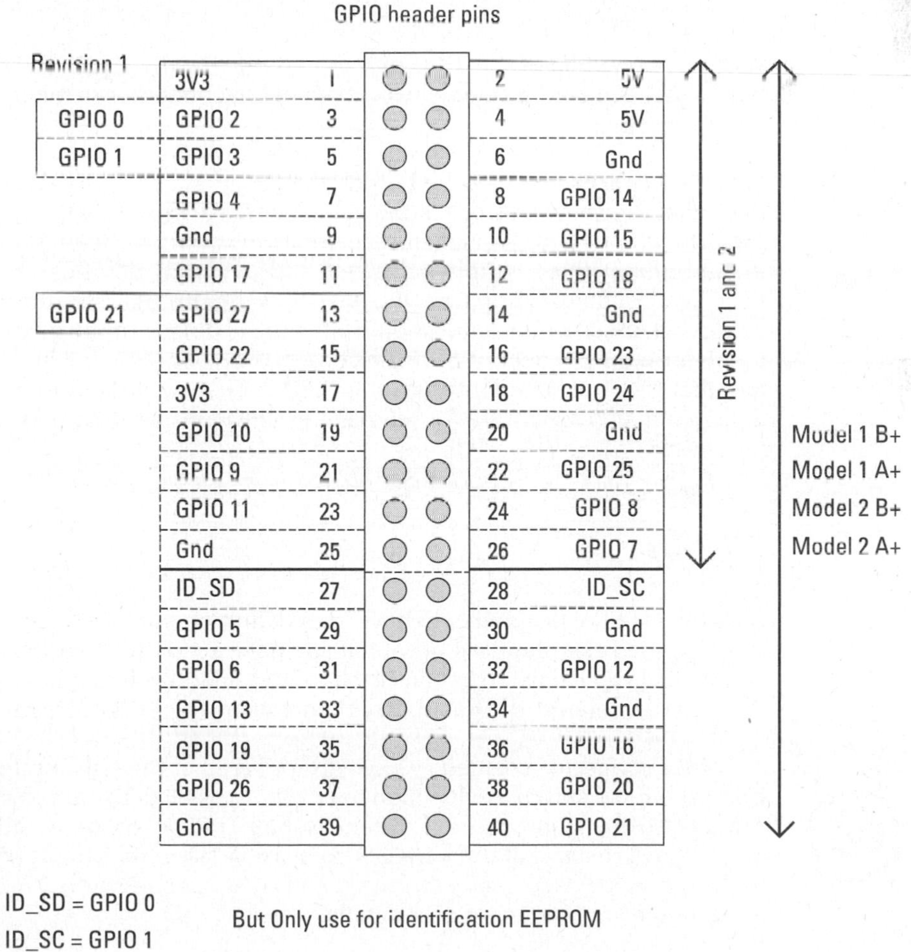

GPIO header pins

Figure 4-3: The GPIO connector pin out.

ID_SD = GPIO 0
ID_SC = GPIO 1

But Only use for identification EEPROM

Connection choice

There is an almost bewildering number of commercial boards, allowing you easy access to the GPIO contacts. Also, there are many designs you can make yourself. These designs tend to fall into two broad categories: those that mount a board directly on the Raspberry Pi's board, and those that connect to the connector with ribbon cable.

Using a direct connector limits the size of the attached board, whereas using ribbon cable does not. However, the ribbon cable connector is specific to the number of pins you have. A 26-way ribbon connector won't fit on a 40-pin header, whereas a 26-way direct connector will.

With the exception of the original Issue 1 of the Raspberry Pi, the GPIO pins have remained on the same physical pin of the connector through subsequent revisions.

Each GPIO pin can be switched inside the processor to perform a different specialist function. This has led to some people designating these pins to these functions, and then labeling the remaining pins as GPIO from 0 upward. In our opinion, this is stupid because it adds an extra, pointless, totally artificial layer of obfuscation that you have to wade through. Another form of confusion arises when some people label these pins with the physical pin number on the connector. So, for example, they refer to pin 3 in the software and that gets translated internally to GPIO 2. That's a little more understandable, but it's no substitute for referring to GPIO pins as what they are in the processor.

Video

All models of the Raspberry Pi have high-definition multimedia interface (HDMI) video as a standard output. If you have a monitor that takes a VGA connector, you'll have to get an HDMI-to-VGA adaptor. If you have a normal TV, you can connect the Raspberry Pi to it using the RCA connector.

This RCA connector seemed to have disappeared in the plus models and the Issue 2, but it's still there. It's hidden in what looks like the audio jack, in a TRRS (Tip, Ring, Ring, Sleeve) system. Not all TRRS leads are wired the same, so you have to check if the wiring is compatible with the Raspberry Pi. Go to www.raspberrypi-spy.co.uk/2014/07/raspberry-pi-model-b-3-5mm-audiovideo-jack for details.

Processor

There is a big leap in the performance of the Raspberry Pi when going to the Raspberry Pi 2 from the Raspberry Pi 1. This is because of a change in the processor chip. The Raspberry Pi 1 used a processor with an ARM6 core; the Raspberry Pi 2 uses a processor with an ARM7 core. The difference between these two processors, as far as performance is concerned, is mainly due to the efficiency with which high-level language instructions, like the C language, can be translated into the machine code instructions the processor actually performs. This performance difference is further boosted by the fact there are four cores in the Raspberry Pi 2 processor, potentially allowing it to run four independent processors at the same time. In addition, the ARM6 was run at a 700 MHz clock speed, and the ARM7 runs at 900 MHz.

The processor in the Raspberry Pi 2 also has a larger level-2 cache. This is an area of very fast on-chip memory where machine code instructions are queued up waiting to be processed. Instructions are transferred to the on-chip memory from the slower off-chip memory in bursts, which are more efficient than single memory accesses, which can speed up processing, in some cases considerably.

The bottom line: The Raspberry Pi 2 runs faster than the Raspberry Pi 1. How much faster depends on many factors, but faster by one and a half to six times is the sort of range you're looking at. This definitely elevates the Raspberry Pi into a useable replacement for a desktop machine.

When the Raspberry Pi 2 was launched, a lot was made about the backward compatibility, but this didn't apply to any code that accessed the GPIO pins — all that kind of code stopped working. The reason was that in the new architecture, all the peripherals — including the GPIO — were located at different addresses in the processor's memory map. Fortunately, most users access these peripherals through one of a number of libraries, so when the library you used was updated, the original programs worked again. However, because most libraries are maintained by individuals, some of the libraries didn't get updated. The situation is very fluid, so check to make sure that any library you want to use has been updated for the Raspberry Pi 2. If it has, it should work with both models of Raspberry Pi.

Figuring Out Which Raspberry Pi You Have

You may not know exactly which Raspberry Pi you have. You can easily see if you have a 26-way or a 40-way GPIO connector, but how can your program tell which pins are available?

In Linux, everything is a file, so there is a way of finding out exactly what you have. Just go to a command-line prompt and type the following:

```
cat /proc/cpuinfo
```

On a Raspberry Pi 1 system, you see the following:

```
Processor       : 0
model name      : ARMv6-compatible processor rev 7 (v6l)
Features        : swp half thumb fastmult vfp edsp java tls
CPU implementer : 0x41
CPU architecture : 7
CPU variant     : 0x0
CPU part        : 0xb76
CPU revision    : 7

Hardware        : BCM2708
Revision        : 0010
Serial          : 00000000a5fb87e8
```

The interesting thing is the revision number, which tells you a lot about your Raspberry Pi. Table 4-2 tells you what the revision number means. The words in parentheses are the factories where the Raspberry Pi boards were made.

Table 4-2	Raspberry Pi Revision Numbers
Revision Number	*Raspberry Pi Version*
0002	Model B Revision 1.0
0003	Model B Revision 1.0 + Fuses mod and D14 removed
0004	Model B Revision 2.0 256MB (Sony)
0005	Model B Revision 2.0 256MB (Qisda)
0006	Model B Revision 2.0 256MB (Egoman)
0007	Model A Revision 2.0 256MB (Egoman)
0008	Model A Revision 2.0 256MB (Sony)
0009	Model A Revision 2.0 256MB (Qisda)
000d	Model B Revision 2.0 512MB (Egoman)
000e	Model B Revision 2.0 512MB (Sony)
000f	Model B Revision 2.0 512MB (Qisda)
0010	Model B+ Revision 2.0 512MB (Sony)
0011	Computer Module (Sony)
0012	Model A+ Revision 2.0 256MB (Sony)

You may notice that revision 0011 is the Computer Module, a Raspberry Pi with a very different form factor. This is a Pi built on a small printed circuit board (PCB) with all the connections brought out on PCB edge connectors. This then plugs into a base board of your own design and is meant for industrial or commercial applications. There is also a blank breakout board to do your development on.

If you look at the CPU info on the Raspberry Pi 2 system, you see four processor blocks in much the same format as the Raspberry Pi 1 — one for each core. The last three entries look like this:

```
Hardware    : BCM2709
Revision    : a01041
Serial      : 000000001664c635
```

The revision number is in an entirely different format with different groups of bits having specific meanings. A collection of bytes is known as a *word*, and the processor in the Raspberry Pi uses words that are four bytes or 32 bits long. Bit 23 in the revision word tells you if the revision number is in the old format or the new. For a new format revision number, this bit will be a 1. The interpretation of the revision number under the new format is given by splitting the word up into bytes in this manner:

```
SRRR MMMM PPPP TTTT TTTT VVVV
```

Where

- ✔ S is one bit giving the revision scheme (0 = old, 1 = new).
- ✔ RRR is three bits indicating the RAM size (0 = 256MB, 1 = 512MB, 2 = 1,024MB)
- ✔ MMMM is four bits giving the manufacturer (0 = Sony, 1 = Egoman, 2 = Embest, 3 = Unknown, 4 = Embest).
- ✔ PPPP is four bits giving the processor (0 = 2835, 1 = 2836).
- ✔ TTTT TTTT is eight bits giving the type (0 = A, 1 = B, 2 = A+, 3 = B+, 4 = Pi 2 B, 5 = Alpha, 6 = Computer Module).
- ✔ VVVV is the four-bit version or revision (0–15).

So, the hex number a01041 in the preceding readout gives the following bit pattern when you write it out in binary:

```
1010 0000 0001 0000 0100 0001
SRRR MMMM PPPP TTTT TTTT VVVV
```

For a quick hexadecimal-to-binary converter and a conversion table, check out www.binaryhexconverter.com/hex-to-binary-converter or search the web for "convert hexadecimal to binary."

So, breaking this down:

- ✔ S is 1, which means it's the new revision scheme.
- ✔ R is 010, which is 2 in binary, and that means the RAM is 1,024MB.
- ✔ M is 0000, which is 0 in binary, and that means the manufacturer is Sony.
- ✔ P is 0001, which is 1 in binary, which means the processor is 2836.
- ✔ T is 0000 0100, which is 4 in binary, which means it's a Raspberry Pi 2 Model B.
- ✔ V is 0001, which is 1 in binary, which means it's version 1.

For information on how to read binary, check out www.dummies.com/how-to/content/digital-electronics-binary-basics.html.

There is a warranty bit that gets set if you attempt to overclock the system. This is to prevent people from overclocking the Raspberry Pi, breaking it, and then claiming it was faulty. This warranty bit is bit 24, but when the Raspberry Pi 2 was introduced, the faster clock and higher voltage required for the processor's core was automatically setting this bit, so the warranty bit has been changed to bit 25 for the Raspberry Pi 2. If you're buying a Raspberry Pi secondhand, check this bit before parting with your cash.

For all the projects in this book, you can use any of the versions of the Raspberry Pi. Newer models will run faster, but this shouldn't have much of an impact because physical computing is heavily involved with human interaction. If you find that something runs too fast, a simple small sleep command will throttle back the speed.

On the upside, faster speed is useful if you're using graphics programs like Gimp to prepare graphics for your programs. And a quad-core machine holds out the possibility of running several programs simultaneously at full speed.

Part II
Working with LEDs and Switches

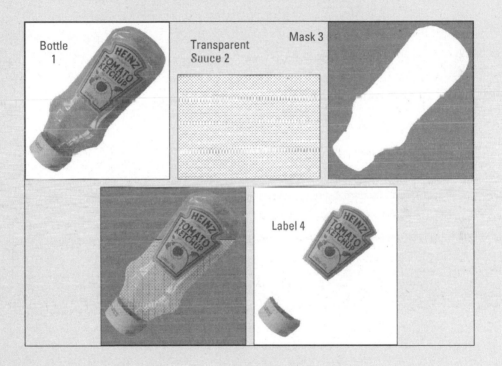

Bottle 1

Transparent Sauce 2

Mask 3

Label 4

In this part . . .

✔ Make projects using LEDs and switches.

✔ Build a sauce bottle simulator.

✔ Construct a bug stomp simulator.

✔ Learn to drive the WS2812b multicolored LED.

✔ Hack a PCB to make the Light Fantastic interface.

✔ Program four full-color games with the Light Fantastic.

Chapter 5

The Sauce Bottle Game

In This Chapter

▶ Making a sauce bottle simulator

▶ Reading a digital input

▶ Creating realistic graphics

▶ Understanding the beginnings of the Pygame framework

The project in this chapter is just about the most fun you can have with a single contact input. Whether you call it catsup, ketchup, or sauce, it's a thixotropic fluid, which means it changes its *viscosity* (runniness) according to the agitation of the fluid.

The Game

The game is simply an interactive sauce bottle where shaking can be sensed by the Raspberry Pi. This is mirrored on the screen by a graphic of the same bottle. However, on the screen, the sauce bottle can be seen to slowly empty in response to the shaking. The idea is to get the bottle emptied in the shortest possible time.

This game is a great introduction to the interaction of hardware and software. Figure 5-1 shows the hardware bottle next to a monitor showing the graphic bottle.

Parts

The parts you need for this project are simple, and you can substitute a wide variety of objects if you don't have exactly the same parts we use. Here are the parts you need:

▶ **Plastic sauce bottle:** We used a Heinz Tomato Ketchup bottle, but you could use another similar plastic bottle.

Figure 5-1:
The finished
game.

- ✔ **6½ feet (2 meters) of twin core cable:** We used microphone shielded cable.

- ✔ **Tilt switch:** The tilt switch consists of a metal ball in a small tube. When the ball rolls down one end, it shorts out the two wires leading into it.

- ✔ **2 single-pin header sockets:** You can use any method of connecting to the general-purpose input/output (GPIO) pins.

- ✔ **Hot melt glue:** You'll need a hot melt glue gun to apply this.

- ✔ **Silicon sealant**

Schematic

The schematic of this circuit (shown in Figure 5-2) is almost trivial, so it's easy to follow.

Always make a schematic whenever you make anything electronic, so you have something to check your construction against.

It doesn't matter which way around you wire the connections on the switch. They just connect and disconnect the GPIO pin 2 to ground. This pin is normally used for the I2C interface. On the board, it's connected to a resistor connected to the 3V3 supply. This is known as a pull-up resistor. It ensures that the logic level on this pin is normally a logic 1, unless the pin is connected to ground, in which case it becomes a logic 0.

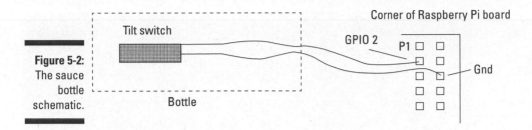

Figure 5-2:
The sauce
bottle
schematic.

Construction

To build this project, follow these steps:

1. **Drill a hole in the top of the bottle for the wire to go in.**

   Our wire was 1.5mm in diameter so we drilled a 2mm hole.

2. **Push the wire through the hole into the bottle.**

   This step is critical. Pushing in the wire from the outside of the bottle is easy. Pushing the wire through the hole from the inside of the bottle is impossible.

3. **With silicon sealant, glue the tilt switch onto the small flexible membrane on the bottle lid, which normally holds back the sauce.**

   Allow the sealant to set.

4. **After the sealant sets, wire the screened cable to the tilt switch, as shown in Figure 5-3.**

   If you haven't used screened cable before, just know that you need to strip off the outer insulation and twist the screen wires together between your fingers. Then tin them by applying a touch of solder, and watch it soak in between the wires. Then trim off the screen a bit to make it tidy. Now strip the inner insulation off the core, twist the wires together, and tin them again. Then make the soldered joints with the switch.

5. **Apply some hot glue over the tilt switch and run it around the base of the cap.**

   Don't overfill it or you'll never get the screw bottle back on the cap.

6. **Screw the cap back onto the bottle and then put a blob of hot glue where the cable comes out of the bottle to fix it.**

   Make sure you leave enough slack in the bottle to remove the cap if any repairs are needed.

Figure 5-3:
Wiring the
screened
cable to the
tilt switch.

7. Attach the other end of the cable to your Raspberry Pi.

You can do this in a variety of different ways with various breakout
boards. Because there are only two wires, we used two single-pin sockets and shells and connected them directly to the GPIO connector, as
shown in Figure 5-4. We soldered the end of the cables to these two
wires and covered the joint with some heat-shrink cable, but you can

Figure 5-4:
Connection
to the GPIO
pins.

use insulating tape if you prefer. Then we carefully placed them on the GPIO connectors before booting up the Raspberry Pi.

As a rule, you should never connect anything to your Raspberry Pi while it's powered up.

Testing

After you've assembled your project, it's time to test the switch. In order to access the GPIO pins, you need a special library. There are a few of these around, but one of our favorites is WiringPi, by Gordon Henderson. There is a Python front end, and it's easy to install.

From the desktop open up a command-line prompt, and type the following:

```
sudo apt-get install python-dev python-pip
sudo pip install wiringpi2
```

That should be it. You can test that it's installed correctly by typing the following:

```
sudo python
import wiringpi2
wiringpi2.piBoardRev()
```

You should see the revision number of your board. However, notice that you have to use the sudo command to access things as the root user. You can still program in the IDLE environment by opening it up and typing the following from a command-line prompt:

```
gksudo idle
```

Then everything you do is as a root user. Get into IDLE like this, open up a new window from the file menu and then type the program in Listing 5-1.

This is a very simple program and shows the basis of reading a GPIO pin. It starts off by importing an instance of the `wiringpi2` library. Then there is a little warning about being a root user. (If the program crashes on the next instruction, it shows that you aren't the root user.) Then the `io.wiringPiSetup()` function is called, which initializes the library. This sets up the pins to use some pin mapping that automatically takes care of the swapping about of pins on this header, which has occurred in the different editions of the board.

Here, GPIO 2 (or GPIO 0 on a Raspberry Pi 1 board) is on connector P1 on pin 3, but it's referred to as pin 8 in the software. It may sound complex, but the point is that pin 8 will access the same pin on the GPIO connector no matter what board revision of the Raspberry Pi you have.

Listing 5-1:   Switch Test

```
#!/ #!/usr/bin/env python
"""
Sauce bottle switch test
"""
import wiringpi2 as io

print "if program quits here start IDLE with 'gksudo idle' from command line"
io.wiringPiSetup()
io.pinMode(8,0) # Physical Pin P1,3 GPIO 2
print "Pin test - Ctrl C to quit"
lastPin = 0
while True :
    pin = io.digitalRead(8)
    if pin != lastPin:
        print "Pin now ", pin
        lastPin = pin
```

Then the io.pinMode(8,0) call makes this pin an input and finally io.digitalRead(8) returns the logic value on this pin. A variable called lastPin holds the previous value on the pin and prevents it from being printed out if it hasn't changed. Run the code and see how the pin state changes with the tilt of the switch. If you don't see any changes, check the wiring and chase down your fault.

The Software

What makes this project really exciting is the combination of good graphics and hardware. In the early days of computers, you had to write code for every line and pixel displayed, but today you can work wonders with digital photographs and image manipulation packages.

In this section, we describe how you can make your own graphics — but there is no need to do this if you don't want to. You can simply download our graphics from the book's companion website (www.dummies.com/go/raspberrypiprojects) if you want to copy exactly what we have.

The idea is that there is a picture of the empty sauce bottle and the software fills it with sauce and then slowly empties it according to how you shake the bottle. You do this by drawing a rectangle of translucent sauce over the bottle and then removing or masking out areas where the sauce should not go. Finally, the label and cap of the bottle are layered over the top to give the illusion that the sauce is actually inside the bottle.

Preparing the graphics

If you want to go it alone and make your own graphics to match your bottle, you have to do a bit of playing about with a graphics application, like Adobe Photoshop (on your desktop or laptop computer) or Gimp (on the Raspberry Pi).

Here are the steps to preparing the graphics yourself:

1. **Using the best digital camera you have access to, take a photograph of your bottle against a white background.**

   Make sure the bottle is at an angle of about 60 degrees.

2. **Save the picture as a high-resolution PNG file.**

   Many cameras create JPGs, so you may have to export the image from your camera and import it onto your computer and then save the image as a PNG using an application like Photoshop.

   All images in the following steps should be saved as PNGs because the JPG image format does not support transparent masks. Also, working at high resolution means any mistakes are minimized when you reduce the picture size later.

3. **Remove any background surrounding the image and replace it with a uniform flat gray.**

4. **Save this image as your base image and call it** `Bottle.png`.

5. **Make a copy of** `Bottle.png`, **and select the gray background.**

6. **Invert the selection and make the selection transparent.**

7. **Save the image and call it** `Mask.png`.

8. **Make another copy of** `Bottle.png` **and paint the same color gray as the background for all of the bottle except the label and the cap.**

9. **Select the gray area and make it transparent.**

10. **Save the resulting image as** `Label.png`.

11. **Make copies of** `Bottle.png`, `Label.png`, **and** `Mask.png` **and place them in another folder called** `Graphics`.

12. **Reduce the image size of all three of the images in the** `Graphics` **folder so that all three pictures are exactly 500 pixels wide.**

13. **Copy the** `Graphics` **folder to the folder you want to have the game in on the Raspberry Pi.**

The trick is to layer these three images along with a rectangle of sauce to build up the image of the half-full sauce bottle, as shown in Figure 5-5.

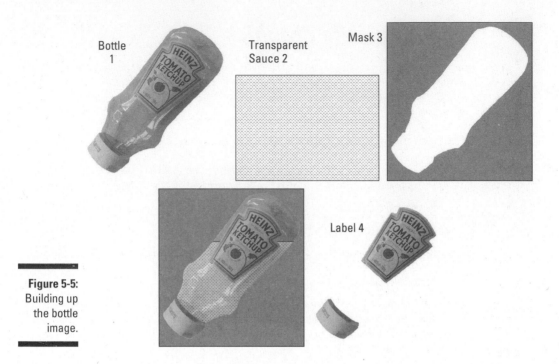

Figure 5-5:
Building up
the bottle
image.

You start with the picture `Bottle.png`, which is the first to be drawn. Then a rectangle of semitransparent sauce is drawn; the height of this rectangle corresponds to how full the bottle is. This rectangle will cover areas outside the bottle image, so in order to remove this, `Mask.png` is drawn on top of it. This mask has a transparent area in the shape of the bottle, so it removes any sauce outside this area. Finally, `Label.png` is drawn so it looks like it isn't being covered by the sauce, which gives the impression that the sauce is inside the bottle. Drawing the sauce as a semitransparent color also adds to this illusion because things like the light reflections off the bottle can still be partly seen through the sauce on the bottom layer, and they're fully seen when the sauce retreats from those reflections. This gives the strong illusion that the sauce is in the bottle.

The rules

The game itself is simple: The bottle starts off full of sauce, and on each shake, a certain amount of sauce is removed and the picture is redrawn. When the bottle is empty, that round of the game is over, and the time it took to empty the bottle is displayed, with a record being kept of the fastest score. There is one more feature that, although it sounds simple, does add quite a bit of code: the game reset, which is triggered by pressing the spacebar. The game reset abandons any current run and refills the bottle.

The game uses the Pygame framework, which allows for easy handling of the keyboard, pictures, and windows. It's included in the standard Raspberry Pi distribution. The code for the game is shown in Listing 5-2.

Listing 5-2: The Sauce Bottle Game

```
#!/usr/bin/env python
"""
Sauce bottle game by Mike Cook
"""
import time, pygame, os, sys
import wiringpi2 as io

print "if program quits here start IDLE with 'gksudo idle' from command line"
io.wiringPiSetup()
io.pinMode(8,0) # Physical Pin P1,3
pygame.init() # initialise graphics interface
os.environ['SDL_VIDEO_WINDOW_POS'] = 'center'
pygame.display.set_caption("The Sauce Bottle")
pygame.event.set_allowed(None)
pygame.event.set_allowed([pygame.KEYDOWN,pygame.QUIT,pygame.MOUSEBUTTONDOWN])

screenWidth = 500
screenHeight = 542
screen = pygame.display.set_mode([screenWidth,screenHeight],0,32)

sBottle = pygame.image.load("Graphics/Bottle.png").convert_alpha()
sLabel = pygame.image.load("Graphics/Label.png").convert_alpha()
sMask = pygame.image.load("Graphics/Mask.png").convert_alpha()

# define the colors to use
cBack =(60,60,60)
pygame.draw.rect(screen, cBack, (0,0,screenWidth, screenHeight),0)
cSauce = (166,30,0) # color of the sauce
returnKey = False ; restart = False

def main():
   global returnKey,restart
   print "Sauce bottle game by Mike Cook"
   full = 100.0 # percent the bottle is full
   highScore = 60.0 # Record time
   while True:
      drawScreen(full)
      print "shake when ready"
      start = time.time()
      while full > 0 :
```

(continued)

Listing 5-2 *(continued)*

```
        while io.digitalRead(8) == 0 and restart == False:
            checkForEvent()
        while io.digitalRead(8) !=0 and restart == False:
            checkForEvent()
        if restart == True :
            full = 0
            print "Reset"
        else :
            full = full - 5.0 #change this number for a faster / slower game
            if full < 0:
                full = 0
            drawScreen(full)
    drawScreen(full) # empty
    if restart == False:
        runTime = time.time() - start
        print"You took ",runTime," to empty the bottle"
        if runTime < highScore:
            print "A new record!"
            highScore = runTime
        print "The record is ",highScore
    else:
        drawScreen(100)
    print "return key for a new game"
    returnKey = False
    while returnKey == False :
        checkForEvent()
    returnKey = False
    restart = False
    full = 100.0

def drawScreen(p) : # draw to the screen
    screen.blit(sBottle,(0,0))
    sauce = pygame.Surface((425,p*4.53)) # maximum sauce
    sauce.set_alpha(170) # transparency of sauce
    sauce.fill(cSauce)
    screen.blit(sauce,(61,11+((100.0-p)*4.53)))
    screen.blit(sMask,(0,0))
    screen.blit(sLabel,(0,0))
    pygame.display.update()

def terminate(): # close down the program
    print ("Closing down please wait")
    pygame.quit() # close pygame
    sys.exit()

def checkForEvent(): # see if we need to quit
    global returnKey,restart
    event = pygame.event.poll()
    if event.type == pygame.QUIT :
```

```
        terminate()
    if event.type == pygame.KEYDOWN :
      if event.key == pygame.K_ESCAPE :
          terminate()
      if event.key == pygame.K_RETURN :
          returnKey = True
      if event.key == pygame.K_SPACE :
          restart = True
    if event.type == pygame.MOUSEBUTTONDOWN :
          print pygame.mouse.get_pos()


if __name__ == '__main__':
    main()
```

The best way to understand this is to look at the functions individually, starting with the last one, checkForEvent, which looks to see if anything has happened that the Pygame framework has picked up in the background. For example, a QUIT event can be the user clicking the close box of the window; if this occurs, the terminate function is called, shutting down everything. Next are the KEYDOWN events, which are picked up if a key is pressed. For example, the Escape key calls the same terminate function as the close box click. The other keys that are of interest simply set variables to indicate that they've been pressed. The way the code works is that this checkForEvent function should be called constantly, as often as possible. If you were in a loop and not calling it, then the program might have thought to have hung. The last event is just for debugging, but we've left it in in case you're adding your own graphics. It simply prints out the *x*- and *y*-coordinates of where the mouse is clicked, which you need to know in order to align and size the sauce rectangle correctly.

The drawScreen function is where all the graphics magic happens, it draws the elements of bottle, sauce, mask, and label just as we describe in the preceding section. It takes in a variable, p, which is the percentage of how full the bottle is, and uses this variable to calculate the size of the sauce rectangle's height. The width is fixed by the maximum extent of the visible area of the bottle. The transparency is set as a value of 170; this is where 255 is fully opaque. You may want to change this value and see how it looks. The rectangle is then drawn with the top representing the top level of the sauce.

Note that in Pygame's windows, the (0,0) coordinate is at the top-left corner and the *y* value increases as you move down the window, which is the opposite of more conventional systems.

The lines at the start of the listing initialize various aspects of the program. It first sets up the hardware GPIO input. Then it sets up the Pygame system and defines the window size. The window size must match your photographs' size. Next the photos are loaded in and the colors are defined. Again, this is an opportunity to change them if you like.

Finally, the `main` function actually plays the game. After setting initial variables and printing out the title, it enters an infinite loop with the `while True:` line. It then draws the picture of the bottle, prints out an invitation to start, and makes a note of the current time so it can calculate the time taken to empty the bottle. The code enters another loop, which repeats as long as the bottle is not full with the `while full > 0:` line. This loop waits for the input to be low and then to be high before removing a bit of the sauce. You can change the amount it removes per shake to make the game longer or shorter. When the bottle is empty, the run is over. The time taken is printed out and checked to see if it's a new fastest score. You can press Return to start again.

Note that the feedback is given in the Python console window, but the game window must have the focus (be the top window) in order for the program to "see" any key presses.

Taking It Farther

You can do even more with this project if you like. Here are some examples:

- You can add sound effects (maybe a squelch for each shake and a fanfare for finishing, with a special one for a new high score). Chapter 13 has a project that uses sound with Pygame so you can see how it's done.

- You can make it so that the timing begins on the first shake of the bottle.

- You can add graphics of the sauce actually squirting out of the bottle.

- You can make the game a two-player game where the players race each other. To do this, you need two bottles and a bigger window.

- You can make the high score permanent by writing it to a file.

- When you get more advanced with handling hardware, you may want to add some flashing red LEDs in the bottle that match the shaking.

What ever you do, there will be a whole lotta shakin' goin' on!

Chapter 6

Stomp!

* *

* *

*N*o matter how complex a project is, the first step is to get an LED flashing. That flashing LED confirms that so much of your system is operating, and then you have a platform to build on.

In this chapter, we show you how you can control LEDs from your Raspberry Pi. There has recently been a big advance for people who want to use a lot of LEDs in their projects: LEDs with built-in controllers, allowing you to easily create colorful projects. We show you how to take advantage of these LEDs in your projects.

Getting Acquainted with the LED

The light emitting diode (LED) was first made available in the mid-1960s and emitted invisible infrared light. An application for LEDs was quickly found in TV remote controls. LEDs work by exciting electrons in a crystal lattice; then, as the electrons lose energy, they emit a photon of light. The wavelength of this light depends on the crystal lattice material, so the drive for visible colors was a drive to find and manufacture semiconductor materials other than silicon and germanium.

An alloy of the metals gallium and arsenic allowed red LEDs to be produced, which was followed slowly over the years by other colors. It wasn't until the 1990s that it was possible to produce a material for blue LEDs. Then about ten years later, you could get a hold of white ones, which work by having an ultraviolet LED shining on a phosphor.

In electronics terms, the LED is a bit of a curiosity in that it isn't a linear device. That means that it doesn't follow Ohm's law, which says that the current increases in proportion to the voltage. With an LED, the situation is like the sauce bottle from Chapter 5: You increase the voltage and the current doesn't increase much; then a threshold is reached, after which a tiny increase in voltage produces a very large increase in current. This means that you can't connect an LED directly to a voltage without it either not working or self-destructing. You have to provide some form of current control, and the simplest way of doing that is to use a resistor in series with the LED.

The value of the series resistor you need to use depends on two factors:

- ✔ The amount of current you want to push through the LED
- ✔ The voltage that is pushing this current

The more current you push through an LED, the brighter it will get. However, there is a limit to how much the LED can take without being fried. For most indicator LEDs, this is 20 mA. So, this is a normal design current to use, but the increase in brightness with current is not proportional.

Well, the increase in brightness with current actually is proportional, but the snag is that the eye doesn't perceive brightness linearly, so the perceived difference between an LED current of 10 mA and 20 mA is not that it is twice as bright but more like only one-third as bright. It is a logarithmic relationship. However, many modern LEDs are high efficiency, which means you can get much brighter for the same amount of current or you can get just as bright for less current.

Calculating the resistor value is simple, but it can be confusing at first. Consider the circuit shown in Figure 6-1, which shows an LED and resistor connected to a voltage source. If you take a meter and measure the voltage across the resistor and the voltage across the LED, both readings will add up to the voltage produced by the voltage source. This sort of thing is known as a *potential divider*.

Now, you want the voltage across the LED to be enough to light it up. It has to be the threshold voltage, known as the *forward voltage drop*. You find this voltage quoted in the data sheet of the LED. (If you don't have a data sheet, you can guess it from the color or, even better, use a nominal resistor of something like 510 R [ohms] and actually measure it with your meter.) Normally, the forward voltage drop for each color LED is roughly the same, with red having the lowest voltage and white having the highest.

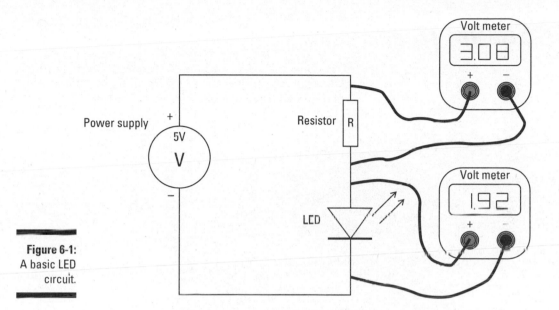

Figure 6-1:
A basic LED circuit.

Once you know the voltage drop across the LED, what's left of the voltage from the supply (that is, the supply voltage minus the LED voltage) is what's across the resistor. If you know what current you want to let flow through the resistor and you know what voltage is across it, you can rearrange Ohm's law and calculate what value the resistor should be. The circuit is a series circuit, so whatever current is flowing through the resistor has to be flowing through the LED, so you can calculate what resistor you need for what current. This can be summarized in the following formula:

Resistance = (Supply Voltage – LED Voltage Drop) ÷ Required Current

When you do this, you'll almost certainly get a value of resistance that is not manufactured. Resistors come in a series of "standard" values, and in this case you pick the standard value that is closest to but higher than the one you calculated. This gives you slightly less current than you designed for, but you won't be able to tell the difference.

You're deciding what current you want to flow and, hence, the brightness. Given that, you calculate the resistance. The actual current is not very critical — don't get hung up on getting exact resistor values. Modern white LEDs are very efficient, and you can get quite a bright output for a few mA, so if you just want an indicator, you don't need much current.

Stomp 1

This project uses LEDs connected directly to the GPIO port. It's a ring of LEDs to play a game we call Stomp. (If you're in the UK, think of this as Stamp.) You can see the finished unit on top of a Raspberry Pi in Figure 6-2.

Figure 6-2:
Stomp 1 LED
ring.

Stomp is a game where lots of bugs are running around, and you have to stomp on them when they pass under your foot. But if there isn't one under your foot when you stomp down, a new bug pops up. The object of the game is to clear all the LEDs in as short a time as possible. The creatures are represented by a ring of white LEDs and the stomping foot by two red LEDs on either side of the ring (red, of course, for blood). You do the actual stomping on a momentary foot switch.

Parts

This project requires a lot of GPIO pins, so you need a Raspberry Pi Model B+, a Raspberry Pi Model A+, a Raspberry Pi 2 Model B+, or a Raspberry Pi 2 Model A+ — in other words, you need a Raspberry Pi with a 40-pin GPIO header. If you have an earlier Pi, Stomp 2, later in this chapter, is for you — it can be run on all models.

Here's what you need to make Stomp 1:

- ✔ A Raspberry Pi with a 40-pin GPIO connector
- ✔ A 2½-x-3¾-inch (60-x-95-mm) stripboard
- ✔ Twenty-four 3mm white LEDs
- ✔ Two 3mm red LEDs
- ✔ A foot-operated momentary switch
- ✔ Twenty-four R1 value resistors for the white LEDs (we used 330R)
- ✔ Two R2 value resistors for the red LEDs (we used 220R)
- ✔ A two-pin header strip
- ✔ A two-pin header socket
- ✔ A thin 0.5m flexible twin core cable
- ✔ A 40-way surface mount header socket

Schematic

This is a simple circuit, but a lot of the impact requires a clean-looking board. That means we've done all the wiring on the underside of the board to make the top side clutter free. You can even use surface mount resistors on the underside of the board if you want, for the ultimate in anti-clutter. The basic schematic is shown in Figure 6-3.

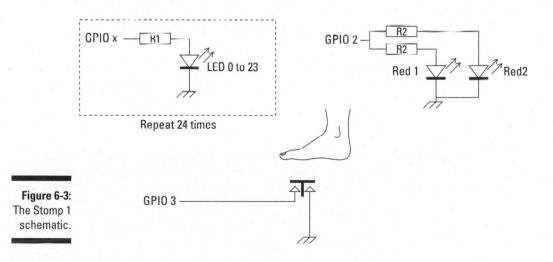

Figure 6-3:
The Stomp 1
schematic.

You can see that the bulk of the circuit is simply an LED connected through current limiting resistors connected to the GPIO pins repeated 24 times, with a different GPIO pin for each LED. The association between the GPIO pin and the LED was partly dictated by the physical layout and the need to make the wires as short as possible, but it isn't important because in software the relationship is defined by a lookup table in the form of a list. The two red LEDs can be driven from the same GPIO pin because you only ever want to turn both of them on at the same time. Finally, the foot switch is connected directly to GPIO 3, which has an onboard strong pull-up resistor so the switch can be on a long length of wire and not suffer from interference pickup.

Design

The only thing to design here is the two values of the LEDs' current limiting resistor. The exact value will depend on the type of LEDs you have and what current looks good. You don't want to pull too much current directly from the GPIO pins. Although 16 mA is the maximum you should draw per pin, there is a rough 55 mA limit on the total current draw from the chip, so we designed the white LED limiting resistor for 1.7 mA. With the 3V3 voltage of the GPIO pins and the 3.0V forward voltage drop of the LEDs we had, this give a resistor value of 330R. For the red LEDs, we gave them 7.5 mA each and used 220R resistors, so they had a 1.7V forward voltage drop.

Check with the LEDs you have to see if the brightness is right before building the circuit.

Construction

The circuit is simple, but if you want to copy exactly what we've done, you need to take some care. We built the prototype on stripboard. Many beginners think that you have to make as many connections as possible with the strips, but this isn't the case. It's fine if some connections work out like that, but don't go overboard trying to make it work this way.

Our main design consideration was to get the LEDs to look as much like a circle as possible, despite being laid out on a 0.1-inch square grid. That was our starting point. Then to fix it to the Pi, we used a twin-row pin header socket. It needs to mount on the underside of the stripboard, so we used a surface mount socket. In fact, we didn't have a 40-pin strip so we cut down a length of 52-pin strip we had. A saw cut to the first waste socket and a quick clean with a fine file were all that was needed.

The circuit laid out is shown in Figure 6-4. We've numbered the columns and rows of the stripboard so we could build up a cutting and wiring list for you to follow. Note the position of the LEDs. There is a very subtle flat on the cathode side of the LED, which is normally the lead that is the shorter of the two. We recommend you make a note of which way around your LEDs are before you get very far with the construction.

Construction should start on the underside of the board, which is shown in Figure 6-5. This shows all the tracks you need to cut. Note that all but two tracks are cut at the hole. A simple circular motion left and right, either side of the hole, with a scalpel is all you need to cut the track. The two red LEDs require a small strip being cut out of the track between the holes. Make two cut lines as close together as possible, and peel off the copper track in between.

On the book's companion website (www.dummies.com/go/raspberry piprojects), there is an image file of Figure 6-5 so that you can print it out full size and lay your board over it. Then you can easily identify the columns and rows. Instead of picking out tracks to cut from the diagram, we've produced a spreadsheet containing a list of tracks to cut. This spreadsheet also contains a list of component placements and a list of wiring links.

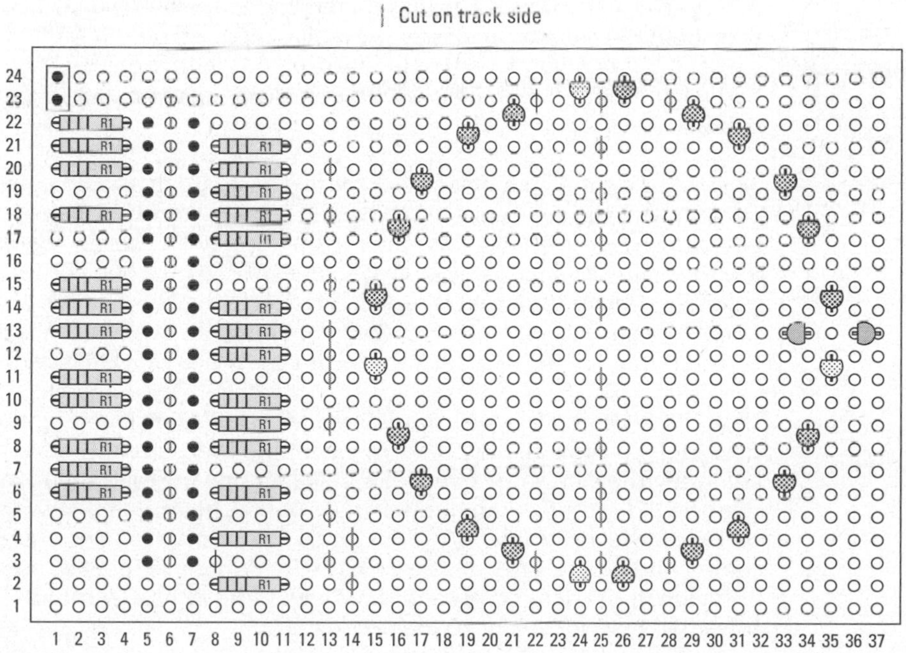

Figure 6-4:
The top side
of Stomp 1.

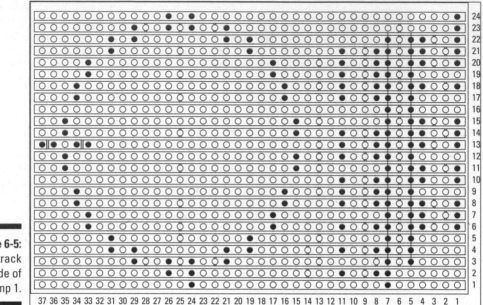

Figure 6-5:
The track
side of
Stomp 1.

The first step is to cut the tracks on the underside of the board. This might take about 30 minutes and requires a bit of concentration. After it was cut, we used the continuity testing function on our multimeter to check that they had been broken and there were no thin whiskers of copper still making a contact.

Next, mount the 40-pin header socket on the board. It should cover the column with the cut tracks and have the small legs covering the track until it almost reaches the hole. Make sure it's placed evenly so the legs on each side are the same distance away from the holes. Then tack one corner with a blob of solder. Check again that it's placed correctly because at this stage it's easy to correct any misalignment by simply melting the one joint. When you're satisfied that it's straight, tack the leg on the other side and check again.

Next is the point of no return, solder all the remaining legs. Flip the board over and solder all the resistors in place, and then carefully add the LEDs, soldering them in one at a time. First, solder one LED and then look to see that the LED stands straight up. If it's crooked, place your iron on the joint and push the top of the LED so it's square and upright. Then you can solder the second leg and snip off the excess wire. You have to make sure that the LEDs are in the right holes, and that they're the right way round. Finally, add the small two-pin header to the board.

All that remains is to wire it up. We've devised the wiring so that it always goes between two points on the board that already have a component in them. We used thin 28 AWG insulated solid core wire for the wiring. Strip just the smallest amount you can from the wire, no more that 2mm or so. Apply your soldering iron to the solder on the component already on the board and push the wire in. Beginners tend to strip too much insulation back. Be constrained, and always cut what you think is too little.

A list of the point-to-point connections is in the spreadsheet on the book's companion website. Also on the website is a multicolored diagram showing all the wiring. This can look like a bit of a mess, but the colors should enable you to pick out the connections one at a time. However, we think it's best just to use the wiring list. You can print it out and cross off each connection as you make the link.

A two-pin header strip is attached to the top end of the board. We made an extension lead with thin flexible microphone wire and finished it off with a two-pin header socket.

Software

While working on another of our Raspberry Pis — one of the types with a 26-way GPIO socket — we ran the following code and it froze out the keyboard and mouse. This is because it was playing about with GPIO pins that shouldn't be altered on earlier revisions, so we put a check in the code to test that it was the right board before the code would run.

Basically, the presence of a bug is held in a list called critters. If a list value contains a 1, that represents a bug; if it contains a 0, that means no bug. The list is rotated each step, and the new list of LEDs is displayed. This gives the appearance of the lights going around in circles. The program is shown in Listing 6-1.

Listing 6-1:   Stomp 1 Game

```python
#!/usr/bin/env python
# Stomp 1
# Author: Mike Cook

import time, random, sys, re
import wiringpi2 as io
from collections import deque
```

(continued)

Listing 6-1 *(continued)*

```
print"if program quits here start IDLE with 'gksudo idle' from command line"
io.wiringPiSetupGpio()
print"OK no crash" ; print" "

numLEDs = 24
stompPos = 18
critters = deque([ 0 for i in range(0,numLEDs) ])
direction = True # direction to run round the ring
#GPIO LED pin numbers for LEDS 0 to 23
pinLED = [20,21,19,26,13,5,11,7,17,4,18,15,14,22,23,24,25,27,8,10,9,6,12,16]
pinRed = 2 #GPIO
stompSwitch = 3 #GPIO
sTime = 0.2
random.seed()


def main():
    if getrevision() < 0x10:
        print"You can only run this on a Pi with a 40 pin GPIO connector"
        sys.exit()
    initGPIO()
    wipe()
    lastSwitch = 0
    print"Stomp on the bugs"
    while True:
        setup()
        startTime=time.time()
        while critters.count(0) != numLEDs:
          switch = io.digitalRead(stompSwitch)
          if lastSwitch != 0 and switch == 0:
              stomp = True
              if critters[stompPos] >0 :
                 critters[stompPos] = 0
              else:
                 critters[stompPos] = 1
          else :
              stomp = False
          showCritters(stomp)
          moveCritters(direction)
          lastSwitch = switch
          time.sleep(sTime)
        wipe()
        print "all gone in ",time.time() - startTime,"seconds"
        print"have another go"
        time.sleep(3)

def moveCritters(wayRound):
    global critters
    if wayRound:
        critters.rotate(1)
    else :
        critters.rotate(-1)
```

```python
def showCritters(stamp):
    for p in range(0,numLEDs):
        io.digitalWrite(pinLED[p],critters[p])
    if stamp :
        io.digitalWrite(pinRed,1)
    else:
        io.digitalWrite(pinRed,0)

def setup():
    global critters,direction,stompPos
    for c in range(0,3):
        choice = random.randint(0, numLEDs -1 )
        while critters[choice] != 0 :
            choice = random.randint(0, numLEDs -1 )
        critters[choice] = 1
    if  random.randint(0,1) == 0:
        direction = True
        stompPos = 19
    else:
        direction = False
        stompPos = 18

def wipe():
    for i in range(0, numLEDs ):
        io.digitalWrite(pinLED[i],0)
    io.digitalWrite(pinRed,0)

def initGPIO():
    for i in range (0, numLEDs ):
        io.pinMode(pinLED[i],1) # to output
    io.pinMode(stompSwitch,0) # to input
    io.pinMode(pinRed,1) # to output

def getrevision():
  revision = "unknown"
  with open('/proc/cmdline', 'r') as f:
    line = f.readline()
    try:
        m = re.search('bcm2708.boardrev=(0x[0123456789abcdef]*) ', line)
        revision = m.group(1)
    except:
        m = re.search('bcm2709.boardrev=(0x[0123456789abcdef]*) ', line)
        revision = m.group(1)
  return revision & 0xff


# Main program logic follows:
if __name__ == '__main__':
    main()
```

A fundamental requirement of the program is that a list should be able to be quickly rotated, clockwise or counterclockwise. To do this, we used Python's double-ended queue (deque) module, and initialized the empty critters list at the start of the code. Each LED in the ring is numbered 0 to 23, and the GPIO pin corresponding to the number is given in the pinLED list. Some global variables are declared before entering the main function.

The first thing the function does is check to make sure the revision number is large enough to have a 40-pin GPIO connector (see Chapter 4). Then the GPIO pins are initialized. (Because GPIO 3 has an external pull-up resistor on the board, there is no need to enable the software one.) Then the wipe function turns off all the LEDs — both those in the ring and the red ones. Finally, an infinite loop is entered that defines a game or round. In this loop, the setup function defines the initial population of bugs by choosing three random locations to place a 1 in the critters list. There is some code to make sure that three different positions are chosen. Then the code chooses a direction to march the bugs for this game and defines the stomp position for each direction. You need to have the "killing field" located just in front of the boot, or red LEDs as you may like to call them.

A record of the system time is made so that the time taken to squash all the bugs can be printed out at the end. Then, a while loop plays the game, continuing until the critters list is full of zeros. The game loop consists of looking at the stomp switch and comparing it to what the switch state was the last time around the loop. This ensures that only the first time the switch is pressed counts as a stomp. The code then looks at the stomp position in the critters list and removes a critter if there is a number 1 in this location; otherwise, it adds a 1 to the list.

The showCritters function is called, which lights up the LEDs corresponding to where the bugs are in the list. The red LEDs are also lit up if the stomp switch has just been activated. Next, the moveCritters function is called, which rotates the critters list. Finally, a delay is called; the sTime variable set up at the start of the code defines how fast the game runs.

When all the bugs have been stomped on, the time taken to clear the ring is printed and a new game is started.

How it plays

In practice, the game plays very well, with a good mixture of tension and reaction. It takes some concentration to rid the circle of bugs. Sometimes we didn't keep our feet on the switch for long enough to register a stomp — we were being far too jittery. All in all, a most enjoyable game — and it was a surprise that we found it easier to clear a ring moving clockwise than counterclockwise.

You may want to take things further, like introducing a small random jitter into the sleep delay to break up any rhythm a player builds up. You may want to add sound effects or keep a high score. You could have more initial bugs in the list or you could reverse the direction of rotation after a fixed time or even after each stomp.

If you only have a Raspberry Pi Model B, you could modify the design to use only 15 LEDs and an input.

Stomp 2

The Stomp 1 game with discrete LEDs is great, but you need a lot of GPIO pins on your Raspberry Pi, and each LED is only one color. Plus, it takes a bit of skill to make. Stomp 2 uses much more ready-built components and is a multicolor game. It's slightly different from Stomp 1 in that it takes three stomps to kill the bugs; each stomp on a bug changes its color, until the last one removes it. In order to get a fine range of colors, you need to know how you control the brightness of an LED (see the nearby sidebar).

Controlling brightness

Although the resistor value sets the maximum brightness for an LED, it's possible to control or fade the brightness down from this maximum. There are two ways of doing this:

✏ **By altering the voltage of the supply:** Unfortunately this approach isn't very satisfactory, because of the nonlinear nature of the LED's current flow. Imagine you can control the voltage smoothly between 0 and 5 volts. For the lower part of the range, below the forward voltage drop, the LED will not be lit. Then, as the voltage is increased past this point, the LED will get brighter very quickly. The increase in brightness will drop off as the voltage approaches the maximum. So, the useful range of control over the brightness is very small.

✏ **By using pulse width modulation (PWM):** This approach simply involves flashing the LED on and off very rapidly. If you do this faster than 32 flashes per second, you can't see the LED flashing due to your persistence of vision. The time you keep the LED on relative to the time it is off is known as the *duty cycle.* Changing this duty cycle changes the apparent brightness of the LED.

Many microcomputer chips have outputs that can automatically generate the PWM signal when you give it the duty cycle you want. The chip in the Raspberry Pi has only two such outputs, and one is used for the sound output, so there is only one output free. So, although it's easy to fade one LED, it isn't that easy to control more than one without extra hardware.

Design

The snag with using a lot of LEDs is that they can take a lot of current. Each WS2812b (see "The WS2182b," later in this chapter) can take about 66 mA, and when you add that up for 24 of them, you get just over 1.5 amps. This is way more than the Raspberry Pi can provide, even if you have a big power supply. So, you need another 5V supply.

The other snag is that the Raspberry Pi is only a 3V3 system; ideally, the LEDs need a 5V data signal, which is just outside the reach of the GPIO lines. However, if the supply voltage is not 5V but just under at 4.8V, this is often enough to allow the Pi's GPIO pin to drive it directly, as long as you put the data signal through a 470R series resistor. This improves the signal shape by damping down ringing on the GPIO signal and preventing reflections on the line.

The LEDs themselves can be driven with 3V3, but they aren't as bright. Besides, 3V3 external power supplies can be hard to come by. The better solution to the driving problem is to use a level shifting circuit. This is a good solution and is guaranteed to give you the best results.

Parts

Here are the parts you need for this game:

- Any Raspberry Pi
- A 2-x-½-inch (48-x-12mm) stripboard
- A 24-pixel WS2182b LED ring
- A foot-operated momentary switch
- Two 5K6 resistors
- A two-pin header strip
- A five-pin header strip
- A two-pin header socket
- A thin 0.5m twin core cable
- A 2.1mm power jack socket
- A 5V power supply with at least 2A capability
- A 2N7000 FET
- A push-button switch
- Five header pin socket leads and shells

The WS2812b

Recently, a component has been introduced that is a game changer as far as hobby projects are concerned. It's the WS2812b or, as branded by Adafruit Industries, the NeoPixel. This isn't just one LED but three in one package — a red one, a green one, and a blue one. But what makes it remarkable is that each package contains not only the three LEDs but also a controller chip that can alter the brightness of each LED. This makes it possible to make an almost unlimited range of colors by mixing these three primary colors in varying amounts. What's more, the controllers are chainable — a serial output of one device feeds into the serial input of the next device. So, you can have several hundred LEDs, all controlled from a single GPIO pin.

The big snag with using the WS2812b with the Raspberry Pi is that the LED requires feeding with a very precisely timed stream of data. Normally, the interrupts that Linux gives to any program would disrupt the timing, and the system wouldn't work. Fortunately, there is a very clever way around this. Unfortunately, the details are very complex and way outside the range of this book. To the rescue comes Jeremy Garff, who has produced a library along with a Python wrapper that makes it very easy to use these LEDs. Under the hood, it uses a DMA channel, direct memory access, which allows simple operations like moving memory from one place to another without the intervention of the computer's processor. This, coupled with the pulse width modulation (PWM) register and an internal FIFO (first in, first out) memory buffer, allows the precisely timed data stream to be generated.

The WS2812b comes in many different products. There are single individual surface mount packages, or you can get them mounted on a tiny PCB for easy soldering. They come in ready-built configurations like an 8-x-8 square matrix or a ring of LEDs. The LED rings are interesting — you can get a small 12-LED ring, a 16-LED ring, or a 24-LED ring. If you want to go even bigger, you can get a ring quadrant so that four together gives you a 60-LED ring. You can even get them in conventional 5mm and 10mm LED packages.

For Stomp 2, we use a 24-LED ring. These have a 66mm outside diameter and are just about the smallest diameter you can get 22 LEDs into.

Schematic

Figure 6-6 shows how this is put together. The level converter is mounted on a small piece of stripboard and connects to the Raspberry Pi through header socket leads. Make sure that your power jack socket matches your power supply output lead.

The wiring is quite simple, and there is an additional switch on this version to act as a reset button. We found it was easy for things to get out of hand with this version of the game with far too many bugs being generated. So, instead of quitting and restarting the program, we thought it would be a good idea to have a simple push button to clear out all the bugs. You can leave out the reset switch altogether if you want. It will have no effect being left open circuit.

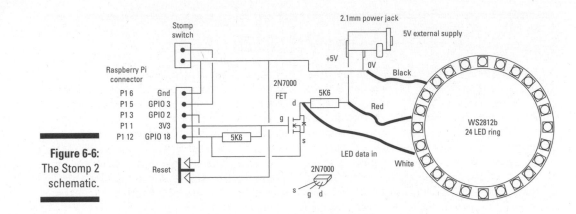

Figure 6-6:
The Stomp 2
schematic.

The 2N7000 FET acts as a noninverting level converter, boosting the 3V3 signal from the Raspberry Pi to a 5V signal for driving the LED's controller. The only GPIO pin you can use on the Pi is GPIO 18, because that's the only one capable of having the PWM register switched to it. The resistor values aren't too critical. Anything between 1K and 10K should be fine.

Construction

There is not too much to the construction — the only tricky bit may be mounting the power jack on the stripboard. The thing is, it simply won't fit on the 0.1-inch pitch of the holes. What we did was put a small router bit in our drill and cut three slots in the stripboard so the connections would fit in. If you don't have a router bit, you can make do with some fine needle files to cut the slots; use the point of the round one to get you started.

When the power jack fits snugly on the stripboard, the rest of the circuit can be built around it. The layout we used is shown in Figure 6-7, and a photograph is shown in Figure 6-8. The power jack has three connections. You need to use only the two in the middle; the one on the side is just used for mechanical stability. Solder it to some tracks, but electrically don't go anywhere with it.

Note that the copper strips run vertically. Make sure you get this right when you cut your stripboard to size. The reset push button we used was a two-wire one. There is room to put a four-connector switch here if you want.

Using opposite corners when wiring these is simplest. The board can be wired to the GPIO connector any way you want. We used two six-way shells to make up a short connector between the GPIO header pins and the five-pin connector on the level shifting board.

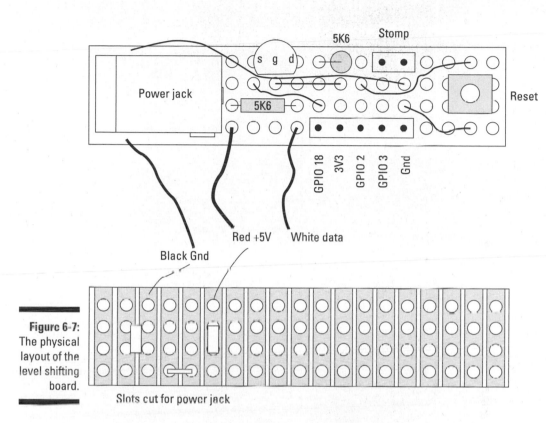

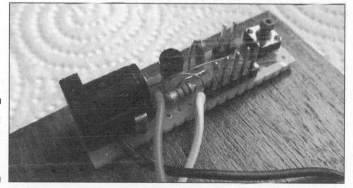

Figure 6-7:
The physical
layout of the
level shifting
board.

Slots cut for power jack

Figure 6-8:
The level
shifting
board.

Finally, we stuck the board and LED ring to a piece of plywood with a generous helping of hot glue. A few coats of medium oak wood staining varnish beforehand made the whole thing look a lot more upmarket than it sounds. A photograph of the finished unit is shown in Figure 6-9.

Figure 6-9:
The finished
Stomp 2
game.

Software

Before you can start using these awesome WS2812b devices, you need to download and install the library to drive them. Do this by typing the following from the command line:

```
wget https://github.com/tdicola/rpi_ws281x/raw/master/python/dist/rpi_ws281x-
            1.0.0-py2.7-linux-armv6l.egg
sudo easy_install rpi_ws281x-1.0.0-py2.7-linux-armv6l.egg
```

Note: armv6l ends in the letter *l* and not the number 1.

Then you need to connect the circuit and run the code in Listing 6-2.

Never plug anything into the Pi while it's powered up. Always shut down, disconnect the power, attach the device, and reconnect the power.

Listing 6-2:   Stomp 2 Game

```python
#!/usr/bin/env python
# Stomp 2
# Author: Mike Cook

import time, random
import wiringpi2 as io
from collections import deque
from neopixel import *
```

```
print"if program quits here start IDLE with 'gksudo idle' from command line"
io.wiringPiSetupGpio()
print"OK no crash" ; print" "

numLEDs = 24
strip = Adafruit_NeoPixel(numLEDs,18,800000,5,False)
sTime = 0.2
critColor = [Color(0, 0, 0),Color(0, 0, 32),Color(0, 32, 0),Color(32, 32, 32)]
stompColor = Color(32, 0, 0)
stompPos = 12
stompSwitch = 3 ; resetSwitch = 2
critters = deque([ 0 for i in range(0,numLEDs) ])
direction = True # direction to run round the ring

def main():
    initGPIO()
    strip.begin()
    wipe()
    lastSwitch = 0
    print"Stomp on the bugs - three stomps to kill"
    while True:
        setup()
        startTime=time.time()
        while critters.count(0) != numLEDs:
            if io.digitalRead(resetSwitch) == 0 :
                resetGame()
            switch = io.digitalRead(stompSwitch)
            if lastSwitch != 0 and switch == 0:
                stomp = True
                if critters[stompPos] >0 :
                    critters[stompPos] -= 1
                else:
                    critters[stompPos] = 3
            else:
                stomp = False
            showCritters(stomp)
            moveCritters(direction)
            lastSwitch = switch
            time.sleep(sTime)
        wipe()
        print "all gone in ",time.time() - startTime,"seconds"
        print"have another go"
        time.sleep(3)

def moveCritters(wayRound):
    global critters
    if wayRound:
        critters.rotate(1)
    else :
        critters.rotate(-1)
```

(continued)

Listing 6-2 *(continued)*

```python
def showCritters(stamp):
    for p in range(0,numLEDs):
        strip.setPixelColor(p, critColor[critters[p]])
    if stamp :
        strip.setPixelColor(stompPos, stompColor)
    strip.show()

def setup():
    global critters,direction
    for c in range(0,3):
        choice = random.randint(0,23)
        while critters[choice] != 0 :
            choice = random.randint(0,23)
        critters[choice] = 3
    if  random.randint(0,1) == 0:
        direction = True
    else:
        direction = False

def resetGame() :
    global critters
    for i in range(0,numLEDs):
        critters[i] = 0
    print"Game restarted"
    while io.digitalRead(resetSwitch) == 0:
        pass # wait until switch released

def wipe():
    for i in range(0,strip.numPixels()):
        strip.setPixelColor(i, Color(0, 0, 0))
    strip.show()

def initGPIO():
    io.pinMode(stompSwitch,0) # input
    io.pinMode(resetSwitch,0) # input

# Main program logic follows:
if __name__ == '__main__':
    main()
```

The overall structure of the code is the same as the Stomp 1 game, but there are some changes needed to drive the WS2812b LEDs. The driver builds up data in a buffer, so whenever you want to change an LED's color, you put the data in the buffer with the setPixelColor method. Nothing will change on the LEDs until you transfer that buffer out to the LEDs using the show method of the library. The data buffer object is set up using the `Adafruit_` `NeoPixel` call. The numbers in the call are explained in the files that came with the library, if you're interested, but it just tells the library how many LEDs to drive, on what pin (you can't change this), and on what frequency. The `False` at the end allows you to invert the output signal in case you use an inverting buffer as a level shifter.

The major change here is that the critters list holds a number, and that number defines the color of the LED. Each time a bug is stomped on, this number is decremented until it reaches 0. Because the LEDs can change color, there is no need for a red stomp LED — you just set the LED at the stomp position to red.

The two games are virtually identical to play, but these LEDs can be too bright to look at directly. This is reflected in the color definitions, but you may want to do what we did and add a diffuser over the LEDs. We used some 0.5mm styrene sheet and cut out a circle with scissors, but a sheet of white paper works nearly as well. You may want to mark the stomp position if you do that.

Have a stomping good time!

Chapter 7

The Light Fantastic

*T*his project is about producing a universal 4-x-4 illuminated switch matrix. Why? Because it's a great base for so many projects with physical interfaces. This chapter shows you how to build and test it, as well as produce a light show with it. In Chapter 8, we show you how to make four games using this interface, as well as a whole host of other uses you can put this to. A photograph of the final project is shown in Figure 7-1.

Figure 7-1:
The finished
Light
Fantastic.

Introducing the Light Fantastic

This interface can be described as an undedicated controller. It consists of 16 push switches, each illuminated by an RGB LED. In Chapter 6, you see how you can use LEDs and, in particular, a long strip of LEDs, all controlled by a single Raspberry Pi pin. Those LEDs in the strip are also available in a normal 5mm LED package, and they're used to create this project.

Before the availability of WS2812b LEDs, constructing a project like this was complex. The multiplexing required meant that it couldn't be done with a Raspberry Pi, because of the time-stealing nature of the Linux core. But with this revolutionary LED, this project is comparatively easy.

There are many ways to build this project, but the one we show you here is simple because it makes use of a readymade printed circuit board. This printed circuit board wasn't designed to use the WS2812b LEDs; instead, it was designed to use the more conventional common anode or common cathode RGB LEDs. We show you how to hack the printed circuit board in order to take this new component.

Here are the components you need:

- Button Pad 4x4–LED Compatible (`www.sparkfun.com/products/7835`)
- Button Pad 4x4–Breakout PCB (`www.sparkfun.com/products/8033`)
- 16 WS2812b 5mm LEDs
- 16 1N4148 or similar diodes
- 16 0.1uF ceramic capacitors
- 470R resistor
- 0.5 meter of 26-way ribbon cable
- 26-way IDC socket (or 40-way if you're using a Raspberry Pi Model B+)
- Four 15mm hexagonal M3 tapped pillars or spacers
- 13 M3 10mm pan-head screws
- 12 M3 10mm countersunk screws
- 21 M3 hex nuts

For the enclosure we used:

- Scrap PCB boards for the side (you can also use ABS or thin plywood)
- 3mm ABS sheet for the base, top cover, and light baffle
- 200mm of 7mm (or so) angle aluminum

The Circuit

There are two parts to the circuit of the Light Fantastic: One is for the switches and is called a switch matrix; the other is for the switch illuminating LED. We start with the LEDs.

LEDs

This is a very simple circuit. It consists of a single string of 16 WS2812b LEDs, chained together, with the data output of one going into the data input of the next. Each LED has a connection to a 5V and ground of a power supply. In most cases, this can be driven directly off the general-purpose input/output (GPIO) pins of the Raspberry Pi, as long as the Pi's power supply can handle an extra amp of current. The only other component is a 0.1uF ceramic decoupling capacitor across the power supply of each LED. The circuit is shown in Figure 7-2.

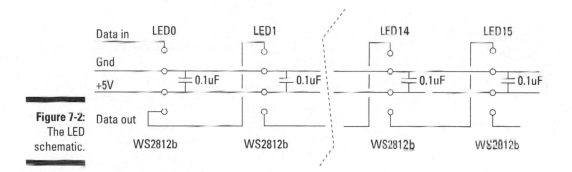

Figure 7-2:
The LED
schematic.

Note: Figure 7-2 shows just 4 of the 16 LEDs for clarity; the other 12 LEDs are wired just the same between the broken doted lines.

Switches

The switch circuit is a bit more complex. It's based around the 4 x 4 silicone button pad sold by SparkFun Electronics, composed of 16 switch covers that have a ring of conduction carbon at the base. The idea is that it fits over a dual ring and spoke track on a PCB; when the cover is pressed, the conducting ring makes contact and shorts out the inner and outer PCB track rings, completing a circuit.

In theory, you could just wire up each switch to a separate GPIO pin, but when you use a lot of keys, you use a lot of inputs, so switches are often arranged in a matrix, as shown in Figure 7-3. In a matrix, there are rows of switch inputs feeding into column outputs. Each switch is isolated with a diode. This component lets the electric current flow only one way; it's important to stop the production of phantom key presses when more than one switch is pressed at once. You can see that although there are 16 switches, only 8 GPIO pins are used. In general for a square matrix, the number of switches you can have is the square of half the number of GPIO pins you use. As you use more GPIO pins, the saving becomes greater.

The price you pay for this efficiency in hardware is that you need to be clever with the software. Basically, the software scans the matrix. It puts one row line high and the others low. Then it looks at each column input in turn, and if an input is found with a logic 1 on it, you know what key is being pressed on that first row. If nothing is found, then that row is made to output a 0 and the next row is set high. Then the inputs are scanned again. This process is repeated until the whole matrix has been scanned. Suppose switch SW9 is pressed. Only when Row 3 is high will there be a high on Column 2.

Here's a small trick to save time seeing if any key is being pressed: Put all the rows high and then if you see a logic high on any column, you know that some key is being pressed. Although this isn't the only way to read a keypad matrix like this one, it's by far the most common and is the method used on the board we're going to hack.

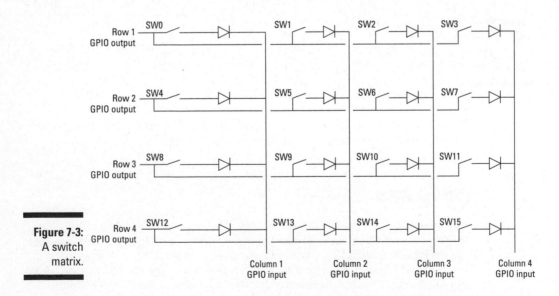

Figure 7-3: A switch matrix.

The PCB

In addition to reading switches in a matrix, you can light LEDs in a similar manner, and that's what the board you're going to hack was originally designed to do. In each row, all the red LEDs are connected together, as are the green and blue components of the RGB LEDs. This is shown in Figure 7-4, along with the pin out of the RGB LEDs used. Also shown are the connector numbers for the rows and columns. Note the switch matrix circuit in addition to the LED circuit on the board. The switch row inputs are marked as S on the connector pads labeled JP.

To convert this into a circuit suitable for the WS2812b LEDs, you need to cut some tracks and add some links in order to convert it into the circuit shown in Figure 7-5. Note how similar it is. What was the blue LED connection on the original board will now be the positive 5V power line. For each row, the green connection is the data input to the first LED, and the red connection is the output from the last LED in the row. Each LED has its data output linked to the data input of the next LED in the row with a wire link.

So, first, you need to make 25 cuts in the tracks of the PCB. The trick is making the correct 25 cuts (see the X's in Figure 7-6). These cuts should be done with a sharp knife or scalpel. Make two cuts in the track close to each other, and then use the blade to remove the small section of track between the two cuts.

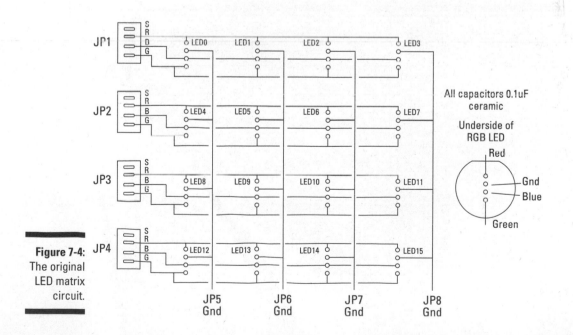

Figure 7-4: The original LED matrix circuit.

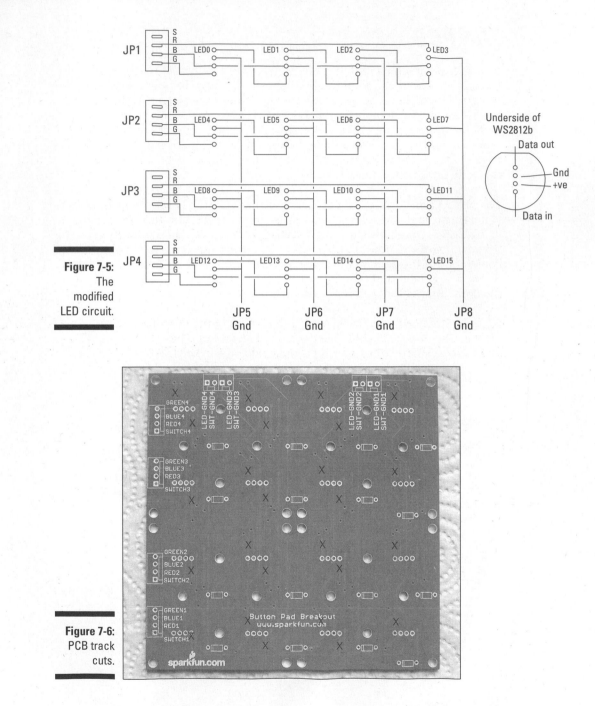

Figure 7-5:
The
modified
LED circuit.

Figure 7-6:
PCB track
cuts.

The only tricky cut is the one on the data output of the first LED on row 1, next to the label Switch 1. This must be between the LED and the track going off to the connector. This is shown in detail in Figure 7-7.

Figure 7-7: Close-up of the bottom-left cut.

Construction

The next step is to solder in all the diodes, which are marked on the board as rectangles with a line at one end. Make sure this line coincides with the line marked on the diode itself.

Now, normally you would insert the diode and solder the other side of the board. However, in this board, the silicone rubber switches will be placed on this track side of the board, so you want as little height on the joints on this side as possible. The technique we used was to fit the diode, and then trim off the lead on the track side flush with the level of the board with a pair of side cutters. Then solder from the component side, letting the solder be sucked down into the hole by capillary action. Be careful not to put too much solder on the joint because you'll get a dome on the wiring side. The silicone rubber can take some distortion, but try to keep it to a minimum. Figure 7-8 shows the three steps in mounting the diodes.

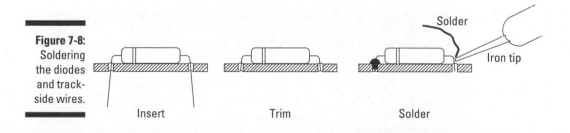

Figure 7-8: Soldering the diodes and track-side wires.

Insert   Trim   Solder

At the next stage, you add the LEDs, pushing them through the other side of the board to the diodes and bending the legs so that the LEDs lie as close as possible to the board. Notice that there's a very subtle flat on the side of the LED that marks the data out connection. The data out and the ground connections are also longer than the other two pins. It's critical that the LEDs are put in the board the right way around. You'll see an exaggerated flat on one side of the legend where the LEDs are to be inserted, as shown in Figure 7-9.

Figure 7-9:
The mounting of the LEDs.

Notice the holes showing in Figure 7-9 with the component wires soldered from the track side and the solder filling the hole but not seeping through. Also, notice the two circles with interleaving spokes that surround the LEDs. These are the two contacts of the switch; the conducting rubber ring on the silicone cover makes contact between the inner and outer ring when the switch is pressed. Keep your fingers off these rings or at least wipe them down with a grease solvent before you fit the silicone cover.

Now that the LEDs are in place, you can wire up each row of LEDs so that the data out of one LED goes into the data in of the next. We used some thin insulated wire to do this. There are three links on each of the four rows.

Finally, you need to solder a ceramic capacitor across the middle two wires of the LEDs. These wires are decoupling capacitors and ensure a smooth power supply for each controller chip in the LEDs. We used a small surface mount capacitor and held it close with fine tweezers while we soldered it onto the pins. If you like, you can use small leaded capacitors — just make sure you bend the leads so that they're as short as possible when soldered up. A photograph of this is shown in Figure 7-10.

Now the rows and columns can be commoned up to complete the circuit. Figure 7-11 shows a diagram of these, as well as where they should be connected to the Raspberry Pi's GPIO pins.

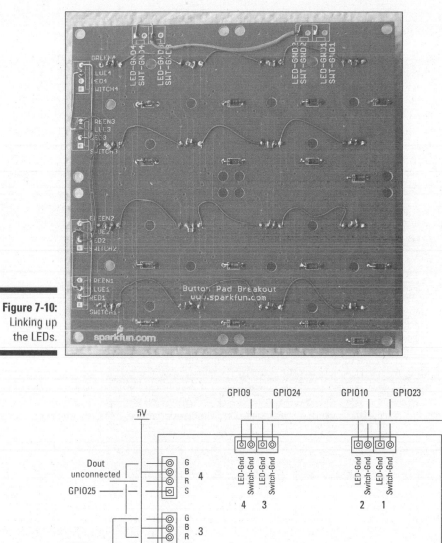

Figure 7-10:
Linking up
the LEDs.

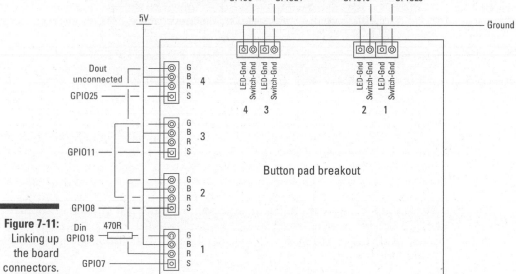

Figure 7-11:
Linking up
the board
connectors.

Connecting to the Raspberry Pi

We decided to use a flying lead from the Light Fantastic board to the Raspberry Pi through a ribbon cable. This allows you to easily attach and detach it. If you have a Raspberry Pi Model B+, you'll need a 40-way IDC connector; otherwise, you need a 26-way one. Either way, you need about half a yard of 26-way ribbon cable; clamp it to the connector, ensuring that the red wire on the cable is pierced by the connector marked with a triangle, as shown in Figure 7-12. Now squeeze it up in the vice and add any strain relief clamp that came with the connector. The red wire is now pin 1 on the GPIO connector and will be the wire in the ribbon connector closest to the edge of the Raspberry Pi board when you plug it in.

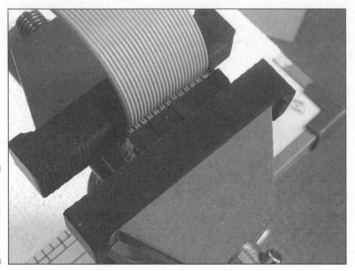

Figure 7-12:
Clamping up
one end of
the ribbon
cable.

Having fitted the connector at one end, you can proceed to wire up the other end to the Light Fantastic board; the connections are shown in Figure 7-13. Strip back the individual wires and cut short those that aren't used. Connect them to the back of the PCB in Figure 7-11. Note the two 5V and two ground connections — wire them both up to reduce any resistance from the connectors. If you don't have a spare amp in your Pi's power supply, connect an external 5V supply to the board and don't connect the 5V on the ribbon cable. When we were finished, we used a double-sided foam pad to stick the ribbon cable to the PCB and stop any mechanical strain from being put on the individual joints.

To finish it off, we put the silicone cover over the LEDs. We fastened it to the PCB with a nut and bolt in the center and middle positions. Don't tighten the nuts too tight, or the silicone will distort. Finally, we attached a 15mm M3 tapped pillar to each corner of the board so that it stood up on the desk while we tested it.

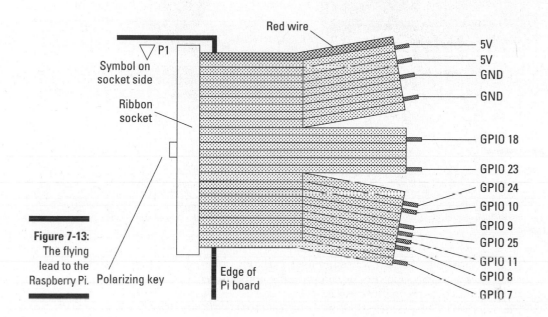

Red wire

5V
5V
GND
GND
GPIO 18
GPIO 23
GPIO 24
GPIO 10
GPIO 9
GPIO 25
GPIO 11
GPIO 8
GPIO 7

∇ P1

Symbol on
socket side

Ribbon
socket

Figure 7-13:
The flying
lead to the
Raspberry Pi.

Polarizing key

Edge of
Pi board

At this point, the electronic construction is complete, and you can use the project just as it is. However, the project looks much better if you surround it with a box. Also, the colors of the LEDs look so much stronger with a black background, and putting light baffles between the keys stop colors from interfering with each other. We describe one way of doing this in the next section, but if you're making this, you may want to skip to the testing stage to see if it works before committing to making the box.

Boxing the Light Fantastic

The project looks much better if it's finished off by putting it in a box. Not only does it look neater, but there is much less glare and the buttons' colors are better defined. The trickiest part about putting a box around it is making the top bezel. Although you can buy four 2 x 2 bezels for the switch cover, they're quite expensive, so we decided to make our own. It would've been simple to laser-cut some thin plywood, but we didn't have access to a laser cutter. If you do have access to one, there is a PDF on the book's website (www.dummies. com/go/raspberrypiprojects) that contains the cutting file.

We used this file to print out the size and position of the 16 square holes and spray-glue mounted it onto some 3mm-thick ABS plastic sheet. Then we used a drill to rough out the holes and a file to give them as neat an edge as we could. It took us about four hours to do this, but a file and a drill is all you need. The only file we had that fit the square holes was a triangular one. Figure 7-14 shows our progress partway through the process.

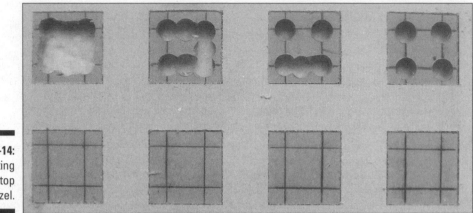

Figure 7-14:
Cutting
out the top
bezel.

The final fitting process involves carefully enlarging the holes one at a time and testing that the button tops slip snugly over the top.

Don't be too worried about the straightness of the edges to the holes. Visually, any small imperfections are masked by the contrast of the two parts, and it looked a lot more precise than it actually was.

We made the base from exactly the same template as the top, only we didn't need to cut out the holes for the switches.

You can make the sides of the box from thin plywood if you like, but we used some scrap fiberglass PCB material, which is strong and thin and machines easily (although it will blunt your tools faster). We think it gives the box a "geek tech" feel. We used strips 26mm wide so that the button tops protruded just 2mm above the top bezel. These were mounted on the base by some 50mm lengths of angle aluminum held in place by two pan-head screws and nuts (see Figure 7-15). The right side had this bracket offset so that the ribbon cable could come out of the side; a small recess in the side was cut in with a file to allow the ribbon cable to go underneath.

We applied a little epoxy to fix the nuts to the brackets so they could be fastened without having access to the inside of the box. On the underside of the top bezel, we fitted some strips of the same ABS plastic we used for the top to shield the lit buttons from each other. They were held in place by model airplane glue (see Figure 7-16). In the central strip, we put a small notch in the center and each end to clear the head of the rubber key fixing screws. Then we carefully painted the top bezel a flat matte black. If we had used plywood for the sides, we would've painted them as well at this stage.

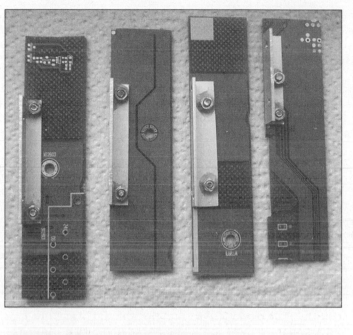

Figure 7-15:
The side
brackets.

Figure 7-16:
Light baffles
on the
underside of
the top.

In theory, the next step is simple: Drill four holes in the base to take the pillars of the PCB assembly. In practice, though, you don't know exactly where to drill them and still have the top bezel square. So, we removed the side panel with the ribbon cable slot, put the bezel on the buttons, and aligned everything nice and square. Then we put some hot glue around the base of the two pillars; when it had set, we disassembled the sides and unscrewed those pillars from the PCB. This left just the base with two pillars glued to it in exactly the right place. Then we took a 2.2mm drill (a 2mm one will do if you haven't got a 2.2mm) and drilled through the pillars into the base. Then we picked off the pillars and the hot glue and drilled out the hole to 3mm.

This meant that the two holes were in exactly the right place. So, we assembled it again with screws through the base into the two pillars — only this time, we left the opposite side off and repeated the glue and drill trick to get the other two pillars in exactly the right place.

Finally, we assembled the box again, left both sides off, and tacked the top bezel to the two remaining sides at the corners, again with hot glue. Then we removed the two sides and the top bezel, now attached to each other, and put a heavy glue fillet around the inside of the sides and top.

Make sure you leave a small unglued area for the other two sides to fit in.

Bringing It All to Life

Now you need to write some software to read the switches and light the LEDs. If you've done the project in Chapter 6, you've installed the NeoPixel Library; if not, turn back to Chapter 6 to see how that's installed.

Because both the NeoPixel library and the reading of switches require access to the GPIO, you need to be in root mode, so open IDLE with `gksudo idle` from the command line. Then type in the code in Listing 7-1 to test them both.

Listing 7-1:   Switch and Lights Test

```
# NeoPixel Light Fantastic
# Switch & lights test
# Author: Mike Cook
import time, random
import wiringpi2 as io
from neopixel import *

print"if program quits here start IDLE with 'gksudo idle' from command line"
io.wiringPiSetupGpio()
print"OK no crash" ; print" "

pinList = [9,24,10,23,7,8,11,25] # pins for keyboard
# LED strip configuration:
LED_COUNT    = 16      # Number of LED pixels.
LED_PIN      = 18      # GPIO pin connected to the pixels
LED_FREQ_HZ  = 800000  # LED signal frequency in hertz
LED_DMA      = 5       # DMA channel to use for generating signal
LED_INVERT   = False   # no need to invert on the Light Fantastic
strip = Adafruit_NeoPixel(LED_COUNT, LED_PIN, LED_FREQ_HZ, LED_DMA, LED_INVERT)

def main():
    initGPIO()
    strip.begin()
    print"Keyboard to LED test - Ctrl C to quit"
    print"pressing key will light up the LED"
```

```python
        wipe() ; key = 1
        while True:
            while keyPressed() == False :
              pass
            newKey = getKey()
            if newKey != -1 :
                key = newKey
                wipe()
            while keyPressed(): # wait for release
                pass
            strip.setPixelColor(key, Color(255, 0, 0))
            x = key % 4
            y = key / 4
            print"key ",key," X=",x," Y=",y
            strip.show()

def initGPIO():
    for pin in range (0,4):
        io.pinMode(pinList[pin],0)
        io.pullUpDnControl(pinList[pin],1) # input enable pull down
    for pin in range(4,8):
        io.pinMode(pinList[pin],1) # output
        io.digitalWrite(pinList[pin],1) # all high

def keyPressed(): #is a key being pressed>?
    pressed = False
    for pin in range(0,4):
        if io.digitalRead(pinList[pin]):
            pressed = True
    return pressed

def getKey():
    key =-1 # -1 = no key
    for outPin in range(4,8):
        io.digitalWrite(pinList[outPin],0) # all low
    for outPin in range(4,8):
        io.digitalWrite(pinList[outPin],1)
        for read in range(0,4):
            if io.digitalRead(pinList[read]):
                key = ((outPin-4) * 4) + read
        io.digitalWrite(pinList[outPin],0) #remove active row
    for outPin in range(4,8):
        io.digitalWrite(pinList[outPin],1) # leave all high
    return key

def wipe():
    for i in range(0,strip.numPixels()):
        strip.setPixelColor(i, Color(0, 0, 0))
    strip.show()

# Main program logic follows:
if __name__ == '__main__':
    main()
```

The setting up of the NeoPixel library should be familiar to you if you read Chapter 6; the difference here is that there are only 16 LEDs. The pinList list is the GPIO pin numbers used for the switch matrix. The first four are the input columns, and the last four are the output rows of the matrix. These pins are initialized in the initGPIO function. Note that the inputs have their pull-down resistors activated so they'll read a steady zero in the event of no key being pressed. The row outputs are all set high in preparation for the next function, keyPressed.

This function's job is just to return a True if a key is being held down and a False if it is not. It assumes that all the rows are high, which they will be after that first function. It does this by initializing a variable pressed to be False and then looking at each column in turn and setting this variable to True if a logic 1 is seen on any of the input columns.

Although sometimes you just want any key indication, when the program knows a key is being held down, it's normal to want to know which key. This is where the getKey function comes in. It starts off by setting all the row outputs to 0. Then a for loop will put them high one at a time. Inside this for loop is another for loop, which reads each column in turn. If a logic 1 is detected, it sets a variable called key to be the index of this inner loop plus four times the index of the outer loop — in other words, the key number. Before the function exits, the code sets all the row outputs high (to a logic 1) for the next time the keyPressed function is called.

The wipe function simply sets each pixel color to black. So, all that remains is the main function. This calls the functions that initializes the key's GPIO pins and the LEDs and sets them all to black. Then it enters an infinite loop where it waits until there is a key press; then it goes off to read the key, wipes the LEDs, and waits for the key to be released. Then the LED corresponding to the key being pressed is set to green and both the key number and its *x*- and *y*-coordinates are printed out before the pixel buffer is transferred to the LEDs with the strip.show function call.

Now, you may have spotted that we said the LED to light up would be green, but we set this up with the line strip.setPixelColor(key, Color(255, 0, 0)), which, as you may expect from Chapter 6, would be red. It turns out, for no explained reason we can tell, that the 5mm version of the WS2812b has the red and green data packets swapped over when compared to the surface mount package used in the LED strips and rings. So, you need to swap red and green in the function call to get the color you expect.

A bit of a show

Now that we have everything working, we finish off this chapter with a bit of a light show. Basically, it consists of eight sequences that you can use to turn on the LEDs and a way of generating a random color. The LEDs turn on one at a time with a small interval between them and then rapidly turn off. This repeats until another key is pressed — the keys are looked at only after the sequence ends, so you have to press a key and hold it until all the lights are off before you can change the sequence.

For each sequence, there are two ways of generating the color: one changing every four steps in the sequence and the other changing every step. The top eight keys evoke the first changing method; the second eight keys evoke the second step.

The way colors are generated here is worth a mention. If you want to generate a random color, setting the red, green, and blue components may seem to be what you would want to do, but that's not the case. Although it will produce random colors, they'll mostly turn out to be fairly washed out.

What you need is another way of representing color. The red, green, blue (RGB) method is often called a color cube, with each color component representing a coordinate in a cubic space. There are several other color models as well; one popular one is known as hue, saturation, value (HSV). The hue is what you would describe as the basic color; the saturation is how intense that color is; and the value is the brightness of the color.

Saturation and value are quite different, although they sound like they may be the same thing. If you were to deal with mixing paints, the hue would be the basic pigment, and the saturation would depend on how much white you added. For a fully saturated color, you would add no white, and for a pale, washed-out color, you would add a lot. Similarly, the value would be how much black paint you added — no black for the full brightness and a lot for a very dim, dark color. This representation of a color is often known as *hex cone space* because the space bounded by these coordinates represents a hexagonal cone. We use a simple function to generate a full-brightness, fully saturated color that is very useful for generating a reasonable set of random colors.

The code for the light show is shown in Listing 7-2. Because this has the key reading functions identical to those in Listing 7-1, to save space they aren't printed here — just copy the function from the previous listing you typed.

Listing 7-2:   The Light Fantastic Light Show

```
# NeoPixel Light Fantastic
# Light sequence
# Author: Mike Cook

import time, random
import wiringpi2 as io
from neopixel import *
```

(continued)

Listing 7-2 *(continued)*

```
print"if program quits here start IDLE with 'gksudo idle' from command line"
io.wiringPiSetupGpio()
print"OK no crash" ; print" "
pinList = [9,24,10,23,7,8,11,25] # pins for keyboard
order =[ [ 0,1,2,3,7,6,5,4,8,9,10,11,15,14,13,12 ],
         [ 0,4,1,5,8,2,12,3,9,6,13,7,10,14,11,15 ],
         [ 9,10,6,5,4,8,12,13,14,15,11,7,3,2,1,0 ],
         [ 12,9,6,3,0,5,10,15,4,8,13,14,11,7,2,1 ],
         [ 12,8,4,0,1,2,3,7,11,15,14,13,9,6,10,5 ],
         [ 0,8,1,9,2,10,3,11,7,15,6,14,5,13,4,12 ],
         [ 12,3,15,0,9,6,10,5,8,7,4,11,13,2,14,1 ],
         [ 12,15,0,3,8,11,4,7,13,1,14,2,9,6,5,10 ], ]

strip = Adafruit_NeoPixel(16,18,800000,5,False)

def main():
    initGPIO()
    strip.begin()
    print"Use the light fantastic keyboard to:-"
    wipe() ; key = 1
    print"press key for demo ",
    print"press and hold until lights go out to change demo"
    while keyPressed() == False :
       pass
    while True:
        newKey = getKey()
        if newKey != 16 :
              print "New sequence ",newKey
              key = newKey
              wipe()
        while keyPressed(): # wait for release
           pass
        if key < 8:
           fill(key, True)
        elif key < 16:
           fill(key-8, False)

def initGPIO():
    # see Listing 7-1 for this function
def keyPressed():
    # see Listing 7-1 for this function
def getKey():
    # see Listing 7-1 for this function
def wipe():
    # see Listing 7-1 for this function

def colorH(angle): # Color returned H=angle, S=1, V=1
    while angle <0 : # get angle in range 0 to 255
        angle += 256
    while angle > 255:
        angle -=256
    if angle < 85:
```

```
        return Color(255 - angle * 3, angle * 3, 0)
    elif angle < 170:
        angle -= 85
        return Color(0, 255 - angle * 3, angle * 3)
    else:
        angle -= 170
        return Color(angle * 3, 0, 255 - angle * 3)

def fill(seq, col):
    startH = random.randint(0,360)
    incH = random.randint(7,35)
    color = colorH(startH)
    for i in range(0,strip.numPixels()):
        if col :
            if (i % 4) == 0 :
                color = colorH(random.randint(0,360))
            else:
                startH += incH
                color = colorH(startH)
        strip.setPixelColor(order[seq][i], color)
        strip.show()
        time.sleep(0.3)
    time.sleep(1.0)
    for i in range(0,strip.numPixels()):
        strip.setPixelColor(order[seq][i], Color(0, 0, 0))
        strip.show()
        time.sleep(0.05)

# Main program logic follows:
if __name__ == '__main__':
    main()
```

The sequence is defined as a list of lists or two-dimensional array called `order`. This sets the order of what lights to turn on in any sequence. Following that, the call to the `Adafruit_NeoPixel` function is the same as the previous listing, except the parameters are placed in the call directly leading to another saving of lines in the listing. The main function is very similar to the previous listing, only this time, at the end, the `fill` function is called. It's called with the second parameter either `True` or `False`, depending on whether the key number is less than eight. This defines the color-changing strategy. The first parameter defines the sequence and, because there are only eight of them, it's kept below eight for key numbers above seven by subtracting eight.

The functions `fill` and `colorH` are the new ones here. The `fill` function does all the work driving the LEDs, and `colorH` does the setting of the color given a number representing the angle H. To make matters simpler, angles are given in 1/256th of a circle to match the resolution of the color in RGB space.

The `fill` function takes in two values: the sequence to use and the way to change the color, either a random color in groups of four, or a chain of blending colors. The color is defined by the H or hue number and is first set to be a random number; then the increment of this number (that is, the amount it's changed each time you want a new number) is set to a random number between 7 and 35.

Next, a `for` loop steps through each position in the sequence in turn, and sets the pixel color, updates the strip, and delays for a short time. Depending on the way the color is changed, either the `startH` variable is incremented or every fourth time around the loop a new color is set. The `%` operator gives the reminder from a division, so `i % 4` is zero every fourth loop.

Before that, the loop index is examined to see if the color needs changing; if it does, it updates the `colorH` variable `startH` calls `colorH` function.

The `colorH` function may look a little strange, but it isn't so bad when you know what's is doing. First, it ensures that the given angle is within the range of 0 to 255. Then it splits the range of possible angles into three, representing the three basic primary colors. Then it generates a color from this primary color and the next one in the sequence. Note that there is always a color component that is zero and a mix of the other two components. The times by three in the color setting statement maps one-third of the circle to the range of the individual color components.

Things to try

You can tinker with this for variety. For example, you might alter the sequence of lights or add more sequences. You can run the original demo from the NeoPixel library. We've added some changes to this and incorporate reading the keyboard to select a sequence and also swapped the red and green to make the colors to be as they were originally intended; that listing can be found on the book's website (www.dummies.com/go/raspberrypiprojects). You could make it so that you show a whole frame of pixels at once or show a sequence of them to make an animation like a firework exploding. You could even read the sequence of frames from a file.

In the next chapter, we show you how to play some games with the Light Fantastic.

Chapter 8

Games for the Light Fantastic

. . . .

In This Chapter

▶ Making more projects with the Light Fantastic keypad

▶ Finding hidden treasure and learning the resistor color code

▶ Making a color sequence sliding block puzzle

▶ Trying your skill at matching colors

▶ Battling logic to get all the lights out

. . . .

Having built the Light Fantastic in Chapter 7, you're ready to have some fun with it. This chapter presents four games, along with ideas for variants and more complex puzzles. Each one is colorful fun.

If you haven't built the Light Fantastic yet, be sure to turn back to Chapter 7. You won't get very far in this chapter otherwise.

A few notes before we begin: The Light Fantastic consists of illuminated push buttons. Each one can be set to a range of colors too subtle for your eye to distinguish. In scientific terms, this is known as better than a "just noticeable difference." The color of each LED is defined by writing a value of the red, green, and blue components of the color into a buffer. When the buffer has been set to what you want to display, it's transferred to the LEDs with the show call. The push buttons and LED positions should match up, as shown in Figure 8-1.

The sequence numbers start at 0 and go to 15, but there is an alternative way of describing a position: with a pair of x- and y-coordinates. This is quite a handy thing to do when you're looking for an adjacent position rather than just the next one in the sequence. In Figure 8-1, you can see how we can convert a sequence number to x- and y-coordinates and back again. You may not have come across the % operation before, but in Python (and many other languages), it's the modulus operation. That means, "Do an integer division, but just give the remainder." Note that the divide operator (/) returns just an integer; if the two numbers involved are integers, it throws away the reminder.

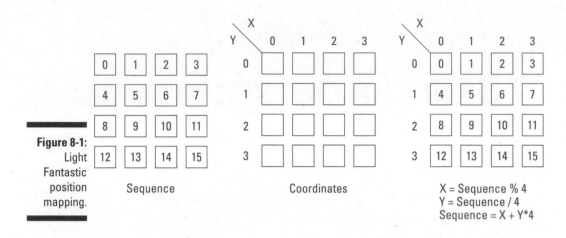

Figure 8-1:
Light
Fantastic
position
mapping.

Sequence

Coordinates

$X = Sequence \% 4$
$Y = Sequence / 4$
$Sequence = X + Y*4$

Finally, in order to save on your fingers some functions that are the same in all programs are not repeated. Instead, after the function definition is a note saying where the function can be copied and pasted from. All these programs require you to enter the IDLE editor by using `gksudo idle` from a command-line window. The programs interact with the user through the Python console window, so keep that the active window (the one with the keyboard focus). All the programs run in an infinite loop, so when you want to quit one, press Ctrl+C. If that doesn't appear to work, click with your mouse on the Python console window to give it the keyboard focus.

Let the games begin!

Treasure Hunt

Treasure Hunt (see Figure 8-2) is a simple game with an educational motive. A treasure has been hidden in one of the squares, and you have to find it. If you guess right and press the right square, it flashes. If you press the wrong square, the square lights up in a color that tells you how many squares you are away, in terms of horizontal plus vertical distance (diagonal distances don't count).

Notice in the diagram that the distance of every square has a number in it. On the Light Fantastic, there are only colors, so the colors that light up are the distance numbers in the resistor color code colors. So in addition to playing a game, you're learning the resistor color code (well, at least up to six).

Resistors have their values marked in colored bands, with each color representing a number. They are as follows:

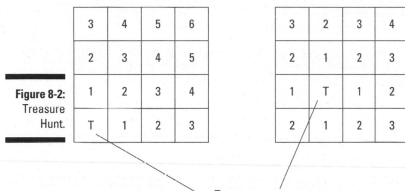

Figure 8-2:
Treasure
Hunt.

Treasure

```
0 Black
1 Brown
2 Red
3 Orange
4 Yellow
5 Green
6 Blue
7 Violet
8 Gray
9 White
```

You need to learn these codes if you're going to work with electronics. Unfortunately, LEDs aren't good at producing brown and orange, and brown can be confused, exactly as it can be with real resistors. It's easy enough to fiddle around with the numbers if you don't like our rendering of the colors.

The code for this game is given in Listing 8-1.

Listing 8-1:   Treasure Hunt

```python
#!/usr/bin/env python
# NeoPixel Light Fantastic
# Treasure Hunt
# Author: Mike Cook
#
import time, random
import wiringpi2 as io

from neopixel import *

print"if program quits here start IDLE with 'gksudo idle' from command line"
io.wiringPiSetupGpio()
```

(continued)

Listing 8-1 *(continued)*

```
print"OK no crash" ; print" "

pinList = [9,24,10,23,7,8,11,25] # pins for keyboard
#   black=0, brown=1, red=2, orange=3, yellow=4, green=5, blue=6
distanceC = [ Color(0,0,0), Color(45,139,0), Color(0,255,0),
              Color(120,255,0), Color(255,255,0), Color(200,0,0),
              Color(0,0,200) ]
treasure = 0 # location of the treasure
strip = Adafruit_NeoPixel(16,18,800000,5,False)

def main():
    initGPIO()
    strip.begin()
    print"Treasure hunt - find the hidden treasure"
    print"pressing a key will show the distance to the treasure"
    wipe() ; key = -1
    while True:
      setBoard() # set up colors to use
      while key != treasure:
        while keyPressed() == False :
          pass
        newKey = getKey()
        if newKey != -1 :
            key = newKey
        while keyPressed(): # wait for release
            pass
        makeMove(key)
      print"puzzle complete - any key for new game"
      while keyPressed() == False :
        pass
      while keyPressed(): # wait for release
        pass
      time.sleep(0.5)
      print"play"

def initGPIO():
    # see Listing 7-1 for this function
def keyPressed():
    # see Listing 7-1 for this function
def getKey():
    # see Listing 7-1 for this function
def wipe():
    # see Listing 7-1 for this function

def setBoard():
    global treasure
    wipe()
    treasure = random.randint(0,15)
    #uncomment to cheat
    #print" treasure at",treasure
```

```
    #strip.setPixelColor(treasure, Color(128, 128, 128))
    #strip.show()

def makeMove(move):
    distX = abs((move % 4) - (treasure % 4))
    distY = abs((move / 4) - (treasure / 4))
    distance = distX + distY
    if move != treasure:
        strip.setPixelColor(move, distanceC[distance])
        strip.show()
    else:
        print"found it"
        flashTreasure()

def flashTreasure():
    for i in range(0,7):
        strip.setPixelColor(treasure, Color(0,0,0))
        strip.show()
        time.sleep(0.3)
        strip.setPixelColor(treasure, Color(0,255,255))
        strip.show()
        time.sleep(0.3)

# Main program logic follows:
if __name__ == '__main__':
    main()
```

The Colors are defined in a list called `distanceC`. For these 5mm packaged versions of the WS2812b LEDs, the `Color` function takes in the color components green, red, and blue. Note that black is defined even though it isn't used in this game, so all the other colors have a list index, which is the same as the color's value in the resistor color code. The main function sets up the LEDs and the switches and prints the instructions to the console.

The `setBoard` function picks a random square to hide the treasure in. Note that there are some cheat lines commented out with # that will show the square number in the console and even light up the treasure square as a light gray color.

When the `main` function has a key press, the key number is passed to the `makeMove` function. This function first calculates the distance to the treasure by adding up the *x* displacement and the *y* displacement; then it checks to see if the move has found the treasure. If it has, the `flashTreasure` function is called. True to its name, it alternates the treasure square between black (unlit) and magenta (a color not otherwise in the game).

If the treasure hasn't been found, the key you pressed is illuminated with a color equal to the distance. The important point here is the use of a list to define a color whose index is the distance color.

You can do more with this game if you like. For example, you could make a more elaborate win celebration, maybe taking the elements of the demo in Chapter 7. You could keep a total of the best score — that is, the fewest moves. You could play the game with a time element, where the score is not simply the number of moves it took you but a measure of the amount of time it took. Because this is such a simple game, you could change it so that you played a number of games — say, six — and it gave you an average score. Finally, you could extend it to a Battleship type of game.

Sliding Block Puzzle

This game is a colorful twist on the sliding-block puzzle game. Normally, you have to get numbered squares into an ascending order, but here it's much trickier. You have to get the colors in the right sequence according to the H value in the HSV color space (see Chapter 7). The correct color sequence is shown at the start; then the colors are scrambled up. Normally, you would have no chance of remembering 15 colors from just one showing, so here there are two ways you can get a hint:

- **Press the blank square, and all the colors that are *not* in the correct order will blink.** This is great for keeping track of how well you're doing.

- **Press a key that is not in line horizontally or vertically with the blank space.** This move would normally be invalid, but here it's a request to repeat the display of the final sequence you're aiming for.

In a normal move, if you press a key that's adjacent to the blank space, it swaps position as you would expect. However, if you press a key that's on the same column or row as the blank, all the colors are pushed up from where you pressed into the blank space, and the blank appears where you made the move.

Listing 8-2 shows the code for this game.

The code follows the overall structure of the previous game in terms of initialization. Here, there are two lists: gameOrder defines the order you have to arrange the colors in, and lightC defines the current colors. At this initial stage, it's set so that they're all black.

Listing 8-2: Sliding Block Puzzle

```python
#!/usr/bin/env python
# NeoPixel Light Fantastic
# Sliding block puzzle
# Author: Mike Cook
#
import time, random
import wiringpi2 as io

from neopixel import *

print"if program quits here start IDLE with 'gksudo idle' from command line"
io.wiringPiSetupGpio()
print"OK no crash" ; print" "

pinList = [9,24,10,23,7,8,11,25] # pins for keyboard
gameOrder =[ 0,1,2,3,4,5,6,7,8,9,10,11,12,13,15,14 ] # working order
lightC = [ Color(0,0,0) for i in range(0,16) ]
strip = Adafruit_NeoPixel(16,18,800000,5,False)

def main():
    initGPIO()
    strip.begin()
    print"Sliding block puzzle - get the lights in the right order"
    print"pressing the unlit block will blink blocks in the wrong place"
    print"pressing a key that does not result in a shift will show the right
            order"
    wipe() ; key = 1
    while True:
      setBoard() # set up colors to use
      while not finished():
        while keyPressed() == False :
          pass
        newKey = getKey()
        if newKey != -1:
            key = newKey
        while keyPressed(): # wait for release
            pass
        makeMove(key)
        showSet()
      print"puzzle complete - any key for new game"
      while keyPressed() == False :
        pass
      while keyPressed(): # wait for release
        pass

def initGPIO():
    # see Listing 7-1 for this function
def keyPressed():
    # see Listing 7-1 for this function
```

(continued)

Listing 8-2 *(continued)*

```python
def getKey():
    # see Listing 7-1 for this function
def wipe():
    # see Listing 7-1 for this function
def colorH(angle):
    # see Listing 7-2 for this function

def setBoard():
    global gameOrder,lightC
    random.shuffle(gameOrder) # mix up the board
    h = random.randint(0,255)
    hInc = random.randint(16,35)
    for i in range(0,15):
        lightC[i] = colorH(h)
        h += hInc
    showSol()

def showSol():
    for i in range(0,16):
        strip.setPixelColor(i, lightC[i])
        time.sleep(0.08)
        strip.show()
    time.sleep(1.0)
    showSet()

def showSet():
    for i in range(0,16):
        #print"game order ",gameOrder[i]
        strip.setPixelColor(i, lightC[gameOrder[i]])
    strip.show()

def finished():
    done = True
    for i in range(0,16):
        #print i," Game order ", gameOrder[i]
        if gameOrder[i] != i:
            done = False
    return done

def showCorrect(): #blink incorrect squares
    for blink in range (0,3):
        for i in range(0,16):
            if gameOrder[i] != i:
                strip.setPixelColor(i,Color(0,0,0))
        strip.show()
        time.sleep(0.5)
        showSet()
        time.sleep(0.3)
```

```
def makeMove(move):
    if lightC[gameOrder[move]] == Color(0,0,0):
        #blank key pressed
        showCorrect()
    else:
        #print"not blank"
        x = move % 4
        y = move / 4
        blank = findBlank()
        if blank[0] == x:
            shuffle(4,blank[1],y,blank[2],move)
        elif blank[1] == y:
            shuffle(1,blank[0],x,blank[2],move)
        else:
            #print" no alignment with blank"
            wipe()
            showSol() # show what you are aiming for

def shuffle(incSize,distance,target,blankPos,move): #move into blank
    global gameOrder
    inc = incSize
    if distance > target:
        inc = -incSize
    while blankPos != move:
        temp = gameOrder[blankPos]
        gameOrder[blankPos] = gameOrder[blankPos + inc]
        gameOrder[blankPos + inc] = temp
        blankPos += inc

def findBlank():
    blank = (-1,-1,-1)
    for i in range(0,16):
        if lightC[gameOrder[i]] == Color(0,0,0):
            blank = (i % 4, i / 4, i)
    if blank == (-1,-1,-1):
            # this should never happen
            print"error blank not found"
    return blank

# Main program logic follows:
if __name__ == '__main__':
    main()
```

The setBoard function first mixes up the gameOrder list, which defines the initial startup position. Then the lightC list is populated by a succession of colors defined by a randomly chosen initial h angle and incremented by a randomly chosen value, incH. When that's finished, the showSol function shows the solution, by simply showing the pixels in the order of the lightC list.

The `while not finished():` line calls the `finished` function, which returns a `true` when the puzzle is complete. It does this by checking that the `gameOrder` list matches the sequence 0 to 15. If any entry in the list fails, the logic variable `done` is set to `false`, and it's this variable that is returned by the function.

So, assuming the puzzle is not complete, the `main` function waits for a key press. When it gets one, it calls the `makeMove` function, which looks to see what sort of move has been made. If it's the blank key, it will call the `showCorrect` function and blink the positions that don't contain the correct color. It does that by alternately blanking the pixels that don't correspond to the right order and then showing the current state of the board with the `showSet` function.

If the move wasn't the blank key, it works out the x- and y-coordinates of the move key and then calls the `findBlank` function, which, as its name implies, returns a *tuple* (a list of numbers in one variable) of the x- and y-coordinates of the blank space. If the blank space is at the same x value as the move, the `shuffle` function is called. This takes the colors between the blank space and the move and shuffles them up one. This function copes with moving the colors along both the x-axis and the y-axis, depending on what's needed. We started out by writing two functions — one to shuffle in the x-axis and the other for the y-axis — but they looked so similar. So we combined them into one and let the axis be defined by the parameters passed to it. This make for very efficient use of code, but it can be a bit tricky to follow at first.

If there is no alignment in either the x- or y-coordinate between the blank space and the move, this is an invalid move and the code responds by showing the solution — that is, the sequence of colors you're aiming for.

When the puzzle is complete, a message is output to the console. On pressing any key, a new game is set up.

You can experiment with changing the range of numbers used for the `incH` variable. Making it a small number makes the game much more difficult, with blue colors starting to look very similar. Making this value too big means you lose any sense of blending between adjacent colors.

Because this is a much longer game than the first one, we suggest that you base any scoring on time rather than the number of moves made. You may want to incorporate an "I give up" combination of keys.

Color Match

Mike Cook wrote this game specifically to annoy someone in an online forum. He was using LEDs without any form of current control and claimed that the intensity of the LEDs had not diminished in three months of continuous operation. It turned out he wasn't measuring it in any way but claimed he could tell by looking. Mike said he couldn't remember the brightness over three seconds let alone three months, so he designed this game to prove it. This is a Light Fantastic version that deals not only with brightness but also with color.

The way this game works is that the center four switches light up for just over a second. Then all goes dark, and two seconds later the perimeter lights are lit up and you have to press the one of the same color as the one lit up in the center. Then the center color, the matching perimeter color, and your guess, if different, flash. If you got it right, there is only one perimeter light flashing — your choice. If you got it wrong, you can see the difference between the color you chose and the central colors. Just to confirm things, a console message is produced as well. If you want to have another look at the colors, you can press one of the central four keys for a sneaky reminder.

The code for this program is shown in Listing 8-3.

Listing 8-3: Color Match

```python
#!/usr/bin/env python
# NeoPixel Light Fantastic
# Color Match
# Author. Mike Cook
#
import time, random
import wiringpi2 as io

from neopixel import *

print"if program quits here start IDLE with 'gksudo idle' from command line"
io.wiringPiSetupGpio()
print"OK no crash" ; print" "

pinList = [9,24,10,23,7,8,11,25] # pins for keyboard
colorOrder = [0,1,2,3,7,11,15,14,13,12,8,4]
colorRange = [ Color(0,0,0) for i in range(0,12) ]
strip = Adafruit_NeoPixel(16,18,800000,5,False)
cheat = False ; target = 0

def main():
    initGPIO()
    strip.begin()
    print"Color Match"
    print"the center four lights will flash a single color"
    print"then you press the match on the outside"
    wipe() ; key = 1
```

(continued)

Listing 8-3 *(continued)*

```
    while True:
      guess = True
      setBoard() # set up colors to choose from
      while guess:
          while keyPressed() == False :
            pass
          newKey = getKey()
          if newKey != -1:
             key = newKey
          while keyPressed(): # wait for release
            pass
          guess = makeMove(key)
      print"another go"
      time.sleep(1.5)

def initGPIO():
    # see Listing 7-1 for this function
def keyPressed():
    # see Listing 7-1 for this function
def getKey():
    # see Listing 7-1 for this function
def wipe():
    # see Listing 7-1 for this function
def colorH(angle):
    # see Listing 7-1 for this function

def setBoard():
    global colorRange,target
    wipe()
    h = random.randint(0,255)
    hInc = 8 # sets how hard it is
    for i in range(0,12):
        colorRange[i] = colorH(h)
        h += hInc
    target = random.randint(0,10)
    showReminder()
    if cheat :
      print target

def showSet():
    for i in range(0,12):
        strip.setPixelColor(colorOrder[i], colorRange[i])
    strip.show()

def showTarget():
    strip.setPixelColor(5, colorRange[target])
    strip.setPixelColor(6, colorRange[target])
    strip.setPixelColor(9, colorRange[target])
```

```
        strip.setPixelColor(10, colorRange[target])
        strip.show()

def showReminder():
    wipe()
    time.sleep(0.4)
    showTarget()
    time.sleep(0.9)
    wipe()
    time.sleep(1.5)
    showSet()

def makeMove(move):
    guess = True
    if move == 5 or move == 6 or move == 9 or move == 10:
        showReminder()
    else:
        guess = False # flash guess and color and right color
        if colorOrder[target] == move:
            print"Yes right"
        else:
            print"No wrong"
        for t in range(0,6):
            wipe()
            time.sleep(0.2)
            strip.setPixelColor(move, colorRange[colorOrder.index(move)])
            strip.setPixelColor(colorOrder[target], colorRange[target])
            showTarget()
            time.sleep(0.4)
    return guess

# Main program logic follows:
if __name__ == '__main__':
    main()
```

Again, following the same template as before, the colorOrder list has in it
the keypad's numbers for the perimeter of the Light Fantastic display. The
colorRange list is used to hold the colors to display. The main function
starts by initializing things and printing out the instructions. The setBoard
function generates a range of colors to act as the potential target and then
chooses one of them at random. Although the initial point in the HSV color
space is chosen at random, the hInc or increment value is fixed. This effec-
tively controls the change between adjacent colors; a value in the listing is
one that we found to give a just noticeable difference over the whole range,
with blue color changes being the hardest to detect. Make this value bigger
for an easier game.

After the colors have been defined, the setBoard function calls the show-Remainder function. This clears the key colors, shows the target color with the showTarget function, wipes that, and then shows the colors around the outside of the keypad with the showSet function.

After all that, back in the main function, the program looks for a key press. There are two actions that can happen as a result of pressing a key: One is to make a guess as to the correct color, and the other is to request a review of the target color. This is decided in the makeMove function. If the move is one of the central keys, it calls the showRemainder function just like at the end of the setBoard function. Then it returns a True value to inform the main function that this round has not yet finished.

If, however, your move is one of the outer keys, that's taken as a valid answer, and a check is made to see if the key you pressed is where the target color was in the colorOrder list. Then your success in matching the color is printed out to the console. Finally, the target color, your guess, and the correct result are flashed. Note that there are two lines that define your guess and the correct color. These are:

```
strip.setPixelColor(move, colorRange[colorOrder.index(move)])
strip.setPixelColor(colorOrder[target], colorRange[target])
```

If you're correct, these two lines will result in setting the same pixel number to the same color. The use of colorOrder.index(move) is a reversal of how you normally use lists. This returns a number that gives the position of where the value of move is in the list.

There are a few things you can tinker with in this program. First, you can alter the sleep delays so you have longer to wait before you see the choice of colors. Unsurprisingly, the longer you have to wait, the harder the game. The order of the color choice also is constantly increasing around the perimeter in order of increasing H color value. You can scramble that by applying a random shuffle to the colorOrder list.

Perhaps the biggest change you can make is in the generation of colors. The eye is much less sensitive to the amounts of blue in a color than to red or green. You could change the H increment value according to the initial H starting point so that if H were clear of the blue content — that is, below a value of 170 — then the hue increment could be smaller. You could change the way the choice colors are generated so that it gets harder as more and more correct answers are given and drops down to easy if a mistake is made. Each degree of difficulty could be marked with a level number. Then you could introduce an element of competition in how high a level you can get.

Lights Out

Lights Out is a fantastic puzzle. We normally implement it on a 3 x 3 grid, but here it's on the 4 x 4 grid of the Light Fantastic. The idea is to turn out all the lights by pressing keys. The snag is that when you press one key, not only is that key inverted but those surrounding it are also inverted. It basically inverts a cross pattern of adjacent keys, but that's clipped if the key is close to the edge. This is shown in Figure 8-3.

The game works on two levels: First, it's about getting all the lights out. But when you get better, the aim is to get the lights out in the minimum number of moves.

You can't just generate any random collection of lights — it has to be a pattern that is solvable. To do this is remarkably simple: You start off with a finished representation of the board and make a number of random moves to generate the start position. The number of moves it took to generate the start position is the number of moves you need to get back to the end position. Each move is fully reversible, so if you press a key twice, you get back to your original position. That applies no matter what keys you press and in what order. Any sequence of key presses is reversed by the same keys in a different order. All you need to do in order to make sure you're getting the minimum number of moves when you're setting up the board is not use any key twice. You can set up a board that is solvable in any number of key presses you like. It turns out that for one or two moves, it's trivial but for three or more moves it becomes increasingly difficult.

The code for the Lights Out game is shown in Listing 8-4.

You should be seeing a pattern in these programs by now. Many of the functions have the same names but do different things, depending on the game. This time, the state of the board is represented by the list light.C. This needs checking to make sure they're all out. One difference here is that you

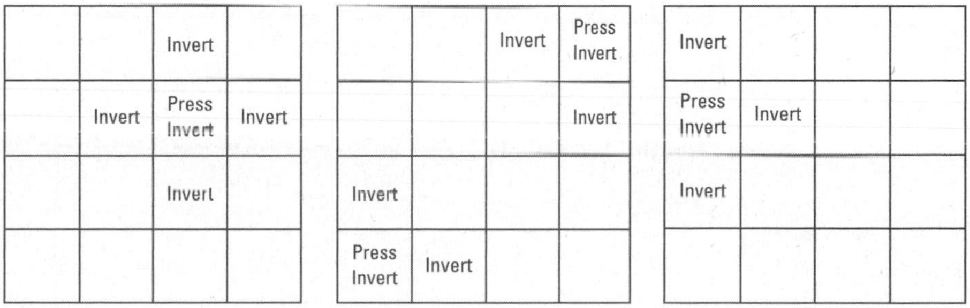

Figure 8-3: Lights Out logic.

Listing 8-4   Lights Out

```
# #!/usr/bin/env python
# NeoPixel Light Fantastic
# Lights Out
# Author: Mike Cook
#
import time, random
import wiringpi2 as io

from neopixel import *

print"if program quits here start IDLE with 'gksudo idle' from command line"
io.wiringPiSetupGpio()
print"OK no crash" ; print" "

pinList = [9,24,10,23,7,8,11,25] # pins for keyboard
litColor = Color(255,0,0)
lightC = [ Color(0,0,0) for i in range(0,16) ]
strip = Adafruit_NeoPixel(16,18,800000,5,False)
cheat = True

def main():
    initGPIO()
    strip.begin()
    print"Lights Out - remove all the lights"
    print"pressing a key will invert the light and others surrounding it"
    playLevel = int(raw_input("Enter the level 3 to 8 "))
    if playLevel < 3 or playLevel > 8 :
        playLevel = random.randint(3,8)
        print"Setting level to ",playLevel
    wipe() ; key = 1
    while True:
     turn = 0
     print"this can be completed in",playLevel,"moves"
     setBoard(playLevel) # set up colors to use
     while not finished():
       while keyPressed() == False :
         pass
       newKey = getKey()
       if newKey != -1:
          key = newKey
       while keyPressed(): # wait for release
          pass
       makeMove(key,True)
       turn += 1
       print"You have had",turn,"turns"
       if turn > playLevel:
          print"taking more than you should"
```

```
        if turn == playLevel:
            print"Well done - minimum number of turns"
        print"puzzle complete - any key for new game"
        while keyPressed() == False :
            pass
        while keyPressed(): # wait for release
            pass

def initGPIO():
    # see Listing 7-1 for this function
def keyPressed():
    # see Listing 7-1 for this function
def getKey():
    # see Listing 7-1 for this function
def wipe():
    # see Listing 7-1 for this function
def colorH(angle):
    # see Listing 7-1 for this function

def setBoard(level):
    global lightC,litColor
    for i in range(0,strip.numPixels()):
        lightC[i] = Color(0, 0, 0)
    h = random.randint(0,255)
    litColor = colorH(h)
    moves = [random.randint(0,15)]
    move = moves[0]
    makeMove(move,False)
    for m in range (0,level-1):
        while  move in moves:
            move = random.randint(0,15)
        moves.extend([move])
        makeMove(move,False)
    showSet()
    if cheat :
        print moves

def showSet():
    for i in range(0,16):
        strip.setPixelColor(i, lightC[i])
    strip.show()

def finished():
    done = True
    for i in range(0,16):
        if lightC[i] != Color(0,0,0):
            done = False
    return done
```

(continued)

Listing 8-4 *(continued)*

```
def makeMove(move,play):
    toggleColor(move,play)
    y = move / 4
    if move -4 >= 0:
        toggleColor(move -4,play)
    if move +4 < 16:
        toggleColor(move +4,play)
    if ((move -1) / 4) == y:
        toggleColor(move -1,play)
    if ((move +1) / 4) == y:
        toggleColor(move +1,play)

def toggleColor(led,play):
    global lightC
    if play: # playing the game
        if lightC[led] == Color(0,0,0):
            lightC[led] = litColor
            strip.setPixelColor(led, litColor)
        else:
            strip.setPixelColor(led, Color(0,0,0))
            lightC[led] = Color(0,0,0)
        strip.show()
        time.sleep(0.2)
    else: # setup the board
        if lightC[led] == Color(0,0,0):
            lightC[led] = litColor
        else:
            lightC[led] = Color(0,0,0)

# Main program logic follows:
if __name__ == '__main__':
    main()
```

need to type in the game level on the keyboard at the start of the game. Once it's set, it'll be the same for all subsequent games.

The loop in the `main` function that plays the game prints a reminder as to how many moves the board can be completed in. Then the `setBoard` function is the one that plays the reverse game to generate the starting position. First, the `lightC` list is cleared. Then a random color for the game is chosen. Next, a list of moves is generated. Notice that after the first move, the `while` loop keeps generating random numbers until it finds one that is not in the list of `moves`. This ensures that the same key is never used more than once. After each unique move has been generated, the `makeMove` function is called. This takes two parameters: one containing the move and the other containing a logic variable that determines if the game is being played or set up.

The `makeMove` function further identifies which positions need to be inverted (or "toggled" as it's called in electronics). These positions are the move, and the positions above, below, left, and right if they're places on the board. Each one identified calls up the `toggleColor` function, which in the setup phase simply sets the move position `lightC` list to the opposite of what it is already. Finally, the `setBoard` function calls the `showSet` function to display the board. Then if the `cheat` variable has been set to `true`, it prints out a list of moves you have to make.

When the `main` function has set up the game, the code loops reading the keys and checking for completion. After each key press, a reminder is given of how many turns you've had. Then when all the lights are out, a congratulation message is printed if you did it in the minimum number of turns.

As always, there are a number of improvements and changes you can make to this basic game. For example, you may want to add a reset button so you can restart the same pattern if you've exceeded the minimum number of turns and want another shot at the same pattern. You need to add an extra list to permanently store the start position in order for this to work.

The biggest change you can make is to change the logic. One such change is that you can restrict the keys you're permitted to press to just the keys that are currently lit. This changes the whole feel of the game.

When generating moves, to get to the starting position you need to filter out those moves that land on a lit position. This is exactly the opposite of how you would play the game. It needs to be opposite so your play can undo what the setup has done.

In addition to restricting what can key be pressed, you could change the patterns of inversions depending on the key pressed. For example, a corner key could invert all four keys in the corner and a side middle key could invert the whole row or column. This can be as asymmetrical as you want. As long as the setup function follows the play logic, the whole concept will work. If you make it too complex, though, you'll have a hard time explaining the rules to the players.

Finally, you could define an ending state to the board, which is not all the lights out. Some of them could be, say, red. Then play in another color — say, green — and have the red lights toggle between blue and red and the others between green and off. Although it may sound complex, it's exactly the same game, just much harder to play.

Exploring a World of Possibilities

There is no need to stop with these four games — there are a whole host of uses you can put the Light Fantastic to. The options we present in this chapter are just a few to give you some inspiration.

The Light Fantastic interface lends itself well to all sorts of variations of the "Whack-a-Mole" game, where lights come on and you have to press the keys as quickly as possible to turn them off. You could have some colors the player should whack and other that the player shouldn't.

You can also make a colorful version of a plumbing game where you have to unblock a drain by maneuvering pipe blocks into place to make the water flow.

How about a snake game that wraps around top and bottom, as well as left and right, of the playing area?

Then there's tic-tac-toe. Normally it's played on a 3-x-3 grid, but there's nothing stopping you from using a 4-x-4 grid. In fact, how about four in a row?

Finally, you don't have to stop at games. You can use the keys to control just about anything, from media players to musical instruments. You have the tools now. Let your imagination flow!

Part III

Developing Advanced Interfaces

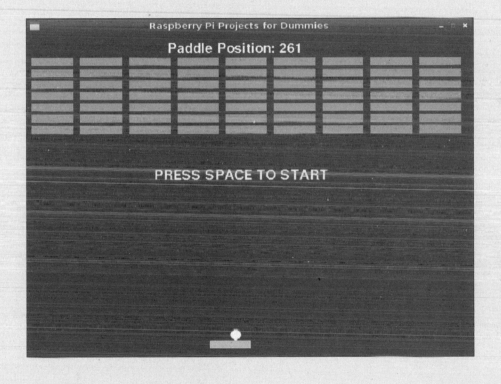

In this part . . .

- ✔ Find out how to read analog signals into the Raspberry Pi and get analog-to-digital conversion techniques.

- ✔ Build a brick in the wall game control.

- ✔ Build a temperature measuring module.

- ✔ See how the Raspberry Pi can interact with the cloud and find out about databases and web servers.

- ✔ Make a data logger.

- ✔ Make a computer vision monitored Connect Four game.

- ✔ Build the Raspberry Jazz Glitter Trio.

Chapter 9

Advanced Interfaces

• •

• •

T he Raspberry Pi general-purpose input/output (GPIO) pins are capable of detecting digital signals — either high or low. The problem is, the world we live in is a lot less black-and-white than that. For example, what if you want to detect light, sounds, temperature, or pressure? A digital signal isn't going to cut it. Instead, you need the ability to detect a *range* of electronic signals, and that's where analog signals come in.

One of the shortcomings of the Raspberry Pi is that it doesn't have any analog inputs. But you can easily solve this problem by using an analog-to-digital converter. In this chapter, you build your own converter, learn about different conversion methods, and write software for each. Toward the end of the chapter, we look at a high-precision analog-to-digital converter microchip.

Converting Analog to Digital

The Raspberry Pi's digital inputs can detect binary signals, which are either high or low represented by either 0V or 3.3V. However, an analog signal consists of a range of voltages. A 5V analog sensor, for example, may output voltages from 1.5V to 5V. An analog-to-digital converter (sometimes known as ADC, A-to-D, or A/D) converts the variable voltage to a reading that can be interpreted by the digital microprocessor or, in our case, the Raspberry Pi.

But how do you determine a variable voltage when all you have is a digital input that has only two states?

One method that is frequently used by microprocessors is to treat the analog sensor like a resistor connected to a capacitor and time how long it takes to charge up a capacitor. Capacitors don't charge instantly; the amount of time they take to charge varies depending on the voltage. Unfortunately, this method isn't very accurate on the Raspberry Pi, because the Linux operating system can't accurately measure clock cycles, so your results would be inaccurate. Additionally, this method works only on analog devices that act as resistors like potentiometers, temperature sensors (thermistors), and photocells.

Another method is to compare the analog voltage to a known reference voltage. Using a device called a *comparator,* we can determine if one voltage is greater than the other. Even though you don't know the analog voltage level, the comparator will tell you when your reference voltage is greater than the analog voltage. By comparing one voltage to the other, you can make a series of calculated guesses to determine the analog voltage.

Figure 9-1 demonstrates how you can increase your known reference voltage and perform series of tests using a comparator. When you receive a positive result from the comparator, you know the analog voltage is somewhere between the current and previous levels.

Figure 9-1:
Use a comparator to compare a known voltage to an unknown voltage in order to determine the unknown voltage.

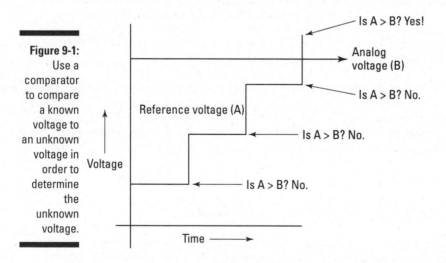

Comparators are often associated with analog-to-digital conversion because of their ability to compare two voltages. A comparator compares the voltage of two inputs and outputs a digital signal indicating which is larger. Figure 9-2 shows a diagrammatic representation of the LM339 comparator, which has four analog inputs and 14 pins in total — 8 inputs, 4 outputs, and 2 pins for +VE and GND. (The LM339 is available from electronics stores or online, and it's very affordable.) The comparator is one of the components you use to build an analog-to-digital converter later in this chapter.

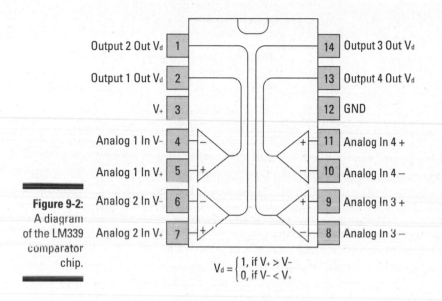

Output 2 Out V_d — 1

Output 1 Out V_d — 2

V_+ — 3

Analog 1 In $V-$ — 4

Analog 1 In $V+$ — 5

Analog 2 In $V-$ — 6

Analog 2 In $V+$ — 7

14 — Output 3 Out V_d

13 — Output 4 Out V_d

12 — GND

11 — Analog In 4 +

10 — Analog In 4 −

9 — Analog In 3 +

8 — Analog In 3 −

$$V_d = \begin{cases} 1, \text{ if } V_+ > V- \\ 0, \text{ if } V- < V_+ \end{cases}$$

Figure 9-2: A diagram of the LM339 comparator chip.

The pulse width modulation (PWM) is the component that enables you to vary the voltage going into the comparator, which makes the method shown in Figure 9-1 possible on the Raspberry Pi. PWM works by regulating energy using a succession of pulses, known as the *pulse train*. By increasing or decreasing the pulse width, you can regulate energy flow. PWM is often used to regulate the brightness of an LED by making the LED blink on and off at different frequencies, which makes it look bright or dim. As long as it blinks faster than the persistence of our vision, you don't see it flickering. The analog-to-digital converter uses PWM to alter the DC voltage of the reference voltage going into the comparator.

Figure 9-3 shows how you can alter the voltage by changing the waveform of the signal. If the average high state of the pulse train is high, then the voltage will be high; if the average high state of the pulse train is low, then the DC voltage will be low.

GPIO 18 on the Raspberry Pi can be configured for PWM. In order to create a digital pulse train, you connect GPIO 18 to the positive end of a comparator and a test voltage to the positive end of the comparator. When the test signal is higher, the comparator will output a positive digital signal; when it's lower, the comparator will output a negative signal.

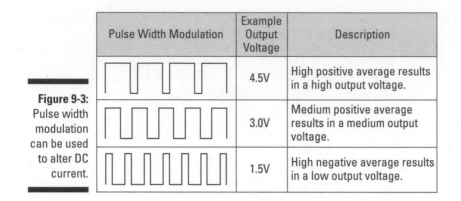

Figure 9-3: Pulse width modulation can be used to alter DC current.

Pulse Width Modulation	Example Output Voltage	Description
	4.5V	High positive average results in a high output voltage.
	3.0V	Medium positive average results in a medium output voltage.
	1.5V	High negative average results in a low output voltage.

We will use a low-pass filter on the PWM signal, which has a smoothing effect and produces a DC output that is connected to the –VE side of the comparator. The filter attenuates the high frequencies and lets through the lower ones. A common method to create a low-pass filter is to use a resistor and a capacitor in series to smooth the signal. The test voltage is connected to the +VE side of the comparator. As shown in Figure 9-4, the output from the comparator tells us whether the test signal is greater or less than the PWM. We can alter the DC current of the input using PWM from the Raspberry Pi, which gives us a method of guessing the test voltage. Later in this chapter, we examine three commonly used methods of guessing the test voltage. You use PWM, a comparator, and a low-pass filter to build an analog-to-digital converter later in this chapter.

Figure 9-4: Use a comparator to convert the PWM waveform into a digital pulse train.

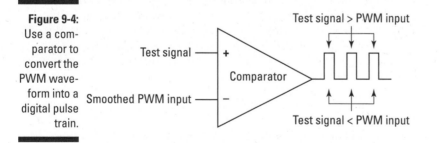

Considering the accuracy of analog-to-digital conversion

The intersection of the analog voltage (A) and the reference voltage (B) is approximate (refer to Figure 9-1). You can get very close to the analog voltage reading, but you'll never get the *exact* reading. Analog-to-digital converters are usually described by their resolution, which represents the range of readings they're capable of producing. For example, an analog-to-digital converter that has a resolution of 8 bits can produce a range of 256 readings ($2^8 = 256$). A 10-bit converter has a resolution of 1,024 ($2^{10} = 1,024$). An analog signal is a range of electronic signals, so the higher the bit rating of the converter, the bigger the range of analog signals it can support.

REMEMBER

The resolution gives you the range of readings it can support, but it isn't an indication of the converter's accuracy. The data sheet of most analog-to-digital converters tells you the converter's accuracy ratings, which describes the potential variance between the analog signal and the digital reading.

TECHNICAL STUFF

These variances are usually given in the unit of least significant bits (LSBs). The LSB is the rightmost bit of a number. For example, a 10-bit number is represented in binary as a ten-digit number of ones and zeroes (for example, 1111111000). The three zeroes are the least significant bits. If a 10-bit analog-to-digital converter has an accuracy of 2 LSB, that means its actual accuracy is 8 bits.

This explains an important difference between an analog-to-digital converter's resolution and its accuracy. The accuracy of an analog-to-digital converter is nonlinear. The extent of the variance changes depending on the voltage. This is called *nonlinearity,* meaning the accuracy is nonlinear to the voltage.

Another aspect of accuracy is *repeatability.* You see during the course of this chapter that all the analog-to-digital converters and methods we use produce a reading that is very close to the analog signal, but that reading is constantly fluctuating. (We explore methods to minimize — or even eradicate — the inaccuracy.) This constant change is called the analog-to-digital converter's *repeatability.* Any analog-to-digital converter can only give a reading of +/–1 LSB.

In this chapter, we compare the accuracy of different conversion methods and make tradeoffs between conversion time, resolution, and the filter to design an analog-to-digital converter that suits your need.

Making sense of a digital reading

You may be wondering, "What does the digital reading mean?" We've explained that analog-to-digital converters can have different resolutions and can produce readings within the range of the resolution. But what does a reading of 524, for example, out of a possible 1,024 actually mean?

In order to make the reading meaningful, you need to understand its relationship to the analog signal. One way to do this is to convert the reading into a value representing the analog voltage. The analog-to-digital converter has a maximum reference voltage. The reference voltage gives you a yardstick to calculate the analog voltage value from the digital reading.

For example if a 10-bit analog-to-digital converter has a reference voltage of 5V and produces a reading of 310, then the analog voltage is

$$(311 \div 1{,}024) \times 5 = 1.519V$$

However, knowing the analog voltage doesn't always mean that much. For example, a potentiometer connected to a 10-bit analog-to-digital converter will produce a reading of 0 when turned all the way to the left and 1,023 when turned all the way to the right. Having a reading between 0 and 1,023 for a potentiometer probably makes more sense to you than a voltage from 0V to 5V, for example. It all depends on what information you require from the analog device.

Understanding the relationship between the digital data you receive from the analog-to-digital converter back to the sensor is an important aspect of your design.

Introducing the Analog-to-Digital Conversion Methods

In this section, we introduce you to three commonly used methods for analog-to-digital conversion. Later in the chapter, we walk you through each method in greater detail.

Each of these methods uses a comparator to compare two voltages and make a series of guesses to try to get as close as we can to discovering the analog voltage.

The ramp method

If an analog sensor has a voltage of 1.75V and you compare it to a known reference voltage that starts at 0V and increments until the reference voltage is greater than the analog voltage, you know that the analog voltage is somewhere between the reading just before 1.75 and after 1.75. This method is known as the ramp method.

The reference voltage in the ramp method starts at zero and increases in small amounts until it's greater than the analog voltage (shown as the trip point in Figure 9-5). To increase accuracy, you can make each step as small as possible, but this adds to the amount of time needed to produce a reading — taking smaller steps means doing more tests on the comparator, which takes time.

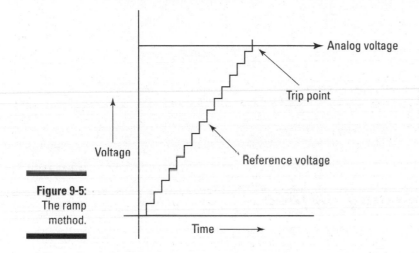

Figure 9-5:
The ramp method.

The successive approximation method

The successive approximation method uses a series of calculated guesses to home in on the answer. The starting point can be half of the maximum voltage and is either increased or decreased depending on whether the comparator has tripped. The increment or decrement value is halved with each guess, as shown in Figure 9-6. As with the ramp method, you can increase the amount of guesses to get a more accurate result, which takes more time.

Successive approximation may look much faster than the ramp method because you can get a very accurate answer in 8 guesses, whereas with the ramp method you could make 1,023 guesses. But successive approximation requires more filtering time — the signal is changing so much between guesses that the filter needs more time to settle. The ramp method takes small increments in one direction, which enables the filter to produce an accurate result with much less settling time. When designed with a fast and accurate filter, successive approximation is faster than the ramp method. Many analog-to-digital conversion chips (like the MCP3008, which we use later in this chapter) use this method for conversion.

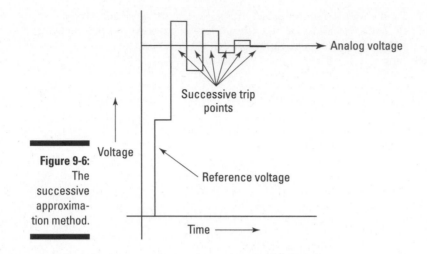

Figure 9-6:
The
successive
approxima-
tion method.

The tracking method

The tracking method uses the ramp method to determine the first value and then tracks the analog voltage using the previous reading as a starting point for the next search, as shown in Figure 9-7. The comparator tells you which direction to search for the analog voltage. Using the previous reading as a starting point reduces the number of steps you need to take. This method is fast if the analog voltage doesn't change very frequently (for example, because you have a temperature sensor that changes fairly slowly over time).

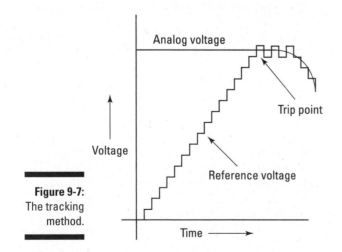

Figure 9-7:
The tracking
method.

Building an Analog-to-Digital Converter

In this section, you build an analog-to-digital converter and write the code for each of the three conversion methods explained in the previous section. The converter uses a comparator (refer to Figure 9-2) and pulse width modulation on the Raspberry Pi, as explained earlier in this chapter, to convert the analog signal to a digital reading on the Raspberry Pi.

Finding the parts you need

To make this project, you need the following parts:

- Five 3K3 ohm 0.5W carbon film resistors ±5 percent
- One 10k ohm 0.5W carbon film resistor ±5 percent
- One 1k ohm 0.5W carbon film resistor ±5 percent
- One 1uF/50V radial electrolytic capacitor
- Two 0.1uF/50V radial electrolytic capacitors
- One LM339 quad comparator (a device used to compare voltages and output the result in a digital signal)
- One Humble PI prototyping board (a prototyping board for the Raspberry Pi from CISECO) or one solderless breadboard (a prototyping board where parts and wires can be connected by clipping them into the board; used for prototyping electronics without having to solder parts together)
- Three 2-pin 0.2-inch (5mm) screw terminals
- Assorted jumper wires for the prototyping board or for the solderless breadboard (*Note:* If you're using a breadboard, use male-to-male for breadboard connections and male-to-female for connecting the bread-board to the GPIO pins. Jumper wires usually come in packs of various quantities, colors, and sizes. Any size will do for this project, but shorter male-to-male [10cm] and longer male-to-female [20cm] are best.)
- One 10K breadboard trim potentiometer

All these parts are readily available from electronic stores or online. We use a Humble PI breakout board from CISECO because it attaches right to the Raspberry Pi GPIO header and has a center power rails and holes arranged in threes, making it a very convenient layout. You can substitute it for a regular prototype board with center rails or a solderless breadboard, but you'll need to make the necessary adjustments because a breadboard has the power rails running down the outside and not down the center.

Since the release of the Raspberry Pi 2 A++, and B++ models, the shape of the board has changed, so some breakout boards (like the Humble PI) no longer fit the Raspberry Pi. However you can use an extra-tall stacking header Raspberry Pi that allows you to connect the Humble PI to the new shape of the Raspberry Pi.

Constructing the circuit

The difficulty level of the prototype board construction will be difficult for a complete beginner because there are around 50 solder points. If you're a total beginner, you may want to opt for the breadboard. However, even if you're a soldering novice, you should be able to construct this prototype.

As with all prototyping, make sure you understand each part before you begin construction. This understanding will help you troubleshoot and test different parts of the circuit during or after the build. Figure 9-8 is the circuit diagram for the analog-to-digital converter.

Take note that in later revisions of the Raspberry Pi, GPIO 21 changed to GPIO 27, but the Raspberry Pi pin number using the in code remains the same.

Understanding the circuit

The left side of the circuit in Figure 9-8 controls the voltage going into pins 6, 8, and 10 of the comparator. You configure the Raspberry Pi pin 18 to the PWM mode and adjust its value from 0 to 1,023. This variable voltage is known as the reference voltage. This moves the voltage going into pins 6, 8, and 10 in small increments from 0V to 5V. The 1uF capacitor and 10K resistor are the low-pass filter (refer to "Converting Analog to Digital," earlier in this chapter, for more details), which converts the PWM pulses into DC current.

The three analog inputs shown in Figure 9-8 can be connected to your analog sensors. We only use one of the analog inputs in this chapter, but we've designed the converter with three inputs to give you more options if you need them for other projects. Later in this chapter, you test this circuit using a potentiometer and a temperature sensor. The comparator compares the voltages of the reference voltage to the analog voltage. When the comparator pins 1, 14, and 13 flip from low to high, you know the reference voltage is greater than the analog voltage. When this happens, the input pins on the GPIO (pins 17, 21, and 4) go high. Each of these pins has a 3K3 pull-up resistor connected to it. Lastly, the comparator is powered by 5V going to pin 3 and is grounded on pin 12.

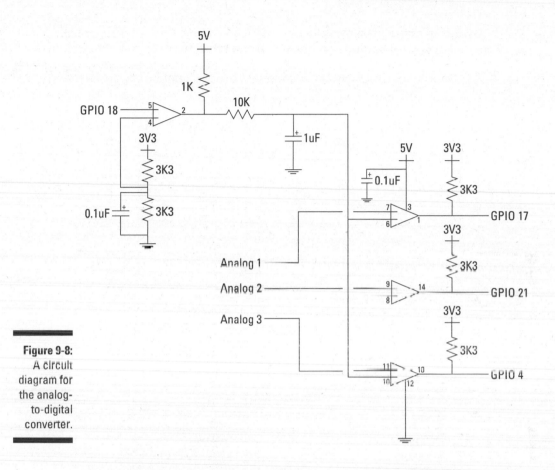

Figure 9-8:
A circuit
diagram for
the analog-
to-digital
converter.

Constructing the circuit

Figure 9-9 shows a grid of the Humble PI prototype board with the *x*- and
y-coordinates of each connection. Each hole in the board is identified by the
row and column numbers given at the top and on the left side of the diagram.
The positive and negative center rails are labeled as + and –. For example,
there is an R1 resistor connected from position E5 to position +5. Table 9-1
shows the position of every component, including jumper wires.

First, place all components onto the prototype board without solder. Double-
check that they're all in the right position and then begin soldering. Be careful not to spill solder over to any adjacent holes. When all the components

are soldered in place, solder in the jumper wires. We recommend placing the jumper wires underneath the board and the electrical components above the board, as shown in Figure 9-10. Some of the jumps can be completed just by using solder to bridge two adjacent pads (for example, M3 to M4).

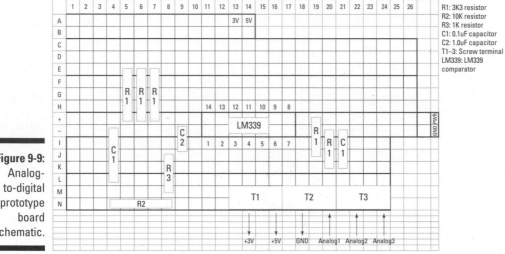

Figure 9-9: Analog-to-digital prototype board schematic.

Table 9-1	Analog-to-Digital Converter Components	
Component	*From*	*To*
LM339	I11	H11
LM339	I12	H12
LM339	I13	H13
LM339	I14	H14
LM339	I15	H15
LM339	I16	H16
LM339	I17	H17
R1	+19	J19
R1	−20	K20
C1	−21	K21
Jumper	K21	K20
Jumper	K20	K19
Jumper	M9	M8

Component	From	To
R2	N4	N8
R3	J8	M8
Jumper	I8	B14
Jumper	M4	N3
C1	−4	L4
C2	−9	I9
Jumper	B14	J9
LM339 pin 1 (GPIO17)	C7	B3
LM339 pin 1 (R1)	J11	D5
LM339 pin 2 (R2)	K12	L8
LM339 pin 3 (5V)	K9	K13
LM339 pin 4 (R1)	K19	K14
LM339 pin 5 (GPIO18)	J15	B4
LM339 pin 6 (R2)	L3	J16
LM339 pin 7 (T2) (analog 1)	L20	J17
LM339 pin 8 (R2)	M3	G17
LM339 pin 9 (T3) (analog 2)	L22	G16
LM339 pin 10 (R2)	N3	G15
LM339 pin 11 (T3) (analog 3)	L24	G14
LM339 pin 12 (GND)	G13	-22
LM339 pin 13 (GPIO4)	C5	B10
LM339 pin 13 (R1)	G12	D7
LM339 pin 14 (R1)	G11	D6
LM339 pin 14 (GPIO21)	C6	B5
T1 (+3V)	L14	B14
T1 (+5V)	L16	B14
T2 (GND)	L18	−24
Jumper	G16	L22
PWR Center Rail (+3V)	+26	B13
GND Center Rail (GND)	−26	−VE

Figure 9-10:
The
Raspberry
Pi analog-
to-digital
converter.

Before powering it up, use a circuit tester to test each connection. Circuit testers can be bought or constructed using an LED circuit. Some multimeters have a circuit tester built in. They consist of a battery connected to a light or a buzzer that indicate when the circuit is closed. The tester has two leads that, when joined, close the circuit and activate the light or buzzer. You can use the circuit tester to test each connection of the analog-to-digital converter. For example, the right side of the 10k resistor should be connected to pins 6, 8, and 10 of the LM339 comparator. In order to test these connections, place one of the circuit tester leads on the right side of the 10k resistor and then touch pins 6, 8, and 10 of the comparator. Your circuit tester will indicate if each of these three circuits is soldered correctly. Use this method to test every connection.

The Humble PI can be powered by external power (refer to the pads on the top-right corner of the board), but we've chosen to power the board directly from the Raspberry Pi by connecting the 3V (A13) to PWR and connecting GND to the negative power rail (–).

The six screw terminals can be used to connect to an analog sensor. There is a screw terminal for the three analog sensors — 5V, 3V, and GND — as shown in Figure 9-9.

Connecting an analog sensor

Now that you have your analog-to-digital converter built, you can connect it to an analog sensor. To start, connect it to a potentiometer (also known as a pot or a trimpot). Connect the left pin of the trimpot to the 3V screw terminal, the middle pin of the trimpot to the Analog 1 screw terminal, and pin 3 of the trimpot to the GND screw terminal (see Figure 9-11).

Figure 9-11: Connecting a potentiometer to the analog-to-digital converter.

Writing the software

In this section, you write code for each of the analog-to-digital conversion methods explained earlier in this chapter. You use C code for the interfaces because it's faster than Python, but we also show you how to call a C program from Python so you can write Python programs to interface with your analog sensors.

Installing WiringPi

You use a GPIO access library called WiringPi to control the PWM and monitor the GPIO digital pins. WiringPi was written by Gordon Henderson and is a GPIO library for the Raspberry Pi. You use it to control the GPIO digital pins and PWM. You also use WiringPi's Serial Peripheral Interface (SPI) library later in this chapter. For more details on WiringPi you can visit Gordon's webpage (www.wiringpi.com).

To install WiringPi, type the following command at the command prompt:

```
$ sudo apt-get install git-
  core
```

If you get any errors here, make sure your Pi is up to date with the latest versions of Raspbian:

```
$ sudo apt-get update
$ sudo apt-get upgrade
```

Install WiringPi:

```
$ cd ~
$ git clone git://git.drogon.
  net/wiringPi
$ cd wiringPi
$ ./build
```

If you aren't able to use git or you're using an operating system other than Raspbian or Debian, you can follow the instructions to install WiringPi. Go to https://git.drogon.net/?p=wiringPi;a=summary. Then look for the most recent (topmost) entry in the shortlog, and click the rightmost link (marked "snapshot") for that entry.

This will download a tar.gz file with a name like wiringPi-98bcb20.tar.gz. Note that the numbers and letters after wiringPi (98bcb20, in this case) will probably be different. They're a unique identifier for each release.

Then enter the following command from the Raspberry Pi command line:

```
tar xfz wiringPi-98bcb20.tar.
gz
cd wiringPi-98bcb20
./build
```

Remember: The actual filename will be different. You have to check the name and adjust it accordingly.

Software for the ramp method

The software for the ramp method is in Listing 9-1. Type the program in and save it to a file called ramp.c.

Listing 9-1: Analog-to-Digital C Program for the Ramp Method

```
/*
 * ramp.c
 * Raspberry Pi Projects For Dummies: Analog-to-Digital Converter
 * Ramp Method
 */
```

```
#include <wiringPi.h>

#include <stdio.h>
#include <stdlib.h>
#include <stdint.h>

float to_volts(int reading, float analog_volts);

int main (int argc, char *argv[])
{
  int one_reading;
  int ramp, reading0, reading1, reading2;
  unsigned char gotReading0, gotReading1, gotReading2;
  const unsigned char A0 = 17, A1 = 21, A2 = 4, pwm = 18;

  if (argc!=2){
    printf ("usage : ramp [single_reading 1/0]\n");
    exit(1);
    }

  one_reading = atoi(argv[1]);

  if (wiringPiSetupGpio () == -1)
  exit (1);

  pinMode (A0,INPUT);
  pinMode (A1,INPUT);
  pinMode (A2,INPUT);
  pinMode (pwm, PWM_OUTPUT) ;
  pwmWrite(pwm, 0);
  delay(40);

  for (;;)
  {
    reading0 =-1;
    reading1 =-1;
    reading2 =-1;
    gotReading0 = 0;
    gotReading1 = 0;
    gotReading2 = 0;

    for (ramp = 0 ; ramp < 1024 ; ramp+=4) // in effect 8 bit
    {
      pwmWrite (pwm, ramp);
      delayMicroseconds(200);

      if(gotReading0 == 0 && digitalRead(A0)== 0){
        gotReading0 = 1;
        reading0 = ramp;
        }
```

(continued)

Listing 9-1 *(continued)*

```
    if(gotReading1 == 0 && digitalRead(A1)== 0){
      gotReading1 = 1;
      reading1 = ramp;
      }

    if(gotReading2 == 0 && digitalRead(A2)== 0){
    gotReading2 = 1;
    reading2 = ramp;
    }
  if(gotReading0 && gotReading1 && gotReading2) break;
}

printf("Reading Ch0 = %d (%2.3fV) Ch1 = %d (%2.3fV) Ch2 = %d (%2.3fV)
\n", reading0, to_volts(reading0,5), reading1, to_volts(reading1,5)
, reading2, to_volts(reading2,5));

if (one_reading) {
  return(0);
    }

pwmWrite (pwm, 0);
delay(40);
}

return 0 ;
}

float to_volts(int reading, float analog_volts)
{
  float volts;
  volts = ((float)reading / 1023) * analog_volts;
  return(volts);
}
```

The program sets GPIO 18 to PWM mode and then loops through each PWM setting starting at 0 and ending at 1,023. To speed it up, we set it to increase in steps of 4. Looping 256 times instead of 1,024 will make the program faster but sacrifice 2 bits of resolution. With each loop cycle, you check the GPIO digital pins to see if one of the comparators has flipped from low to high and, if so, save the reading for that sensor. When all three sensor values have been read or you reach the end of the loop, the program writes the results to the screen and goes again into the loop to get the next reading.

Compile the program using the following command:

```
$ sudo gcc -o ./ramp ramp.c -l wiringPi
```

You pass a parameter of 0 or 1 to the program that determines whether the program will print only one reading or multiple readings. If it's the latter, you press Ctrl+C to quit. Now run the program from the command line using the following command:

```
$ ./ramp 0
```

You see the output printed to the screen for each of the three analog channels. Adjust the trimpot by turning the knob left and right, and watch the value of channel 0 move up and down. Then stop adjusting the potentiometer and observe the results. Notice that even though the potentiometer is not changing, the reading fluctuates. The spread between the minimum and maximum reading we get is about 8, as shown here:

```
Reading Ch0 = 540
Reading Ch0 = 536
Reading Ch0 = 544
```

Our goal is to try get to a steady reading with little to no fluctuation. One way you can reduce the fluctuation is to refine the granularity of the PWM cycle. The ramp.c program loops through 0 to 1,023 PWM setting in increments of 4 as per the following line of code:

```
for (ramp = 0 ; ramp < 1024 ; ramp+=4) // in effect 8 bit
```

It will loop 256 times, which equates to 8-bit accuracy ($2^8 = 256$). With the fluctuation, we're losing around 3 bits, so our converter is, in effect, a 5-bit converter. You can improve this by taking smaller increments and increasing the loop cycle to the full 1,024 settings available on the Raspberry Pi PWM. Change the following line to:

```
for (ramp = 0 ; ramp < 1024 ; ramp+=1) // in effect 10 bit
```

Recompile and run the program. You should now see a more accurate result. Our results are as follows:

```
Reading Ch0 = 197
Reading Ch0 = 198
Reading Ch0 = 199
Reading Ch0 = 202
Reading Ch0 = 197
Reading Ch0 = 197
```

The spread of the fluctuation is now 5. We've improved the accuracy of the analog-to-digital converter, but we paid a price in time. The converter is now half the speed it was originally, and it's noticeable.

Another change you can make to improve accuracy is to adjust the settling time given to the circuit with every change of the PWM cycle. The first of the following two lines changes the PWM value and the second pauses the program for 200 microseconds while the circuit settles.

```
pwmWrite (pwm, ramp);
delayMicroseconds(200);
```

Change the 200 to 500 and recompile and run again. Our results improved to a spread of only 2. However, there is an even more noticeable degradation to the performance of the conversion.

```
Reading Ch0 = 178
Reading Ch0 = 178
Reading Ch0 = 180
```

A third modification that could be made is to fine-tune the low-pass filter by reducing the cut-off frequency. The settling time is governed by the action of the filter. Again, there's a performance trade-off to be made because the lower the cut-off frequency, the longer it takes for the resulting voltage to ramp up to the final value. This would mean changing the 1uF capacitor and the 10k resistor, which would require a change to the circuit, so for the purposes of this chapter we won't go into the different options here.

Software for the successive approximation method

Listing 9-2 is the code for the successive approximation method. The program performs eight guesses at the analog voltage. With each guess, the comparator tells you if you're higher or lower than the analog voltage, and then the next guess is either increased or decreased by half the previous increment. With each guess, you home in on the answer. Type the program in and save it to a file called succ.c.

Listing 9-2:   Analog-to-Digital C Program for the Successive Approximation Method

```
/*
 * succ.c
 * Raspberry Pi Projects For Dummies: Analog-to-Digital Converter
 * Successive Approximation Method
 */
#include <wiringPi.h>

#include <stdio.h>
#include <stdlib.h>
#include <stdint.h>
```

```c
int successive(char ch);
float to_volts(int reading, float analog_volts);

int main (int argc, char *argv[]){
  int one_reading;
  int reading0, reading1, reading2 ;
  const unsigned char A0 = 17, A1 = 21, A2 = 4;

  if (argc!=2){
  printf ("usage : succ [single_reading 1/0]\n");
  exit(1);
  }

  one_reading = atoi(argv[1]);

  if (wiringPiSetupGpio () == -1)
    exit (1) ;

  pinMode (A0,INPUT);
  pinMode (A1,INPUT);
  pinMode (A2,INPUT);
  pinMode (18, PWM_OUTPUT) ;

  for (;;){
    reading0 =-1;
    reading1 =-1;
    reading2 =-1;
    reading0 = successive(A0);
    reading1 = successive(A1);
    reading2 = successive(A2);

    printf("Reading Ch0 = %d (%2.3fV) Ch1 = %d (%2.3fV) Ch2 = %d (%2.3fV) \n",
    reading0, to_volts(reading0,5), reading1, to_volts(reading1,5),
    reading2, to_volts(reading2,5));

    if (one_reading==1)
      return(0);
  }
  return 0 ;
}

int successive(char ch){
  int reading = 512; // start at the midpoint
  int x = 256,i,pwm = 18;
  for(i=0; i<8; i++){
    pwmWrite(pwm,reading);
    delayMicroseconds(3000);  // settling time
    if(digitalRead(ch) == 0){
      reading=reading-x;
        }
```

(continued)

Listing 9-2 *(continued)*

```
    else {
       reading=reading+x;
       }
    x=x/2; //narrow the search
    }
  return (reading);
}

float to_volts(int reading, float analog_volts)
{
  float volts;
  volts = ((float)reading / 1023) * analog_volts;
  return(volts);
}
```

Compile the program using the following command:

```
$ sudo gcc -o ./succ succ.c -l wiringPi
```

You pass a parameter of 0 or 1 to the program that determines whether the program will print only one reading or successive readings. If it's the latter, you press Ctrl+C to quit. Now run the program from the command line using the following command:

```
$ ./succ 0
```

Using this method, you can obtain the same result as the ramp method, except with the ramp method you could potentially have to make 256 guesses as opposed to 8 using this method. One major disadvantage of this method is the settling time (3,000 microseconds) that the circuit needs before it takes a new reading. This is due to the fact that we're making large jumps in voltage with each guess. The ramp method, however, increments the voltage in small increments in the same direction so you can dramatically reduce the settling time (75 microseconds).

Here's is a comparison of the total potential settling time of each method:

Total settling time for the ramp method:

$256 \times 75 = 19,200$ microseconds

Total settling time for the successive approximation method:

$3,000 \times 8 = 16,000$ microseconds

Even though the ramp method takes many more guesses, it's only marginally slower than successive approximation.

As with the ramp method, a number of factors will affect the accuracy of the conversion. In the preceding section, we explain how you can fine-tune the settling time, the granularity of the PWM settings, and the low-pass filter. The same applies with this method.

You can increase or decrease the amount of guesses it makes by adjusting the 8 in this form loop statement to your desired value:

```
for(i=0; i<8; i++){
```

Software for the tracking method

The tracking method starts by using the ramp method (or successive approximation, it doesn't matter which) to find and track the analog voltage. Then it uses the previous reading as a starting point to search for the next reading. This way, it can track the analog voltage and reduce the number of overall readings, which can make this method faster than the other methods.

The software for the tracking method is shown in Listing 9-3. Type the program and save it to a file called track.c.

Listing 9-3: Analog-to-Digital C Program for the Tracking Method

```
/*
 * track.c
 * Raspberry Pi Projects For Dummies: Analog-to-Digital Converter
 * Tracking Method
 */


#include <wiringPi.h>

#include <stdio.h>
#include <stdlib.h>
#include <stdint.h>

// Declare functions
int track(char ch, int direction);

int main (int argc, char *argv[])
{
  int one_reading;
  int reading0 = 0, reading1 = 0, reading2 = 0;
  const unsigned char A0 = 17, A1 = 21, A2 = 4;
```

(continued)

Listing 9-3 *(continued)*

```c
    if (argc!=2 && argc!=3){
      printf ("usage : ramp [single_reading 1/0]\n");
      printf ("                [previous_reading1 (0-1023) (optional)]\n");
      printf ("                [previous_reading2 (0-1023) (optional)]\n");
      printf ("                [previous_reading3 (0-1023) (optional)]\n");
      exit(1);
      }

  one_reading = atoi(argv[1]);
  if (argc>=3){
    reading0=atoi(argv[2]);
    }

if (argc>=4){
    reading1=atoi(argv[3]);
    }

if (argc>=5){
    reading2=atoi(argv[4]);
    }

  if (wiringPiSetupGpio () == -1)
  exit (1);

  pinMode (A0,INPUT);
  pinMode (A1,INPUT);
  pinMode (A2,INPUT);
  pinMode (18, PWM_OUTPUT) ;

  for (;;)
  {
    reading0 = track(A0, reading0);
    reading1 = track(A1, reading1);
    reading2 = track(A2, reading2);
    printf("Reading Ch0 = %d Ch1 = %d Ch2 = %d \n", reading0, reading1,reading2);
    if (one_reading==1)
      return(0);
  }
return(0);
}


int track(char ch, int reading)
{
  int gotReading, direction, digital_read;
  pwmWrite (18, reading);
  delayMicroseconds(4000);
  if (digitalRead(ch)==1){
    direction=1;
    }
```

```
  else{
    direction=-1;
    }
  gotReading=0;
  while (!gotReading){
    reading=reading+direction;
    pwmWrite (18, reading);
    delayMicroseconds(500);
    digital_read=digitalRead(ch);
    if ((digital_read==1 && direction==-1) ||
        (digital_read==0 && direction==1)){
      gotReading=1;
      }
    if (reading<0){
      reading=0;
      gotReading=1;
      }
    if (reading>1024){
      reading=1023;
      gotReading=1;
      }
    }
  return(reading);
}
```

Compile the program using the following command:

```
$ sudo gcc -o ./track track.c -l wiringPi
```

The program takes up to four parameters. The first parameter determines whether the program will print one reading and quit or continue forever printing readings to the screen until you press Ctrl+C. The second to fourth parameters are the starting points for each analog sensor (which is a value between 0 and 1,023). You can use these parameters if you want to call this program from a Python program where the Python program stores the previous reading and passes it to this program to obtain a new reading. This is used in the Breakdown game, later in this chapter.

The program calls the track routine for each of the three analog sensors passing the previous reading as a parameter. The track routine first sets the PWM cycle to the previous reading and tests the comparator. This determines which direction you track to find the next reading. If the comparator is positive, the PWM cycle needs to increase until the comparator flips negative; if the comparator is negative, the search heads in the other direction until the comparator flips positive (refer Figure 9-7).

We set the wait time on the first read to 4,000 microseconds so you give the circuit enough initial settling time. When the tracking starts, we decrease the wait time to 500 microseconds because the changes between readings will be smaller.

As with the other two methods, you can fine-tune the accuracy by changing the wait times, speeding it up by increasing the increment/decrement value between readings and reducing the cut-off frequency of the low-pass filter.

Now that you've completed the software for the three methods, compare the results and speeds of each method. Fine-tune them using the parameters we describe to try get the most accurate readings. In the next two sections, you use the analog-to-digital converter on two different projects. The first project uses a potentiometer to control the paddle of the Breakdown game. You use the reading of the potentiometer to control the horizontal positioning of the paddle. The more the reading fluctuates, the more unstable the paddle will appear. Speed is also an important factor for the Breakdown game. You don't want the digital conversion to slow down the game and make it unplayable.

In the other project, you use the analog converter to read the temperature from a *thermistor* (temperature sensor). In order to calculate the temperature, we need an accurate voltage reading across the sensor. In this project, speed is less important, but accuracy is very important.

Using a Potentiometer to Control the Breakdown Game

In this section, you use a potentiometer to control the paddle (or blocker) of the Breakdown game, a legendary game from the 1970s. The objective is quite simple: You use the blocker that moves left and right to deflect a ball and send it back up to eliminate some more bricks. The objective is to clear all the bricks.

Use the potentiometer circuit you construct earlier in this chapter to move the paddle left and right. This shows a good visual representation of the accuracy of your analog-to-digital converter. If your reading fluctuates, you see the paddle jump or shake. If your analog-to-digital conversion takes too long, the game will slow down and become unplayable. Use this game as an exercise to determine which conversion method best suits the game's needs.

Listing 9-4 is configured to call the ramp program you develop in the "Software for the ramp method" section, earlier in this chapter. However, you can change it to call the successive approximation or tracking programs as follows:

- ✔ If you want to change methods, then change the METHOD constant at the top of the program to T for tracking or S for the successive approximation method.

- ✔ You can set the minimum and maximum boundaries of your analog readings using the MIN_PADDLE and MAX_PADDLE variable settings at the beginning of the program. Depending on which potentiometer you're using, you could have different boundaries within the 0 to 1,023 PWM range.

Type the following program in to a file called breakdown.py and save it in your user directory of your Raspberry Pi. The program calls the analog-to-digital conversion C programs, which should also be in your user directory.

Listing 9-4:   Breakdown Game Using a Potentiometer to Control the Game Paddle

```
#!/usr/bin/env python
"""
Raspberry Pi Projects For Dummies: breakdown game
using a potentiometer to control the paddle
for the Raspberry Pi
"""
import os
import sys
import subprocess
import re
import pygame

# Color constants
BLACK = (0,0,0)
WHITE = (255,255,255)
YELLOW  = (200,200,0)
BRICK_COLOR = (0,200,0)

# Game State Constants
STATE_BEGIN = 0
STATE_PLAYING = 1
STATE_WON = 2
STATE_GAME_OVER = 3
PADDLE_DELAY=5
METHOD = "R"
MIN_PADDLE=0
MAX_PADDLE=850
```

(continued)

Listing 9-4 *(continued)*

```
class breakdown:

    def get_paddle_position(bo):
            if METHOD=="T":
                    output = subprocess.check_output(["~/track","1",str(bo.
               reading)])
            elif METHOD=="R":
                    output = subprocess.check_output(["~/ramp","1"])
            elif METHOD=="S":
                    output = subprocess.check_output(["~/succ","1"])
            elif METHOD=="M":
                    output = subprocess.check_output(["~/mcp3008", "1"])

            s = re.search("Ch0 =\s+([0-9a-f]+)", output)
            if s:
                    x = (float(s.group(1))/float(MAX_PADDLE-MIN_PADDLE)*615)
                    bo.reading = int(x)

    def display_message(bo,message,x,y):
            txt_format = bo.font.render(message,False, WHITE)
            bo.screen.blit(txt_format, (x,y))

    def run(bo):
            pygame.init()
            bo.screen = pygame.display.set_mode([640,480])
            pygame.display.set_caption("Raspberry Pi Projects For Dummies")
            bo.clock = pygame.time.Clock()
            bo.font = pygame.font.Font(None,30)
            bo.reset_game()
            while 1:
                    for event in pygame.event.get():
                            if event.type == pygame.QUIT:
                                    sys.exit
                    bo.clock.tick(50)
                    bo.screen.fill([0,0,0])
                    if bo.paddle_no>PADDLE_DELAY:
                            bo.get_paddle_position()
                            bo.paddle.left=bo.reading
                            bo.paddle_no=0
                    else:
                            bo.paddle_no=bo.paddle_no+1
                    #If you want to use the keyboard to control the paddle
                    #uncomment the following lines
                    keys = pygame.key.get_pressed()
                    #if keys[pygame.K_LEFT]:
                    #    bo.paddle.left -= 5
                    #if keys[pygame.K_RIGHT]:
                    #    bo.paddle.left += 5
                    if keys[pygame.K_SPACE] and bo.state == STATE_BEGIN:
```

```
                        bo.ball_direction = [5,-5]
                        bo.state = STATE_PLAYING
            elif keys[pygame.K_RETURN] and (bo.state == STATE_GAME_OVER
    or bo.state == STATE_WON):
                        bo.reset_game()
            if bo.state == STATE_PLAYING:
                        bo.ball.left += bo.horizontal
                        bo.ball.top  += bo.vertical
                        if bo.ball.left <= 0:
                                bo.ball.left = 0
                                bo.horizontal = -bo.horizontal
                        elif bo.ball.left >= 624:
                                bo.ball.left = 624
                                bo.horizontal = -bo.horizontal
                        if bo.ball.top < 0:
                                bo.ball.top = 0
                                bo.vertical = -bo.vertical
                        elif bo.ball.top >= 464:
                                bo.ball.top = 464
                                bo.vertical = -bo.vertical
                        for brick in bo.bricks:
                                if bo.ball.colliderect(brick):
                                        bo.vertical = -bo.vertical
                                        bo.bricks.remove(brick)
                                        break
                        if bo.ball.colliderect(bo.paddle):
                                bo.ball.top = 442
                                bo.vertical = -bo.vertical #If ball
    hits the edge of the paddle send it back in the same direction
                                if bo.ball.left <  bo.paddle.left or
    bo.ball.left > bo.paddle.left+45:
                                        bo.horizontal = -bo.
                                horizontal
                        elif bo.ball.top > bo.paddle.top:
                                bo.state = STATE_GAME_OVER
                        if len(bo.bricks) == 0:
                                bo.state = STATE_WON
            elif bo.state == STATE_BEGIN:
                        bo.ball.left = bo.paddle.left + bo.paddle.width / 2
                        bo.ball.top  = bo.paddle.top - bo.ball.height
                        bo.display_message("PRESS SPACE TO START",180,200)
            elif bo.state == STATE_GAME_OVER:
                        bo.display_message("GAME OVER - PRESS ENTER TO PLAY
    AGAIN",100,200)
            elif bo.state == STATE_WON:
                        bo.display_message("WINNER! PRESS ENTER TO PLAY
    AGAIN",100,200)
            for brick in bo.bricks:
```

(continued)

Listing 9-4 *(continued)*

```
                        pygame.draw.rect(bo.screen, BRICK_COLOR, brick)
            pygame.draw.rect(bo.screen, YELLOW, bo.paddle)

            pygame.draw.circle(bo.screen, WHITE, (bo.ball.left + 8,
    bo.ball.top + 8), 8)
                            bo.display_message("Paddle Position: "
        +str(bo.reading),200,10)
            pygame.display.flip()

    def reset_game(bo):
            bo.reading    = 0
            bo.state      = STATE_BEGIN
            bo.paddle     = pygame.Rect(300,458,60,12)
            bo.ball       = pygame.Rect(300,442,16,16)
            bo.vertical=-5
            bo.horizontal=5
            bo.paddle_no=0
            y = 35
            bo.bricks = []
            for i in range(7):
                    x = 5
                    for j in range(9):
                            bo.bricks.append(pygame.Rect(x,y,60,12))
                            x += 70
                    y += 17

if __name__ == "__main__":
        breakdown().run()
```

To run the program, type **startx** from the Raspberry Pi command line and open an LXTerminal window. At the command prompt, type the following commands to start the game:

```
$ cd ~
$ python breakdown.py
```

The program will start up as shown in Figure 9-12. The paddle isn't very stable so you need to fine-tune your analog-to-digital conversion methods and experiment to find one that best suits the game. Your goal is to find a conversion method that's fast and that has an acceptable level of fluctuation.

Paddle Position: 261

PRESS SPACE TO START

Figure 9-12:
The
Breakdown
game being
controlled
by a poten-
tiometer
connected
to the
analog-
to-digital
converter.

Creating an Analog Temperature Sensor

In this section, you use the analog-to-digital converter you construct earlier in this chapter to tell the temperature. The analog temperature sensor you use is a TMP36, shown in Figure 9-13.

The TMP36 is a low-voltage, centigrade temperature sensor. It provides an analog voltage output that is linearly proportional to the temperature. It's very easy to use. Just connect 2.7 to 5.5 VDC, and it produces the analog voltage on the output pin.

In this project, it's important for your digital converter to produce an accurate reading. Depending on how frequently you want to read the temperature, you can increase the settling time of the low-pass filter of the converter to improve accuracy. The speed of the conversion is probably less important to you than it was with the Breakdown game. The software that you wrote earlier in this chapter provides you with a reading between 0 and 1,023. You can calculate the voltage using the following formula:

Analog Voltage = (Analog-to-Digital Reading ÷ 1,023) × 5

where Analog-to-Digital Reading is the reading from the analog-to-digital converter and 5 is the reference voltage we're using with the analog-to-digital converter.

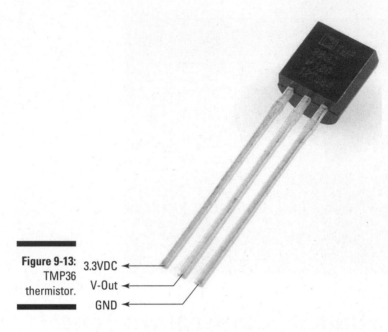

Figure 9-13:
TMP36
thermistor.

3.3VDC ◄

V-Out ◄

GND ◄

The temperature formula for the TMP36 sensor is as follows:

Temperature = (Sensor Reading Millivolts – 500) ÷ 10

A volt is equal to 1,000 millivolts, so for our purposes, we use the following formula:

Temperature = ([Analog Voltage × 1,000] – 500) ÷ 10

For example, if the analog-to-digital converter gives you a reading of 144, the calculation is as follows:

Analog Voltage = (144 ÷ 1,023) × 5

Analog Voltage = 0.70381

Temperature = ([0.70381 × 1,000] – 500) ÷ 10

Temperature = 20.831°C

Constructing the circuit

Here are the parts you need to build this circuit:

- ✔ **A TMP36 sensor:** This is a wide-range, low-power (between 2.7V and 5.5V) temperature sensor that outputs an analog voltage that is proportional to the ambient temperature.

- ✔ **A solderless breadboard:** A solderless breadboard is a prototyping board where parts and wires can be connected by clipping them into the board. It's used for prototyping electronics without having to solder parts together.

- ✔ **Assorted jumper wires for a solderless breadboard:** Use male-to-male for breadboard connections and male-to-female for connecting the breadboard to the GPIO pins. Jumper wires usually come in packs of various quantities, colors, and sizes. Any size will do for this project, but shorter male-to-male (10cm) and longer male-to-female (20cm) are best.

As per Figure 9-13, connect pin 1 (left) to 3V, pin 2 to the analog-to-digital converter (refer to "Building an Analog-to-Digital Converter" section of this chapter), and pin 3 (right) to ground.

Writing the software

Listing 9-5 is the Python software for the TMP36 that uses the successive approximation method program built in the "Software for the successive approximation method" section of this chapter.

Listing 9-5: Python Code for the TMP36 Analog Sensor Using an Analog-to-Digital Converter

```
#!/usr/bin/env python
"""
Raspberry Pi Projects For Dummies: TMP36 thermistor
using successive approximation and an analog-to-
digital converter
for the Raspberry Pi
"""
```

(continued)

Listing 9-5 *(continued)*

```
import os
import sys
import subprocess
import re

output = subprocess.check_output(["~/succ","1"])
s = re.search("Ch0 =\s+([0-9a-f]+)", output)
if s:
        x = float(s.group(1))
        analog_voltage=(x/1023)*5
        temperature = ((analog_voltage * 1000) - 500) / 10
        fahrenheit = temperature*1.8+32
        print "Temperature = " + str(round(temperature,2)) + "C " +
                str(round(fahrenheit,2)) + "F"
else:
        print "Invalid reading"
```

Run the program and check that the reading is correct:

```
$ python tmp36.py
Temperature = 19.4C 66.93F
```

The program prints both Celsius and Fahrenheit temperature values. If your reading is high, make sure that the reference voltage on the analog-to-digital converter is exactly 5V. Use a multimeter to make sure that you're getting exactly 5V from pin 2 of the Raspberry Pi. When you have an accurate reading, pinch the TMP36 with your fingers and watch the temperature rise as the sensor warms up from your body heat.

Compare the results of the successive approximation method to the ramp and tracking methods by changing the following line of code:

```
output = subprocess.check_output(["/home/succ","1"])
```

Change `succ` in the preceding line of code to `ramp` for the ramp method and `track` for the tracking method.

Interfacing with an Analog-to-Digital Microchip

In this section, you use a high-precision analog-to-digital converter that performs the digital conversion external to the Raspberry Pi. The microchip you use is the MCP3008. It performs the analog-to-digital conversion and outputs a digital reading to the Raspberry Pi. The MCP3008 is an 8-channel 10-bit converter and is capable of conversion rates of up to 200 kilo samples per second (ksps), with a conversion time of 10 microseconds.

Figure 9-14 shows the pin allocation of the MCP3008 and how it maps to the GPIO pins on the Raspberry Pi. Use the semicircular indentation on the MCP3008 to orient yourself to the diagram. The eight pins down the left side are eight analog inputs. And the pins down the right side provide the chip with power, ground, a reference voltage, and the various connections required for the serial peripheral interface (SPI). The communication between the Raspberry Pi and MCP3008 is handled by SPI, which is a full duplex serial communication link. The Raspberry Pi supports the SPI protocol and has pins assigned for it on the Raspberry Pi GPIO header.

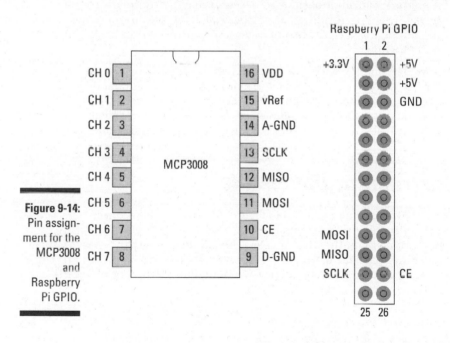

Figure 9-14: Pin assignment for the MCP3008 and Raspberry Pi GPIO.

In this section, we show you how to interface a temperature sensor and a potentiometer so you can compare the readings you get from the MCP3008 with the analog-to-digital converter you build earlier in this chapter.

Assembling the parts you need

Here are the parts you need:

- ✔ **An MCP3008:** This is a high-precision 10-bit 8-channel analog-to-digital converter. You could also use the MCP3004, which has four analog inputs instead of eight.

- ✔ **A TMP36:** This is a wide-range, low-power (between 2.7V and 5.5V) temperature sensor that outputs an analog voltage that is proportional to the ambient temperature.

- ✔ **A 10K breadboard trim potentiometer**

- ✔ **A solderless breadboard:** A solderless breadboard is a prototyping board where parts and wires can be connected by clipping them into the board. It's used for prototyping electronics without having to solder parts together.

- ✔ **Assorted jumper wires for a solderless breadboard:** Use male-to-male for breadboard connections and male-to-female for connecting the breadboard to the GPIO pins. Jumper wires usually come in packs of various quantities, colors and sizes. Any size will do for this project, but shorter male-to-male (10cm) and longer male-to-female (20cm) are best.

Constructing the circuit

Construct your circuit as shown in Figure 9-15. Be careful to orient the TMP36 thermistor the right way around (refer to Figure 9-13 for pin assignment). The potentiometer in the diagram uses the middle put as the analog output. The two outer pins of the potentiometer connect to +3.3V and Ground. The temperature sensor is connected to channel 1, and the potentiometer is connected to channel 0 of the MCP3008.

Writing the software

In order to enable SPI on the Raspberry Pi, you need to edit the following file and comment out the `spi-bcm2708` line as shown in Figure 9-16.

From the Raspberry Pi commend line type the following:

```
sudo nano /etc/modprobe.d/raspi-blacklist.conf
```

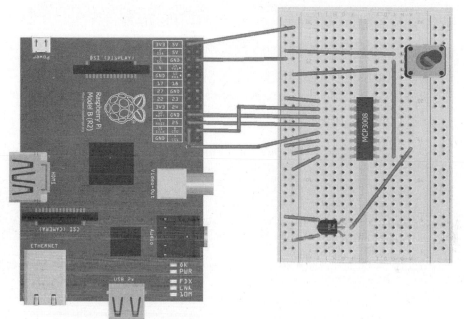

Figure 9-15:
How to connect the MCP3008 to your Raspberry Pi GPIO.

Figure 9-16:
Enable SPI by removing it from the blacklist.

Press Ctrl+X, then press Y, and finally press Enter to save and exit. Then reboot your Raspberry Pi by typing the following:

```
$ reboot
```

If you haven't already installed the WiringPi library, refer to the "Installing WiringPi" sidebar earlier in this chapter. You use the mcp3008 subroutine within WiringPi to interface with the MCP3008 chip.

Listing 9-6:   C Code for a Potentiometer and Temperature Sensor Connected to an MCP3008

```c
/*
 * mcp3008.c
 * Raspberry Pi Projects For Dummies: MCP3008
 * Analog-to-Digital Converter
 * Potentiometer and temperature sensor
 */

#include <wiringPi.h>
#include <mcp3004.h>

#include <stdio.h>
#include <stdlib.h>
#include <stdint.h>

#define BASE 100
#define SPI_CHAN 0

int main (int argc, char *argv[]){
  int tmp,pot, one_reading;
  float analog_voltage, temperature, fahrenheit;

  if (argc!=2){
    printf ("usage : msp3008 [single_reading 1/0]\n");
    exit(1);
    }

  one_reading = atoi(argv[1]);

  mcp3004Setup (BASE, SPI_CHAN);
  while (1) {
    pot = analogRead (BASE+0);
    tmp = analogRead (BASE+1);
    analog_voltage=((float)tmp/1023)*3.3;
    temperature = ((analog_voltage * 1000) - 500) / 10;
    fahrenheit = temperature*1.8+32;
    printf ("Ch0 = %d Ch1 = %d Temperature = %2.2fC %2.2fF \n",
    pot, tmp, temperature, fahrenheit);
    if (one_reading) return(0);
    }
}
```

The code obtains an analog reading from channels 0 and 1 and then calculates the temperature based on the analog reading in the `tmp` variable. For more details regarding the theory behind the TMP36 sensor, please refer to the "Creating an Analog Temperature Sensor" section, earlier in this chapter. Compile and run the program from the Raspberry Pi command line as follows:

```
$ gcc -o ./mcp3008 mcp3008.c -l wiringPi
$ ./mcp3008 0
```

The program should print to screen something similar to this:

```
Ch0=92 Ch1=216 Temperature = 19.68C 67.42F
Ch0=92 Ch1=216 Temperature = 19.68C 67.42F
Ch0=92 Ch1=216 Temperature = 19.68C 67.42F
```

The Ch0 and Ch1 values are the raw readings from the MCP3008 chip. These readings are values in the range 0 to 1,023. The temperature is calculated using the reading from Ch1.

If you created the Breakdown game (refer to "Using a Potentiometer to Control the Breakdown Game," earlier in this chapter), you can configure the Breakdown game to use the potentiometer reading from the MCP3008. Change the METHOD constant to M as follows:

```
$ cd /home
$ sudo nano breakdown.py
```

Edit the METHOD constant as follows:

```
METHOD = "S"
```

Exit and save by pressing Ctrl+X, pressing Y, and then pressing Enter.

Chapter 10

Raspberry Pi in the Sky

Sensors can generate enormous amounts of data that need to be stored, monitored, and analyzed. In this chapter, we explore Internet service providers that do just that. Later in the chapter, we show you how to log temperature data into a database and view it through a web browser.

Understanding the Cloud

An abundance of services are available through the Internet that can be used by the Raspberry Pi. Increasingly, we're seeing everyday appliances and sensors connecting to a network providing us with real-time information from and control over those devices. The Raspberry Pi is very good at interfacing with sensors through the general-purpose input/output (GPIO) ports. Its small form factor, processing capability, and simple connectivity to the Internet makes the Raspberry Pi the perfect fit for this new world of connected devices called the *Internet of Things*.

Connecting to the cloud

Storing sensor data on the Internet requires a connection of some kind to the service provider. Each service provider specifies how to connect to its service and how to send sensor information. The service provider usually requires you to apply for an account or create a user profile, and some charge a fee depending on what services you choose.

In this chapter, we show you the following two free options for storing and viewing sensor data on the Internet:

✔ Storing data in a Google Docs spreadsheet

✔ Creating an online dashboard and alerts using PrivateEyePi

For each of these projects, you use the DS18B20 temperature sensor to collect temperature readings. In the next section, we describe how to interface to the DS18B20 sensor that will be used for the basis of the temperature reading you'll send to each service provider.

Assembling the parts you need

In this project, you use the readily available DS18B20 temperature sensor. Here are all the parts you need to construct your temperature sensor and link it to your Raspberry Pi:

✔ **A DS18B20:** This sensor looks like a transistor, but it's actually a highly accurate one-wire temperature sensor.

✔ **A 4.7k ohm 0.5W carbon film resistor ±5 percent**

✔ **A solderless breadboard:** A solderless breadboard is a prototyping board where parts and wires can be connected by clipping them into the board. It's used for prototyping electronics without having to solder parts together.

✔ **A variety of jumper wires:** You need male-to-male for breadboard connections and male-to-female for connecting the breadboard to the GPIO pins. Jumper wires usually come in packs of various quantities, colors, and sizes. Although you need only 6 for this project, having 20 to 30 of each should see you through most projects. Any size will do for this project, but shorter male-to-male (10cm) and longer male-to-female (20cm) are best.

Constructing the temperature sensor

Besides the power and ground connections, all you need to do is connect the 4.7k ohm pull-up resistor between the signal and power, as shown in Figures 10-1 and 10-2.

Be sure to use pin 7 on the Raspberry Pi for the sensor connection. The software you use to interface with the DS18B20 is hard-coded for pin 7, so you can't use another pin for this sensor.

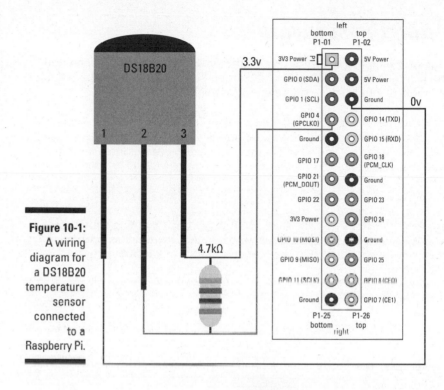

Figure 10-1:
A wiring diagram for a DS18B20 temperature sensor connected to a Raspberry Pi.

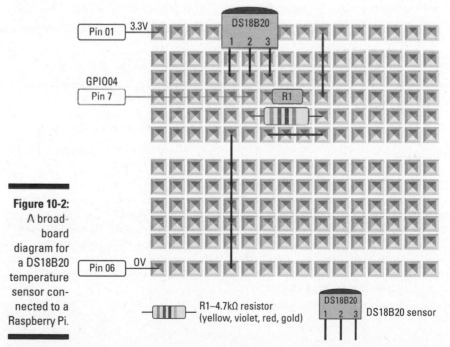

Figure 10-2:
A bread-board diagram for a DS18B20 temperature sensor connected to a Raspberry Pi.

R1—4.7kΩ resistor (yellow, violet, red, gold)

DS18B20 sensor

Writing the software

The software required to interface with the DS18B20 has already been written and is built into your Raspberry Pi kernel. You'll be using an application called modprobe to retrieve the temperature value.

Log into your Raspberry Pi using the root user for this chapter so you don't run into permission issues during installations. If you don't have a root user or don't know whether you have one, you can easily create one using the following command:

```
sudo passwd root
```

It's also a good idea to protect your Raspberry Pi by disabling root access via Secure Shell (SSH). SSH can be used to connect to your Raspberry Pi from a remote location. Edit the SSH configuration file by typing the following command:

```
sudo nano /etc/ssh/sshd_config
```

Then look for a setting called PermitRootLogin and change it to no as follows:

```
PermitRootLogin no
```

Save the file by pressing Ctrl+X, pressing Y, and pressing Enter. Then log out or restart your Raspberry Pi and use the root user and password you just created.

In the next few sections, you edit files on your Raspberry Pi. If you don't know how to work with editors on the Raspberry Pi, use Table 10-1 and practice creating new files, editing content, and saving files.

At the Raspberry Pi command prompt, type the following two commands:

```
modprobe w1-gpio
modprobe w1-therm
```

One of the nice features of the DS18B20 sensor is that it has a unique number that allows you to use multiple sensors and uniquely identify the temperature of each sensor. The preceding command interfaces with the sensor and retrieves the temperature, which it then writes to a new directory on the Raspberry Pi. This directory can be found in /sys/bus/w1/devices/. In order to check whether this file was created, you can do a directory listing by typing the following command:

```
ls /sys/bus/w1/devices/
```

Table 10-1   Useful File-Editing Commands Using the nano Editor

Description	Sample Linux Commands
Navigate to the desired directory	`cd /home`
Create a new file	`nano newfile.py`
Edit the file	Use the keyboard to create the content of the file.
Save the file	Press Ctrl+X, press Y, and then press Enter.
Create a new folder (directory)	`mkdir /home/temp`
Copy the file	`cp newfile.py /home/temp`
Change directory	`cd /home/temp`
Delete the file	`rm newfile.py`

You should see a directory that correlates to the unique number of your sensor. Every sensor has a unique number, so it won't be the same as our file, but it will be similar to this:

```
28-0000040be5b6
```

Take note of this number for use later in this chapter. If you don't see a directory with lots of numbers and letters like this one, do the following:

1. **Check your circuit wiring.**

2. **Make sure that you have the correct resistor.**

   You need to have a 4.7k ohm resistor (sometimes written as 4k7 ohm). Check your resistor by looking at the colored bands on it. If there are four bands, your resistor should have bands in this order: yellow, violet, red, and gold. If there are five bands, look for: yellow; violet; black; brown; and brown, red, gold, or silver for the fifth band.

3. **Feel the temperature gauge with your finger.**

   If it feels hot, you have it wired back to front.

If you see the new directory, navigate into it and view the contents of the w1_slave file, which will contain the temperature value. (Remember to replace our number with yours.)

```
cd /sys/bus/w1/devices/28-0000040be5b6
nano w1_slave
```

You see the contents of the `w1_slave` file, which contains the temperature data in Celsius. In our example (shown in Figure 10-3), the temperature is 20.812°C. Press Ctrl+X followed by N to exit.

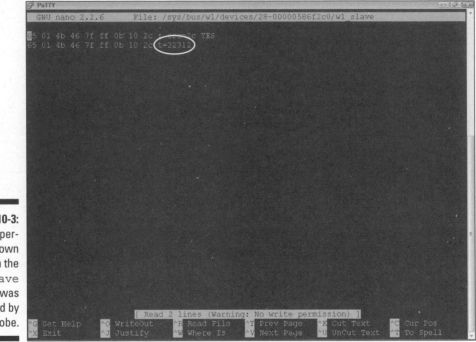

Figure 10-3:
The temperature shown in the `w1_slave` file that was created by modprobe.

Now that you've completed testing your circuit and you have the sensor working, you can proceed to the next sections about interfacing with public cloud service providers.

Storing Data in Google Docs from Your Raspberry Pi

In this section, we send the temperature readings obtained from the temperature sensor you build in the last section to a Google Docs spreadsheet that gives you access to your sensor data from anywhere on the Internet. The main prerequisite for sending data to Google Docs is having a Gmail address. But we don't recommend using your Raspberry Pi's web browser (Midori) because it's very slow. Instead, use a computer or device that you normally use for browsing the web.

Creating a new Google Docs spreadsheet

Using a PC or a device you normally use to browse the web (but not your Raspberry Pi), go to `https://docs.google.com/spreadsheet`.

Enter three new column headings — Temperature, Date, and Unit — and give the spreadsheet a name, as shown in Figure 10-4. Take note of the document key that is contained in the URL. The URL will look something like this:

```
https://docs.google.com/spreadsheet/ccc?key=0Ah0775EeJVAAp0BATBJha0RyUTBiOU1JRS1
              BVThKcmc#gid=0
```

The document key is the bold part of the preceding URL, which starts after `key=` and ends before `cmc#gid=0`.

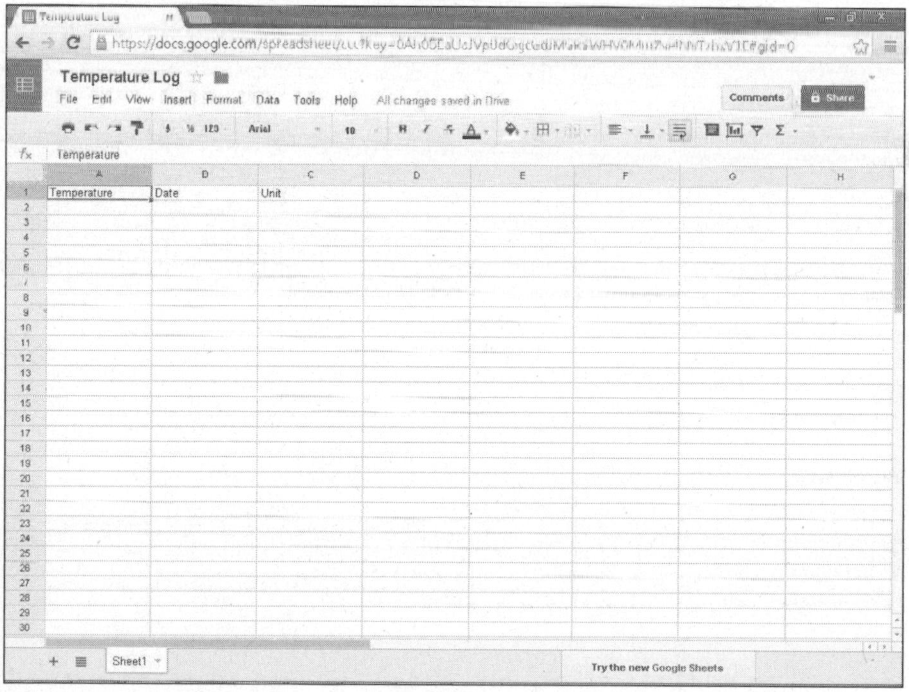

Figure 10-4:
A new spreadsheet in Google Docs.

Creating an authentication token

You're using Google's OAuth 2.0 for devices to authenticate your Raspberry Pi to the Google spreadsheet service. For more details on OAuth 2.0 for devices, go to `https://developers.google.com/accounts/docs/OAuth2ForDevices`. The authentication process requires that you authorize your Raspberry Pi to write data to Google Docs. Authorizing the Raspberry Pi is a one-time three-step process.

Step 1: Creating a client ID

To create a client ID, start by using a web browser to navigate to `https://console.developers.google.com`. Then follow these steps:

1. **Click Create Project.**

   The screen shown in Figure 10-5 appears, prompting you to enter a project name and project ID.

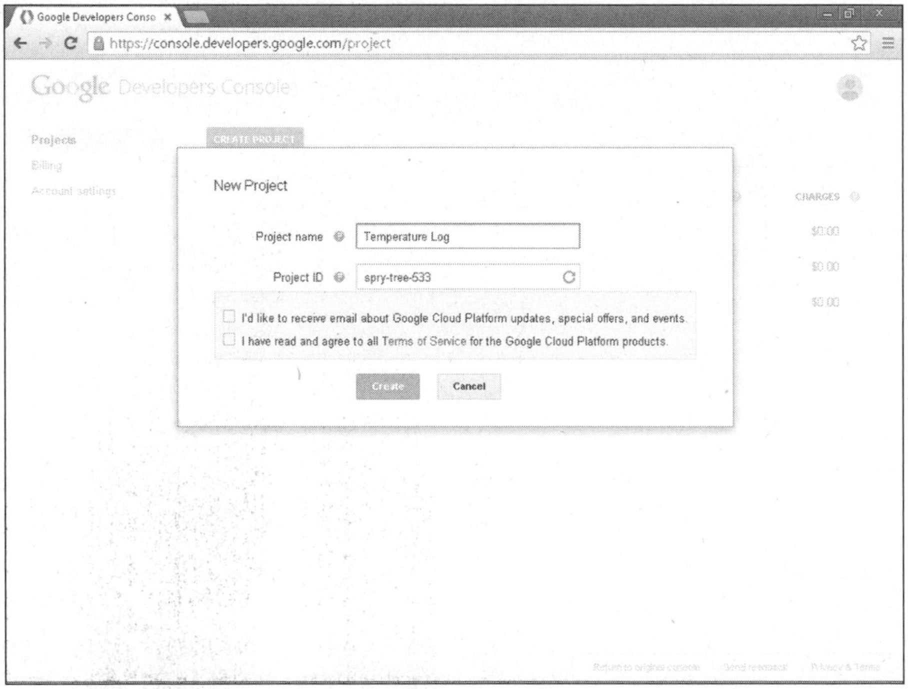

Figure 10-5:
Enter a proj-
ect name.

2. **Enter the project name (as shown in Figure 10-5), and leave the project ID whatever Google made up for you.**

3. **Click Create.**

   A screen providing the menu options for your new project appears.

4. **Click APIs & Auth from the menu bar on the left, and then click Credentials.**

   The screen shown in Figure 10-6 appears.

5. **Click the Create New Client ID button.**

   The screen shown in Figure 10-7 appears.

6. **Click the Installed Application radio button, and click the Create Client ID button.**

   A screen showing your client ID and client secret appears. It looks like Figure 10-8.

   You use these two codes later in this section.

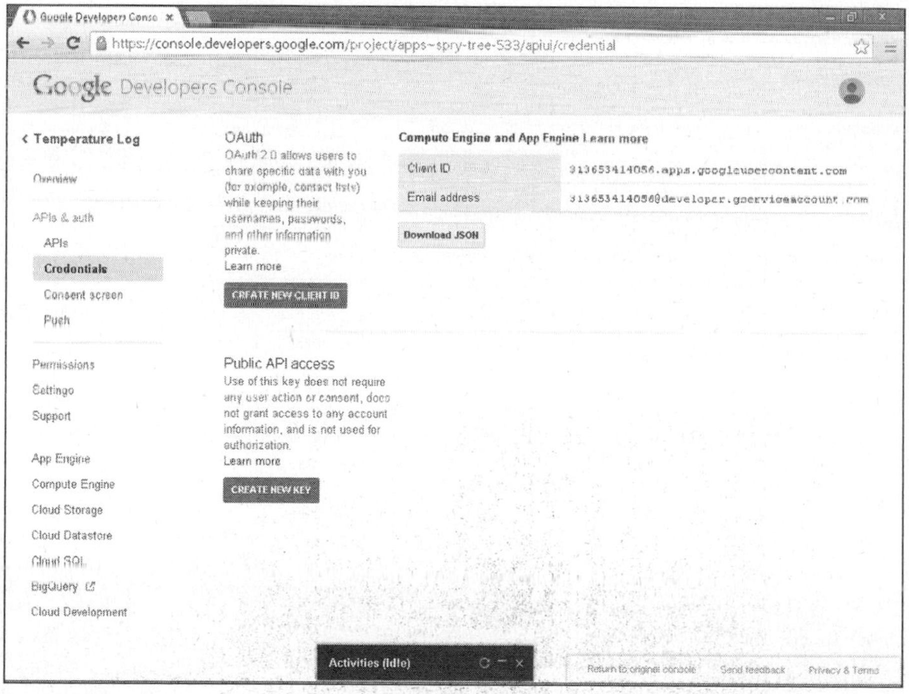

Figure 10-6: The Credentials menu option.

Figure 10-7:
Create a
new client
ID.

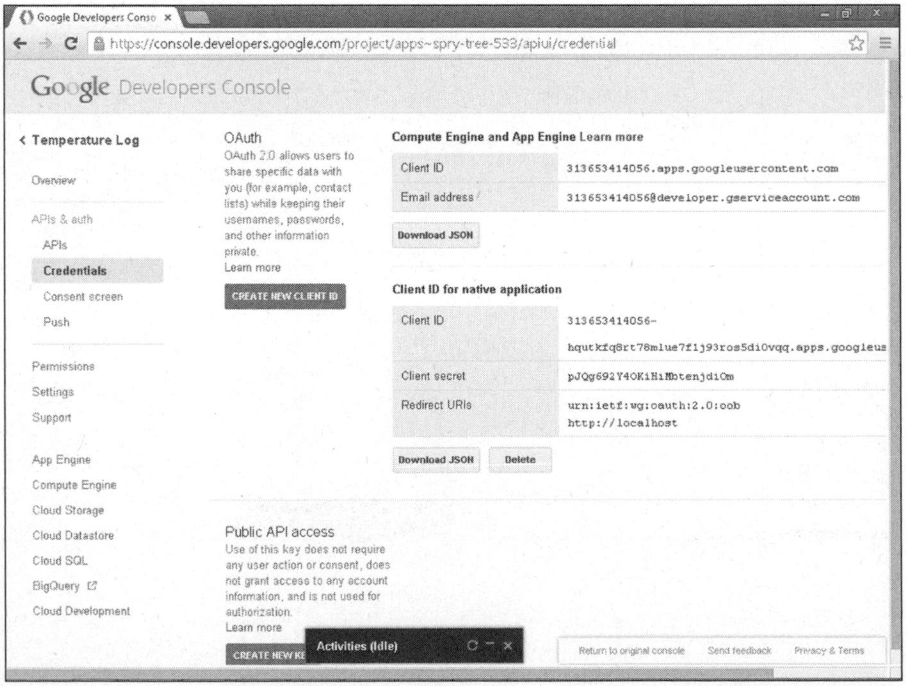

Figure 10-8:
Client ID
and Client
Secret
codes.

7. **Click the Consent Screen option in the menu on the left.**

   A screen showing your email address and a project name appears.

8. **Enter your email address in the Email Address field and enter a description like "Temperature Log" in the Project Name field and click Save.**

Step 2: Initializing the token for your Raspberry Pi

You need to download and run the Python program that will log the temperature sensor values to the spreadsheet. The first time you run the program, it prompts you to go to a URL and enter a code (see the next section), which, when entered, gives the program access to the spreadsheet.

On the Raspberry Pi, log in as the root user and type the following commands:

```
$ cd /home
$ apt-get install python-gdata
$ git clone git://github.com/gadjetnut/rpipfd.git
$ cd rpipfd
$ git clone git://github.com/guyc/py-gaugette.git
$ ln -s py-gaugette/gaugette gaugette
```

This process downloads all the software you need. Three Python programs in particular are important for understanding how the software works:

- **templogger_gdocs.py:** The main program that takes the temperature reading from the sensor and sends it to the Google Docs spreadsheet.

- **ds18b20.py:** The interface program for the temperature sensor. It contains a function called GetTemperature that takes two parameters: Fahrenheit and directory. When Fahrenheit is set to True, this function returns a temperature reading in Fahrenheit. When Fahrenheit is set to False, it returns a Celsius reading. The directory parameter is the directory name of your DS18B20 that you recorded in the "Constructing the temperature sensor" and "Writing the software" sections, earlier in the chapter.

- **gdocs.py:** Contains the functionality to authenticate with Google Docs. This was largely adapted from libraries developed by Guy Carpenter (http://guy.carpenter.id.au/gaugette).

Before you run the temperature logger, you need to do some configuration. At the command prompt of your Raspberry Pi, perform the following steps:

```
$ nano templogger_gdocs.py
```

As shown in Figure 10-9, edit the following configurations:

- ✔ **ds18b20_dir:** Enter the unique directory for your DS18B20 sensor that you took note of in the "Constructing the temperature sensor" section.

- ✔ **client_id:** Enter the client ID you obtained in the section "Step 1: Creating a client ID."

- ✔ **client_secret:** Enter the client secret you obtained in the section "Step 1: Creating a client ID."

- ✔ **spreadsheet_key:** Enter the spreadsheet key you obtained in the "Creating a new Google Docs spreadsheet" section.

- ✔ **fahrenheit:** Set this to False if you want a Celsius reading; otherwise, leave it set to True for a reading in Fahrenheit.

Press Ctrl+X, press Y, and then press Enter to save. Now run the database logger from the command line using the following command:

```
$ python templogger_gdocs.py
```

You're prompted to go to www.google.com/device and enter a code that is displayed on the screen, as shown in Figure 10-10.

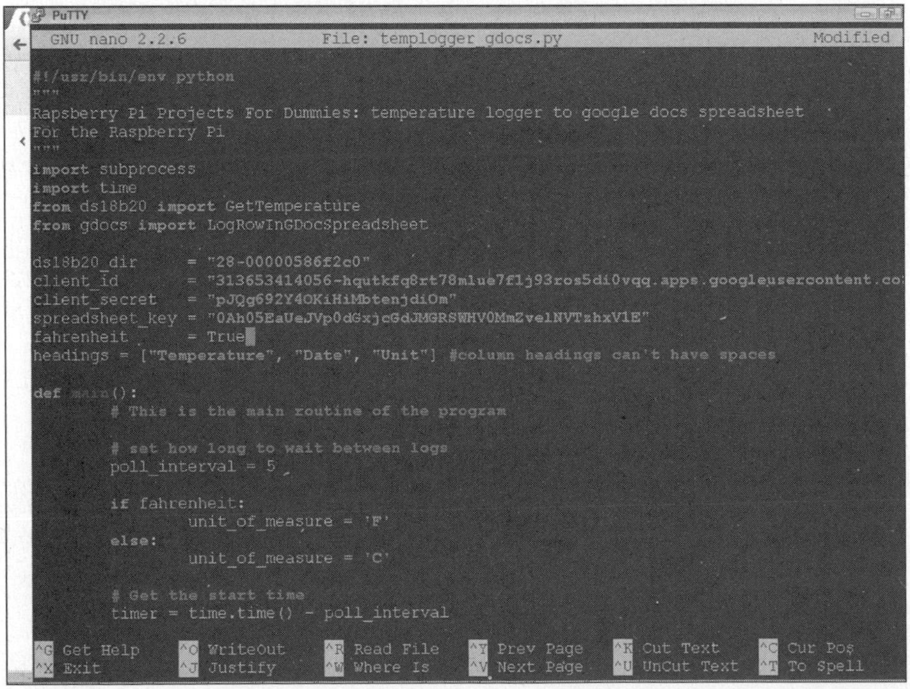

Figure 10-9: An example of the completed configurations.

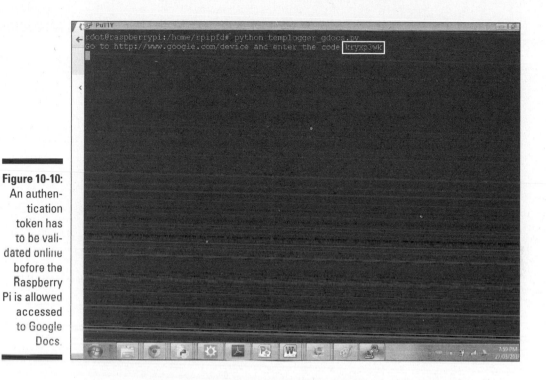

Figure 10-10:
An authen-
tication
token has
to be vali-
dated online
before the
Raspberry
Pi is allowed
accessed
to Google
Docs.

Step 3: Authenticating the token online

Open a web browser, go to `www.google.com/device`, and enter the code given to you on your Raspberry Pi, as shown in Figure 10-11. Click the Allow Access button. You should get the following message:

```
Success! You've authorized Project Default Service
Account. Please return to your device to continue.
```

Return to your Raspberry Pi, which automatically resumes and starts logging temperature values to the spreadsheet. You see the temperature reading written to the screen on the Raspberry Pi as follows:

```
Temperature of 73.06F logged
Temperature of 73.06F logged
Temperature of 73.06F logged
```

Finally, open the spreadsheet and check that the temperature values are being recorded in the spreadsheet, as shown in Figure 10-12.

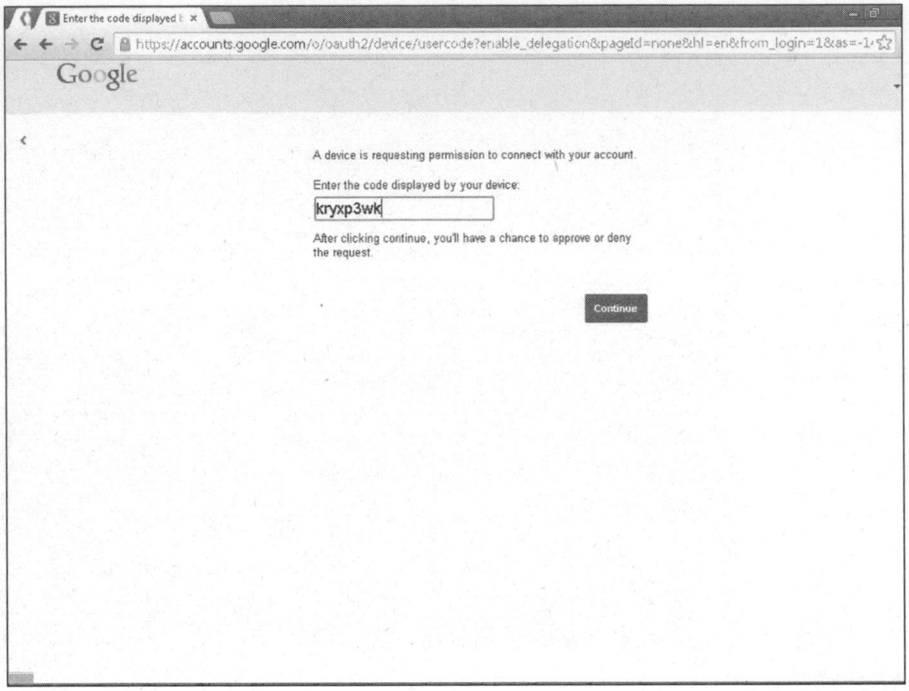

Figure 10-11: Validate your token from the Raspberry Pi online.

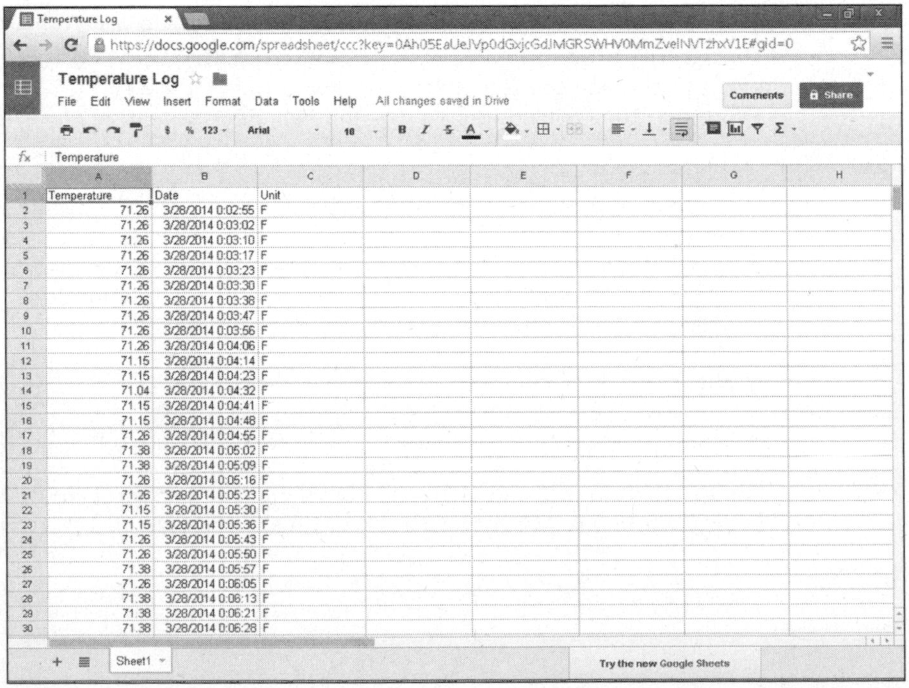

	A	B	C
1	Temperature	Date	Unit
2	71.26	3/28/2014 0:02:55	F
3	71.26	3/28/2014 0:03:02	F
4	71.26	3/28/2014 0:03:10	F
5	71.26	3/28/2014 0:03:17	F
6	71.26	3/28/2014 0:03:23	F
7	71.26	3/28/2014 0:03:30	F
8	71.26	3/28/2014 0:03:38	F
9	71.26	3/28/2014 0:03:47	F
10	71.26	3/28/2014 0:03:56	F
11	71.26	3/28/2014 0:04:06	F
12	71.15	3/28/2014 0:04:14	F
13	71.15	3/28/2014 0:04:23	F
14	71.04	3/28/2014 0:04:32	F
15	71.15	3/28/2014 0:04:41	F
16	71.15	3/28/2014 0:04:48	F
17	71.26	3/28/2014 0:04:55	F
18	71.38	3/28/2014 0:05:02	F
19	71.38	3/28/2014 0:05:09	F
20	71.26	3/28/2014 0:05:16	F
21	71.26	3/28/2014 0:05:23	F
22	71.15	3/28/2014 0:05:30	F
23	71.15	3/28/2014 0:05:36	F
24	71.26	3/28/2014 0:05:43	F
25	71.26	3/28/2014 0:05:50	F
26	71.38	3/28/2014 0:05:57	F
27	71.26	3/28/2014 0:06:05	F
28	71.38	3/28/2014 0:06:13	F
29	71.38	3/28/2014 0:06:21	F
30	71.38	3/28/2014 0:06:28	F

Figure 10-12: The Google Docs spreadsheet temperature log populated by the Raspberry Pi.

Creating a Dashboard and Temperature Alerts Using PrivateEyePi

In this section, you create an online temperature dashboard and define rules that will trigger email alerts to you based on the temperature reading. In this section, the Raspberry Pi sends temperature readings to PrivateEyePi, where you can view the temperature and a 24-hour graph on your dashboard. Additionally, each temperature reading is checked against a set of customizable rules that allow you to create temperature email alerts.

Follow these steps:

1. **Go to www.privateeyepi.com, click the New User link, enter your details, and click the Update button.**

2. **Click the GPIO menu option and click Add.**

   The screen shown in Figure 10-13 appears.

3. **Type 7 in the Number field, enter a description in the Description field, and click Update.**

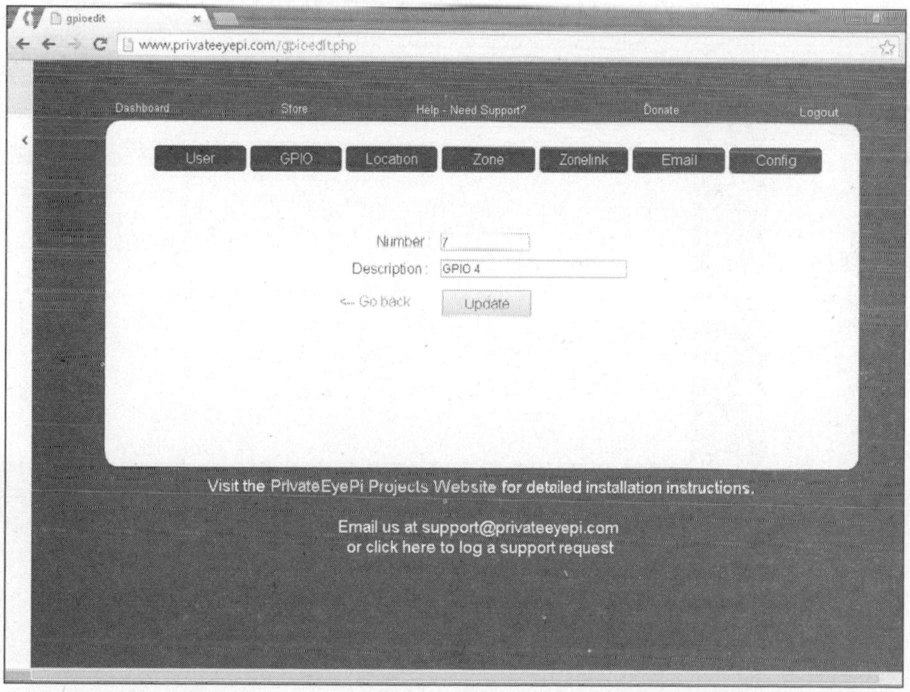

Figure 10-13: Configure the GPIO port on the PrivateEyePi website.

4. **Click the Location menu option.**

The screen shown in Figure 10-14 appears.

5. **In the Description field, enter a description of the location of the temperature sensor, and click Update.**

6. **Download the software that will poll the sensor and send the values to the PrivateEyePi web service.**

If you completed the previous section, you can skip this step. Otherwise, type the following command at the Raspberry Pi command prompt:

```
cd /home
git clone git://github.com/gadjetnut/rpipfd.git
```

The preceding commands download the software into the `/home/rpipfd` directory.

7. **Edit the `globals.py` file in order to enter your username and password that you used earlier on the PrivateEyePi website.**

At the Raspberry Pi command prompt, type the following:

```
cd /home/rpipfd
nano globals.py
```

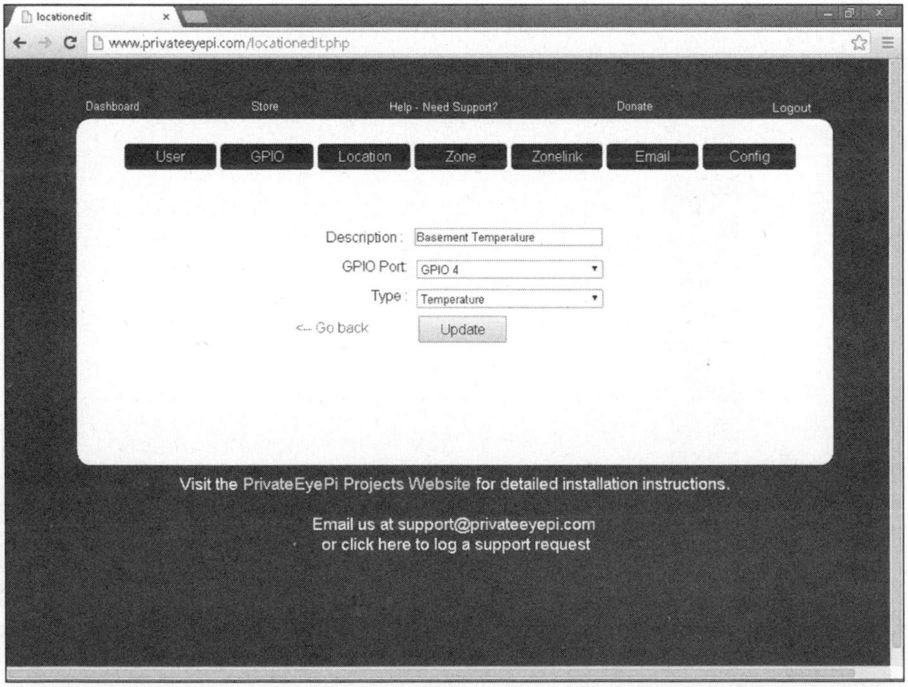

Figure 10-14: Configure the location of the sensor.

As shown in Figure 10-15, enter the user and the password in between the quotes. The user is the email address you used in the signup process from the PrivateEyePi website.

Page down until you see the `DallasSensorNumber` settings (see Figure 10-16). You need to set the GPIO number to 7 in between the brackets (for example, `DallasSensorNumber(7)`). Look for `DallasSensorDirectory` and replace the numbers you see in the file with your own numbers (refer to the "Constructing the temperature sensor" section, earlier in this chapter), as shown in Figure 10-16.

If you want your temperature to be displayed in Fahrenheit instead of Celsius, find the line that says `Fahrenheit=False` and change it to `Fahrenheit=True`.

8. Press Ctrl+X, press Y, and then press Enter to exit.

Now you're ready to run the script and view the temperature on your PrivateEyePi dashboard display. At the Raspberry Pi command prompt, type the following:

```
cd /home/rpipfd
python templogger_pep.py
```

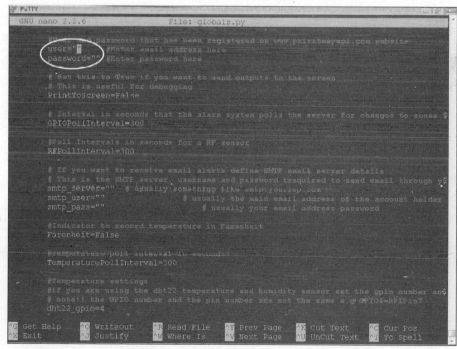

Figure 10-15:
User and password for the Private EyePi website.

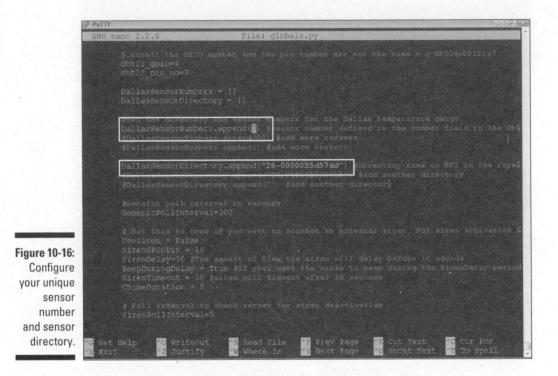

```
GNU nano 2.2.6                    File: globals.py

#.note!! the GPIO number and the pin number are not the same e.g GPIO4=RPIPin7
dht22_gpio=4
dht22_pin_no=7

DallasSensorNumbers = []
DallasSensorDirectory = []

#Set the directory and sensor numbers for the Dallas temperature gauge
DallasSensorNumbers.append(7)    #sensor number defined in the number field in the GPS
#DallasSensorNumbers.append(80)  #add more sensors.
#DallasSensorNumbers.append() #add more sensors.

DallasSensorDirectory.append("28-0000055d57dd")  #directory name on RPI in the /sys$
#DallasSensorDirectory.append("")    #add another directory
#DallasSensorDirectory.append("")    #add another directory

#Generic poll interval in seconds
GenericPollInterval=300

# Set this to true if you want to connect an external siren  Put siren activation $
UseSiren = False
SirenGPIOPin = 18
SirenDelay=30 #The amount of time the siren will delay before it sounds
BeepDuringDelay = True #if your want the siren to beep during the SirenDelay period
SirenTimeout = 30 #siren will timeout after 30 seconds
ChimeDuration = 5

# Poll interval to check server for siren deactivation
SirenPollInterval=5

^G Get Help    ^O WriteOut    ^R Read File    ^Y Prev Page    ^K Cut Text    ^C Cur Pos
^X Exit        ^J Justify     ^W Where Is     ^V Next Page    ^U UnCut Text  ^T To Spell
```

Figure 10-16:
Configure your unique sensor number and sensor directory.

Using a web browser, go to www.privateyepi.com and log in using your email and password. You're directed to your dashboard, where you see your temperature displayed, as shown in Figure 10-17. You can switch on the graph by selecting Settings from the dashboard and then selecting the Config menu option.

You can create rules and actions for each of your sensors. This is useful for creating a temperature sensor alert if the temperature reaches a certain threshold or drops below a threshold. Follow these steps:

1. **From the dashboard, click Settings and then select the Rules option.**

2. **Click the Add button and configure a rule and action as shown in Figure 10-18.**

   In this example, we configured a rule to send an email when the temperature reading on GPIO 4 is between 0 and –10. (Your email details need to be configured in the globals.py file.)

   Alternatively, you could choose to send an email if the temperature reaches or exceeds 30°C, for example, which may be an indication of a fire or a problem with the heating system in your house.

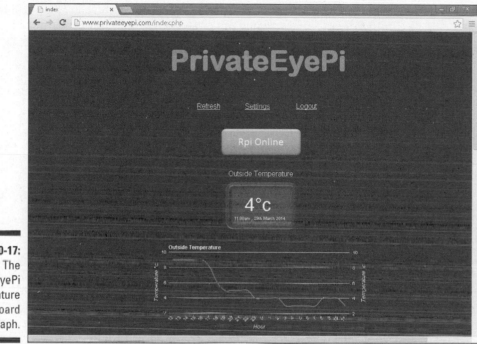

Figure 10-17:
The
PrivateEyePi
temperature
dashboard
with graph.

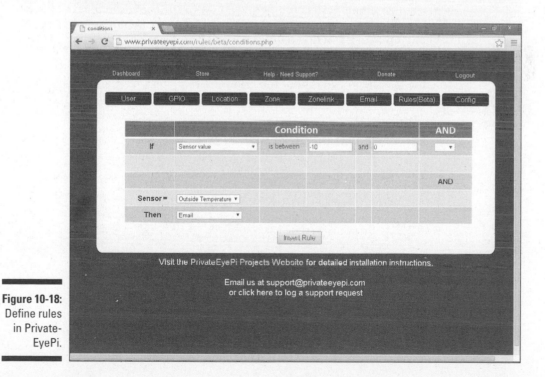

Figure 10-18:
Define rules
in Private-
EyePi.

You can define as many rules as you need and you can also combine up to three rules by clicking the AND drop-down box on the right side of the screen. For example, you may not want alerts during the day or you may want them only on specific days of the week.

PrivateEyePi also has alarm system functionality for the Raspberry Pi so you can configure alerts to be triggered only if the alarm is armed (refer to `www.projects.privateeyepi.com` for more details).

For more details on how to configure PrivateEyePi rules and actions, visit `www.projects.privateeyepi.com`.

Creating a Database Logger

Logging data to the cloud is one way to log data, but you may want to take matters into your own hands and do it yourself. In the next section, you develop your own data-logging application and web page to display the data. You install a database and web server on your Raspberry Pi and write some code to log to the database and then some HTML and PHP code to view the data. Figure 10-19 shows how all the components fit together.

In the next few sections, we cover topics about which entire books have been written. Our intent here is to provide you with the tools you need to further your knowledge in these areas. By following each of the upcoming sections, you end up with a working database-logging application. You can build on these basics by modifying the code to add new functionality.

Use the Internet to search for more information. It's a wonderful resource for developers seeking knowledge on how to solve problems or in need of reference material.

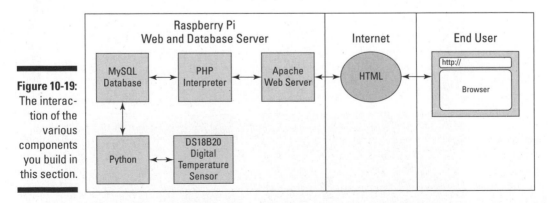

Figure 10-19: The interaction of the various components you build in this section.

Understanding web servers and databases

A web server contains the content (text, pictures, links, tables, and so on) for a website. It sends the content to a web browser upon request from the web browser. The content can be static or dynamic. Static content on a web page does not change (like a book). Dynamic content changes automatically over time, and the content usually comes from a content management system (CMS) of sorts. An example of a website with dynamic content is a newspaper website that is continuously updated with new stories.

In this section, you create a dynamic webpage that displays the temperature and temperature log, as shown in Figure 10-20.

A database is used to store and query information (data). It's capable of storing data and retrieving it at a rapid rate. In this section, we use a database to log the temperature sensor data and return the data to the web page, which displays the temperature data to the user (refer to Figure 10-20).

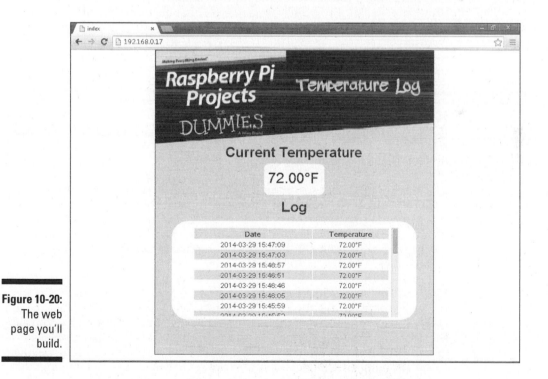

Figure 10-20: The web page you'll build.

Explaining HTML and server-side scripting

A web page is served from the web server to the browser using Hypertext Markup Language, more commonly known as HTML. Your web browser interprets the HTML and displays it. The web browser interprets the HTML and translates it into graphics, text, links, and tables, but HTML is not a programming language — it's a *markup* language. There are, however, programming languages that can run in the browser. JavaScript, for example, is a very popular development language that is inserted into the HTML code and executed in the browser.

Many books have been written on each of these topics, most of which are beyond the scope of this chapter, but here we share with you the fundamentals of each that provide you with a platform to further your database knowledge. Try to understand each line of code and experiment with your own modifications.

For this project, you retrieve data from a database and send it to the web browser as HTML. Programming languages that perform this function are called *server-side languages* because they reside and are executed on the web server (refer to Figure 10-19). There are a number of reasons why you want to perform this action on the server side and not on the *client side* (the browser). The most important reason is security. It's incredibly risky to expose your data layer to the public Internet. Another reason to perform it on the server side is that you don't know what's running on the client side, so you can run into incompatibility issues with all the different operating systems, PCs, tablets, smartphones, and so on that use browsers. That's why it's good practice to keep the client side as simple as possible (using HTML) and do your database programming on the server side.

There are a number of server-side scripting languages you could use (for example, PHP, Perl, ASP, or JSP). You use Hypertext Preprocessor (PHP) in this project. From the browser, you call a PHP file the same way you call an HTML file, except it has a `.php` extension (for example, `index.php` instead of `index.html`). Figure 10-19 shows interaction between the browser, web and database servers, and PHP interpreter.

When a PHP file is requested, the web server passes the file to the PHP interpreter, which executes the PHP code and typically passes back HTML, which the web server sends back to the browser to display. In Listing 10-1, you can see an example of a PHP file that resides on the web server that displays either `Hello world` or `I love Raspberry Pi`, depending on the result of a random number. This demonstrates how PHP can create the dynamic web pages described earlier. Most of Listing 10-1 is normal HTML except the sections demarcated with `<?php` and `?>` that mark the beginning and end of the PHP code. You don't need to type this program in, but we've provided it to show you the difference between PHP and HTML. You code in PHP and HTML later in this chapter.

Listing 10-1: An Example of PHP Code That Resides on the Web Server

```
<!DOCTYPE html>
<html lang="en">
<head>
    <title>An example PHP application</title>
</head>
<body>
    <?php
    random_number=rand(1,2);
    if (random_number==1){
            echo "Hello world";
    }
    else {
        echo "I love Raspberry Pi";
    }
    ?>
    </body>
</html>
```

In Listing 10-2, you can see the HTML that was sent back to the browser. Notice that the PHP code is not present anymore. Only the result (that is, I love Raspberry Pi) was sent back to the browser. This is the basic principle of how server-side scripting works. You build on this principle later in this chapter when you use PHP to read and write to a database.

Listing 10-2: The HTML That Is Sent to the Web Browser

```
<!DOCTYPE html>
<html lang="en">
<head>
    <title>An example PHP application</title>
</head>
<body>
    I love Raspberry Pi
</body>
</html>
```

Delving into database basics

You store the data from the sensor in a database. Think of a database as a collection of lists of data. Each list is known as a *table.* Each table has a number of columns, and each line item in the list is called a *row* (refer to Figure 10-21).

Column Column Column

Temperature	Date	Unit
73.06	03/01/2014 20:41	F
73.06	03/01/2014 20:41	F
73.06	03/01/2014 20:42	F
72.72	03/01/2014 21:27	F
72.72	03/01/2014 21:27	F
72.72	03/01/2014 21:27	F
72.84	03/01/2014 21:28	F
72.84	03/01/2014 21:28	F
72.84	03/01/2014 21:28	F

Column names
Row
Row
"
"
"
"

Figure 10-21: A depiction of a temperature log database table with rows and columns.

A database can store and retrieve large amounts of data very quickly. In this section, you create a new table called `TemperatureLog` that contains the temperature values coming from the temperature sensor. In addition to the temperature value, you store other information, such as date, time, and unit of measure (Celsius or Fahrenheit). These data elements will be columns in the table. The fourth column is a unique identifier for every row called `temp_id`. It isn't strictly required for this project, but it's good practice to create a unique identifier, called the *primary key,* for each row. We configure `temp_id` to automatically increment every time a new row is inserted in the database.

The `TemperatureLog` table will have four columns: `temp_id` (primary key), `temperature`, `date/time`, and `unit_of_measure`. Date and time can be stored in the same column using the `DateTime` data type. Next, think about how you'll manipulate the data. This helps you understand which columns need to be indexed. An *index* allows the database to find and sort data very quickly. The ability to sort the temperature log by date and time is important for reporting, so you'll create an index on the `date/time` column. Lastly, think about how to describe the content of each of the columns (for example, alphanumeric, numeric, date/time, size, and so on). These are called *data types.*

Installing MySQL, PHP, and Apache

After you've done some basic database design planning, go ahead and create the table. You'll be installing Apache (a very popular web server), MySQL (a database management system), and PHP (see the "Explaining HTML and server-side scripting" section, earlier in this chapter). All are open-source software and work very well on a Raspberry Pi.

You'll be using the root user in this chapter so you don't run into permission problems. Start off by logging into your Raspberry Pi as the root user. At the command prompt, type the following commands:

```
apt-get update
apt-get install apache2
apt-get install php5
apt-get install php5-mysql
apt-get install mysql-server mysql-client
apt-get install python-mysqldb
```

During the installation, you'll be prompted to enter a password for the root user in MySQL.

Creating the data logger

Now you're ready to create the temperature log table. At the Raspberry Pi command prompt, type the following:

```
$ mysql -u root -p
```

Enter the password you configured earlier during the installation. This will take you into the command-line interpreter of MySQL. Here you can issue SQL commands to MySQL. Standard Linux commands will no longer work when you're in the MySQL interpreter. Type **exit** or **quit** to return to the Linux command prompt.

Next, create a new database by typing the following:

```
mysql> CREATE database sensor_logs;
```

Type in the USE command to tell MySQL that all subsequent commands will relate to the temperature_log table:

```
mysql> USE sensor_logs;
```

Next, create a user and password, which you use again later, and assign all privileges to that user.

TIP

We don't recommend changing the username and password at this point because we refer to the user "dblogger" with a password of "password" and it's also contained in the code. When you have it working, you can come back and change the password and edit the code with the new password, if you want.

Create the user and password as follows:

```
mysql> CREATE USER 'dblogger'@'localhost' IDENTIFIED BY 'password';
mysql> GRANT ALL PRIVILEGES ON sensor_logs.* TO 'dblogger'@'localhost';
mysql> FLUSH PRIVILEGES;
mysql> quit
```

Now log back in using the user you just created and create the new table:

```
mysql -u dblogger -p
mysql> USE sensor_logs;
mysql>CREATE TABLE temperature_log (temp_id INT NOT NULL AUTO_INCREMENT,
temperature DECIMAL(10,2), date DATETIME, unit_of_measure CHAR, PRIMARY
KEY (temp_id));
```

Check that the table was created successfully by typing the following:

```
mysql>SHOW TABLES;
```

As shown in Figure 10-22, you should see the new table listed in the database.

Last, create an index on the Date column so that you can search and sort easily by date:

```
mysql>CREATE  INDEX idx_date  ON temperature_log(date);
```

Now make sure that you're happy with the new table you've created (see Figure 10-23):

```
mysql>SHOW COLUMNS IN temperature_log;
```

Log out of MySQL by typing **quit**.

If you made some mistakes and want to delete the table and start again, use the DROP statement:

```
mysql>DROP TABLE temperature_logs;
```

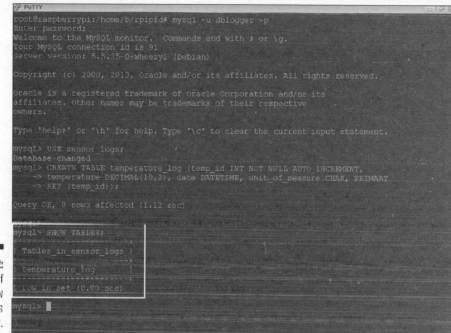

Figure 10-22:
Results of
a SHOW
TABLES
command.

Figure 10-23:
Column
view of the
tempera-
ture_log
table.

Be very careful with this command because there is no option to undo it and you don't get a warning message that all data in the table will be deleted.

Developing a sensor logger

The next step is to log data into the database from the temperature sensor you built earlier. You accomplish this by using Structured Query Language (SQL) syntax. SQL is made up of commands that closely resemble spoken language. Here are some examples of SQL statements. The following SQL statement will return the first name, surname (last name), and grade of all students with a surname of Evans:

```
SELECT firstname, surname, grade FROM student WHERE surname = "Evans"
```

The following SQL statement creates a new row of data in the student table:

```
INSERT INTO student (firstname, surname, grade) VALUES ("Jonathan",
"Evans", "A");
```

The following SQL statement changes the grade of all students that have a surname of Evans to B:

```
UPDATE student SET grade = "B" WHERE surname="Evans"
```

Notice the use of surname in the preceding WHERE clauses. Earlier in the chapter, we describe how to create an index to sort data and how to make searching data quicker. Surname would be an ideal candidate for an index. If surname were not indexed, the database engine would scan through the entire table looking for students with the surname of Evans. However, by creating an index on the surname column, the database engine will be able to sort through and pull out the relevant records much more quickly. However, don't create an index on many columns because every index adds overhead to the performance of the table. This is why planning your database tables, fields, and indexes is important.

Your database logger application will use two SQL statements: an INSERT statement to log the data and a SELECT statement to retrieve the data that will be displayed on a web page.

You use a Python program called templogger_db.py to log the temperature readings to the database. If you didn't download the chapter software earlier, you need to download the software using the following commands:

```
$ git clone git://github.com/gadjetnut/rpipfd.git
```

Edit the file and observe its contents by typing the following:

```
$ cd /home/rpipfd
$ nano templogger_db.py
```

Input the sensor directory name for your DS18B20 sensor (refer to the "Constructing the temperature sensor" section, earlier in this chapter), as shown in Figure 10-24.

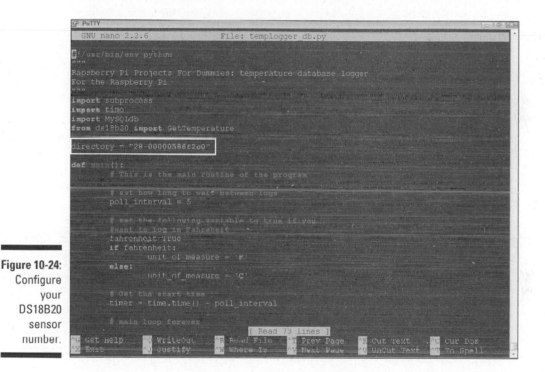

Figure 10-24:
Configure your DS18B20 sensor number.

Page down in the code and observe how the program works. The program starts execution at `def main():` by setting the poll interval to five seconds (`poll_interval = 5`). This means you store a temperature reading in the database every five seconds.

Next, you configure whether you want a Celsius or Fahrenheit temperature to be stored (`fahrenheit=True or False`). The program then goes into a loop that logs the temperature every five seconds. The program uses a function in the `ds18b20.py` program called `GetTemperature` that will run the modprobe application to obtain a reading from the sensor. If you're interested in seeing how the sensor information is retrieved, edit `ds18B20.py`, which is in the same directory as `templogger_db.py`.

Next, the program logs temperature readings to the database using a sequence of database commands: `connect`, `create cursor`, `insert`, `commit`, and `close`. The `MySQLdb.connect` statement creates a new database connection, where you pass to it the IP address of the database server (`localhost`), the database user name (`dblogger`), the password (`password`), and the name of the database you want to open (`sensor_logs`).

Next, prepare a `cursor` object to execute the SQL statement, followed by execution of the statement. The `commit` statement writes the data to the database, and the `close` statement closes the database connection.

Exit and save by typing the following:

```
CTRL-x together, followed by pressing 'Y', then followed by pressing ENTER
```

Run the program:

```
$ python templogger_db.py
```

The program prints temperature readings to the screen and also writes those values into the database. After the program has logged a few readings, quit by pressing Ctrl+C. Go back into MySQL and view the data that has been logged by typing the following commands:

```
$ mysql -u dblogger -p (then type the password)
$ mysql> USE sensor_logs;
$ mysql> select * from temperature_log;
```

The rows that were inserted into the database will be listed in a table, as shown in Figure 10-25.

Creating a dynamic web page

In this section, you create a web page that displays the temperature log you created in the previous section on a web page. In the "Installing MySQL, PHP, and Apache" section of this chapter, you install PHP and Apache. You use both in this section to create a web page to display your temperature readings. Check that the Apache installation worked. Open a browser either by typing **startx** and opening a browser on your Raspberry Pi, or by using another PC connected to your network, and type in the IP address of your Raspberry Pi as the URL.

You should see a web page that says `It works!`, as shown in Figure 10-26.

```
PuTTY
owners.

Type 'help;' or '\h' for help. Type '\c' to clear the current input statement.

mysql> USE sensor_logs;
Reading table information for completion of table and column names
You can turn off this feature to get a quicker startup with -A

Database changed
mysql> select * from temperature_log;

| temp_id | temperature | Date                | unit_of_measure |
|       1 |       72.00 | 2014-03-29 18:12:21 | F               |
|       2 |       72.00 | 2014-03-29 18:12:28 | F               |
|       3 |       71.00 | 2014-03-29 18:12:46 | F               |
|       4 |       71.00 | 2014-03-29 18:12:48 | F               |
|       5 |       72.00 | 2014-03-29 18:12:50 | F               |
|       6 |       72.00 | 2014-03-29 18:12:52 | F               |
|       7 |       72.00 | 2014-03-29 18:12:53 | F               |
|       8 |       75.00 | 2014-03-29 18:12:55 | F               |
|       9 |       79.00 | 2014-03-29 18:12:57 | F               |
|      10 |       82.00 | 2014-03-29 18:13:00 | F               |
|      11 |       81.00 | 2014-03-29 18:13:02 | F               |
|      12 |       80.00 | 2014-03-29 18:13:04 | F               |
|      13 |       80.00 | 2014-03-29 18:13:06 | F               |
|      14 |       78.00 | 2014-03-29 18:13:08 | F               |
|      15 |       78.00 | 2014-03-29 18:13:10 | F               |
|      16 |       77.00 | 2014-03-29 18:13:12 | F               |
|      17 |       77.00 | 2014-03-29 18:13:13 | F               |
|      18 |       76.00 | 2014-03-29 18:13:15 | F               |
|      19 |       76.00 | 2014-03-29 18:13:17 | F               |
|      20 |       76.00 | 2014-03-29 18:13:19 | F               |
|      21 |       75.00 | 2014-03-29 18:13:21 | F               |
```

Figure 10-25: Temperature readings in the database.

You can find the IP address of your Raspberry Pi by typing the following:

```
/sbin/ifconfig
```

The output will look something like this:

```
wlan0 Link encap:Ethernet HWaddr d8:eb:97:18:16:ef
      inet addr:192.168.0.2 Bcast:192.168.0.255 Mask:255.255.255.0
```

Your IP address is the number provided after `inet addr:`, which in this case is 192.168.0.2.

Now that you have your web server up and running, you work with the following two PHP files to retrieve and display the data on a web page:

- **dbreader.php:** Contains two functions: `DisplayTemperatureLog` displays the temperature log, and `DisplayTheLatestTemperature` displays the last temperature stored in the log.

- **temptest.php:** The second PHP file calls both of these functions and displays the data that the functions return on a web page.

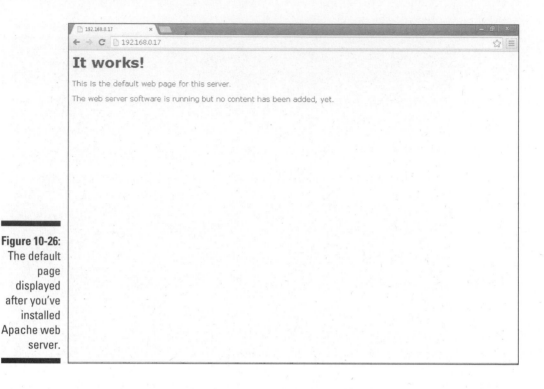

Later in this section, you create a nicer-looking web page using HTML that
reuses the dbreader.php, but be concerned with the functionality, not the
look. PHP files need to be located in the web server's directory (/var/www),
so you need to copy both the files into that directory as follows:

```
$ cd /home/rpipfd
$ cp dbreader.php /var/www
$ cp temptest.php /var/www
```

Before you run these programs, edit them and observe their contents. At the
command line, type the following:

```
$ cd /home/rpipfd
$ nano dbreader.php
```

Read through the PHP code and you see similarities to the Python code you
used earlier to log temperature readings to the database. The syntax is very
different, but the essence of the database commands is the same. A new connection to the database is made with the following statement:

```
$mysqli = new mysqli("localhost", "dblogger", "password", "sensor_logs");
```

Read the database using the following statement:

```
$res = $mysqli->query("SELECT * FROM temperature_log ORDER BY date
DESC");
```

The preceding SQL statement returns all the temperature readings and sorts them in descending order by date. This operation is very fast, even though the table may contain millions of rows. The reason for the high speed at which SQL can sort these rows goes back to the index you created on the Date column. The rest of the function loops through all the records until it reaches the num_rows_to_display value. The following section loops through the data:

```
for ($row_no = 0; $row_no < $res->num_rows/
&& $row_no < $num_rows_to_display; $row_no++)
    {
        echo "<tr>";
        $res->data_seek($row_no);
        $row = $res->fetch_assoc();
    }
```

The echo statements send the HTML back to the web server and then on to the web browser to get displayed. Press Ctrl+X, press N, and press Enter to exit without saving.

Next, open the other PHP file that will call each of the two functions and display the data on the web page:

```
$ cd /home/rpipfd
$ nano temptest.php
```

The contents of this program are very simple. All this program does is call the two functions in dbreader.php and display the contents on the screen. Press Ctrl+X, press N, and press Enter to exit without saving.

Now return to the browser you used earlier and type the following URL:

```
http://IPaddress/temptest.php
```

where *IPaddress* is the IP address of your Raspberry Pi.

The latest temperature and a table containing the temperatures over the past calendar day will be displayed on the web page, as shown in Figure 10-27.

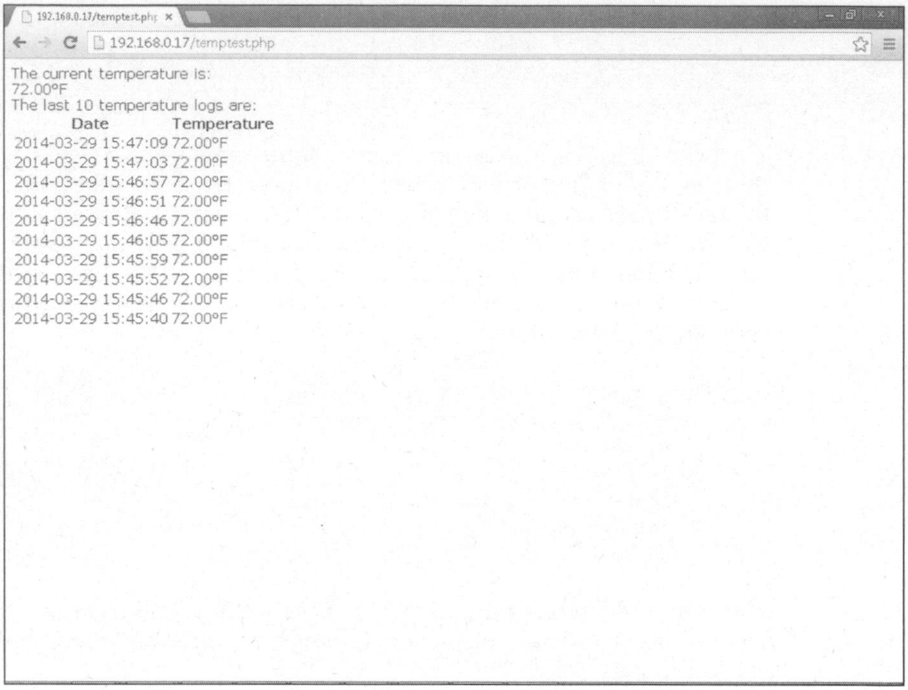

192.168.0.17/temptest.php
192.168.0.17/temptest.php
The current temperature is:
72.00°F
The last 10 temperature logs are:
Date Temperature
2014-03-29 15:47:09 72.00°F
2014-03-29 15:47:03 72.00°F
2014-03-29 15:46:57 72.00°F
2014-03-29 15:46:51 72.00°F
2014-03-29 15:46:46 72.00°F
2014-03-29 15:46:05 72.00°F
2014-03-29 15:45:59 72.00°F
2014-03-29 15:45:52 72.00°F
2014-03-29 15:45:46 72.00°F
2014-03-29 15:45:40 72.00°F

Figure 10-27: The raw data from the database log is displayed on a web page.

The data displayed in Figure 10-27 is accurate, but it doesn't look very nice. Next, we use more sophisticated HTML in `index.php` to make look and feel more professional. `index.php` is the default file that the web server will look for when it receives a request from a web browser. For example, you only have to type **http://ipaddress** into your browser, and it will display this page.

Edit `index.php` and observe its contents. Look carefully for `<?php` and `?>`, which demarcate the start end of the PHP code that the PHP interpreter will execute before sending the HTML back to the browser. At the beginning of the file, you can see that we're including `dbreader.php`, which contains the two functions that are called later in the file in sections starting with `<?php`. To make the web page look better, we've included a background picture that is referred to on the line with the following code:

```
<img id="Ggeo18" src="RPIPFDTLBanner.png" alt="">
```

TIP

Unless you know how to code HTML, the content of the file isn't easy to read and won't make much sense to you. Other than knowing the HTML basics, you don't need to know how to code HTML. Few people code HTML like you would code PHP or Python. This is because there are graphical tools that are much better suited to creating HTML than coding it in a code editor. The tool that we used to create `index.php` is called SiteSpinner Pro, but a number of other very good tools on the market will do the job.

Exit the file by pressing Ctrl+X, and pressing N to quit without saving. Copy `index.php` and the picture file to the web server as follows:

```
$ cd /home/rpipfd
$ rm /var/www/index.html
$ cp index.php /var/www
$ cp RPIPFDTLBanner.png /var/www
```

Now return to your browser and navigate to the IP address of your Raspberry Pi (`http://ipaddress`). You should see the final product, as shown in Figure 10-28.

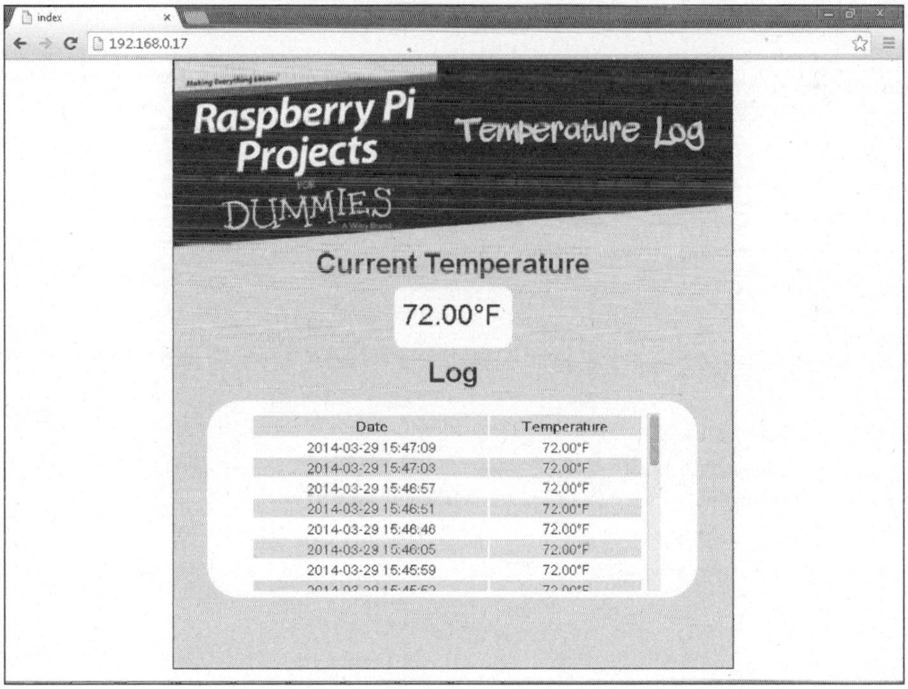

Figure 10-28: The final temperature log web page.

Chapter 11

Webcam and Computer Vision

. . . .

In This Chapter

▶ Setting up a webcam or Raspberry Pi camera module

▶ Looking at images

▶ Creating image files

▶ Using a webcam to detect motion

▶ Looking at image recognition

▶ Interpreting color

▶ Making a Connect Four game using computer vision

. . . .

*I*n this chapter, we show you how to give your Raspberry Pi vision using a webcam or the Pi Camera Module. Using image-processing techniques, you can use the Raspberry Pi to analyze images to identify things like motion, colors, and shapes. Here, we show you how computer images are created and how you can look into the images for information about them.

Note: Throughout this chapter, we provide instructions and code for both a webcam and the Raspberry Pi Camera module. We use the term *camera* to refer to either your webcam or your Raspberry Pi camera. If you're using Secure Shell (SSH) and Putty to connect to your Raspberry Pi, you won't be able to do the sections of this chapter that require graphical views that aren't supported in SSH, but you can view images using FTP. Please ensure that you're on the latest Raspbian Wheezy image and have recently performed an update:

```
$ sudo apt-get update
$ sudo apt-get upgrade
```

Setting Up the Webcam or Raspberry Pi Camera Module

Setting up a webcam is as easy as plugging it into the USB port on your Raspberry Pi or an attached USB hub.

We strongly recommend that you use a powered USB hub for your webcam because the Raspberry Pi can't support much more than a keyboard and a mouse on its own power supply.

You can check the compatibility of your webcam with the Raspberry Pi at www.elinux.org/RPi_USB_Webcam. When you have your webcam plugged in and you've powered up your Raspberry Pi, type the following commands to see if your webcam is listed in the listing:

```
$ lsusb
$ ls /dev
```

You should see two listings similar to Figure 11-1. We're using a Creative Technology, Ltd., webcam (as shown by the first circle in Figure 11-1). In the second listing, look for video0 (also circled in Figure 11-1). If you see both of these, you know your webcam is working. If you don't, try shutting down the Raspberry Pi, unplugging the webcam, plugging it back in, and starting up again.

```
root@raspberrypi:/# lsusb
Bus 001 Device 002: ID 05e3:0608 Genesys Logic, Inc. USB-2.0 4-Port HUB
Bus 001 Device 001: ID 1d6b:0002 Linux Foundation 2.0 root hub
Bus 001 Device 003: ID 0b05:1786 ASUSTek Computer, Inc. USB-N10 802.11n Network
Adapter [Realtek RTL8188SU]
Bus 001 Device 004: ID 05e3:0608 Genesys Logic, Inc. USB-2.0 4-Port HUB
Bus 001 Device 005: ID 041e:4095 Creative Technology, Ltd
root@raspberrypi:/# ls /dev
autofs          loop6              ram13    tty1    tty3    tty5    urandom
block           loop7              ram14    tty10   tty30   tty50   v4l
btrfs-control   loop-control       ram15    tty11   tty31   tty51   vc-cma
bus             MAKEDEV            ram2     tty12   tty32   tty52   vchiq
cachefiles      mapper            ram3     tty13   tty33   tty53   vc-mem
char            media0            ram4     tty14   tty34   tty54   vcs
console         mem               ram5     tty15   tty35   tty55   vcs1
cpu_dma_latency mmcblk0           ram6     tty16   tty36   tty56   vcs2
disk            mmcblk0p1         ram7     tty17   tty37   tty57   vcs3
fb0             mmcblk0p2         ram8     tty18   tty38   tty58   vcs4
fd              net               ram9     tty19   tty39   tty59   vcs5
full            network_latency   random   tty2    tty4    tty6    vcs6
fuse            network_throughput raw     tty20   tty40   tty60   vcsa
input           null              root     tty21   tty41   tty61   vcsa1
kmsg            ppp               shm      tty22   tty42   tty62   vcsa2
log             ptmx              snd      tty23   tty43   tty63   vcsa3
loop0           pts               sndstat  tty24   tty44   tty7    vcsa4
loop1           ram0              stderr   tty25   tty45   tty8    vcsa5
loop2           ram1              stdin    tty26   tty46   tty9    vcsa6
loop3           ram10             stdout   tty27   tty47   ttyAMA0 video0
loop4           ram11             tty      tty28   tty48   ttyprintk xconsole
loop5           ram12             tty0     tty29   tty49   uinput  zero
root@raspberrypi:/#
```

Figure 11-1:
A listing of USB peripherals, including the USB webcam.

For a list of supported webcams go to www.elinux.org/RPi_USB_Webcams.

If you have a Raspberry Pi camera module, make sure it's connected and you've switched on the camera module setting. You should have received setup instructions with your camera; refer to www.raspberrypi.org/camera for detailed instructions on installing the camera module.

Test your camera by typing one of the commands in the following sections, position the camera toward yourself, smile, and press Enter. You should have a wonderful portrait of yourself saved to a file called test.bmp. You use this technique of taking pictures throughout this chapter.

Taking a picture with a webcam

To take a picture with a webcam, use the following command:

```
fswebcam -d /dev/video0 -q -r 1024x768 test.bmp
```

fswebcam is a utility that's included in the Raspbian image. Take a close look at the command to understand what each part does. The -d option is the device name. (Earlier, we had you look for the video0 file in the /dev directory.) The -q option is a quiet option that does not display any text to the screen during operation. The -r option sets the resolution to 1,024 pixels wide by 768 pixels tall. Finally, you gave it the filename test.bmp to save the picture to.

For a full list of options, pass the --help option, and all the options will be written to the screen:

```
$ fswebcam --help
```

Taking a picture with the Raspberry Pi camera module

To take a picture with the Raspberry Pi camera module, use the following command:

```
raspistill -o test.bmp -t 1 -w 1024 -h 768 -e bmp
```

raspistill is a utility written specifically for the Raspberry Pi camera. The -o is for output, followed by the filename where we want the picture to be stored (test.bmp). The -t is how many seconds it waits before taking a picture (the default is 5 seconds). As you may have guessed, -w is the width and -h is the height of the picture.

For a full list of options, pass the --help option, and all the options will be written to the screen:

```
$ raspistill --help
```

Viewing pictures on the Raspberry Pi

Viewing pictures on the Raspberry Pi is best done through X, as follows:

```
$ startx
```

Then double-click the lxTerminal icon on the desktop and enter the following command that will view a picture:

```
$qinv -f test.bmp
```

qinv is a utility that displays images. If it isn't installed, you can type the following to install it:

```
$ sudo apt-get install qiv
```

Understanding Images

A picture may be worth a thousand words, but in this section, we use almost a thousand words to describe images. Here, we explain, resolution, color spaces, color models, and file types.

Resolution

Resolution is a term that's usually associated with the dimensions and pixel count of an image. Think of an image as a two-dimensional matrix of pixels. In the previous section, you created a 1,024 x 768 image using your camera. Your picture contains 1,024 columns and 768 rows, and a total of 786,432 pixels (1,024 × 768 = 786,432).

Resolution is often incorrectly used to determine the clarity of a picture, but the image size does *not* determine its clarity. Instead, the number of dots per inch (dpi) or an image's spatial resolution is a better determinant of clarity.

For example, compare the 1,024 x 768 pictures created by a webcam to the 1,024 x 768 pictures created by the Raspberry Pi camera module. The Raspberry Pi camera is a 5-megapixel camera, which means it can produce images with 5 million pixels. The webcam was designed to produce images that can be sent easily over the Internet. Even though you may be able to get 1,024 x 768 resolution from the webcam, the clarity and sharpness of the image doesn't compare to the camera picture.

Color spaces

The number of colors, or *color space,* is measured in bits per pixel (bpp). The higher the number of bits per pixel, the more colors it represents and the larger the picture file. A 1-bpp pixel can store 2 (2^1) colors (if you're old enough, you may remember monochrome monitors, which were 2-bit), a 2-bpp pixel can store four (2^2) colors, and a 24-bpp pixel can store a staggering 16,777,216 (2^{24}) colors. 24 bpp is also known as 24-bit or *true color. Deep color* (30/36/48-bit) is measured in the billions of colors per pixel.

If you're using a Raspberry Pi camera, the picture you took earlier was in 24 bit. If you're using a fairly cheap webcam like we are, it's unlikely that the webcam will support 24-bit, but some of them can.

Color models

A color model is the mathematical method of representing the color. There are a whole range of different color models, but a very popular one is the RGB model, where a color is made up of different intensities of red, blue, and green (known as channels). Another popular color model is hue, saturation, and value (HSV) or hue, saturation, and lightness (HSL). You use the RGB and HSV models throughout this chapter.

For each of these models, a pixel is described using three numbers (one number per channel). For example the color red in a 24-bit color space would be represented by the following combination of red, blue, and green: [255,0,0]. There are a total of 256 different shades of red, blue, and green that, when blended together, produce a total of 16,777,216 (or 256 × 256 × 256) colors. In Python, we call [255,0,0] a *tuple* (a number of values separated by commas). The tuples are stored sequentially in the image file, one per pixel.

Image file types

Different file types have been created to store the multitude of image types; BMP, JPG, and GIF are three popular ones. There are so many different file types because of the massive range of color spaces, color models, and compression algorithms. Every file type was designed with a particular goal in mind. Some were created for image clarity, others were created for web pages, and others were created especially for your webcam to make it easy to share videos and pictures over the Internet. Our research for this book led us to discover *78 different image file types,* and we're certain there are more we didn't find.

In this chapter, you start by using the BMP file format, mainly because its simplicity makes it a great starting point for understanding how to create and process image files. Later, you use a Python image library that shields you from the complexities of each file type and gives you a powerful set of imaging tools.

Check out the image file type comparison chart at `http://en.wikipedia.org/wiki/Comparison_of_graphics_file_formats`.

Creating an Image File

Enough of the theory — let's get on with writing some code and working toward the goal of computer vision! In this section, you write some Python code to create a BMP image file. You create an image at the lowest possible level without the help of a camera, scanner, or image programming library. You're writing the bits and bytes into a file to create an image.

A BMP file is basically made of up two sections: a header and the image data. The header describes the file type (24-bit color space, RGB model, and so on). Table 11-1 shows the data that makes up the header.

As you can see from this table, you need to store data in very specific sizes (2 and 4 bytes). This requires you to use data types that match both the size of the data and the content of the data (character, string, or number). In order to do this, it helps to understand data types in Python.

Also important is the type of the file. The file you create is known as a *binary file.* A binary file is different from a text file that contains characters. The binary file contains bits and bytes. When you write the Python program, it's important to write binary data into the file and not text data. You do this using a byte array and a function called `pack_into()`.

Table 11-1		BMP File Header Information
Offset	*Size (Bytes)*	*Description*
0	2	The header field used to identify the type of BMP file.
2	4	The size of the BMP file in bytes.
6	2	Not used.
8	2	Not used.
10	4	The offset in bytes where the image data starts.
14	4	The size of the header.
18	4	The bitmap width in pixels.
22	4	The bitmap height in pixels.
26	2	The number of color planes.
28	2	The number of bits per pixel, which is the color depth of the image. Typical values are 1, 4, 8, 16, 24, and 32.
30	4	The compression method being used.
34	4	The image size.
38	4	The horizontal resolution of the image (pixels per meter).
42	4	The vertical resolution of the image (pixels per meter).
46	4	The number of colors in the color palette.
50	4	The number of important colors used, or 0 when every color is important. Generally ignored.

Refer to the Python reference manual for how to interpret strings as packed binary data: http://docs.python.org/2.7/library/struct. html?highlight=pack_into#struct.Struct.pack_into.

Start by opening a new Python program in your home directory. At the Raspberry Pi command prompt, type the following commands:

```
$ cd ~
$ nano createbmp.py
```

Then type the program code in Listing 11-1.

Listing 11-1:   Create an Image File

```python
#!/usr/bin/env python
"""
Raspberry Pi Projects For Dummies: create a BMP image
For the Raspberry Pi
"""

import struct
from ctypes import *

def main():
        image_size=(1024*768*3)+54
        data = create_string_buffer(image_size)
        rt=struct.pack_into('<s',data,0,"B")
        rt=struct.pack_into('<s',data,1, "M")
        rt=struct.pack_into('<i',data,2, image_size)
        rt=struct.pack_into('<i',data,10, 54)
        rt=struct.pack_into('<i',data,14, 40)
        rt=struct.pack_into('<i',data,18, 640)
        rt=struct.pack_into('<i',data,22, 480)
        rt=struct.pack_into('<h',data,26, 1)
        rt=struct.pack_into('<h',data,28, 24)
        rt=struct.pack_into('<i',data,34, image_size)
        pcnt=54
        row_cnt=0
        color=0
        alt=0
        for x in range (0, 1024*768):
                if row_cnt>=1024:
                        row_cnt=0
                        color=color+1
                        if color>=255: color=0
                rt=struct.pack_into('<B',data,pcnt, color)
                rt=struct.pack_into('<B',data,pcnt+1, 255-color)
                rt=struct.pack_into('<B',data,pcnt+2, 0)
                pcnt=pcnt+3
                row_cnt=row_cnt+1
        print str(len(data))+" bytes written to file"
        f=open('mypic.bmp', 'wb')
        f.write(data)
        f.close()

if __name__ == "__main__":
        main()
```

In the program in Listing 11.1, you start by creating a buffer of the size you need. In this case, you create a 24-bit image file. The image has 1,024 x 768 pixels, and each pixel is 3 bytes. The size of the header is 54 bytes. Next, you use the `create_string_buffer` function to create a buffer into which we pack our binary data. The ten `pack_into` function calls create the mandatory header file information. The first parameter in the `pack_into` function call specifies the data type. There are three data types in the header:

- ✔ **String,** denoted by `<s`
- ✔ **Integer** (size 4), denoted by `<i`
- ✔ **Short** (an integer of size 2), denoted by `<h`

The second parameter of the `pack_into` function is the buffer into which we're packing the binary data. The third parameter is the offset (refer to Table 11-1), and the last parameter is the actual data itself that we're storing in the file.

The second part of the program (within the `for` loop) creates the image file data. You can see it starts at position 54 after the header information, and it loops for every pixel (1,024 x 768), writing 3 bytes per pixel (24 bits per pixel). The BMP file format is stored in BGR, not RGB, so the blue value is packed first, then the green, and finally the red. To make the image more interesting, the color is incremented after every row and you reverse the green image color (255-color) to give a beautiful blue and green rainbow. We set the red color to 0, so that's why we see only blue and green in the image.

Figure 11-2 shows how the file is built from the bottom, left to right. This build pattern is quite common for image file types, but it isn't standard across all image types.

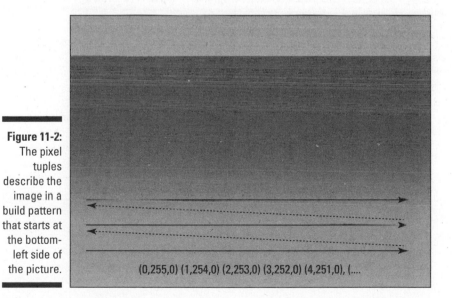

Figure 11-2:
The pixel tuples describe the image in a build pattern that starts at the bottom-left side of the picture.

(0,255,0) (1,254,0) (2,253,0) (3,252,0) (4,251,0), (....

The last part of the program is the code that writes the data (`f.write(data)`) into a file.

Save the file by pressing Ctrl+X, pressing Y, and then pressing Enter to save and exit. Now run the program using the following command:

```
$ python createbmp.py
```

The program should print the number of bytes written:

```
2359350 bytes written to file
```

Detecting Motion with a Webcam

In this section, we introduce you to an image-processing library for Python called OpenCV. It allows you to work with most image types without having to understand the complexity of the file formats and compression algorithms. It also contains many advanced functions that allow you to process images more easily.

In the following Python program, pictures are taken continuously by the webcam. Each new image is compared to the previous image, and a difference in pixels between the two images is summed into a total, which is compared to a threshold. If the pixel difference between the two images exceeds the threshold, we conclude that there has been sufficient change in the images to identify that a motion has taken place.

There are two variables you can use to fine-tune the motion detector. The first is the pixel difference threshold, and the second is the amount of pixels that we sample. We don't need to sample every pixel (which is good, because this allows the program to run faster). We've set the pixel difference threshold to 100,000 and the pixel sample to 3,000, which produced good results for both a webcam and the camera module. We've dropped the resolution to 320 x 240, which also speeds up the program because the webcam can take pictures faster at a lower resolution and there are fewer pixels to process.

Open a new Python program in your home directory. At the Raspberry Pi command prompt, type the following commands:

```
$ sudo apt-get install libopencv-dev python-opencv
$ cd ~
$ nano motion.py
```

Then type the program code in Listing 11-2.

Listing 11-2:   Python Code for a Webcam Motion Detector

```python
#!/usr/bin/env python
"""
Raspberry Pi Projects For Dummies: webcam motion detection
For the Raspberry Pi
"""
import cv2
import os
import struct

#Uncomment the following line if you are using a Pi Camera
#import picamera

import time

def main():
#if the pixel color difference between the images is
#greater than the threshold then motion is detected
threshold=100000

#set the number of pixels to compare
no_pixels=3000

diff=0
first=True
while True:

        #Uncomment these four lines if you are using a Raspberry Pi
        #camera module and comment out the fswebcam line below

        #camera = picamera.PiCamera()
        #camera.resolution = (320, 240)
        #camera.capture('current.jpg')
        #camera.close()

        os.system("fswebcam -d /dev/video0 -q -r 320x240 current.jpg")

        current_image = cv2.imread('current.jpg')
        if (first):
                prev_image=current_image
                first = False
                continue
        cnt=0
        diff=0
        width = current_image.shape[1]
        height = current_image.shape[0]
        for i in range(0, width):
                for j in range(0, height):
                        cnt=cnt+1
                        if cnt==(width*height)/no_pixels:
```

(continued)

Listing 11-2 *(continued)*

```
                        pixel1 = current_image[j][i]
                        pixel2 = prev_image[j][i]
                        diff=diff+abs((int)(pixel1[2])
                        -(int)(pixel2[2]))
                        diff=diff+abs((int)(pixel1[0])
                        -(int)(pixel2[0]))
                        diff=diff+abs((int)(pixel1[1])
                        -(int)(pixel2[1]))
                        cnt=0
        if diff>threshold:
                print "Motion detected:"+str(diff)+". . .resetting"
                first=True
                continue
        print "Difference:"+str(diff)
        prev_image=current_image

if __name__ == "__main__":
        main()
```

If you're using a Pi Camera, you need to uncomment the `import camera` line near the top of the program by removing the # at the beginning of the line.

The threshold and the pixel sample rate can be fine-tuned with the two variables: `threshold` and `no_pixels`. As we mention earlier, we set them to 100,000 and 3,000, respectively. The first few lines of the main loop (starting with `while True:`) are the code that takes a picture either using the webcam or Raspberry Pi camera. Lines that are commented out start with a #, which tells the Python interpreter not to execute these lines of code. If you're using the camera module, uncomment the four lines that start with `camera` and comment out the `fswebcam` line.

After the picture has been taken, the following line of code loads the picture into an OpenCV object that you can use to compare the pixels:

```
current_image = cv2.imread('current.jpg')
```

When there are two images to compare, the width and height of the image are determined and the main processing loops start:

```
for i in range(0, width):
                for j in range(0, height):
```

The next two lines are important because they give you access to the pixel color *tuples* (three numbers describing the RGB colors) of every pixel in the sample.

```
pixel1 = current_image[j][i]
pixel2 = prev_image[j][i]
```

The j and i variables are the *y*- and *x*-axis coordinates of the image, respectively. The pixel1 and pixel2 variables contain the color tuples of the pixel at the j and i coordinate as shown here:

```
pixel1=[245,232,84]
pixel2=[230,220,75]
```

You can determine the difference between these two pixels by subtracting the colors from each other and summing the absolute difference. In this example, the difference would be 15 + 12 + 9 = 36. You do this for every pixel in the sample, which produces a grand total difference, which is compared to the threshold in the last if statement of the program. If the threshold is exceeded, the program will print "Motion detected. . . ."

Working with Image Recognition

In this section, we create a Python script that can detect circles within an image. You use this function extensively in the next section where it's used to detect the tokens of a Connect Four game. You want to detect not only circles but also the color. We explain how to detect color in the previous section; here, we build on that knowledge.

OpenCV has a library of feature detection functions that can be found at http://docs.opencv.org/modules/imgproc/doc/feature_detection.html.

You're using the Hough Transform Circles technique that was invented in 1959 by Paul Hough and later patented by the U.S. Atomic Energy Commission. Luckily, you don't need to do much programming because the folks at OpenCV have already done all the hard work. We've found that the routine is very good at detecting circles of common size, but we got less accurate results detecting circles of different sizes in the same image. In a Connect Four game, we only need to be able to detect tokens of the same size, so it works very well for that purpose.

Start by finding some round objects of the same size, like Connect Four tokens or coins, as shown in Figure 11-3. Create an image of the objects called shapes.jpg using your webcam or Raspberry Pi camera (refer to "Setting Up the Webcam or Raspberry Pi Camera Module").

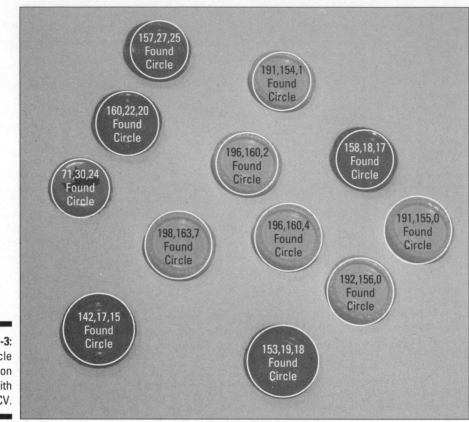

Figure 11-3:
Circle
detection
with
OpenCV.

The program in Listing 11-3 processes the image you created and creates a new image called `detectedcircles.jpg`. It also automatically displays the new image, so make sure you're within X and running an lxTerminal window. To go into X, type the following command at the command prompt:

```
$ startx
```

Then double-click the lxTerminal icon on the desktop and enter the following command, which will create a new Python script:

```
$ cd ~
$ nano circles.py
```

Then type in the code in Listing 11-3.

Listing 11-3:   Python Script to Detect Circles with OpenCV

```python
#!/usr/bin/env python
"""
Raspberry Pi Projects For Dummies: detect circles
For the Raspberry Pi
"""

import cv2.cv
import numpy as np

def main():
        img = cv2.imread('shapes.jpg',0)
        img = cv2.medianBlur(img,0)
        circles = cv2.HoughCircles (img,cv2.cv.CV_HOUGH_GRADIENT, 1,minDist=40,
                param1=30, param2=20, minRadius=35, maxRadius=50)

        circles = np.uint16(np.around(circles))
        img = cv2.imread('shapes.jpg')
        for i in circles[0,:]:
                # draw the circles
                cv2.circle(img,(i[0],i[1]),i[2],(0,255,0),2)
                x=i[0]
                y=i[1]
                Red=img[i[1],i[0],[2]]
                Green=img[i[1],i[0],[1]]
                Blue=img[i[1],i[0],[0]]
                cv2.putText(img,str(int(Red))+","+str(int(Green))+","+/
                str(int(Blue)), (x-40,y), cv2.FONT_HERSHEY_SIMPLEX, /
                .5, 0)
                cv2.putText(img,"Found Circle", (x-50,y+30),/
                cv2.FONT_HERSHEY_SIMPLEX, .5, 0)
        cv2.imwrite('detectedcircles.jpg', img)
        cv2.imshow('detected circles',img)
        cv2.waitKey(0)
        cv2.destroyAllWindows()

if __name__ == "__main__":
        main()
```

Run the program from the command line, and a window similar to Figure 11-3 appears. For each circle that it detects, it draws a graphical circle around the image and writes the text `Found Circle` and a number that corresponds to the RGB color of the center pixel of the circle. The program likely won't work perfectly the first time you run it because there are a number of parameters that fine-tune the minimum spacing between circles, and minimum and maximum diameter.

If you get an `AttributeError: rint`, this is because it hasn't detected any circles. You'll need to fine-tune it.

The first two lines of the main program open the `shapes.jpg` image that is located in the same directory as the program (≈) and convert it to an 8-bit black-and-white picture that is required by the `HoughCircles` function. The third line contains the call to the `HoughCircles` function. There are three parameters that you need to fine-tune this function:

- ✔ `minDist` is the minimum distance you want between the center of each of the circles.
- ✔ `minRadius` is the minimum radius you want for a circle.
- ✔ `maxRadius` is the maximum radius for a circle.

If the function finds circles that do not meet these criteria, it will exclude them from the list. The next line creates an array (list) of all the circles and stores it in a variable called `circles`. The next line opens the image again and discards the previous black-and-white image. Then there is a `for` loop that loops through each of the circles that were found by the `HoughCircles` function and plots a graphical circle at the coordinates and with the radius it detected. The program writes the RGB color code and `Found Circle` text within each circle (refer to Figure 11-3).

If the program is not detecting the circles correctly, fine-tune it by adjusting the three parameters accordingly.

Interpreting Color

In the last two sections, we examine the RGB subcomponents of a pixel to determine the color of a pixel. The RGB color model, however, is not best for detecting color. A better version of the RGB color model is HSV, sometimes called HSL. In the "Building a Connect Four Game Using Computer Vision" section of this chapter, you need to be able to detect the red and yellow colors of differing brightness. To the human eye, all the pieces in a Connect Four game appear either red or yellow, but their brightness differs vastly depending on the lighting conditions, shadows, and angle of the camera. Using the RGB color model, the number ranges of different shades of the same color differ substantially. However, using the HSV model, the hue (the main representation of color) remains constant. The shadows will likely affect the value or maybe the saturation.

We've modified Listing 11-3 to perform an HSV conversion and use it to distinguish between red and yellow circles in Listing 11-4. Instead of printing the RGB color within the circle, it will now print the HSV values. Instead of printing `Found Circle`, it will print the color interpretation of the red or yellow circle. If you have different color tokens in your image, fine-tune color ranges until you get accurate interpretations.

The program in Listing 11-4 processes the image you created and creates a new image called detectedcircles.jpg (see Figure 11-4).

The program will also automatically display the new image, so make sure you're within X and running an lxTerminal window. To go into X, type the following command at the command prompt:

```
$ startx
```

Then double-click the lxTerminal icon on the desktop and enter the following command to create a new Python script:

```
$ cd ~
$ nano circles2.py
```

Now type the code in Listing 11-4.

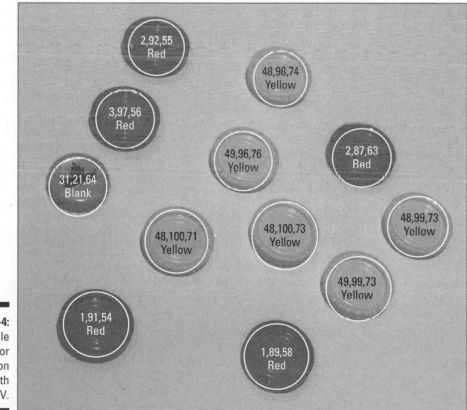

Figure 11-4:
Circle
and color
detection
with
OpenCV.

Listing 11-4:   Python Script to Detect Circles and Red or Yellow Colors

```python
#!/usr/bin/env python
"""
Raspberry Pi Projects For Dummies: detect circles and color
For the Raspberry Pi
"""

import cv2.cv
import numpy as np

def rgb2hsv(r, g, b):
    r, g, b = r/255.0, g/255.0, b/255.0
    mx = max(r, g, b)
    mn = min(r, g, b)
    df = mx-mn
    if mx == mn:
        h = 0
    elif mx == r:
        h = (60 * ((g-b)/df) + 360) % 360
    elif mx == g:
        h = (60 * ((b-r)/df) + 120) % 360
    elif mx == b:
        h = (60 * ((r-g)/df) + 240) % 360
    if mx == 0:
        s = 0
    else:
        s = df/mx*100
    v = mx*100
    return h, s, v

def main():
        img = cv2.imread('shapes.jpg',0)
        img = cv2.medianBlur(img,0)
        circles = cv2.HoughCircles(img,cv2.cv.CV_HOUGH_GRADIENT,1,minDist=100 /
,param1=30,param2=60,minRadius=45,maxRadius=75)
        circles = np.uint16(np.around(circles))
        img = cv2.imread('shapes.jpg')
        for i in circles[0,:]:
                # draw the circles
                cv2.circle(img,(i[0],i[1]),i[2],(0,255,0),2)
                x=i[0]
                y=i[1]
                Red=img[i[1],i[0],[2]]
                Green=img[i[1],i[0],[1]]
                Blue=img[i[1],i[0],[0]]
                hsv=rgb2hsv(Red, Green, Blue)
                Hue=round(hsv[0])
```

```
            Sat=round(hsv[1])
            Value=round(hsv[2])
            if ((Hue>=320) or (Hue>=0 and Hue <=25)) and (Sat>50):
                    token="Red"
            elif (Hue>=30 and Hue<=60) and (Sat>50):
                    token="Yellow"
            else:
                    token="Blank"
            cv2.putText(img,str(int(Hue))+","+str(int(Sat))+","+str(int( /
Value)), (x-40,y), cv2.FONT_HERSHEY_SIMPLEX, .5, 0)
            cv2.putText(img,token, (x-30,y+30), cv2.FONT_HERSHEY_SIMPLEX,
            .5, 0)
    cv2.imwrite('detectedcircles.jpg', img)
    cv2.imshow('detected circles',img)
    cv2.waitKey(0)
    cv2.destroyAllWindows()

if __name__ == "__main__":
    main()
```

The code explanation is the same as the code explanation in the "Working with Image Recognition" section, except for the code starting at this line:

```
hsv=rgb2hsv(Red, Green, Blue)
```

This line calls the rgb2hsv function within the program with the RGB parameters. The function performs the mathematical conversion and returns the HSV equivalent of the color. The next few if statements compare the HSV values to the number ranges for red and yellow. If your tokens are a different color, adjust these values until you get the correct readings for your colors.

Many color wheels are available online that will help you determine the RGB and HSV values for all the colors in the color model. You can use sites like www.colorizer.org to determine the color numbers for ranges of colors.

Building a Connect Four Game Using Computer Vision

In this section, you use a webcam or Raspberry Pi camera to give your Raspberry Pi a view of a real-life Connect Four game. Using what you learned in the previous sections of this chapter, you can detect the movement of pieces and the color of each piece to give the Raspberry Pi enough information to play against a human opponent. We've added speech to the program so the Raspberry Pi can announce whose turn it is and which moves it wants you to make for it.

This section requires some coding that is more in depth than the rest of the chapter. The code listing is quite long, but you can download it from `www.dummies.com/go/raspberrypiprojects`. Let's get started!

Start off by calibrating your webcam and the Connect Four grid. Fill most of the positions on the grid with tokens and try to evenly space out the red and yellow pieces (or whichever color tokens you have); leave some blank. Position your webcam evenly in front of the grid and take some 640 x 480 pictures (refer to "Setting Up the Webcam or Raspberry Pi Camera Module," earlier in this chapter), until you're satisfied that the grid occupies most of the picture. Try to use a white or neutral background, and don't use any patterns that contain circles other than the grid within the picture. Run your sample images through the program in Listing 11-4 until you have every circle correctly identified (see Figure 11-5).

You need to fine-tune these values in the `HoughCircles` function call:

 ✔ `minDist` is the minimum distance you want between the center of each of the circles.

 ✔ `minRadius` is the minimum radius you want for a circle.

 ✔ `maxRadius` is the maximum radius for a circle.

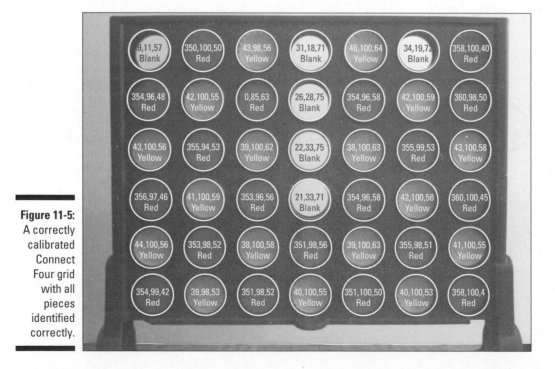

Figure 11-5:
A correctly calibrated Connect Four grid with all pieces identified correctly.

After it's calibrated, you're ready to move on to the actual game itself. You need to install OpenCV (if you haven't done that already in the previous sections):

```
$ sudo apt-get install libopencv-dev python-opencv
```

The program makes use of a program called mpg321 to play the MP3 files that the computer uses to communicate with the player:

```
$ sudo apt-get install mpg321
```

Now code the program in Listing 11-5 by typing the following:

```
$ cd ~
$ nano c4.py
```

Listing 11-5:   Connect Four Game Using Computer Vision

```python
#!/usr/bin/env python
"""
Raspberry Pi Projects For Dummies: Connect Four Game Using Computer Vision
For the Raspberry Pi
"""

import cv2
import cv2.cv
import numpy as np
import struct
import math
import sys
import os
from operator import itemgetter, attrgetter

#Uncomment this line of you have a Pi Camera
#import picamera

import time
import random
global circles
global human_color
global computer_color


def rgb2hsv(r, g, b):
    r, g, b = r/255.0, g/255.0, b/255.0
    mx = max(r, g, b)
    mn = min(r, g, b)
    df = mx-mn
    if mx == mn:
        h = 0
```

(continued)

Listing 11-5 *(continued)*

```
    elif mx == r:
        h = (60 * ((g-b)/df) + 360) % 360
    elif mx == g:
        h = (60 * ((b-r)/df) + 120) % 360
    elif mx == b:
        h = (60 * ((r-g)/df) + 240) % 360
    if mx == 0:
        s = 0
    else:
        s = df/mx*100
    v = mx*100
    return h, s, v


def calculate_a_move(c4grid):
    global human_color
    global computer_color
    max_found=0
    best_move=0
    #find best move for the computer
    #first we determine the max amount in row
    rt=check_for_4_in_a_row(c4grid)
    if rt[0]!=1:
        max_found=rt[2]
    for x in range (0,7):
        for y in range (0,6):
            if  (y==5) or (c4grid[x,y]=="B" and/
            c4grid[x,y+1]!="B"):
                #Reevaluate if a disc in this position
                #will yield more in a row
                c4grid[x,y]=computer_color
                rt=check_for_4_in_a_row(c4grid)
                c4grid[x,y]="B"
                if rt[0]==1:
                    return(x+1)
                if rt[2]>max_found:
                    max_found=rt[2]
                    best_move=x+1
                #check if human needs to be blocked
                c4grid[x,y]=human_color
                rt=check_for_4_in_a_row(c4grid)
                c4grid[x,y]="B"
                if rt[0]==1:
                    return(x+1)
                break

    if best_move==0:
        best_move=random.randint(1,7)
    return(best_move)
```

```
def check_for_4_in_a_row (c4grid):
    max_found=0
    max_found2=0

    #look for vertical
    best_move = [0,0]
    for x in range (0,7):
            found=1
            max_found=1
            for y in range (1,6):
                    if (c4grid[x,y]=="Y" or c4grid[x,y]=="R") and/
                    c4grid[x,y]==c4grid[x,y-1]:
                            found=found+1
                            if c4grid[x,y]=="Y":
                                    max_found=max_found+1
                    else:
                            found=1
                    if found==4:
                            return([1,1,x,c4grid[x,y]])
            if max_found > 1:
                    max_found2=max_found2+max_found

    #look for horizontal
    for y in range (0,6):
            found=1
            max_found=1
            for x in range (1,7):
                    if (c4grid[x,y]=="Y" or c4grid[x,y]=="R") and/
                    c4grid[x,y]==c4grid[x-1,y]:
                            found=found+1
                            if c4grid[x,y]=="Y":
                                    max_found=max_found+1
                    else:
                            found=1
                    if found==4:
                            return([1,2,y, c4grid[x,y]])
            if max_found > 1:
                    max_found2=max_found2+max_found

    #look for diagonal bottom left top right
    startx=0-(6-4)
    for z in range (0,6):
            x=startx
            y=5
            max_found=1
            found=1
            while y>=1:
                    if x>0 and x<=6-1:
                        if (c4grid[x,y]=="Y" or c4grid[x,y]=="R") and/
```

(continued)

Listing 11-5 *(continued)*

```
                        c4grid[x+1,y-1]==c4grid[x,y]:
                                found=found+1
                                if c4grid[x,y]=="Y":
                                        max_found=max_found+1
                        else:
                                found=1
                if found==4:
                        return([1,3,x,c4grid[x,y]])
                x=x+1
                y=y-1
        startx=startx+1

        if max_found > 1:
                max_found2=max_found2+max_found

#look for diagonal bottom left top right
startx=0-(6-4)
for z in range (0,6):
        x=startx
        y=5
        max_found=1
        found=1
        while y>=1:
                if x>0 and x<=6-1:
                        if (c4grid[x,y]=="Y" or c4grid[x,y]=="R") and/
                        c4grid[x+1,y-1]==c4grid[x,y]:
                                found=found+1
                                if c4grid[x,y]=="Y":
                                        max_found=max_found+1
                        else:
                                found=1
                if found==4:
                        return([1,3,x,c4grid[x,y]])
                x=x+1
                y=y-1
        startx=startx+1

        if max_found > 1:
                max_found2=max_found2+max_found

#look for diagonal bottom right to top left
startx=6+(6-4)
for z in range (0,6):
        x=startx
        y=5
        max_found=1
        found=1
        while y>=1:
                if x>0 and x<=6-1:
```

```
                          if (c4grid[x,y]=="Y" or c4grid[x,y]=="R") and/
                          c4grid[x-1,y-1]==c4grid[x,y]:
                                    found=found+1
                                    if c4grid[x,y]=="Y":
                                            max_found=max_found+1
                          else:
                                    found=1
                     if found==4:
                                    return([1,4,x,c4grid[x,y]])
                     x=x-1
                     y=y-1
          startx=startx-1

          if max_found > 1:
                     max_found2=max_found2+max_found

     return([0,"",max_found2])

def check_for_new_move(prev_grid, c4grid):
     for x in range (0,7):
          y=0
          while y<=5 and prev_grid[x,y]=="B":
                     y=y+1
          if y>0 and c4grid[x,y-1]<>"B":
                     new_token=c4grid[x,y-1]
                     return([x, new_token])
     return([0,""])

def process_image(new_game):
     global circles

     c4grid = np.empty((7, 6), dtype=object)
     no_empty_slots=0

     #If you are using a Raspberry Pi Camera
     camera = picamera.PiCamera()
     camera.resolution = (640, 480)
     camera.capture('c4grid.bmp')
     camera.close()

     #If you are using a webcam
     #os.system("fswebcam -d /dev/video0 -q -r 640x480 c4grid.bmp")

     if new_game:
               img = cv2.imread('c4grid.bmp',0)
               img = cv2.medianBlur(img,0)
               circles = cv2.HoughCircles(img, cv2.cv.CV_HOUGH_GRADIENT,/
               1,40,param1=20/ ,param2=30, minRadius=25, maxRadius=50)
               circles = np.uint16(np.around(circles))
     img = cv2.imread('c4grid.bmp')
```

(continued)

Listing 11-5 *(continued)*

```
grid = []
for i in circles[0,:]:
        x=i[0]
        y=i[1]
        Red=img[i[1],i[0],[2]]
        Green=img[i[1],i[0],[1]]
        Blue=img[i[1],i[0],[0]]
        hsv=rgb2hsv(Red, Green, Blue)
        Hue=round(hsv[0])
        Sat=round(hsv[1])
        Value=round(hsv[2])
        if ((Hue>=320) or (Hue>=0 and Hue <=25)) and (Sat>50):
                token="R"
        elif (Hue>=69 and Hue<=165) and (Sat>50):
                token="G"
        elif (Hue>=30 and Hue<=60) and (Sat>50):
                token="Y"
        else:
                token="B"
                no_empty_slots=no_empty_slots+1

        grid.append([0,0,x,y,token, img[i[1],i[0]]])

temp = sorted(grid, key=itemgetter(2))

xcounter=0
prev=(int)(temp[0][2])
for i in temp:
        if abs(prev-(int)(i[2]))>20:
                xcounter=xcounter+1
        i[0]=xcounter
        prev=(int)(i[2])

temp = sorted(grid, key=itemgetter(0,3))
ycounter=-1
prev=(int)(temp[0][0])
for i in temp:
        if prev<>(int)(i[0]):
                ycounter=0
        else:
                ycounter=ycounter+1
        i[1]=ycounter
        prev=(int)(i[0])

for i in temp:
        x=i[0]
        y=i[1]
        if x>=0 and x <=6 and y>=0 and y<=5:
                c4grid[x, y]=i[4]
```

```
        return(c4grid, no_empty_slots)

def wait_for_play(c4grid):

        prev_grid = c4grid
        no=0
        new_move_detected=False
        while not new_move_detected:
                rt=process_image(0)
                c4grid=rt[0]
                print "C4 Grid:"
                for y in range (0,6):

                        print c4grid[0,y] , ",", c4grid[1,y],", /
" , c4grid[2,y],",",c4grid[3,y], ",",c4grid[4,y],",",c4grid[5,y],",",c4grid[6,y]

                rt=check_for_new_move(prev_grid, c4grid)
                if rt[1]!="":
                        print "New move detected in column "+str(rt[0]+1)/
                        + " color "+rt[1]
                        prev_grid=np.copy(c4grid)
                        new_move_detected=True
        return(c4grid)

def play_mp3(mp3_no):
        if (mp3_no>=1 and mp3_no<=7):
                mp3_file="slot"+str(mp3_no)+".mp3"
        elif mp3_no==8:
                mp3_file="mymove.mp3"
        elif mp3_no==9:
                mp3_file="yourmove.mp3"
        elif mp3_no==10:
                mp3_file="letsplay.mp3"
        elif mp3_no==11:
                mp3_file="youwin.mp3"
        elif mp3_no==12:
                mp3_file="letsplayagain.mp3"
        elif mp3_no==13:
                mp3_file="badluck.mp3"

        os.system('mpg321 -q '+mp3_file)

        return

def main():
    global human_color
    global computer_color

    humans_turn = True
    human_color="R"
```

(continued)

Listing 11-5 *(continued)*

```python
    computer_color="Y"
    new_game=True
    winner=False
    play_grid = np.empty((7, 6), dtype=object)

    while True:
        while new_game==True:
                rt = process_image(1)
                if rt[1]==7*6:
                        new_game=False
                        winner=False
                        play_grid=rt[0]
                time.sleep(2)

        print "Empty grid detected, let's play!"
        play_mp3(10)
        play_mp3(9)

        while True:
                play_grid = wait_for_play(play_grid)
                rt = check_for_4_in_a_row(play_grid)
                if rt[0]==1:
                        print "four in a row"
                        if rt[3]==human_color:
                                play_mp3(11)
                                play_mp3(12)
                        else:
                                play_mp3(13)
                                play_mp3(12)

                        new_game=True
                        humans_turn = True
                        break;

                if not humans_turn:
                        play_mp3(9)
                        humans_turn=True
                else:
                        play_mp3(8) # my move
                        rt = calculate_a_move(play_grid)
                        play_mp3(rt)
                        humans_turn=False

if __name__ == "__main__":
        main()
```

Starting at the `main()` section, there are a few variables you can change in order to configure the color for the human and the color for the computer. If you use colors other than red or yellow, do a search for *R* and *Y* and replace with your colors. The game is programmed for the standard grid of seven across by six down. The program then enters the main loop, which has two sub loops: one for determining the start of a new game (that is, an empty grid), and one for game play. Notice a number of `play_mp3` function calls throughout the program. These play the sounds for the Raspberry Pi to communicate with the human. You can download these files from `www.dummies.com/go/raspberrypiprojects`. The computer moves are communicated to the human who must perform the moves on the computer's behalf. The computer's intelligence is limited to the following:

- Detecting a change in game state when a piece is dropped into the grid
- Determining whether the computer needs to block the human from getting four in a row
- Determining the computer's best move by calculating which move will produce the most in a row for the computer.

The computer does not

- Detect whether an incorrect move has occurred. (You can cheat!)
- Think ahead more than one move (either for blocking or for its own game strategy).

When an empty grid has occurred, the computer announces "Let's play!" and the main game play loop starts. The game play loop consists of the following steps:

1. **Wait for a move to occur.**

2. **Once a move has occurred, check for four in a row.**

3. **Either tell the human to move or calculate a computer move.**

Starting at the top of the program, here's is an explanation of each function:

- `rgb2hsv` converts the RGB color model to HSV (see the "Interpreting Color" section, earlier in this chapter).
- `calculate_a_move` determines the best move for the computer, which includes either blocking the human or calculating a move that yields the most tokens in a row for the computer.
- `check_for_4_in_a_row` scans the grid to determine whether there are four tokens in a row vertically, horizontally, or diagonally. This function also serves the `calculate_a_move` function by returning the maximum number of tokens in a row for the computer for each possible move.

✔ check_for_new_move scans through the grid in memory to determine if it has changed.

✔ process_image is very similar to the calibration program you wrote earlier. It's responsible for taking a picture of the grid, finding the circles, determining the color and position of each piece, and storing the grid in memory. This function contains the HoughCircles function that you need to change to match the values you calibrated earlier. The HoughCircles function returns a long list of all circles, so this function also sorts each circle by *x*- and *y*-coordinate to determine its position in the grid.

✔ wait_for_play loops and continuously checks for new moves. It also prints the grid that the computer has in memory to the screen so you can verify that the computer is "seeing" each piece correctly.

✔ play_mp3 plays each MP3 file using the mpg321 external program call. If you'd prefer to see the move written to the screen and not spoken, this would be a good place to replace the os.system call with a print command. You can download these files from www.dummies.com/go/raspberrypiprojects.

Chapter 12

The Raspberry Jazz Glitter Trio

This is a fun project that creates a free jazz trio inside your Raspberry Pi. (Some people joke that free jazz got its name because no one would ever pay for it. True, jazz is an acquired taste and a little goes a long way, but this is a fascinating little project nevertheless.) The project points a webcam at a glitter lamp, the kind that features glitter floating in a liquid. The camera acts as a high-resolution multicolor sensor. It uses the data gathered from the glitter lamp to trigger the sounds for the project, thus creating free jazz.

Meeting the Gang

The photograph in Figure 12-1 shows our version of the Raspberry Pi jazz glitter trio. Yours may be a bit different because of the exact materials you're able to gather, but it shows you what you're aiming for.

It consists of two main components — a cheap webcam and a glitter lamp — which we picked up from a home bargain/thrift store for less than $10 for the pair. These are cheap, generic devices and are widely available online, including on eBay.

The lamp

The glitter lamp we chose was the smallest we could find. It's about 5 inches tall and contains silver glitter suspended in a liquid. When the lamp is still, the glitter slowly floats up. When the lamp is turned upside down, a tilt switch in the base triggers a circuit to start one minute of random pulsing of three different colored light-emitting diodes (LEDs), illuminating the glitter from the lamp's base. As the glitter drifts and tumbles, some pieces catch the light from the LEDs and sparkle. Because the LEDs are in different positions, different bits of glitter get illuminated with different colors.

In this project, you use this effect to trigger jazz sounds. Both the lamp and the webcam are mounted in a box. The box includes a back shield so that only the glitter is picked up and stray light is reduced. (Construction plans of the box are included as part of the project.)

The webcam

Webcams come in all sorts of shapes, sizes, and resolutions. For this project, get the cheapest one you can find. The resolution doesn't matter much for this project, so a low-resolution webcam will do the trick. Here's what to look for in a webcam for this project:

- ✔ **Compatibility:** The most important thing is that the camera be supported by the Raspberry Pi's Python-based software, which usually seems to support low-cost generic cameras.

- ✔ **Access to the interior of the webcam:** You need to be able to physically get into the camera so you can mount it. Look for a webcam with small screws on the outside of the case rather than an all-in-one molded type of case. You're going to be hacking into the USB power lead to power the glitter lamp's LEDs.

- ✔ **Manual focus:** Make sure that the webcam has a manual-focus lens. The fixed-focus types are hard to adjust for very small distances, which is what you need for this project.

You can buy the webcam we used at http://uk.farnell.com/trust/ 17003/webcam-exis-trust-uk/dp/1860369. For a complete list of Raspberry Pi USB webcams, check out www.elinux.org/RPi_USB_ Webcams.

Testing the Webcam

The first step is to test whether your webcam works and is supported by the software. Create a directory for the project called glitter, either from the desktop or by typing the following from your home directory (or wherever you want to work):

```
mkdir glitter
cd glitter
```

Next, download the support files you need by typing the following:

```
sudo wget http://www.cl.cam.ac.uk/downloads/freshers/image_processing.tar.gz
```

To extract the files, you just type the following:

```
sudo tar -xf image_processing.tar.gz
```

This gives you the support software and some basic tutorial files on how to use the software, but for the time being, ignore these and install the Python libraries. First, navigate to the libraries directory. Then install the libraries by typing the following two lines:

```
sudo cd library
sudo make install
```

This executes a script that moves all the files and the library code into the necessary places in Python's file system.

Now you're ready to try out the camera. Create a file, using the code shown in Listing 12-1, and store it in your `glitter` directory. Give it the title of `camTest.py`, plug in your webcam, change the directory of the prompt to the `glitter` directory, and run the file by typing the following:

```
python camTest.py
```

Listing 12-1:   Camera Test

```
from imgproc import *
import time

my_camera = Camera(320, 240)
my_image = my_camera.grabImage()
my_view = Viewer(my_image.width, my_image.height, "WebCam")
while True:
  my_view.displayImage(my_image)
  time.sleep(0.1)
  my_image = my_camera.grabImage()
```

Reading step-by-step through this listing gives you an idea of what's going on. First, you have to import the module that supports the webcam, as well as the time module. Then you define an instance of the `Camera` class and say what size you want it to be. Here, it's only 320 x 240 pixels, so it's not very high resolution. (Later, you make this even smaller.) Next, the listing grabs an image from what the camera is currently seeing and defines a `view` window for later displaying this image on the screen. Last, the program goes into an endless loop of displaying the image, sleeping (or delaying) for 0.1 second, and then getting a new image.

The result of this listing is that you see the image from your webcam in the top-left corner of the screen. If this fails, your webcam is probably not supported by Raspberry Pi and you'll have to get another one to do this project.

If your webcam works, check that you can focus to half an inch or so. If you can't, you may be able to adjust the lens when you take the camera apart.

Hacking the Glitter Lamp

You can set up your camera pointing to the glitter lamp and turn it on manually — this will give you some idea of what the finished project will sound like. However, by hacking the glitter lamp and the camera, you get a neat compact unit all powered off the USB connection, and you can easily invert the lamp to get the glitter all mixed up again.

You may have to modify these instructions depending on how your lamp and camera are constructed.

Note: At this point, you may want to skip to the software section, and get the system going without doing any hardware hacking. Feel free to skip ahead and come back to this section later.

Assembling the necessary parts

Besides a glitter lamp and a suitable webcam (covered earlier in this chapter), here's a list of the parts we used:

- ¼-inch plywood or medium-density fiberboard (MDF) to make the box — two pieces measuring 3 x 5 inches and one piece measuring 3 x 2 inches
- ¾-x-16-inch strip of pine for the box sides
- A tack switch with ¼-inch plunger
- A 3-inch length of ⅜-inch angle aluminum
- Matte black paint
- Four 18mm M3 tapped hexagonal pillars
- Ten 10mm pan-head M3 screws
- Two M3 nuts
- Wood glue, hot glue, and connecting wire

The glitter lamp we bought is shown in Figure 12-2. It was powered by three self-contained coin cell batteries.

Except for the battery compartment, we could see no way into the lamp, so eventually we resorted to drastic measures and cut all around the base with a saw, leaving it looking a bit truncated, as shown in Figure 12-3.

This left the electronics in the other half of the lamp. In Figure 12-4, the photograph on the left shows the circuit board in the plastic assembly, and the photograph on the right shows the removed printed circuit board (PCB). That long component on the top is the tilt switch; it consists of a small metal ball inside a tube that makes a circuit between the two wire ends when the lamp is tilted past a certain angle.

Figure 12-2:
Our original
glitter lamp.

Figure 12-3:
The glitter
portion of
the lamp.

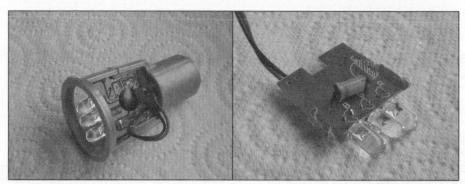

Figure 12-4:
The elec-
tronics of
the lamp.

In this project, you need to remove the tilt switch and solder a normal push
button in its place. Extend the power wires by soldering two new wires to
the PCB, and then solder two other wires about 6 inches long to the connections where you removed the tilt switch. Bend the LEDs so that they point
up. You're going to mount this under the lamp's glitter section, as shown in
Figure 12-5.

Figure 12-5:
The LEDs
mounted on
the base.

Making the box

Figure 12-6 shows the schematic of the box into which you'll place the lamp and webcam.

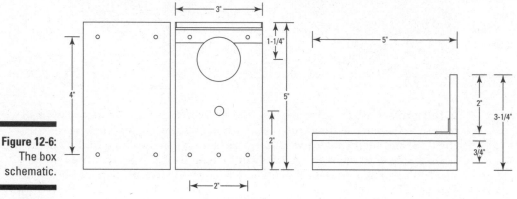

Figure 12-6:
The box
schematic.

If your camera or glitter lamp are materially different from the ones we used, you may have to modify these instructions to suit what you have.

To make the box, follow these steps:

1. **Cut two pieces of 5-x-3-inch MDF or plywood.**

2. **In the top piece, cut a 1½-inch hole at one end to take the diameter of the clear base of the glitter lamp, and then cut a tapered hole to which the camera can be attached.**

   We did this by first drilling a 10mm hole and then enlarging it to 12mm by drilling only partially through the wood. This allowed us to use the thick-domed plastic plug (which normally attaches the camera to its stand) to attach the camera to the board.

3. **Drill a ⅛-inch hole for the tack switch to poke out of and four ⅛-inch holes in each corner for the supporting pillar.**

   When we did this, we also clamped the base and top together so the holes lined up.

4. **Cut a 2¾-inch piece of ¼-inch angled aluminum for the back screen support, and drill two ⅛-inch holes ½-inch from each side on both faces of the aluminum.**

   Mark the holes on the top through the holes in the aluminum, so they line up correctly.

5. **Cut part of a semicircle in the aluminum so you can get the back screen close to the glitter lamp.**

We used a round back file for this.

6. **Use ¾-inch strip pine to make the sides, and glue them to the top.**

7. **Use 18mm tapped pillars between the top and the base to hold it all together.**

8. **Cut a 3-x-2-inch back screen from the wood and mount it on the aluminum angle with two screws and nuts. Then paint the whole thing matte black.**

   You can use another color if you want, but black cuts down the stray reflected light, especially from the back shield.

   The idea is that the LEDs are placed under the large hole and the glitter lamp is glued in the lid of the box. We used a small ring from the lower part of the lamp that we cut off previously.

9. **Cut a *chamfer* (beveled edge) on the inside of the lamp's ring with a scalpel or sharp hobby knife so that it fits snugly over the ring surrounding the LEDs. Push this ring onto the base of the lamp and screw the box together.**

10. **Using hot glue or silicon sealant, glue the lamp to the top of the box.**

11. **When the glue or sealant has set, unfasten the box and apply another fillet of glue to the underside.**

12. **Put some glue on the base of the ring and again assemble the box so the ring is secured in the right place, as shown in Figure 12-7.**

Figure 12-7:
The lamp/
electronics
assembly.

Adding the camera

To take the camera apart, first we unscrewed the plastic plug that holds the camera to its clip or stand. Then we unfastened the screws in the body. (In the case of our camera, there were four small star-head screws.)

You want to tap off the 5V and ground coming from the USB lead that powers it with a pair of wires. You need to take this power to the LEDs in the box. With the camera enclosure removed, you can see the red and black wires carrying the USB power. Solder two new wires onto this and drill two 1mm holes in the plastic case so these wires can pass out of the camera body.

You also have to drill two matching holes in the top of the box for them to pass through. Reassemble the camera and, with the round plastic plug, attach the camera to the top of the box and pass the wires through the lid.

Connect the two wires from the LED board to a tack switch with a ¼-inch-long top and glue that in place in the center hole in the top. From the underside, the wiring should look something like that shown in Figure 12-8.

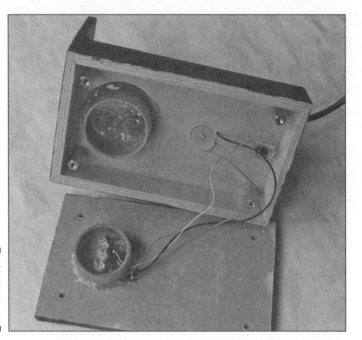

Figure 12-8:
The wiring
of the
project.

Testing

After you have the hardware built, it doesn't do any harm to give it a quick test. You can plug it into your Raspberry Pi and run the program in Listing 12-1 just to make sure that the camera still works. Then push the tack switch that replaced the tilt switch and make sure that the LEDs pulse for about a minute.

Letting the Band Play

There are two more things you need before you can get a performance out of this band: sound samples and software. The way these are brought together determines how the project works. You need to define an array of pixels to sample from the glitter image. When these points reach a certain brightness and color, the sounds are triggered.

Gathering the sounds

First, you have to gather the sounds for the trio. We did a web search for individual sounds for each instrument: sax, bass, and drums. There are many free sound sample sites, but the one we found most useful was www.freesound.org because you can search for specific sounds and listen to them before downloading. We looked for short samples, mainly single notes, from each of the three instruments. We got 16 samples for bass and drums and 22 samples of the sax. (You can use more, but you'll have to make minor changes to the software if you do.)

We used Audacity (a free downloadable audio editor and recorder, available at http://audacity.sourceforge.net) to *top* and *tail* each sample (that is, to cut out any long silence at the beginning and end of the sample). Also, while chopping the samples up, we converted them into a mono sample in order to save memory space. This is a bit of an iterative process: After you hear the results, you may want to go back and get different types of sounds.

Finally, after a bit of trial and error, we placed the samples in directories at the same level as the code called sax, drums, and bass. Each sample is called soundX.wav, where the X is replaced by a number, starting at 0 and incrementing up to the biggest sample number.

Writing the software

The idea behind the code is that, from the image, 16 pixels in a 4 x 4 grid will be monitored for color. When a bright red, green, or blue color is detected, a sound is triggered. In the case of drums or bass each pixel monitored triggers a fixed sample, but the sax triggering is slightly more complex. The sax sound triggered depends on both the number of the pixel triggering it and an offset. The offset is incremented on each sax trigger, and when it reaches a limit, it resets back to 0. We found this approach necessary to introduce a bit of variety into the music produced. (Although a repetitive drum and bass note sounds fine, the sax, being a solo instrument, needs a bit of variety to keep it interesting.)

Because you're using only 16 pixels out of the whole image, you don't need a very big image. We used a 160-x-120-pixel image. This still results in an image of 19,200 pixels, which is quite a lot of memory for a small embedded processor, especially considering that you're only interested in 16 of the pixels. Each pixel has 3 bytes of memory associated with it — one each for the red, green, and blue signals. To add a bit of interest, after a pixel triggers a sound, the program draws an outline around that pixel so you can see what's happening. All this is done in the code shown in Listing 12-2.

Listing 12-2:   The Glitter Band

```python
from imgproc import *
import time
import os, pygame, sys

pygame.init()
pygame.mixer.quit()
#pygame.mixer.init(frequency= 44100, size=8, channels = 8, buffer= 2048 )
pygame.mixer.init()
print"loading Sound files"
samplesSax = [pygame.mixer.Sound("sax/sound"+str(i)+".wav") for i in range
             (0, 22)]
samplesBass = [pygame.mixer.Sound("bass/sound"+str(i)+".wav") for i in range
             (0, 16)]
samplesDrum = [pygame.mixer.Sound("drums/sound"+str(i)+".wav") for i in range
             (0, 16)]
print"finished"
my_camera = Camera(160, 120)
my_image = my_camera.grabImage()
my_view = Viewer(my_image.width, my_image.height, "WebCam")
monX = [ int(p * 32) for p in range(1,5)]
monY = [ int(p * 24) for p in range(1,5)]
saxOffset = 0

def main():
 global my_image
 while True:
    my_image = my_camera.grabImage()
    for x in monX:
        for y in monY:
            surround(x,y,(0,0,0))
    #my_view.displayImage(my_image)
    #time.sleep(0.1)
    #print" "
    for x in monX :
        for y in monY :
            red, green, blue = my_image[x, y]
            if green > 248 :
              #print green," green at ", x, y
```

```
            sampleSax(x,y)
          if red > 225 :
            sampleDrum(x,y)
            #print red," red at ", x, y
          if blue > 240 :
            sampleBass(x,y)
            #print blue," blue at ", x, y
      my_view.displayImage(my_image)

def sampleSax(x,y) :
    global saxOffset
    number = saxOffset + ((x / 32)-1) + (4 *((y /24)-1))
    samplesSax[number].play()
    surround( x,y-3, (0,255,0) )
    saxOffset += 1
    if saxOffset >5 :
        saxOffset = 0
def sampleBass(x,y) :
    number = ((x / 32)-1) + (4 *((y /24)-1))
    samplesBass[number].play()
    surround( x+3,y, (0,0,255) )
def sampleDrum(x,y) :
    number = ((x / 32)-1) + (4 *((y /24)-1))
    samplesDrum[number].play()
    surround(x-3, y, (255,0,0) )

def surround(x, y, col):
    global my_image
    my_image[x-1,y] = col
    my_image[x-1,y+1] = col
    my_image[x-1,y-1] = col
    my_image[x,y+1] = col
    my_image[x,y-1] = col
    my_image[x+1,y] = col
    my_image[x+1,y+1] = col
    my_image[x+1,y-1] = col

if __name__ == '__main__':
    main()
```

The program uses the pygame module to handle the sound samples and starts off by loading them in. This could take a few seconds, so a `print` statement is used just to give the user the confidence that the program hasn't crashed. Each instrument is loaded into its own array. Then the camera is initialized, as are the arrays containing the *x*- and *y*-coordinates of the pixels to monitor.

The main function consists of an infinite loop that grabs an image, examines the target pixels, and calls the functions to trigger the sounds. Note that in this function, there are a number of `print` statements commented out with a hash symbol (#). These will be skipped, but if you want to see the progress of the program, simply remove the # from one or more of these lines.

Reading through the main function, you see that first an image is grabbed, and then each target pixel is surrounded with a black outline. Then each of the target pixels is examined in turn. The pixel values from the image are extracted into the variables red, green, and blue. These variables are then tested to see if they exceed a threshold value. If they do, the appropriate call is made to a function that actually does the triggering. These thresholds were derived from experimentation and have a bearing on the note density of the music. Feel free to play around with these values.

The sample functions take the *x*- and *y*-coordinates of the triggering pixel and turn them into a number from 0 to 15. Then the appropriate sample number is triggered. Also, the triggered pixel is surrounded by the trigger color. If one pixel triggers more than one sound, it will be left surrounded with the last color detected.

The result is that when you run the program, the image returned is such that none of the pixels can trigger the notes. Then when the button is pressed, the LEDs start pulsing and the sounds start being triggered. The degree of change depends on how long it was since you last inverted the lamp. The glitter moves fast at first, but quickly settles down into a slow, steady wandering. If you leave it too long, all the glitter will float to the top and nothing will be triggered. If you have trouble with sound being triggered with no LED illumination, try moving the project out of direct light or arrange some sort of top shade for it.

Playing variations on a theme

Now comes the interesting part: You can make variations on this code that can change the whole project, hopefully for the better. Simply renaming the sound samples, so they're in a different order, can have an effect on the music produced. Try adjusting the threshold values that cause the triggering as well. Then you could define three different arrays of pixels to sample for each instrument, or increase the number of samples for each instrument.

How about triggering a solo mode where the sax plays much longer phrases? Another set of samples could be switched in order to do this. Better yet, why stick with the traditional trio lineup? You can use any sounds you like, from instruments to sound effects to longer phrase loops. Free jazz was never quite so free!

Part IV

Making the Raspberry Pi Your LEGO's Magic Brick

In this part . . .

- ✔ Connect the Raspberry Pi to LEGO MINDSTORMS.
- ✔ Build an infrared handset simulator.
- ✔ Build your own LEGO sensors.
- ✔ Use LEGO sensors and motors directly from the Raspberry Pi.
- ✔ Build an interactive luck-free dice game.

Chapter 13

The Pi Meets LEGO

*L*EGO has been a popular toy since its invention in 1949, but it has never been more popular than it is today. This is due, in part, to the LEGO company's continual development and ability to reinvent itself, just like the toys it makes. LEGO Technic has always been a great way to learn the basics of mechanical engineering, and lately, the MINDSTORMS series of robotic construction has propelled it successfully into the new century. In this part, we look at some of the ways you can enhance the latest MINDSTORMS set, the EV3, by using the Raspberry Pi. In this chapter specifically, we explore how the Raspberry Pi can communicate with the EV3 control brick.

Exploring the MINDSTORMS Range

The LEGO MINDSTORMS EV3 Intelligent Brick is the fourth incarnation of the robot-building concept, and, in keeping with the improvements in technology, it's the most sophisticated yet. Although the mechanical (plastic) parts are compatible with earlier versions, the electronic control brick and the sensors and motors it uses have limited compatibility.

The first system, called LEGO MINDSTORMS Robotics Invention System, was launched in 1999. It was followed by the NXT in 2006 and the NXT 2.0 in 2009. Those two systems differ only in the parts supplied with the sets and the software used on the control bricks. The control bricks themselves are identical. Finally, the EV3 launched in 2013 using a much more powerful processor with more memory and limited compatibility with previous systems.

The EV3 can be used with all the sensors of the NXT system, but nothing of the original Robotics Invention System. These three controllers are shown in Figure 13-1. For the purposes of this book, the original MINDSTORMS brick is obsolete, so we concentrate on the EV3 system.

Programming the control brick has always involved using some sort of graphics-based language, with increasing sophistication through the LEGO generations. The languages are based on the LabView graphical programming language used widely in industry for software-based instrumentation. If you are new to the EV3 system, we suggest that you take time to get familiar with the basic operation of it using the supplied software before exploring the extensions that the Raspberry Pi makes possible.

Hackers have also developed several alternative text-based programming languages for the bricks. However, the EV3 system offers, for the first time, the ability for third-party systems to interact with the control brick instead of overriding or replacing the native brick software. In this chapter, we explore some of the ways you can use your Raspberry Pi with an unmodified EV3 system.

There are four basic ways to access the LEGO MINDSTORMS EV3 Intelligent Brick:

- Wi-Fi
- USB
- Bluetooth
- Infrared (IR)

Figure 13-1: The three generations of LEGO control bricks.

Wi-Fi and USB are interchangeable and are used for downloading programs to the control brick and uploading data from it. Wi-Fi requires the separate purchase of a specific Wi-Fi dongle.

When it comes to interacting with the Raspberry Pi, Bluetooth and IR are the best ways to control or interact with a robot remotely. They allow much more sophisticated programs to be written than would otherwise be possible simply by using the brick's graphical language alone. They also open up the possibility of using hardware attached to the Pi to control the LEGO system.

Up to eight EV3 control bricks can communicate with each other by exchanging messages over Bluetooth. However, this mechanism can also be used to allow the Raspberry Pi to send and receive messages from the EV3 brick. These messages can be programmed to trigger actions or to get data back from the robot's sensors. These messages can be controlled by a program running on the Raspberry Pi; in this chapter, we show you how to use Python to do this.

The EV3 set comes with a small handheld IR remote control that is capable of sending some commands to the IR sensor. The remote control can transmit on four different "channels" and can be picked up by the IR sensor. This is a dual-purpose sensor — it's also capable of detecting the distance to an object by detecting IR reflection off the object. The Raspberry Pi can be made to generate IR messages and send them to the control brick from its own programs.

In the following sections, we cover Bluetooth and IR messages in greater detail.

Bluetooth messages

The EV3's language has a messaging block to send and receive messages. Most of the flow control blocks in the LEGO language can use the reception of a message to trigger the execution of a section of a program. So, it would be very useful if you could send and receive these messages with the Raspberry Pi. You need two things to do this:

- A Bluetooth interface on your Raspberry Pi
- Some knowledge of the message structure in order to make sense of the messages

We cover these requirements in the following sections.

Bluetooth Pi

The simplest way to give your Raspberry Pi Bluetooth capability is to fit it with a Bluetooth USB dongle. It should be fitted directly to one of the Pi's USB sockets and not to a USB hub.

You can get a variety of different types of USB dongles, but the vast majority use really only two chipsets. Unfortunately, only one of these chipsets will work with the Raspberry Pi and, surprisingly, it's the cheaper one! To find a list of the increasingly large range of recommended devices, check out `www. elinux.org/RPi_USB_Bluetooth_adapters`.

To see what type of dongle you have, plug in the dongle, boot up the Raspberry Pi, and log in. From the command line, type the following:

```
lsusb
```

You see a list of devices attached to the USB ports. One of them should read something like this:

```
Cambridge Silicon Radio, Ltd Bluetooth Dongle
```

If yours is a Broadcom or any other manufacturer, try to get a Cambridge one because, as of this writing, the others may not work properly. That said, the Linux software in the Raspberry Pi is constantly evolving, so try what you have first, and if you have trouble, then get a Cambridge chip set.

To get started using your Bluetooth dongle, follow these steps:

1. **Install the necessary software by typing the following from a command line:**

   ```
   sudo apt-get update
   sudo apt-get upgrade
   sudo apt-get install bluetooth bluez-utils blueman
   sudo apt-get install python-serial
   ```

   The first line gets a list of the latest packages, the second line installs them, and the third line installs the Bluetooth-specific applications.

2. **Reboot the system and type** lsusb **again, just to make sure things are working.**

   Occasionally, a dongle won't power up, so check to make sure it's working before you proceed.

3. **Type** startx **to get into the desktop.**

   You should see a Bluetooth icon in the bar at the bottom-right of the screen. If you don't, look for it under the Preferences menu.

4. Click the Bluetooth icon.

The Bluetooth Devices dialog box appears (see Figure 13-2). You may see several unknown devices listed in the dialog box. Don't worry about them — they aren't real, but we haven't found a way of getting rid of them permanently.

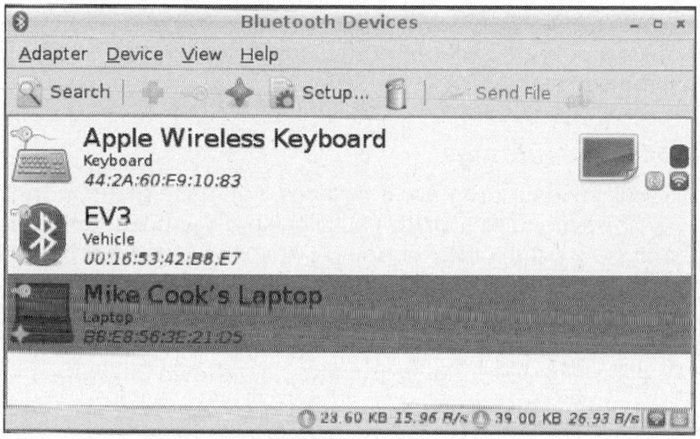

Figure 13-2:
The
Bluetooth
Devices
dialog box.

5. Turn on your EV3 brick and make sure the Bluetooth is enabled and visible.

Don't select the iPhone option. See the instructions that came with the EV3 brick if you don't know how to change the Bluetooth settings.

6. In the Bluetooth Devices dialog box, click Search in the toolbar at the top.

After a short time, the EV3 brick appears.

7. Click the brick to highlight it and then click Setup in the toolbar.

8. Choose the pairing option with a custom pass key, type 1234, and click Continue or Forward.

The LEGO brick makes a sound and asks you to confirm the keys.

9. Select the check box and press the middle button.

The brick and the Raspberry Pi should now be paired. You won't have to do this again.

10. While you're at it, pair up your computer or laptop and Raspberry Pi as well.

It's a very convenient way of swapping files between the two systems.

11. **Right-click the EV3 entry in the Bluetooth Devices dialog box and select Connect to Serial Port.**

You should get the following message:

```
Serial port connected to /dev/rfcomm0
```

This last step has to be done each time you boot up your Pi or when you leave the desktop and return to it.

Now you can treat the Bluetooth dongle just like any other serial port in any programs you write.

The anatomy of a message

Before you can send and receive messages, you have to know the format they use. At the time of this writing, LEGO hasn't published the message specification, so we did a little snooping to see what it was. By looking at the messaging blocks in the EV3 language, you can see that each message box has a name and contents. The contents can be Boolean, text, or a number, so the message must contain both the contents or payload and the message box name. The results of the investigation are shown in Figure 13-3.

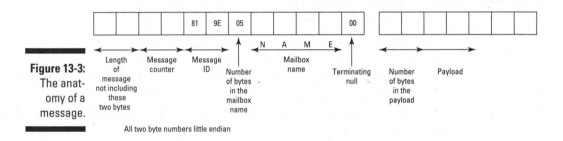

Figure 13-3: The anatomy of a message.

The message starts with two bytes that give the number of bytes in the rest of the message. This, like all other two-byte numbers in this system, are in the *little endian* format, which means that the least significant byte of the two-byte number is first and the most significant byte is second.

If the numbers are arranged the other way round, that's called *big endian*. Much metaphorical blood has been spilled by proponents of the two systems as to which is fundamentally better. We're in the big endian camp ourselves, but there you go.

The next two bytes are a message counter. When the bricks are talking amongst themselves, the message counter doesn't appear to change. The same goes for the next two bytes, the message ID. Then there is a single byte that gives the number of bytes in the mailbox name. The name then follows as a null terminated string. Note that the number of bytes includes the null. Finally, the next two bytes give the number of bytes in the payload, followed by the payload or message itself.

Sending a message

In principle, it's very easy to send a message to the EV3 brick. Just put together a character list that matches the format we just described and then send it character by character to the serial port. Take a look at that in practice with Listing 13-1, which sends four text messages to a mailbox called "Brick."

Listing 13-1:   Composing and Sending a Text Message

```python
#!/usr/bin/env python
# Compose a message for Lego Bluetooth
# and send it - Mike Cook
import serial
import time

EV3 = serial.Serial('/dev/rfcomm0')
print "sending EV3 a Bluetooth message"

def main():
 for t in range(0,4) :
    m = messageG("Brick","See Me "+str(t))
    print "sending :- ", "See Me "+str(t)
    messageSend(m)
    time.sleep(2.0)
 EV3.close()
# end of main

# Function definitions
def messageSend(message):
    if EV3.isOpen() == True :
      for n in range(0, 2 + ord(message[0]) + (ord(message[1]) * 256 )):
        EV3.write(message[n])

def messageG(boxName,message): # generate a text message
    length = len(boxName) + len(message) + 10
    btMessage = [ chr(0) for temp in range (0,length)] # initial blank
    btMessage[2] = chr(1)
    # message ID
    btMessage[4] = chr(0x81)
    btMessage[5] = chr(0x9E)
    btMessage[6] = chr(len(boxName) + 1)
    btMessage[7:7+len(boxName)] = boxName
    payloadPointer = 8 + len(boxName)
    btMessage[payloadPointer] = chr((len(message) + 1) & 0xff)
    btMessage[payloadPointer + 1] = chr((len(message) + 1) >> 8)
```

(continued)

Listing 13-1 *(continued)*

```
        btMessage[payloadPointer + 2:len(message)] = message
        endPoint = payloadPointer + len(message) + 1
        btMessage[0] = chr((endPoint & 0xff))
        btMessage[1] = chr(endPoint >> 8)
        return btMessage
if __name__ == '__main__':
    main()
```

The first thing this code does is open the Bluetooth serial port to the LEGO brick. Then the main function composes four messages reading "See Me" with a number appended. It generates a text message using the messageG function, which first calculates the length of the message and initializes a blank message containing all null characters. Then the message counter is set to 1 and the message ID numbers are set. Then the sixth element in the list is set to the length of the box name plus one (to accommodate the null at the end) and the box name is inserted in the list from the seventh position.

Next, a variable called payloadPointer is calculated to give the position of the last part of the message. This is an intermediate value and makes the calculations that follow a little easer to write down. Then the length of the message string is placed in the two bytes, giving the number of bytes in the payload, and the text is inserted in the message just like the box name was.

Finally, the endpoint of the message is calculated and the first two bytes of the message, giving the overall message length, are set. The complete message is then returned from this function. All that remains to be done is to send the message with the messageSend function, which writes the bytes one by one to the serial port. Note that this function used the first two bytes of the message to see how many bytes to send.

In order to test this, you need to put a simple program on the LEGO brick. This program is shown in Figure 13-4.

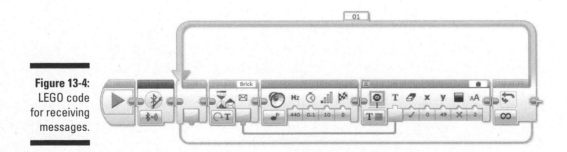

Figure 13-4: LEGO code for receiving messages.

This program first turns on the Bluetooth system. Then, when a message is updated, it makes a brief sound and displays the message. Run the code on the LEGO brick first, followed by the Raspberry Pi python program, and you'll see the message displayed on the LEGO brick.

The payloads for the two types of message are very similar. A logical message has a simple one-byte payload of a zero for False or a one for True. A numeric message is just four bytes that make up a floating point number. Even if the number is an integer, it's always encoded as a floating point number. In order to send these other types of messages, we've written a function to generate them, shown in Listing 13-2. (You won't need these two other types of messages in the project later in this chapter, but if you ever need them, this is how it's done.) This code is very similar to the generate message function messageG in the previous program, but it takes in a text string that determines what sort of message is generated.

Listing 13-2: Function for Generating All Three Message Types

```python
import struct

def messageGuin(boxName,message, messageType): # generate any message
    mType = False
    if messageType == "text" :
        length = len(boxName) + len(message) + 10
        mType = True
    if messageType == "logic" :
        length = len(boxName) + 12
        mType = True
    if messageType == "number" :
        length = len(boxName) + 16
        mType = True
    if mType :  # only go on if message type is valid
        btMessage = [ chr(0) for temp in range (0,length)] # initial blank
        btMessage[2] = chr(1)
        # message ID
        btMessage[4] = chr(0x81)
        btMessage[5] = chr(0x9E)
        btMessage[6] = chr(len(boxName) + 1)
        btMessage[7:7+len(boxName)] = boxName
        payloadPointer = 8 + len(boxName)
        if messageType == "text" :
            btMessage[payloadPointer] = chr((len(message) + 1) & 0xff)
            btMessage[payloadPointer + 1] = chr((len(message) + 1) >> 8)
            btMessage[payloadPointer + 2:len(message)] = message
            endPoint = payloadPointer + len(message) + 1
        if messageType == "logic" :
            btMessage[payloadPointer] = chr(2)
            btMessage[payloadPointer + 1] = chr(0)
```

(continued)

Listing 13-2 *(continued)*

```
        if message == True :
            btMessage[payloadPointer + 2] = chr(1)
        endPoint = payloadPointer + 2
    if messageType == "number" :
        btMessage[payloadPointer] = chr(4)
        btMessage[payloadPointer + 1] = chr(0)
        btMessage[payloadPointer + 2:] = struct.pack('f',message)
        endPoint = payloadPointer + 4

    btMessage[0] = chr((endPoint & 0xff))
    btMessage[1] = chr(endPoint >> 8)
    return btMessage
else :
    print "Message type is not one of text, logic or number"
     return "error"
```

First, the message type is checked and the appropriate length of blank message is generated. Then the function proceeds as before until it comes to generating the payload, where again different payloads are generated depending on the message type. (We go into more detail about these other message types in the next section.)

Receiving a message

Receiving a message is quite simple: You have to read the bytes in from the serial port. The number of bytes you have to read is given in the first two bytes you get. You have to wait until the serial port has at least two bytes in the buffer, read them, and then you know how many more you have to read.

The more complex part is in decoding what you read, which involves splitting up the message into the two pieces of information it contains (known as *parsing*): mailbox name and payload.

One important thing to realize is that you can't tell from looking at the payload what sort of message it is. That means you have to know in advance what sort of message you're expecting. One way to get around this problem is to arrange things so that certain mailbox names always send the same sort of data payload. Assigning mailbox names that match the data names makes this more clear, although it isn't required.

In the next example, we use the mailbox names Text, Logic, and Number to deliver data of the same type as the name. If you look at Figure 13-5, you see the LEGO EV3 code to send three types of messages, one after the other, each having a different data type. You need to run this on your LEGO brick.

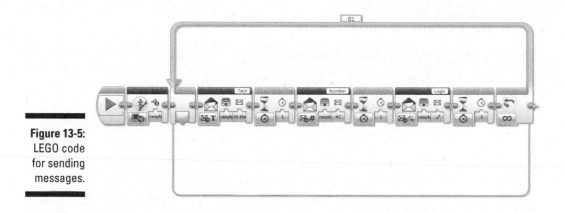

Figure 13-5:
LEGO code
for sending
messages.

Note that you need the computer connected to the brick in order to get the drop-down menu to show the message sender's name. You can't see all of this name on the screen when you make the brick's program.

The messages are continuously sent and the data is the same each time it's sent. In order to receive this on your Raspberry Pi, you need to run the code in Listing 13-3.

Listing 13-3:   Simple Message Receive

```python
#!/usr/bin/env python
# Simple receive of message by Mike Cook
import serial
import time
import struct

EV3 = serial.Serial('/dev/rfcomm0')
EV3.flushInput()
print "Receiving EV3 Bluetooth messages"
box = "Mail Box"

def main():
    while 1:
        rx = readMessage()
        decodeMessage(rx)
    EV3.close()

# Function definitions
def readMessage():
    global box
    while EV3.inWaiting() <2 :# hold until message starts to arrive
      continue
    inMessage = EV3.read(2)
```

(continued)

Listing 13-3 *(continued)*

```python
        messageBytes = ord(inMessage[0]) + ( ord(inMessage[1]) *256 )
        while EV3.inWaiting() < (messageBytes ):
          continue
        inMessage = inMessage + EV3.read(messageBytes )
        box = inMessage[7 : 7 + ord(inMessage[6])-1]
        payloadPointer = 9 + ord(inMessage[6])
        message = inMessage[payloadPointer:]
        return message

def decodeMessage(payload) :
    print "Message from box",box,"is a",
    if box == "Text" :
        print "text message saying",
        print  payload

    if box == "Logic" :
        print "logic message of",
        logic = False
        if ord(payload[0]) == 1 :
            logic = True
        print logic

    if box == "Number" :
        print "number with a value of",
        val = struct.unpack('f',payload)
        value = val[0] # to convert from a tuple
        print value
    print

if __name__ == '__main__':
    main()
```

The `main` function repeatedly reads messages and decodes them. The `readMessage` function reads in the bytes from the serial port and extracts the mailbox name, which is used to set a global variable called `box`. It also extracts the payload and returns it to the calling program. Then the `decodeMessage` function uses the global variable `box` to decide how to decode the payload. It also prints out the mailbox name and value of the payload it received.

The `readMessage` function works just like the reverse of the generate message function we saw in Listing 13-1. Bytes from the message are read into a string called `inMessage`, and then the mailbox's name string and payload string are extracted from that. The `decodeMessage` function then handles the payload string according to its type. A text message is simply printed out, whereas a logic message sets a Boolean variable called `logic`, initially to `False`. If it finds a `one` in the payload string, it changes the variable to `True`.

The numeric message is a little more complex to cope with. As we mention before, it's in a floating point format. In order to convert it into a number, you have to use the `struct` functions. The `struct.unpack` function converts the string given in the second parameter to a number type given in the first parameter. Just to throw a curveball into the mix, this function returns a tuple, even if the string contains only one value. Therefore, the next line extracts a single floating point variable called `value` from the tuple.

If you run this code, you should see the messages being sent back from the LEGO brick. Here's an interesting experiment to do: Change the LEGO code to send not the number 42 but the number 42.1. You may be surprised to see that the number being read back on the Raspberry Pi is not 42.1, but 42.0999984741. This is to be expected. Many beginners are shocked to discover that floating point numbers are only an approximation. This can sometimes be masked by rounding when you print out the number, but it's worth remembering that if you want anything to be absolutely accurate, stick to integer-type variables.

Armed with this information, you can now pass information between the brick and the Raspberry Pi. You can use this to gather data or control what your LEGO creation does. In the next chapter, you see a full-blown application of control using message passing.

Infrared messages

The other way of getting information to the LEGO brick is by using infrared. Unlike the Bluetooth system, however, IR is one-way. That is, you can send messages into the brick, but the brick can't send information out.

The IR sensor can receive key presses generated from the handheld remote that comes as part of the EV3 set. There are five push buttons and one four-position slider. The slider sets the channel it transmits on and has four positions. At the time of this writing, LEGO had not published the protocol for this remote controller, so we had to do a bit of playing around with sensors and an oscilloscope to reveal how it works.

The IR beam is *modulated* (turned on and off rapidly) at a rate of 38 KHz. This is a common frequency for many TV remote control systems, although other frequencies from 32 KHz to 42 KHz are used as well. This modulation allows the amplifier at the receiving end to reject signals that are not modulated and, therefore, not get swamped by interfering IR light from daylight or artificial light. This technique of modulation gives the remote control a good range.

The LEGO system works entirely on bursts of six IR pulses, and the data is encoded by the length of the gap after each burst. For example, all messages begin with a start bit that consists of a burst of six pulses of IR followed by a gap equivalent to 39 pulses. Similarly, a logic one is six pulses followed by a 21-pulse gap, and a logic zero is six pulses followed by a 10-pulse gap. At the end is a stop bit, which is the same as the start bit. If a button is held down, the codes repeat every 80 milliseconds (mS). This is summed up in Figure 13-6.

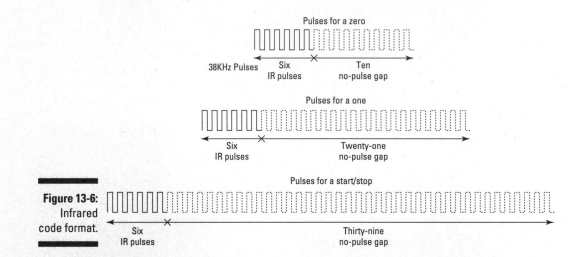

Figure 13-6: Infrared code format.

By using a good oscilloscope, we were able to map what was being produced by each push button. We discovered that changing the channel slider switch changes only a few of the bits in the code being sent. The horizontal bar button on the EV3 remote produced a continuous stream of codes until it was pressed again, whereas each of the other buttons produced one repeating code value when it was pressed and another when it was released. All the release codes were the same for all the buttons in that channel.

Armed with this information, we can duplicate what the remote controller produces directly from the Raspberry Pi, thus allowing programmatic control of the production of the codes. To do this, you need to build a small IR transmitter board and install and customize a software package.

The Raspberry Pi infrared transmitter

Peering into the smoked plastic cover of the EV3 remote controller shows two infrared LEDs offset by about 45 degrees, as well as a small green LED that comes on when it's sending. Infrared LEDs take more current than visible ones, and the forward voltage drop is so low that you can happily power two LEDs in series from 5V.

We designed a simple circuit using one of the general-purpose input/output (GPIO) pins to switch a transistor to allow the LEDs to turn on and off. The schematic is shown in Figure 13-7. When the GPIO pin is low, the transistor is off and no current flows through the LEDs. When the GPIO pin is high, current flows into the base of the transistor, turning it on. This means that current can flow from the collector to the emitter of the transistor, allowing the three LEDs all to turn on.

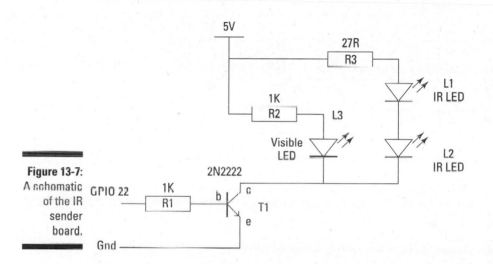

Figure 13-7: A schematic of the IR sender board.

The resistor in series with each LED is important. It limits the current flowing to a safe level. Note that R3, the resistor controlling the IR LEDs, is much smaller than you normally see. This is because IR LEDs can take much more current than visible ones. We made the R2 resistor quite high so the LED is not very bright. Feel free to drop this to 220R if you want the visible LED brighter.

Here are the parts you need for this circuit (the component's reference number shown on the diagrams is in parentheses):

- ✔ Two 1K resistors (R1–R2)
- ✔ One 27R resistor (R3)
- ✔ One 2N2222 transistor or similar NPN transistor (T1)
- ✔ Two 5mm IR LEDs (L1–L2)
- ✔ One 2mm red LED (L3)
- ✔ One 11-x-5-hole stripboard with strips running horizontally

We built this on a small piece of stripboard. The physical construction is shown in Figure 13-8. There are four breaks in the copper strips on the reverse side. Three you can break at a hole, but the fourth should be a break between the holes. You can do this with a scalpel or sharp hobby knife. Make two cuts as close as possible together and then peel the copper away between the cuts.

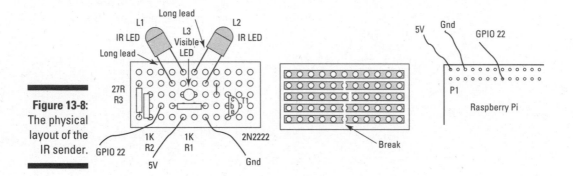

Figure 13-8: The physical layout of the IR sender.

The three wires — 5V, Gnd, and GPIO 22 — were connected to the Raspberry Pi's GPIO plug through individual flying leads with pin header sockets on both ends, although you can use any form of breakout board or connector to make this connection. A photograph of the final board is shown in Figure 13-9.

Figure 13-9: The final IR sender board.

Installing the Linux infrared remote control

Next, you have to install the Linux infrared remote control (LIRC) package that will generate IR codes according to a configuration file. The LIRC has been developed for people who want to control electronic consumer products, but the vast collection of ready-defined protocols didn't include the EV3 brick, so we had to design a custom file. The LIRC package has been designed to both transmit and receive IR communications, but here you're concerned only with sending, so you don't have to bother with the receiving side.

First, you have to get the package onto your machine. This is easily done by typing the following:

```
sudo apt-get install lirc
```

Then when this is installed, you have to add the following two lines to the /etc/modules file:

```
lirc_dev
lirc_rpi gpio_in_pin=23 gpio_out_pin=22
```

Note that you can do this from the desktop if you navigate to the etc directory and choose the Open Window as Root option. Then modify the /etc/lirc/hardware.conf file to read like Listing 13-4.

Listing 13-4:   The Contents of /etc/lirc/hardware.conf

```
# /etc/lirc/hardware.conf
#
# Arguments which will be used when launching lircd
LIRCD_ARGS="--uinput"

#Don't start lircmd even if there seems to be a good config file
#START_LIRCMD=false

#Don't start irexec, even if a good config file seems to exist.
#START_IREXEC=false

#Try to load appropriate kernel modules
LOAD_MODULES=true

# Run "lircd --driver=help" for a list of supported drivers.
DRIVER="default"
# usually /dev/lirc0 is the correct setting for systems using udev
DEVICE="/dev/lirc0"
MODULES="lirc_rpi"

# Default configuration files for your hardware if any
LIRCD_CONF=""
LIRCMD_CONF=""
```

Finally, you have to change the /etc/lirc/lircd.conf to be like Listing 13-5.

Listing 13-5:   The Contents of /etc/lirc/lircd.conf

```
begin remote

  name  Lego_EV3
  bits            16
  flags SPACE_ENC
  eps            30
  aeps          100
# see text for note on frequency
  frequency 38000

  header        158   1026
  one           158   552
  zero          158   263
  ptrail        158
  gap          1206

      begin codes
# EV3 remote codes
          beacon1       0x4006
          beacon2       0x5004
          beacon3       0x6002
          beacon4       0x7000
          release1      0x010E
          key1c1        0x8117
          key2c1        0x8124
          key3c1        0x8142
          key4c1        0x818E
          release2      0x110F
          key1c2        0x9116
          key2c2        0x9125
          key3c2        0x9143
          key4c2        0x918F
          release3      0x210C
          key1c3        0xA115
          key2c3        0xA126
          key3c3        0xA140
          key4c3        0xA18C
          release4      0x310D
          key1c4        0xB114
          key2c4        0xB127
          key3c4        0xB141
          key4c4        0xB18D
      end codes

end remote
```

This last file controls the code and the format of the IR being sent. There are lots of other ways of using IR to send messages, and LIRC can cope with most of them. The first part defines the sort of code to produce with a flag saying that it's *space encoded* (that is, the space after the burst of pulses defines what the data will be). The header, one, and zero are the format of the data, with the time being defined in terms of microseconds. So, a one is a 158 uS burst of IR followed by 552uS of gap, or nothing. This relates to the number of pulses in the data format.

To get LIRC to accept the new control codes in this file, type the following in at the command line:

```
sudo /etc/init.d/lirc stop
sudo /etc/init.d/lirc start
```

The frequency of the modulation is defined in the file, but when we tried it, we got a frequency of 45.2 KHz despite setting it to 38 KHz. We had to put in a frequency of 32,000 in order to get the 38 KHz out. It turns out that there was an issue in the kernel on the Raspberry Pi, and it caused the timing to be wrong. However, it was corrected at about the same time we found the trouble. To check what version of kernel you have, type the following at the command line:

```
uname -rv
```

If the answer is any earlier than

```
3.12.18+ #677 PREEMPT Mon Apr 28 22:45:00 BST 2014
```

you should update your kernel by typing the following and checking again:

```
sudo apt-get update
sudo rpi-update
```

The error in the kernel affects not only the frequency but also the accuracy of the gaps. However, the transmitter still seemed to work with the uncorrected gaps.

The names we gave to each key are based on the number that is detected by the EV3 brick. So, key1c3 is short for key 1 on channel 3. The code for a key release is the word *release* followed by the channel number, and the four beacon modes are defined by the word *beacon* followed by the channel number. Feel free to change these names if something else makes more sense to you. For example, the release key is detected as zero in the LEGO brick, so you might want to label those keys K0c. Similarly, the beacon message is seen as the key 9 by the brick. However, you might want to label the keys after the keys on the remote like redTop, blueBottom, and so on.

Driving the infrared codes

IR codes are produced from the command line, so if you want to use these codes from some language, you should do it by calling the operating system. A simple example of this is shown in Listing 13-6. This simply sends out a beacon signal on channel 4.

Listing 13-6:   Infrared Beacon

```
#!/usr/bin/env python
'''
Sending IR Beacon message - by Mike Cook
'''
import time
import os

print "Sending Beacon message"
while 1 :
    os.system("irsend SEND_ONCE Lego_EV3 beacon4")
    time.sleep(0.08) # time between repeats
```

You see that the os.system call takes a string with the irsend parameters in it. Don't be tempted to use the send continuous commands — they don't work by simply repeating the command as you may expect. Instead, substitute other repeat codes in place of the commands.

In order to test this, you need a very simple LEGO model, as shown in Figure 13-10. This is basically just the IR sensor mounted on a motor. If you put into the brick the program shown in Figure 13-11, the sensor turns to face the emitter board. It's quite an eerie sensation — it feels like the robot is alive. Test out this model using the supplied IR remote if you have any trouble.

If that goes well, you can test out the other keys with the code in Listing 13-7, which simply cycles through the key presses. Note that it shows how you can change what the program sends by building up a command string.

The key names are held in a list called button, and the channel to use is held in a variable called ch. These two strings are concatenated to a fixed string to make up the command. To see this on the brick, put the program in Figure 13-12 into the LEGO controller.

Now it's time to do something fun with this setup.

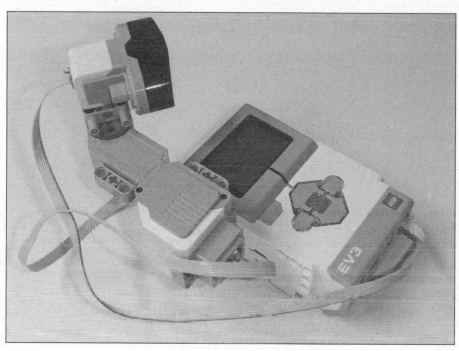

Figure 13-10:
The LEGO
model for
the tracker.

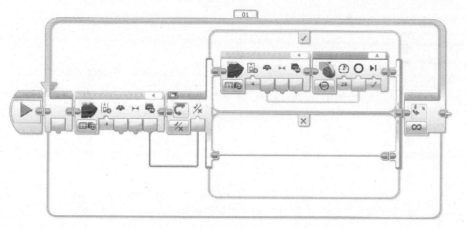

Figure 13-11:
The LEGO
program for
the tracker.

Listing 13-7: Key Test Program

```python
#!/usr/bin/env python
'''
IR test IR2
testing config file at
/etc/lirc/lircd.conf
Tests buttons
'''

import time
import os

os.system("sudo /etc/init.d/lirc stop")
os.system("sudo /etc/init.d/lirc start")

ch = "c3" # channel
button = [ "key1", "key2"; "key3", "key4"]
while 1 :
    for b in range(0,4) :
        os.system("irsend SEND_ONCE Lego_EV3 " +button[b]+ch)
        print"sent ",button[b]+ch
        time.sleep(0.8)
        os.system("irsend SEND_ONCE Lego_EV3 release"+ch)
        time.sleep(1.5)
```

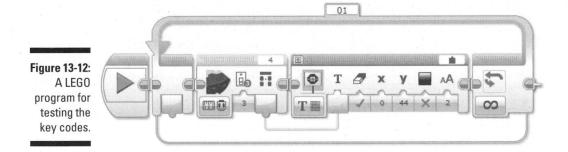

Figure 13-12:
A LEGO
program for
testing the
key codes.

Creating a Tug-of-War LEGO Robot

The Tug-of-War LEGO Robot is a fun way to incorporate a program on the Raspberry Pi with action on a LEGO system. Basically, it's a two-player reaction game, with the score being kept by a LEGO robot.

Here's how it works: The robot is placed on top of a long thin box on a line drawn halfway across. The Raspberry Pi puts up the word *Ready* on the screen. After a random interval, this changes to *Go* and a noise is generated. The first player to react by pressing a keyboard key wins, and the LEGO robot moves a small distance in the losing player's direction. If a player presses a key before the sound, he has jumped the gun and the other player gets the robot to move for her. Eventually, the robot falls off the box and indicates the winner. (The box should be only a few inches high to prevent any damage to the robot. If you aren't willing to risk any sort of a fall for your robot, you can just tape a winning line on a table and place the robot on that instead.)

We leave it up to you which robot to use. There are plenty of simple two-motor robots you can build. If you're stuck for a design, use the TRACK3R robot from your computer's LEGO software. The box to click is called EV3 Getting Started, and it's located at the bottom right of the main page. There is no need to add all the tools — you just want the basic movement.

All that is required of the robot is that it be able to move in a straight line backward and forward in response to the IR remote key press. Then program it with the very simple program shown in Figure 13-13.

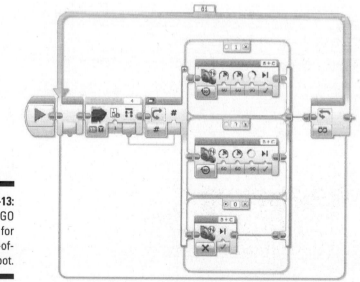

Figure 13-13:
The LEGO program for the Tug-of-War Robot.

You can change how far the robot moves in response to each key press very easily by changing the number of degrees of movement. This affects the length of time a game runs and depends on the physical size of the space you have to run it in. You can also build in a handicap system by making the robot move more in one direction than the other. This is useful in a kids-versus-adults situation.

We put an extra condition to stop the motors when the release key was detected. This shouldn't have been necessary, but we found that, without it, the motors sometimes hunted a little (made continuous small movements left and right) when they were supposed to have stopped. Test it out with the handheld remote before going on to controlling it with the Raspberry Pi.

Next, you have to program the Raspberry Pi to play the game and control the robot. Before you start, you have to make sure you have a directory called `sounds` in the same directory as this code, and that it contains an .ogg sound file called `gun`. Despite the name, the file can be any short, sharp sound. The code to play the game is shown in Listing 13-8 and is written in Python with Pygame.

Listing 13-8:   The Tug-of-War Raspberry Pi Code

```python
#!/usr/bin/env python
'''
 Lego-powered Tug-of-War
 Reaction Time Game By Mike Cook
'''
import time
import random
import os, pygame, sys

pygame.init()                       # initialize graphics interface
pygame.mixer.quit()
pygame.mixer.init(frequency=22050, size=-16, channels=2, buffer=512)
goSound = pygame.mixer.Sound("sounds/gun.ogg")

os.environ['SDL_VIDEO_WINDOW_POS'] = 'center'
pygame.display.set_caption("Lego Tug of War Reaction Game")
pygame.event.set_allowed(None)
pygame.event.set_allowed([pygame.KEYDOWN,pygame.QUIT])
cBackground =(0,255,255)
cText = (255,0,0)
textHeight = 38
font = pygame.font.Font(None, textHeight)

screenWidth = 350
screenHeight = 160
screen = pygame.display.set_mode([screenWidth,screenHeight],0)
```

```
random.seed()
player1 = False # keyboard inputs
player2 = False
space = False

def main():
    global player1, player2, screen
    print "Tug of War"
    draw_screen()
    while True : # play the game
        updateWords("            ")
        while space == False :
          checkForEvent()
        updateWords("Ready")
        player1 = False
        player2 = False
        go = time.time() + 1.5 + ( random.random() * 5 )
        while go > time.time() :
            checkForEvent()
        # check for jump the gun
        if player1 == True or player2 == True :
            player1 = not(player1)
            player2 = not(player2)
            updateWords("Jumped the gun")
            time.sleep(2)
        else :
            updateWords("Go")
            goSound.play()
        while player1 == False and player2 == False and space == True:
          checkForEvent()
        if space == True :
          if player1 == True :
            updateWords("Player 1 wins")
            winner = "key1c1"
          else :
            updateWords("Player 2 wins")
            winner = "key2c1"
          os.system("irsend SEND_ONCE Lego EV3 "+winner)
          time.sleep(0.08)
          os.system("irsend SEND_ONCE Lego_EV3 release1")
          time.sleep(2.0)
          checkForEvent() # remove losing player's key
        else :
            updateWords("Game ends")
            time.sleep(2)

def draw_screen():
    screen.fill(cBackground) # blank screen
    drawWords("Q - Player 1",10,2)
```

(continued)

Listing 13-8 *(continued)*

```python
        drawWords("P - Player 2",10,30)
        drawWords("Space - New Game",10,60)
        updateWords("Ready")

def updateWords(words) :
        pygame.draw.rect(screen,cBackground, (0,100,screenWidth,textHeight), 0)
        drawWords(words,120,100)
        pygame.display.update()

def drawWords(words,x,y) :
        textSurface = pygame.Surface((len(words) * (textHeight / 2),textHeight))
        textRect = textSurface.get_rect()
        textRect.left = x
        textRect.top = y
        pygame.draw.rect(screen,cBackground, (x,y,len(words) * (textHeight
                    /2),textHeight), 0)
        textSurface = font.render(words, True, cText, cBackground )
        screen.blit(textSurface, textRect)

#pygame house keeping
def terminate(): # close down the program
        print "Closing down please wait"
        pygame.quit() # close pygame
        sys.exit()

def checkForEvent(): # see if we need to quit
        global player1, player2, space
        event = pygame.event.poll()
        if event.type == pygame.KEYDOWN :
            if event.key == pygame.K_q :
                player1 = True
            if event.key == pygame.K_p :
                player2 = True
            if event.key == pygame.K_SPACE :
                space = not(space)
        if event.type == pygame.QUIT :
            terminate()

if __name__ == '__main__':
    main()
```

The `main` function is where all the action is, with the other functions supplying support. Keyboard presses generate Pygame events, and there are three you're looking for here. The two players' reaction keys — P and Q — are placed at opposite ends of the keyboard for maximum separation, and the spacebar is for stopping and starting the game. Before looking at the `main` function, take a quick look around at the others.

The `draw_screen`, `drawWords`, and `updateWords` functions are all concerned with writing text into the Pygame window. The `checkForEvent` function sets logic variables whenever one of the target keys is pressed and monitors for a click in the close box of the window. If one is detected, the `terminate` function is called and the program ends.

The `main` function is basically one big loop that starts by blanking out any message from any previous game and then pauses until the spacebar is pressed. This controls whether a round of the game will be played. If it is, the window displays the word *Ready* and the players ready themselves to be the first to react. The heart of the game is the following line:

```
go = time.time() + 1.5 + ( random.random() * 5 )
```

This sets up a random delay for a minimum of 1.5 seconds and a maximum of 6.5 seconds into the future. The `random.random` function returns a floating point value so the time isn't restricted to whole numbers of seconds. If you want to change the range of the delays, change the number 5 to something bigger or smaller.

A `while` loop holds until this time has expired, checking all the time that no player has pressed early. If a player has pressed early, the other player is declared the winner. Otherwise, the word *Go* appears on the screen and the sound is generated. When the first player to react is detected, a message saying who has won is placed in the window and the IR signal is sent to move the LEGO robot. The losing player probably also reacted, so another call to `checkForEvent` is made to remove that key from the events buffer. If it isn't removed, the losing player will be accused of jumping the gun in the next round.

Going on from Here

You can do plenty more with this game if you want! For a start, there is a small bug that shows itself if both players jump the gun: The first to do so is declared the winner. You could conclude that the second player deserves to lose, or you could change that situation to one you prefer.

Another change you may like to make is to add more sounds to the game, like cheers and applause to mark one player winning. Or you may want to keep track of how many rounds one player has won over the other and declare a winner in the program's window instead of having the robot fall off a box. You could even make the robot do something when one player has won, like perform a victory dance or fire off a red or blue ball, depending on who has won.

You can do many other things with the IR message capability. When the Raspberry Pi can command the IR control, you have many exciting possibilities. For example, how about making a joystick input on the GPIO pins of the Pi and having that control the IR keys? Or why not make a graphics console where you have access to all the keys on all the channels on one screen? You can even write a sequencer so you can send the IR commands in a long but repeating sequence.

In the next chapter, we look at incorporating what we know about Bluetooth messages to create a unique project.

Chapter 14

The LEGO Dice Game

*T*his project plays a rather unusual dice game — unusual because it involves skill, not luck. Players take turns trying to reduce a heap to exactly nothing. The number removed from the heap each turn is indicated by turning a dice with the required number on the top face. Now, here's the rub: You can't use the same number as the previous player, nor can you use the number that the previous player had on the bottom face. The game as described here pits you against the computer, and by the power of LEGO, the computer can actually place the dice with its turn number uppermost. Confused? Don't worry — we explain the game to you in detail in this chapter.

Introducing the Dice Game

We first saw the dice game described in Ian Stewart's book *The Cow Maze*. It's one of the few games that involve dice but no element of luck. In this game, the top number on the dice is used to indicate by how much a target number (or *heap* as we call it) should be reduced. The winner is the first to reduce the heap to exactly zero or get the opponent to overshoot zero. What makes this a game of skill is that, on any turn, the only numbers you *can't* use are the number already shown on the top of the dice and the number on the bottom side of the dice. This restriction is what makes the game interesting.

The game is a two-player game and can be played quite simply by two players, but in order to computerize the game, there are two major problems to overcome:

- ✔ We need to get the computer to be able to sense which way up the dice is placed.
- ✔ More difficult, we need to get the computer to place the dice in the right position to indicate its own move.

This project has a rather novel way of solving both problems.

A dice has some interesting properties, and one of the more useful of these is that opposite sides of a dice always add up to a total of 7. That's the vital piece of information you need to know in order to write a program for the computer to be able to identify the complete orientation of the dice. In the LEGO EV3, there is a color sensor that is capable of identifying seven different colors, as well as no color at all. This is one more color than we actually need.

The playing mechanism is a bit more problematic. It needs to be able to turn a dice through 90 degrees. Most robot arms don't have the degrees of freedom to do this, so we had to come up with another solution. Instead of lifting up the device, rotate it and then place it down. This solution throws the dice but in such a way that we can control exactly what the top face will be. The whole machine is shown in Figure 14-1.

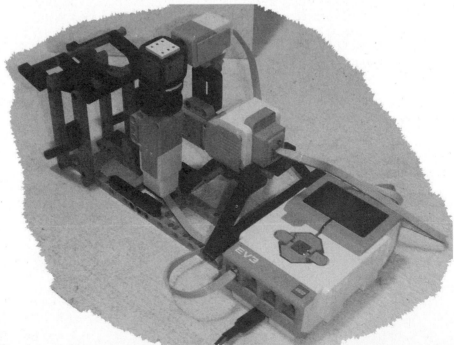

Figure 14-1:
The dice
game
machine.

By working through the elements one at a time, you can make your own dice game and even be able to beat it, while the game seems to be unbeatable to all other players.

Understanding the Game Theory

This sort of game is known as a *solved game.* Given any starting position and perfect play, a winner can be determined without actually playing the game. In the case of the dice game, for any given size of heap, with any dice facing uppermost, the current player is guaranteed to win or lose if he plays the game correctly. Of course, it's easy to lose and a bit harder to win, but the point is that the outcome of the game is fixed given this information.

The combination of heap size and top dice number determines if the next player can win. If he can, this is known as a *winning position,* and as long as he makes the right moves, there is nothing an opponent can do to stop him from winning. If the current heap size and top dice number indicate a losing position, there is nothing a player can do to convert this into a winning position, except by his opponent making a mistake and deviating from perfect play.

Many games fall in this class. Examples include tic-tac-toe (called noughts and crosses in the UK), checkers (called draughts in the UK), four in a row, and nim, to name but a few.

The winning strategy for the dice game is formed by a complete analysis of the game from every starting position and heap number. This may sound like a daunting task, but it's easy to build a table showing these results. For example, if the heap is 1 and the current top dice number is 1 or 6, then this is a losing position and any valid move must overshoot zero. However, if the heap is 1 and the top dice is any other number but 1 and 6, the next player can choose a value of 1 and win. This is a winning position. If, on the other hand, the dice has 1 or 6 uppermost, the only move left to the next player will force an overshoot of zero and, therefore, he has lost. This is a losing position.

You can apply the same analysis for a heap of 2. For any combination of dice positions, you find that all positions are winning by playing either a 2 to win directly or, if a 2 is not available, playing a 1 will force the next player into overshooting and thus losing. When you extend this to 7, you get a table of moves shown in Table 14-1, which shows the size of the heap in each column against the current dice top number in each row. The body of the table shows the move. An L indicates that you're in a losing position and it doesn't matter what you play; otherwise, it shows the number to play (that is, the dice number to turn to the top) in order to win or maintain a winning position. In some places, more than one number is shown; this means you can play any of these numbers and still be in a winning position. Notice that it doesn't matter which way the dice is up because each line indicates two opposite sides of the dice.

Table 14-1	Analysis of the Moves for a Heap of 1 to 7						
Heap Size **Dice Up**	**1**	**2**	**3**	**4**	**5**	**6**	**7**
1 or 6	L	2	3	4	5	3	2, 3, 4
2 or 5	1	1	3	4	L	3, 6	3, 4, 6
3 or 4	1	1, 2	L	L	5	6	2, 6

All well and good, but the heap can be any number you like so this playing matrix must be extended. The next stage is to extend the table to heap sizes up to 16, as shown in Table 14-2.

Table 14-2	Analysis of the Moves for a Heap of 8 to 16								
Heap Size **Dice Up**	**8**	**9**	**10**	**11**	**12**	**13**	**14**	**15**	**16**
1 or 6	4	L	5	2, 3	3, 4	4	5	3	2, 3, 4
2 or 5	4	L	1	3	3, 4	4	L	3, 6	3, 4
3 or 4	L	L	1, 5	2	L	L	5	6	2

Table 14-2, along with Table 14-1, shows what to play for any position of the dice for a heap from 1 to 16. Note how a heap size of 9 is a losing position no matter what the state of the dice is. Now something very interesting happens if we extend this analysis for the next nine heap sizes, shown in Table 14-3.

Table 14-3	Analysis of the Moves for a Heap of 17 to 25								
Heap Size **Dice Up**	**17**	**18**	**19**	**20**	**21**	**22**	**23**	**24**	**25**
1 or 6	4	L	5	2, 3	3, 4	4	5	3	2, 3, 4
2 or 5	4	L	1	3	3, 4	4	L	3, 6	3, 4
3 or 4	L	L	1, 5	2	L	L	5	6	2

You see that this playing matrix is exactly the same as Table 14-2. When you get a repeat pattern like this, you know it has to keep on repeating forever, for every successive 9 increases in the heap size.

Why is this important? Well, given any heap size and current dice position, you can repeatedly subtract 9 from the heap until you get into the range of 16 or less and then, if you can memorize the matrix, you know what to play. It gives a surprisingly small number of moves to memorize given the apparent complexity of the game, and you can cut this down even further by memorizing only one number when you have the choice of two or three numbers. This repeat also makes it much easer to implement the playing matrix for programming into the computer.

So, analysis of this game reveals a playing strategy that is not obvious or simplistic, but also is not very complex either.

Detecting Dice

In this section, we look at the detection of the dice state. There are a few ways to do this, but the way we chose to do it is to use the EV3's color detector. Each color returns a number. To make things simple, we used the color numbers 1 to 6 to represent the dice numbers 1 to 6. The sensor also returns a zero if nothing is in front of the sensor. Figure 14-2 shows how the dice numbers relate to the colors, as well as the LEGO part numbers for the tiles and dice body.

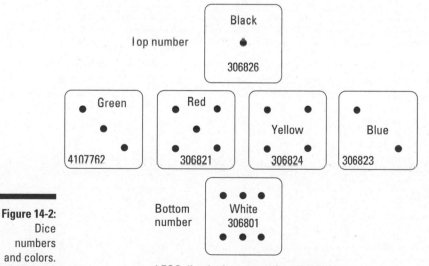

Figure 14-2:
Dice
numbers
and colors.

The color sensor is positioned so that it can detect one of the dice sides. If we know one side of the dice, we can calculate the other side because opposite sides add up to 7. The dice is positioned on a rotating table. If it's rotated by 90 degrees clockwise, we can find two more dice sides. This is all the information we need in order to calculate the numbers on the top and bottom of the dice. Figure 14-3 shows a table of the clockwise sequence of the side dice numbers for each top number.

Top number   Clockwise side sequence

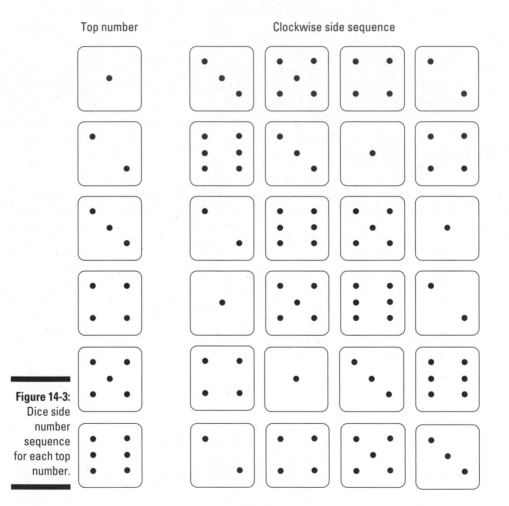

Figure 14-3: Dice side number sequence for each top number.

Note that complementary numbers — that is, dice numbers that add up to 7 — or, in other words, opposite sides of the dice, are simply the reverse sequence. So, given two side numbers, we can use this information in a lookup table to find the top number. This is illustrated in the simple Python program shown in Listing 14-1.

Listing 14-1:   Finding a Top Dice Number

```
#!/usr/bin/env python
# Look up dice orientation - By Mike Cook
                                # side sequence
diceLookup = [ [ 3, 5, 4, 2, 3],   # for 1 on top
               [ 6, 3, 1, 4, 6],   # for 2 on top
               [ 2, 6, 5, 1, 2],   # for 3 on top
               [ 1, 5, 6, 2, 1],   # for 4 on top
               [ 4, 1, 3, 6, 4],   # for 5 on top
               [ 2, 4, 5, 3, 2] ] # for 6 on top

print "Find top number by two side values"
while True :
  first = input('first number ')
  second = input('second number ')
  top = -1
  topTry = 0
  while top == -1 and topTry < 6:
    for n in range(0, 4):
       if diceLookup[topTry][n] == first and diceLookup[topTry][n+1]
           == second :
           top = topTry + 1
    topTry += 1
  if top == -1 :
    print "numbers are not in clockwise sequence"
  else :
    print 'top of dice is ',top
```

This code uses a list of lists, or two-dimensional array, to hold the sequence, but notice how the last number in the list is the same as the first. This makes the code easy by taking care of any wraparound when searching the list. Given two numbers entered from the keyboard, the list is searched until the two numbers are found next to each other in the list. When these two numbers are found, the row they're found on gives you the top number of the dice. The rows are numbered for 0 to 5 and the dice is numbered 1 to 6 so, in fact, the real top number is the row number plus one.

Looking at the Playing Mechanism

In this section, we take a look at the dice-playing mechanism. The aim is to place the dice with a new number on the top, a number that is the "right" one according to the playing matrix. Now, the rules of the game preclude the use of the current top or bottom number, so the mechanism only has to flip the dice over on its side. The dice is on a rotating platform anyway, so that can be used to move the dice into the throwing position and a motor can then flick it off onto a static platform. If you get this landing platform right, the dice will move only 90 degrees and not roll over any more.

The dice

The dice is the key to making the game. LEGO used to produce a whole series of games that involved a dice. This series was discontinued in 2013 but is still available from many outlets, as well as on popular auction sites. One of the cheaper games, Magikus, provides an ideal dice along with the colored tiles for the sides. You can also get the dice and colored tiles from online auction sites, but we found a discount game that was cheaper than buying the separate parts. The only snag is that the colored tiles don't have the dot markings found on dice.

To rectify this, we used a 3mm drill to mark the sides with dots by just drilling the point of the bit in about 1mm. Then we used black paint to fill the holes — all except the black tile, where we used white paint. This made it easy for a human to see the dice number but didn't interfere with the color sensor's output. Rather than use a fine brush, we used a solid wire from a resistor to transfer a drop of paint into the recess left by the drill.

We found it convenient to clamp two blocks to the drill press so that the drill was just 3mm in from the corner. Then each tile that needed a dot in the corner was placed between the blocks, drilled, rotated, and drilled again. In that way, all the corner dots could be drilled consistently. Then the blocks were adjusted so that the "center side" dots could be drilled; finally, the center dots were drilled. This arrangement, along with the dice side measurements, is shown in Figure 14-4; a photograph of the finished dice is shown in Figure 14-5.

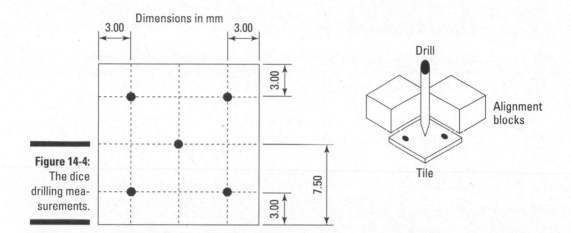

Dimensions in mm

Figure 14-4:
The dice drilling measurements.

Figure 14-5:
The finished dice.

The mechanism

All the parts for the rest of the mechanism can be found in the LEGO MINDSTORMS EV3 set. The best way of documenting a LEGO model is with step-by-step build instructions, but there are two problems with this:

- ✔ It will take up many more pages than this chapter has room for.
- ✔ Creating these instructions isn't easy.

There is a free, official LEGO application called LEGO Digital Designer (LDD) that allows you to make 3D interactive LEGO models. Once complete, LDD can produce a construction sequence. The big snag with this approach is that, although it works for a lot of models, technic beams, especially when tilted, can be almost impossible to construct. The tolerances in the software are much tighter than the hardware, so some models are impossible to construct virtually. Also, sometimes the rotation tools simply don't work or rotate around a wholly unexpected axis.

The construction of the dice-playing mechanism is shown in the digital designer model as three separate parts, but they all fit together like the photograph in Figure 14-1. Go to www.dummies.com/go/raspberrypiprojects to download the digital model and generate your own step-by-step instructions. Note that there is the odd connecting peg that doesn't fit in the model, but these pegs are in the file and it's quite obvious where they should go.

One important aspect of the design is the dice landing platform. We tried many designs of this until we got it right. We found that the platform couldn't be horizontal because it gave too much roll to the dice and the dice ended up being flipped more than 90 degrees. By angling the platform, it reduced the tendency of the dice to roll, and the retaining bar at the top of the platform stops the dice from rolling any more than is required. This produces an almost perfect throw, but very, very occasionally the dice ends up in the wrong orientation or bouncing off the platform altogether. Fortunately, for the purposes of the game, there is a graphical representation of the dice on the screen, which is always the last word in what the computer's move should be.

One problem with the cables that connect the EV3 devices to the control block is that they're pretty stiff. This could be an issue with the medium motor that has to be moved by the large motor to flick the dice. We replaced this with a flexible ribbon cable connector, as described in Chapter 13. Alternatively, we found that by lifting the robot and platform off the table a bit higher, the throwing arm cable didn't snag.

We tried putting some alignment strips on the rotating table to get the dice into exactly the right position, but in the end it only interfered with the angle at which the dice slipped off the table and changed the flipping characteristics. So, your best bet is to place the dice as square on as you can to the sensor. We've found this isn't too critical in practice.

Writing the Code

The code for this project is in two parts: One part runs on the LEGO brick, and its job is to report back the sensor readings and control the motors according to messages sent to it by the Raspberry Pi. It's the code on the Raspberry Pi that controls the playing of the game and responds to the moves a player makes and decides what move the computer should make. It also keeps track of the score so it knows when a game is over. Finally, this code generates a graphic representation of both the current state of the dice and the heap.

The EV3 code

The code that goes into the EV3 brick can be downloaded from www.dummies.com/go/raspberrypiprojects, but it's also shown in Figure 14-6. Basically, it's a large loop that receives a message from the Raspberry Pi via Bluetooth and displays that message on the screen. Then a switch block is used to perform the appropriate actions and a message is sent back to the Raspberry Pi with either some data or text saying the action has been performed.

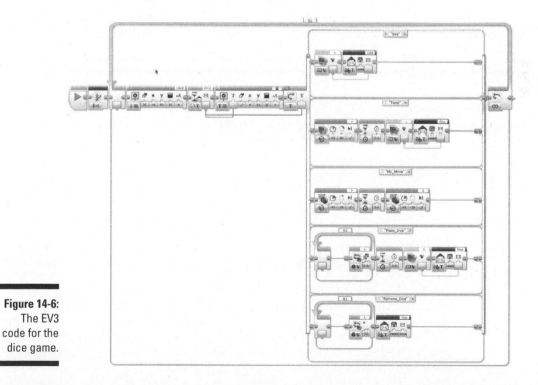

Figure 14-6:
The EV3
code for the
dice game.

The commands are relatively simple but still a bit more complex than they could be in order to minimize the communications between the Raspberry Pi and the control brick. Instead of continually asking the control brick to report what the color the sensor sees, and the Raspberry Pi making the decision of whether the dice has been replaced or removed, the brick waits and only sends a message back when the dice is in place or has been removed.

We found that the command names shouldn't have spaces in them in order to operate the switch block correctly. This technique proved to be very successful.

Following are descriptions of all the commands. Note that these are all implemented as text messages for simplicity:

- ✔ **See:** Simply reports the color seen by the color sensor and returns it immediately.

- ✔ **Twist:** Rotates the dice platform clockwise by 90 degrees, so that another side of the dice faces the color sensor. Sends back a message indicating the color of that new side.

- ✔ **Place_Dice:** Waits until the dice is placed on the platform and then returns a message showing the color reported by the color sensor.

- ✔ **Remove_Dice:** Waits until the dice has been removed (as determined by the color sensor reading 0) and then sends a fixed text message saying "Gone."

- ✔ **My_Move:** Triggers the throwing of the dice onto the landing platform. This command is the only one that does not return a message.

The Raspberry Pi code

The job of the code in the Raspberry Pi is to actually play the game and give commands to the LEGO in order for it to read a player's move and make the computer's move. It draws a graphical representation of the dice reconstructed from the information given by the color sensor. It also displays the heap number and graphically depicts it by drawing stacks of coins, with the same number of coins as the heap size. This software keeps track of the player's move and works out the computer's response. Finally, it adds some sound effects to the game.

At the start of the game, you're asked to remove the dice from the sensor if it's already on and replace it at the starting position. The computer then generates a heap number based on this starting position. It generates a heap with a value that is a winning position for you. This means if you play the perfect game, you'll win; otherwise, the first deviation from this perfect game that you make will mean the computer will win.

Resources

Before you begin, you need some sound and graphics resources. These are stored in directories called `sounds` and `images` at the same directory level as the game code. For the sounds, you need the following files:

- ✔ `laugh.ogg`: Sound effect when the computer wins
- ✔ `applause.ogg`: Sound effect when you win
- ✔ `ching.ogg`: Sound effect when the heap is drawn

The graphics files are a bit more complex. First, you need the image of a coin taken at an oblique angle. We photographed a euro 20-cent piece and used a graphics package to make the surroundings transparent. Then you need the component parts to make up the image of the dice. We made an isometric drawing of the top of the dice and its right-hand side, for each number; we also gave these sides the actual color of the LEGO dice tiles, so the drawn representation matches closely the real dice. There is no need to have files for the left-hand side of the dice because you can reuse the right-hand side drawing simply by flipping the image horizontally when it's drawn by the software.

The best way to create these dice components is to use a vector drawing package, like Inkscape, and first draw a cube. Then draw grid lines on it and make a copy of the top and side. Populate all nine locations of the dice dots and remove the grid lines. Then copy these two elements six times each, and delete the dots on each piece until you have the appropriate number pattern showing. Then apply a flood fill of the matching color. Note that you also need a dice graphic where the faces are unknown, for the start of the game; we used texture patterns for this, but you could draw one with question marks on each side. You need to use a PNG file format for these dice elements because you need to make the background transparent. This can be done with an online image editor such as `www.online-image-editor.com` or any other graphics editor with these capabilities.

These parts are shown in Figure 14-7. Then we saved them individually from the drawing package as PNG files and used an image editor to make the backgrounds transparent. The images for the top of the dice should be called `t0.png` to `t6.png` with the zero being the unknown top. Likewise the side images should be called `s0.png` to `s6.png`. We made the dice tops 148 x 148 pixels and the disc sides 100 x 162 pixels, but the size isn't critical. Also, the coins were 90 x 44 pixels in size. If you don't want to do this, all the graphics and sound files are available for download from `www.dummies.com/go/raspberrypiprojects`.

The code is written in Python and uses the Pygame extension library. Instead of presenting it as one big lump of code, we'll present it as a series of functions. You should type these into the same file using your favorite Python editor (we used IDLE). The listings should be assembled into the final file by typing each listing in front of the previous listing, so we're starting with the bottom of the file and working up.

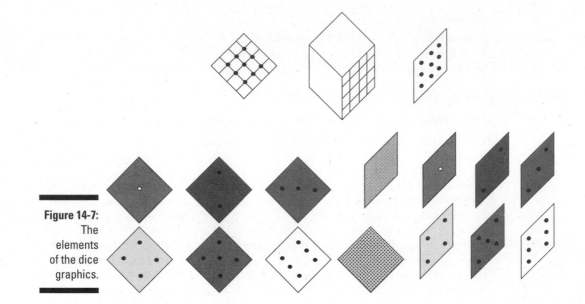

Figure 14-7:
The
elements
of the dice
graphics.

The purpose of this code is to produce a graphics-based interface to the game, as shown in Figure 14-8. The program draws the representation of the current size of the heap and draws the current state of the dice as understood by the program. In the very odd occasion when the computer's turn is not executed correctly, the graphics of the intended move should always be taken as the correct move.

So, let's start writing the code by looking at some basic housekeeping functions required by Pygame, shown in Listing 14-2.

Listing 14-2: Dice Game: Housekeeping Functions

```
#pygame housekeeping
def terminate(): # close down the program
    print "Closing down please wait"
    EV3.close() # close the port
    pygame.quit() # close pygame
    sys.exit()

def checkForEvent(): # see if we need to quit
    event = pygame.event.poll()
    if event.type == pygame.QUIT :
        terminate()

if __name__ == '__main__':
    main()
```

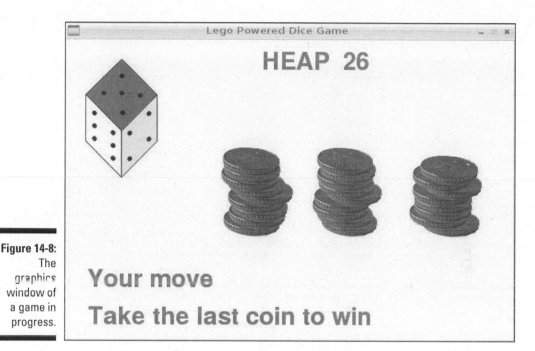

Figure 14-8:
The
graphics
window of
a game in
progress.

These are almost standard and appear in a lot of our code — just two functions. The first function is called when the program quits, closes open files, and exits. The second function monitors for any events in the Pygame system and acts on them. In this program, the only events we're bothered about are the shutdown or quit events, like the Escape key or a click in the close box of the window.

Next comes the code for talking to the bricks. Listing 14-3 is for sending and receiving messages, as well as generating message blocks.

Listing 14-3:   Dice Game: Talking to the LEGO Brick

```
# Talking to the brick
def init(): #set up messages to the brick
    global see, twist, play, place, remove
    see = messageG("Brick","See")
    twist = messageG("Brick","Twist")
    play =  messageG("Brick","My_Move")
    place = messageG("Brick","Place_Dice")
    remove = messageG("Brick", "Remove_Dice")

def readMessage() :
    n = 0
    while n < 2 :# hold until message starts to arrive
```

(continued)

Listing 14-3 *(continued)*

```
        n = EV3.inWaiting()
        checkForEvent()
    inMessage = EV3.read(2)

    messageBytes = ord(inMessage[0]) + ( ord(inMessage[1] ↩
                ) *256 )
    while EV3.inWaiting() < (messageBytes ):
      checkForEvent()
    inMessage = inMessage + EV3.read(messageBytes )
    payloadPointer = 9 + ord(inMessage[6])
    message = inMessage[payloadPointer:]
    return message

def messageSend(message):
    if EV3.isOpen() == True :
      for n in range(0, 2 + ord(message[0]) + ↩
           (ord(message[1]) * 256 )):
        EV3.write(message[n])
    else :
        print"Serial port not open"
def messageG(boxName,message): # generate a message
    length = len(boxName) + len(message) + 8
    btMessage = [ chr(0) for temp in range (0,length)] ↩
                # initial blank
    btMessage[2] = chr(1)
    # message ID
    btMessage[4] = chr(0x81)
    btMessage[5] = chr(0x9E)
    btMessage[6] = chr(len(boxName) + 1)
    btMessage[7:7+len(boxName)] = boxName
    payloadPointer = 8 + len(boxName)
    btMessage[payloadPointer] = chr((len(message) + 1) & 0xff)
    btMessage[payloadPointer + 1] = chr((len(message)+ 1) ↩
           >> 8)
    btMessage[payloadPointer + 2:len(message)] = message
    endPoint = payloadPointer + len(message) + 1
    btMessage[0] = chr((endPoint & 0xff))
    btMessage[1] = chr(endPoint >> 8)
    return btMessage
```

Each of the commands that is going to be sent to the LEGO brick are defined in the `init` function. This is done by calling the `messageG` function, which generates the message block of data. Note that this takes in both the message text and the name of the message box that it's delivered to. For a full explanation of the structure of a message, see the previous chapter. The `readMessage` function is simplified in that here there is no interest in retrieving the mailbox name; it just returns the payload in the form of a list of characters.

The next block of code concerns the Pygame drawing functions and is shown in Listing 14-4.

Listing 14-4:   Dice Game: Screen-Drawing Functions

```python
# Pygame graphic functions
def drawDice(top) :
    pygame.draw.rect(screen,cBackground, (0, 0, 150, 200), 0)
    screen.blit(diceTop[top],[0,0]) # draw dice
    screen.blit(diceSide[currentDice[0]],[48,48])
    screen.blit(pygame.transform.flip(diceSide ⊃
                    [currentDice[3]] ,False,True),[0,48])
    pygame.display.update()


def drawHeap(size):
    chingSound.play()
    pygame.draw.rect(screen,cBackground, (194,50,400,215), 0)
    drawWords("HEAP  " + str(size), 262, 10)
    x = [ 212, 334, 465 ]
    y = 220
    h = 0
    w = 0
    if size < 1 :
        return
    while size != 0 :
        screen.blit(coin,[x[h] + heapWobble[w],y])
        size -= 1
        w += 1
        h += 1
        if h > 2 :
            h = 0
            y -= 10
    pygame.display.update()


def blank_screen():
    screen.fill(cBackground) # blank screen
    pygame.display.update()


def drawFeedback(feedback) :
    pygame.draw.rect(screen,cBackground, (30,300,570,textHeight), 0)
    drawWords(feedback,30,300)
    pygame.display.update()


def drawWords(words,x,y) :
    textSurface = pygame.Surface((len(words) * ⊃
                (textHeight / 2),textHeight))
    textRect = textSurface.get_rect()
    textRect.left = x
    textRect.top = y
    pygame.draw.rect(screen,cBackground, (x,y,len(words) ⊃
                    * (textHeight /2),textHeight), 0)
    textSurface = font.render(words, True, cText, cBackground)
    screen.blit(textSurface, textRect)
```

The drawDice function takes in the number on the top of the dice and draws an isometric view of the dice. It uses the global list currentDice to see what numbers to draw for the sides. This list is updated whenever a new dice position occurs. The drawHeap function takes in the heap size and draws the word *Heap* along with its size in the playing window. It then goes on to draw the heap as a stack of coins in three piles.

There is nothing significant about the three piles — it just makes them fit in the window better. However, the stacks of coins are staggered for a bit of visual interest. The same staggering is kept throughout a game so that when a smaller number of coins are drawn, they appear to have been removed from the top of each heap. The amount of displacement for each coin is held in a list called heapWobble, and a new list is generated whenever a new heap is generated.

The drawFeedback function is used to give the human player feedback on the game's progress. This is one line on the screen, and the function blanks out any previous messages before writing the new one. This function calls the drawWords function that handles the nitty-gritty of rendering text onto the bitmapped area of the window.

Next, we have the functions that handle the interaction between the game and the LEGO control brick and act as an interface for hardware. These functions deal with finding the current dice orientation and positioning the dice for the computer's move, as shown in Listing 14-5.

Listing 14-5: Dice Game: Interacting with the Hardware

```
# Interacting with hardware definitions
def getStartDice() : # read the sensor
    messageSend(see)
    face = readNumber()
    if face != 0 :
        drawFeedback("Please remove the dice")
        messageSend(remove)
        getAck()
        time.sleep(0.8)
        drawFeedback("Now replace it with start number")
    time.sleep(0.5)
    messageSend(place)
    return getTop(readNumber()) # get the top positions

def getTop(face) : # identifies the dice top number
    global currentDice
    currentDice[0] = face
    currentDice[2] = 7 - currentDice[0]
    time.sleep(1.0) # time for hand to clear
```

```
        messageSend(twist)
        face = readNumber()
        currentDice[1] = face
        currentDice[3] = 7 - currentDice[1]
        top = findTopFromSides(currentDice[0],currentDice[1])
        return top

def readNumber() :
    number = readMessage()
    dice = ord(number[0]) - 0x30
    return dice

def getAck():
    if(readMessage() == "Gone") :
        return True
    else :
        return False

def computerPlay(move) : # move dice into correct place
    twists = -1
    for t in range(0, 4) :
        if currentDice[t] == move :
            twists = t
    while twists != 0 :
        messageSend(twist)
        getAck() # not interested in the sensor
        adjustCurrentDice()
        time.sleep(0.25)
        twists -= 1
    messageSend(play) # throw the dice
    time.sleep(1) # wait until it is done

def adjustCurrentDice() :
    global currentDice
    tempDice = copy.deepcopy(currentDice)
    currentDice[0] = tempDice[1]
    currentDice[1] = tempDice[2]
    currentDice[2] = tempDice[3]
    currentDice[3] = tempDice[0]

def findTopFromSides(first, second):
    top = -1
    topTry = 0
    while top == -1 and topTry < 6:
        for n in range(0, 4):
            if diceLookup[topTry][n] == first and
                diceLookup[topTry][n+1] == second :
                top = topTry + 1
        topTry += 1
    return top
```

The `getStartDice` function is the procedure used at the start of the game. If the dice is in front of the sensor, the game says it should be removed. Then the dice needs to be placed in front of the sensor. This then becomes the starting position. When the dice is in place, it returns the value acquired from the next function, `getTop`, which passes the number of the face in front of the sensor and updates the `currentDice` list. Then the dice platform is rotated by 90 degrees, and the next face of the dice is read. Having acquired the value of all four sides of the dice, the `findTopFromSides` function finds the top number of the dice in the same way as we've already seen in Listing 14-1. The `readNumber` function extracts a single-digit number from the text message, whereas the `getAck` function simply reads a message returning `true` or `false` if it's the string `Gone`. In this code, no use is made of this returned value.

The last two functions to consider in this block are concerned with the computer playing a move. The `computerPlay` function takes in a move number to make. This number must then be maneuvered into the throwing position, and the throwing command must be given. The function uses the `currentDice` list to find out how many 90-degree twists to give the dice platform to bring it into the right place. After each twist, the `currentDice` list is updated by the `adjustCurrentDice` function so that the correct dice sides can be drawn after the throw. This is done simply by shifting the entries in the list by one place to the left. Note the need to use the `copy.deepcopy` function to get a temporary duplicate of the list.

The next block of code consists of the functions that play the game. These functions, shown in Listing 14-6, set up the heap and make the computer's move.

Listing 14-6:   Dice Game: Setup and Play

```
# Game playing definitions
def generateHeap(start) :
    global heapWobble
    total = 9 # impossible win start
    line = index[start] # the opening position line in the move table
    # now choose another total heap that is not a ⊃
          losing position
    while(moveMatrix[line][total] == 128) :
        total= random.randint(8, 16) ⊃
                          # generate a winnable position
    total = total + ( random.randint(1, 4) * 9 ) ⊃
                    # pick a multiple of 9 of this
    for n in range(0,54):
      heapWobble[n] =  random.randint(0,20) - 10
    return total
```

```
def computerMove(target, top):
    modTarget = target
    while modTarget > 16 : # reduce target to final table
        modTarget -= 9
    potMove = moveMatrix[index[top]][modTarget]
    moveToMake = potMove # gets overridden if ⊃
                          not a dice number
    if potMove > 6 : # a potential move has a choice
      if potMove == 7 : #move is 2 or 3 or 4
        moveToMake = random.randint(2, 4)
      if potMove == 8 : # move is 2 or 3
        moveToMake = random.randint(2, 3)
      if potMove == 9 : # move is 3 or 4
        moveToMake = random.randint(3, 4)
      if potMove == 10 : # move is 3 or 6
        moveToMake = random.randint(3, 4)
        if moveToMake == 4 :
          moveToMake = 6
      if potMove == 11: # move is 3 or 4 or 6
        moveToMake = random.randint(3, 5)
        if moveToMake == 5:
          moveToMake = 6
      if potMove == 12 : # move is 1 or 2
        moveToMake = random.randint(1, 2)
      if potMove == 13 : # move is 2 or 6
        moveToMake = random.randint(1, 2)
        if moveToMake == 1 :
          moveToMake = 6
      if potMove == 14 : # move 1 or 5
        moveToMake = random.randint(1, 2)
        if moveToMake == 2 :
          moveToMake = 5
      if potMove == 128 : # losing move so select ⊃
                           a random move
        moveToMake = random.randint(1, 6)
        #print "losing position for me" # uncomment to ⊃
                             see if you are winning
      while moveToMake == top or moveToMake == 7-top :
        moveToMake = random.randint(1, 6)
    return moveToMake
```

Both these functions make use of the move matrix (refer to Tables 14-1 through 14-3). However, the computer version of this table has numbers in it representing various things. A number between 1 and 6 indicates the move to make; a number between 7 and 14 indicates there is a choice of moves, and the specific number defines what those choices are; finally, a value of 128 shows that this is a losing position.

The generateHeap function starts off assuming a heap of 9, which is a totally unwinnable position no matter what number is currently on the top. The code then generates a random number between 8 and 16 until it finds one where the heap size and the current top number of the dice produces a winnable position. Then this is multiplied by a random multiple of 9 to make the heap bigger and add a bit of variety to the game. Finally, the function generates the heapWobble list for the staggering of the coin pile graphics.

The last function, computerMove, is where the computer's move is worked out. It takes in the current size of the heap and the current top number on the dice. It then repeatedly subtracts 9 from the heap until it is 16 or less. Then it looks up the potential move by extracting it from the two-dimensional list of the playing matrix. The first index decides what line on the table to use; this depends on the top number. The second index is the reduced heap value.

Now that number is interpreted by a pile of if statements. For example, if the number 10 is drawn from the moveMatrix table, that means the playing number should be either 3 or 6. A random number between 3 and 4 is generated; if it turns out to be 4, the code sets the move to 6. If the number is 128, that's a losing position, so a random move is generated. This must still be a legal move so while the moveToMake variable is an illegal move, random numbers are repeatedly generated until a legal move is found.

The last function to consider is the main function. This is the loop that defines the whole game. It's implemented as a state machine — in other words, there are a number of phases in play, setup, player move, computer move, player win, computer win, and end of game, and each one of these phases has a number in the variable gameState. This function is shown in Listing 14-7.

Listing 14-7:   Dice Game: The Main Loop

```
def main():
 init() # Initialize variables
 blank_screen()
 drawDice(0)
 gameState = 0
 while True : # play the game
    checkForEvent()
    if gameState == 0 : # new game send out introduction
        drawWords("Take the last coin to win", 30,350)
        drawFeedback("Welcome to the dice game")
        time.sleep(1)
        drawFeedback("Put the dice on the sensor")
        move = 0
        move = getStartDice()
        lastMove = move
```

```
        drawDice(move)
        random.seed() # seed random number generator
        heap = generateHeap(move);
        drawHeap(heap)
        drawFeedback("Now make your first move")
        messageSend(remove)
        getAck()
        time.sleep(0.8)
        gameState = 1 # introduction over

    if gameState == 1 :  # players move
        move= 0
        while move == 0 or move == lastMove or ⊃
move == 7-lastMove :
            while move < 1 or move > 6 :
                messageSend(place)
                move = getTop(readNumber())
            if move == lastMove or move == 7-lastMove :
                print"can't play this number"
                move = 0
                drawFeedback("You cannot use "+ ⊃
str(lastMove)+" or "+ str(7 - lastMove)+ " . Try again")
                messageSend(remove)
                getAck()
        heap -= move
        drawDice(move)
        drawFeedback("Your move was "+ str(move))
        drawHeap(heap)
        time.sleep(1.5)
        if heap == 0 :
            gameState = 4 # player wins
        if heap < 0 :
            gameState = 5 # computer wins
        lastMove = move;
        if gameState == 1 : # if we are still playing
            gameState = 2 # computer's move next

    if gameState == 2 : # Computer's move
        move = computerMove(heap,lastMove)
        drawFeedback("My move of " + str(move))
        computerPlay(move) # play the move
        currentDice[0] = 7 - lastMove # bottom number is ⊃
                                      now in position 0
        drawDice(move)
        lastMove = move;
        heap -= move
        drawHeap(heap)
        time.sleep(2)
        if heap == 0 :
            gameState = 5
```

(continued)

Listing 14-7 *(continued)*

```
        if heap < 0 :
            gameState = 4
        if heap > 0 :
            drawFeedback("Your move ")
            gameState = 1

    if gameState == 4 : # Player wins
        applauseSound.play()
        drawFeedback( "WOW you won - well done")
        gameState = 6

    if gameState == 5 : #Computer wins
        laughSound.play()
        drawFeedback("I win again . . .")
        gameState = 6

    if gameState == 6 : # end of game
        time.sleep(3)
        drawFeedback('Have another go')
        time.sleep(2)
        gameState = 0
```

This is the longest function in the program, but it breaks up into a number of small state sections, or game phases, so it's best to consider them one at a time.

For most of the game, the gameState variable will alternate from 1 to 2, representing the player's move or the computer's move. Higher values represent the end of the game and the outcome, and they draw the appropriate feedback and trigger the appropriate sound effects. A gameState variable value of 0 represents the setup phase.

To kick things off, there are a few lines that do one-off initialization. The init function is called to set up the lists used as messages to the LEGO brick, the window is cleared, and a blank dice is drawn. Then the while True loop is an infinite loop that will repeatedly play all the moves of a game and play multiple games.

If the gameState variable is a 0, then this is the setup phase of the game. It makes sure that there is no dice in front of the sensor and then asks the player to put the dice down in the starting position. It then reads the dice and draws a picture of it. This starting dice state is used to generate a heap size that is winnable by the player. The code then asks the player to make the first move, and the gameState variable is set to 1.

The main purpose of the if gameState == 1 section is to get the player's move, but it must be a legal move (one that is not the same as the previous move or a use of the number the dice is sitting on). This is achieved by putting the code into a `while` loop that keeps repeating until a legal move has been made. When a move is made, that number is subtracted from the heap and a check is made to see if the game is over. This is determined by looking at the heap size. A heap size of 0 indicates the player has won; a negative heap size indicates the computer has won. If neither of those two things has happened, then the `gameState` variable is advanced to 2, the computer's move.

The computer works out its move by giving the current heap size and last move to the `computerMove` function. The side dice face corresponding to the computer's move is then rotated into the correct place for throwing. Then it's thrown and the dice graphic is updated. Then the move is evaluated by subtracting it from the heap to see if anyone has won. If not, the `gameState` variable is set back to the player's move value of 1.

The end of game values of the `gameState` variable print messages to the screen and play sound effects depending on whether the player has won or lost. A value of 4 indicates that the player has won, and a value of 5 shows that the computer has won. These both change the state to the final value of 6, which invites the player to play again and then sets the `gameState` variable back to 0.

All that remains is the initialization of the variables, lookup tables, and loading in of sound and graphics. This is shown in Listing 14-8.

Listing 14-8: The Dice Game: Initialization

```python
#!/usr/bin/env python
'''
 Lego powered Dice Game
 By Mike Cook
'''
import serial
import time
import random, copy
import os, pygame, sys
import struct

EV3 = serial.Serial('/dev/rfcomm0', timeout=1)
EV3.flushInput()

pygame.init()              # initialise graphics interface
pygame.mixer.quit()
pygame.mixer.init(frequency=22050, size=-16, ⊃
                  channels=2, buffer=512)
chingSound = pygame.mixer.Sound("sounds/ching.ogg")
applauseSound = pygame.mixer.Sound("sounds/applause.ogg")
laughSound = pygame.mixer.Sound("sounds/laugh.ogg")
```

(continued)

Listing 14-8 *(continued)*

```python
os.environ['SDL_VIDEO_WINDOW_POS'] = 'center'
pygame.display.set_caption("Lego Powered Dice Game")
pygame.event.set_allowed(None)
pygame.event.set_allowed([pygame.KEYDOWN,pygame.QUIT])
cBackground =(255,255,255)
cText = (255,0,0)
textHeight = 48
font = pygame.font.Font(None, textHeight)
screenWidth = 600
screenHeight = 400

screen = pygame.display.set_mode([screenWidth,screenHeight],0)

diceTop = [ pygame.image.load("images/t"+str(num)+".png" ⊃
              ).convert_alpha() for num in range(0,7)]

diceSide = [ pygame.image.load("images/s"+str(num)+".png" ⊃
              ).convert_alpha() for num in range(0,7)]

coin = pygame.image.load("images/coin.png").convert_alpha()

print "Lego Dice"
currentDice = [0 , 0, 0, 0]
heapWobble = [ random.randint(0,20) - 10 for n in range(0,54)]
moveMatrix = [
[0, 128, 2, 3, 4, 5, 3, 7, 4, 128, 5, 8, 9, 4, 5, 3, 7],
[0, 1, 1, 3, 4, 128, 10, 11, 4, 128, 1, 3, 9, 4, 128, 10, 9],
[0, 1, 12, 128, 128, 5, 6, 13, 128, 128, 14, 2, 128, 128, 5, 6,2]
          ]

index = [ 0, 0, 1, 2, 2, 1, 0]  # input the current state ⊃ of the
              dice to read what line on the move matrix to use

diceLookup = [ [ 3, 5, 4, 2, 3],  # side sequence for 1 on top
               [ 6, 3, 1, 4, 6],  # for 2 on top
               [ 2, 6, 5, 1, 2],  # for 3 on top
               [ 1, 5, 6, 2, 1],  # for 4 on top
               [ 4, 1, 3, 6, 4],  # for 5 on top
               [ 2, 4, 5, 3, 2] ] # for 6 on top

see = "see"
twist = "twist"
play = "play"
place = "place"
remove = "remove"
```

First, the Python modules needed are imported. Then the Bluetooth connection to the LEGO brick is established and the buffers are cleared out. Next comes the Pygame initialization for the sound, window, text, and graphics. Note that the graphics for the dice side and top are loaded into a list from files in the images directory, whereas the coin is a single file.

Next come the definitions of the global variables that allow the playing of the game. The `moveMatrix` list consists of three lists, each for use with a different top face number. The values in the list of moves is coded as the move to make if it's between 1 and 6 or a number representing a choice of moves, or the value 128 representing the state when there is no winning move to make from this position. The zero at the start of the list is just a dummy value so that the list index number and the current heap size match up.

The `index` list informs the code doing the move lookup which list of the three to use given the current top state of the dice. The `diceLookup` list contains the sequence of numbers on the side of the dice when rotated clockwise for every top dice number. Note that the first and last numbers are the same so that the code can be made simpler by not having to cope with wraparound.

Finally, the five strings that define the messages sent to the LEGO brick are defined as global variables with dummy data. The `init` function will assign the real data to it later. It can't be done at this stage because it involves other functions that can't be called yet.

Play

All that remains is to play the game. It works even better if you can memorize the playing matrix so that you can win every time and astound your friends.

Customizing the Code

Like all projects, you can customize this game to your heart's content. Here are some ideas you may want to implement.

The simplest modification is to change the sound effects. You could even add some extra ones. For example, the computer can speak instructions for your move and tell you when you've made an illegal move. You can record all the numbers and get the move spoken. If you're feeling adventurous, you can write a function that takes several samples of numbers being spoken and speaks the heap size. You'll just have to record extra number parts like "teen," "twenty," and so on.

Another idea is to remove the coins one at a time from the heap to make the animation a bit more interesting. You may even want to write a small sequence where the top coin off each heap rises up and disappears off the top of the screen. In fact, you don't have to stick to coins — the heap could be anything drawn in any arrangement you like. Remember, though, that if you want to use random positions, you should use a `heapWobble`-like list of positions so that the heap doesn't keep rearranging itself whenever anything is removed from it.

If you really want to take it to another level, how about a LEGO robot that scurries around the room to find the dice, picks it up, detects what it is, and makes its own move? That would be a challenge, indeed, but we're sure it can be done somehow. If you manage to do that, email us the results!

Chapter 15

LEGO Direct

*I*n the previous two chapters, we show you ways to communicate with the LEGO MINDSTORMS EV3 Intelligent Brick. In this chapter, we get a lot more hacky and look at controlling motors and reading sensors directly from the Raspberry Pi.

You can make your own cables that are much more flexible than the official cables, and we show you how in this chapter. Finally, when using the Raspberry Pi with a LEGO system, you can save on battery power and customize your project to your liking, and we cover all that in the pages that follow.

Creating a Reset Button for the Raspberry Pi

A reset button on the Raspberry Pi may not seem obvious, and we never needed one until we started playing around with Bluetooth, but it's a great idea for when everything is stuck. (Sure, you can just yank out the power lead, but that isn't really recommended because it could cause trouble with your SD card.) Even though there is no reset button on the Raspberry Pi, provision has been made for fitting one from revision 2 of the board. You can see it in the form of two holes to the left of the HDMI socket — it's very easy to solder a two-pin header there. The idea is that when these two lines are shorted together, the Raspberry Pi's processor is reset.

You can use a jumper link to temporarily connect these two lines together when needed, keeping the jumper on one pin for normal operation. However, you can go for the deluxe method and wrap a tact push button's wires around a two-pin header to produce an actual button. As an alternative, you can solder a button directly into the two holes. Make sure you have a two-wire push button because there are many four-wire ones out there. Figure 15-1 shows some photographs of this. On the right is a tact push button wired to a two-pin socket; on the left, it's mounted on a two-pin header soldered into the Raspberry Pi's board.

Figure 15-1:
Raspberry
Pi reset
buttons.

Making Batteries Last Longer

Having done a few projects using the LEGO EV3 system, we noticed that the batteries didn't last very long. In fact, during development, the brick would often sit there doing nothing for long periods while we concentrated on the Raspberry Pi aspect of the software. Turning the brick on and off takes some time — about 30 seconds to power up and 45 seconds to power down — so you tend not to do it too often. Although there are rechargeable batteries for mobile use, static LEGO machines like the dice game in Chapter 14 can get away with a tethered power supply.

The LEGO system runs off 6 AA batteries; at 1.5V each, that adds up to 9V. All the solutions we found to this problem online involved some very ugly soldering of wires directly onto the battery springs. We thought that this was a bit too intrusive. Plus, it was difficult to swap between a power supply and batteries. So, we wanted something that would look like a AA battery and allow us to connect wires to it. While thinking, "What is about the size of a AA battery?," we came up with the answer: "A AA battery!"

The battery cover at the bottom of the EV3 brick has a small flange that covers a U-shaped hole in the body of the brick. This hole is just about long enough to put a long-reach 2.1mm power jack through, so all we had to do was to attach a matching socket into something that was the same length as a AA battery. However, it isn't quite as easy as that because the spring that holds the battery in place tends to apply a snapping force to the center of any tube. After a few false starts, we hit upon the solution, shown in Figure 15-2.

All this system has to do is to connect the positive end of your external power supply to the top-right spring in the battery compartment and the negative end to the top-left spring. The basic idea is that a surface-mount power-jack socket lines up with the center notch in the battery compartment and attaches to the negative connector of the brick. It's held in place by a styrene tube, which fits around the narrow pip on the battery holder's spring positive connector. This pip is what causes trouble — it's too narrow to allow a stable fitting. The tube and the left-hand side of the PCB fit around the pip, preventing it from producing any sideways movement and holding the assembly stable. The positive connection from the jack socket is wired to the full battery's body with a wire soldered to the body. Note the positive connection is the main body of the battery with the negative connection just the end.

To make this project, you need the following parts:

- ✔ Two old dead AA batteries (the plastic-covered type, not the painted type)
- ✔ A surface-mount 2.1mm power-jack socket
- ✔ A 7mm x 30mm piece of single-sided PCB material

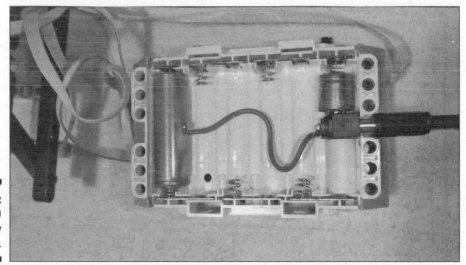

Figure 15-2:
The LEGO
brick battery
eliminator.

✔ A styrene tube with an outside diameter of 20mm x 11mm

✔ 70mm of 24-gauge (or thicker) insulated wire

✔ A long-reach 2.1mm power-jack plug

✔ A small amount of epoxy resin

✔ A 9V regulated mains power supply (an SPS-8041 or similar)

To build the battery eliminator, follow these steps:

1. **Take the two batteries and strip off all the plastic covers, leaving just the bare metal.**

2. **Using a small hacksaw, gently saw off the last 16mm of the negative end of one of the batteries.**

   Make sure you catch the black stuff that comes out in a paper towel. You'll find that you've also sawed through a rod that runs down the center of the battery.

   The black stuff is a compressed paste of manganese dioxide with carbon powder added for increased conductivity. The sticky stuff surrounding the center negative electrode is composed of zinc powder in a gel containing the potassium hydroxide electrolyte wrapped up in a layer of cellulose or a synthetic polymer.

3. **Remove all the black stuff, leaving just the center electrode.**

   We did this by putting a small screwdriver in and scratching the black stuff out. It comes out very easily.

   Make sure you catch all the black stuff and don't get it in your mouth. Don't dispose of this in the normal household garbage; instead, place it in a resealable plastic bag and put it with your other dead batteries for proper disposal.

4. **Bend down the central electrode rod until it nearly touches the case.**

5. **Slip the piece of PCB material into the tube and push it as far in as it will go.**

6. **Solder the electrode rod to the PCB material.**

7. **Take a small amount of epoxy resin and fix the PCB into the battery case. Let it set for 24 hours.**

8. **Make sure the surface mount socket lines up with the center of the hole in the LEGO brick when the battery retaining spring is compressed about halfway. Then solder the surface mount socket in place on both sides.**

9. **Solder an insulated wire from the center pin of this socket to the body of the other whole battery.**

Clean up the area first with glass paper and make the joint quickly with a soldering iron. Don't allow the battery to heat up too much, and allow it much longer than usual to cool down. The bulk of the battery means it will absorb more heat before you can solder it.

10. **Cut 20mm of styrene tube and fit it over the PCB material. Then place it in the battery holder.**

    The construction is shown in Figure 15-3. A photograph is shown in Figure 15-4.

11. **Wire up a long 2.1mm power jack with the center pin as the positive and attach it to your 9V power supply.**

    We used an SPS-8041 selectable switch mode supply set to 9V for this. You may want to cut off the small flange in the battery cover that covers up the hole for the power jack, or you may want to leave your LEGO unmodified and just operate the brick with no back cover. The choice is yours.

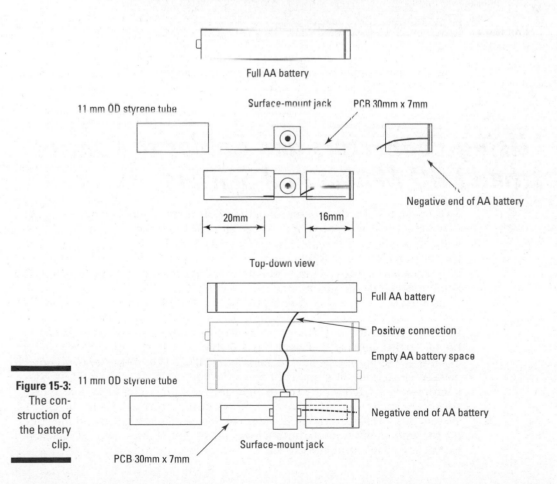

Figure 15-3: The construction of the battery clip.

Figure 15-4:
The battery
clip.

Now you can happily power your EV3 brick during development and quickly change to batteries when needed.

Using Connectors and Cables to Control the LEGO Motors and Sensors

If you want to have direct control of the LEGO motors and sensors, you have to get electrical access to them. All the electronic components in the EV3 and NXT systems are connected to the control brick using a six-way connector called an RJ12. The RJ12 is very similar to the RJ11 connector — the only difference is that the RJ11 uses only four of the six wiring positions of an RJ12. Sometimes an RJ12 connector is called a 6P6C RJ11; this stands for six positions and six connectors (whereas the normal RJ11 is a 6P4C connection).

Although these are both standard connectors in the electronics industry, the LEGO designers added a small tweak to make things a bit difficult (or as LEGO would probable say, to ensure the MINDSTORMS system was not connected to things it should not be connected to). The RJ11 and RJ12 connectors have a latch on the top to allow for the cable to be locked into the socket. Normal connectors have this connector in the center, but the LEGO system has it offset on the right side. There was an old RJ11 telephone connector with an offset latch, but that was offset on the other side, so making extra cables isn't straightforward.

RJ12 cables are normally crimped onto the connectors. You get a special size-6 core flat cable and strip off the outer insulation. Then you put the insulated wire ends into a plug and crimp it with a special tool. This does two things:

- ✔ It distorts a plastic bar to push against the wires and acts as a mechanical clamp.

- ✔ It pushes the blades on the back of the plug's contacts through the plastic of the wire's insulation to make a contact.

Done properly, this produces a good durable connection. The only snag is that the double insulation tends to make the resulting cables a bit stiff, which can sometimes cause problems when connecting parts that move.

There are several things you can do with the leads to improve them or allow electrical access to the signals, some of them more straightforward than others:

- ✔ **Hack an existing lead.** This approach is perhaps the simplest one to take. You have a lead with two ends, so you can simply cut it in half, and you have two ends to solder your extension wires onto. If you want to extend the cable to use more flexible wires, you can cut the cable close to the connector and insert a length of stranded wires with thinner insulation. Make sure you cover any exposed joints with insulating tape or, better yet, a dab of liquid insulation tape.

- ✔ **Use a normal RJ12 and crimp tool, but move the latch over to the right side.** We've seen this method advocated on some websites, but we haven't had much success with this technique ourselves. The idea is that, after you've fitted the cable, you slice off the tab with a sharp knife and glue it on the side using polystyrene model airplane glue, using an existing socket as a guide so you get it in the right place. You have to be very careful not to permanently glue the cable into the socket; plus, the springiness of the latch is in question after the gluing.

- ✔ **Get some real connectors.** In our opinion, the best approach is to get some real connectors, ones designed for the job. Unfortunately, there isn't a great deal of choice with suppliers — we could only find one source, but they're available on both sides of the Atlantic. In the United States, go to www.mindsensors.com; in Europe, go to www.active-robots.com. Here, you can buy sockets and readymade leads, as well as the plug connectors.

   However, if you're going to make your own lead, you need a crimping tool, and the only way we know of accommodating the offset latch is to modify an existing crimping tool. Crimping tools can be quite expensive, but if you choose the right one, it's not only cheap but also easy to modify.

The LogiLink crimp tool is inexpensive and made from bright orange plastic, so it's simple to modify. It crimps four-position, six-position, and eight-position connectors. The two halves unscrew, and it's comparatively easy to file a larger slot in the six-position hole to accommodate the offset latch. We used a small square needle file to do this. Figure 15-5 shows the slot filed away on the front piece. Note that you also need to file the back piece. You have a connector of the right size in the LEGO set, so it's easy to file the crimper so that the plug fits in snugly.

We found that the best wire to use was ribbon cable. The vast majority of ribbon cable is 0.1-inch pitch, but it's too big for these connectors so what you want is 1mm pitch cable. All you need to do is cut the cable off square, insert it into the socket, insert the socket in the crimper, and squeeze. For a bit of added resilience, we added a small spot of Gorilla Glue to the cable underneath the clamping bar. We left this a few hours to set before flexing the cable.

Using this method, you can make flexible two-ended cables of exactly the right length for your model. Or you can make single-ended cables for attaching your LEGO parts to other electronics or your Raspberry Pi.

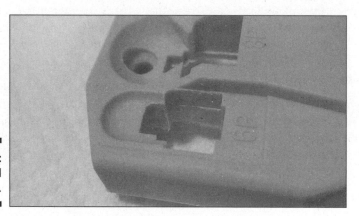

Figure 15-5:
Crimp tool
modification.

Reading and Commanding

There are basically two different sets of signals you can get on the LEGO control brick:

- **Sensors:** You read information from these. They're labeled A through D.
- **Actuators or motors:** You command these to move. They're labeled 1 through 4.

Each has a different set of electrical connections. Figure 15-6 shows the signals on the two types of LEGO peripherals. Note that this is oriented with the latch on the underside. The colors used on a standard LEGO cable for each wire are also shown in Figure 15-6.

The motor lead

The LEGO motor basically consists of two components:

✔ A geared motor capable of clockwise or counterclockwise rotation

✔ A rotary sensor giving pulses in response to the motor movement

The motor is geared, through a multigear train, so it turns many times before the movement is transmitted to the outside world.

To get a motor to move, you apply a voltage across the Motor Power 1 and 2 lines. This should be 9V, but the voltage isn't too critical. To make it reverse direction, you need to swap the polarity of these two lines. To stop the motor, you can do one of two things:

✔ **Remove the power by removing the voltage from these lines.** When you do this, the motor will coast to a stop.

✔ **Make the two power lines be the same voltage — either both 0V or both 9V.** This is not the same as disconnecting the voltage. Instead, it's like connecting the two motor wires together. This results in the motor stopping very quickly by means of what is known as *regenerative breaking* or *flywheel breaking*.

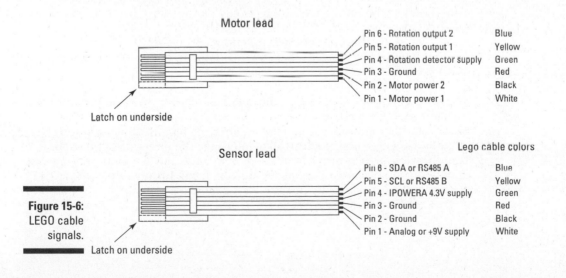

Figure 15-6: LEGO cable signals.

Motor lead

Pin 6 - Rotation output 2	Blue
Pin 5 - Rotation output 1	Yellow
Pin 4 - Rotation detector supply	Green
Pin 3 - Ground	Red
Pin 2 - Motor power 2	Black
Pin 1 - Motor power 1	White

Latch on underside

Lego cable colors

Sensor lead

Pin 6 - SDA or RS485 A	Blue
Pin 5 - SCL or RS485 B	Yellow
Pin 4 - IPOWERA 4.3V supply	Green
Pin 3 - Ground	Red
Pin 2 - Ground	Black
Pin 1 - Analog or +9V supply	White

Latch on underside

Flywheel breaking works because an electric motor that is turning is actually acting like a generator and is producing a voltage that is in the opposite direction of the voltage required to make the motor turn in that direction. So, by connecting the two wires of the motor, you're using the voltage generated by the movement of the motor to try to drive the motor backward. This is like a power shutdown and stops the motor much faster than just letting it coast to a stop.

You may have noticed the two stop modes in the LEGO language — the `break at end` can be `true` or `false`. This is a simple way of saying "stop by coasting" or "stop by flywheel breaking."

The other control the motor has in the LEGO language is the power. (This used to be called speed, but power is a more accurate description.) You can reduce the power sent to a motor and, thus, see a speed drop by very rapidly turning the motor on and off. This happens hundreds of times a second. By changing the relative time the motor is on and off (known as the *duty cycle*), you can reduce the power fed into the motor.

For example, at 500 times a second, the motor is turned on and off every 0.002 second or 2 milliseconds (mS). If the motor is on for 1 mS and off for 1 mS, the power will only be 50 percent of full power. This rapid switching of the motor and changing the duty cycle is known as pulse width modulation (PWM) and is a common way of backing off the power on motors. Depending on the mechanical load the motor is under, the speed will also drop. The off part of the cycle is normally a flywheel breaking type rather than coasting type.

The last part of the motor is the rotary sensors, which give feedback on the actual movement of the motor. Applying power to the motor is great, but it may be jammed up or one motor may actually spin faster than another even if they're given the same voltage. Each motor is fitted with a rotational sensor. The sensor works similarly to a mouse with a ball: Any movement rotates a disc with holes that block and unblock one of two infrared beams. These beams produce pulses that can be related to the motor's actual movement.

The beams are quite accurate — you get one pulse for every degree of rotation. In fact, there are two pulse outputs that are 90 degrees out of phase with each other (known as a *quadrature arrangement*). By looking at which pulse line changes first, you can also determine the direction of rotation. These pulses on their own can be used to find how much a motor has moved, even if it isn't powered and is moved only by hand. However, the pulses can't be used to find the absolute position of the motor — only the relative motion or how much it has moved.

The sensor lead

The sensor leads, connecting to the sensor ports A through D, carry a very different sort of signal. Pin 3 is ground and pin 4 is positive, and they carry the power supply for the sensor. The new EV3 sensors communicate using the serial RS485 protocol at normal TTL logic levels. Communication between brick and sensor can be complex, as you see later in this chapter.

Rolling Your Own Motor Control

In order to control LEGO motors directly from the Raspberry Pi, you have to convert the signals available on the Pi's general-purpose input/output (GPIO) pins into signals suitable for driving the motor. The GPIO pins, when used as outputs, can provide only a very small current (16 mA at 3.3V). The LEGO motor needs a voltage of 9V at a current of 60 mA when under no load, and up to 2,000 mA when it's stalled. In order to make the motor turn in either direction, any driving circuit needs to be able to swap the polarity of the voltage on the motor's wires. In order to get regenerative breaking, a circuit needs to be able to connect the two wires from the motor together. A circuit that can do this is called an *H-bridge circuit*; it's composed of two half H-bridges.

A half H-bridge is simply what you get with a *changeover switch* (a switch that can be connected to either one of two poles or positions). With each pole connected to the two polarities of the motor's power supply, you can make an H-bridge (as shown in Figure 15-7) using only switches.

The common connector of each switch is connection to one wire of the motor, as you can see in Figure 15-7a — one switch is up and the other is down, so the current flows through the motor and causes the motor to turn in a clockwise direction. If the two switches are reversed, so switch 1 is down and switch 2 is up, the current flows through the motor in the opposite direction and the motor rotates in the opposite direction, as shown in Figure 15-7b. Finally, in Figure 15-7c, both switches are down and the two motor wires are

Figure 15-7: An H-bridge made from switches.

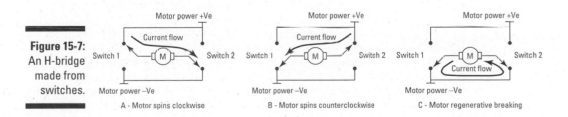

A - Motor spins clockwise   B - Motor spins counterclockwise   C - Motor regenerative breaking

connected together allowing regenerative breaking to occur. Note that this would also happen if both switches were up; if they're both connected to the same voltage level, they're in effect connected together.

Making it move

The only problem with an H-bridge made from switches is that you would have to physically switch them. You could use relays to make the contacts, but there is a pure electronic method that does not involve any moving parts. Fortunately, this is such a common circuit that many integrated circuits are available with this configuration, so you don't need to make one from individual parts.

If you just want to control the direction of the motor, all you need is an H-bridge circuit. But if you want to control the power/speed of the motor, you need to apply some PWM to the voltage. Unfortunately, the Raspberry Pi is not very well endowed with PWM signals — there are just two on the processor, and you can only get to both of them on the plus model's GPIO pins; the earlier models could access only one. These pins are also used for generating sound so if you're controlling a motor, the Raspberry Pi can't make any sound. Although each motor can have its own PWM control, with a Raspberry Pi 2, there is a sneaky trick that will work with all models to control two motors with one PWM pin. The way this works is to use logic gates to pass or block signals to the H-bridge switches. The gates we've chosen to use are called *NAND gates* (which stands for Not AND), and they're among the most common gates.

Logic gates have rules for what their output will be when presented with all the possible different combinations of inputs. In words, an AND gate will have a true output when input A *and* input B are true. A NOT gate has an output that is *not* the input, so if the input is true, the output is false, and if the input is false, the output is true. A NAND gate is an AND gate followed by a NOT gate.

All this gets very wordy, and you can quickly become muddled, so it's normal to have a table that shows every possible combination of inputs and the output results. This is known as a *truth table;* three such tables are shown in Figure 15-8.

The AND gate has two inputs — A and B — so there are four different possible combinations, each with its own row in the table. The symbol for an AND gate is shown below the table. Similarly, because the NOT function has only one input, there are only two lines. Sometimes this function is called a *logic inverter* or just an *inverter* for short. Finally, a NAND gate simply has the

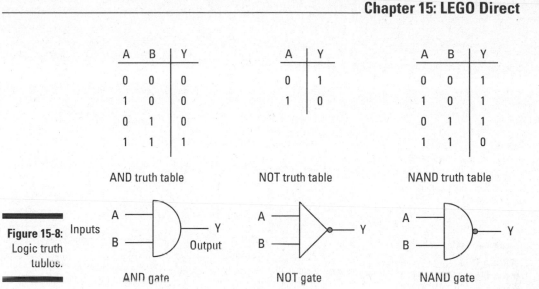

A	B	Y
0	0	0
1	0	0
0	1	0
1	1	1

AND truth table

A	Y
0	1
1	0

NOT truth table

A	B	Y
0	0	1
1	0	1
0	1	1
1	1	0

NAND truth table

Figure 15-8: Logic truth tables.

Inputs — A, B / Output — Y

AND gate   NOT gate   NAND gate

output of the AND gate inverted. Notice how the symbol for the NAND gate takes the filled circle from the output of the inverter and combines it with the body of the AND gate symbol.

Perhaps one of the more mind-boggling aspects of digital logic is that, when you have a NAND gate, everything else can be made up from this one function. That means that circuits that add up numbers, circuits that count, circuits that remember . . . all the circuitry of your microprocessor or any computer can be made up of NAND gates. No other functions are necessary. However, showing you how this can happen would take up a whole other book.

So, why do you need to know about NAND gates here? Well, we use them to send PWM signals or not send them into the H-bridge inputs to control the motor. Figure 15-9 shows the motor-activating part of an interface circuit for the Raspberry Pi to control a LEGO motor. With this circuit, you can control two motors. This circuit can also be used to control any sort of low-power DC motor.

The circuit consists of two interface circuits: the H-bridge and the NAND gate. In fact, the 74HC00 contains four NAND gates, and the SN754410 contains two H-bridge circuits (or, to be more accurate, it contains four [or quad] half H-bridge circuits). There are two supply voltages for this chip: One is for controlling the logic signals, and the other is for driving the motor. The motor supply can be anything up to 36V, but for a LEGO motor you should stick to between 9V and 12V. The negative of the motor's supply must be connected to the ground connection of this circuit.

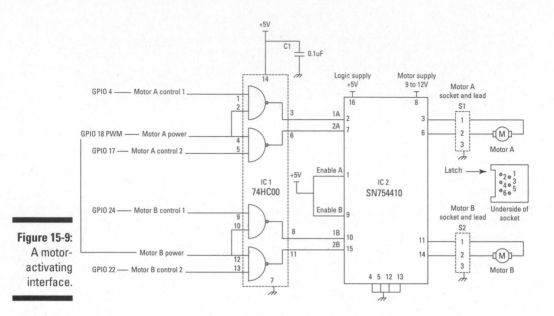

Figure 15-9:
A motor-activating interface.

The enable lines of the two H-bridges are connected to the logic supply so that they're always on. You can apply the PWM to these lines, but then power control is less effective because the motor will coast through the off parts of the cycle. If you want, you can connect these enable lines to another Raspberry Pi pin to shut down the motors altogether, but there isn't much reason for this because the other pins will allow you full control of the motor.

Each of the two control lines for the motor passes through an NAND gate, which has the effect of "gating" the PWM signal. When the PWM signal is low, both control lines to the H-bridge are high, so the motor is in the breaking mode irrespective of what state either of the control lines is in. However, when one control line is high, and the other is low, the rapid PWM signal is applied to the H-bridge control input corresponding to the high motor control, with the other H-bridge input being permanently high. This is exactly what you need for power control, as well as directional control.

This circuit can drive the LEGO motors in the LEGO Technics and the LEGO Power series, as well as the original MINDSTORMS motors. However, the NXT and EV3 motors have another trick up their sleeves: built-in rotational feedback.

Note how the motor's voltage is shown as 9V to 12V. The LEGO motor is capable of being run at 12V. But even so, the H-bridge circuit can cut the applied voltage down by as much as 3V, so even supplying the bridge with 12V, the motor gets only a touch over 9V anyway. So, if you supply the drive circuit with 12V, it will act like a very fresh battery; if you supply it with 9V, it will act like a partly discharged battery.

Knowing where it is: Motor feedback

The built-in sensor is known as an *quadrature incremental rotary encoder,* and produces pulses, as shown in Figure 15-10. These signals are 90 degrees out of phase from each other. By looking at the relative positions of the edges, you can determine the direction of rotation.

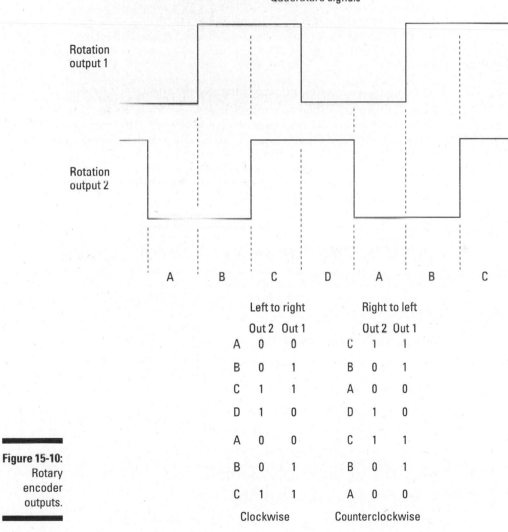

Quadrature signals

	Left to right		Right to left	
	Out 2	Out 1	Out 2	Out 1
A	0	0	C 1	1
B	0	1	B 0	1
C	1	1	A 0	0
D	1	0	D 1	0
A	0	0	C 1	1
B	0	1	B 0	1
C	1	1	A 0	0
	Clockwise		Counterclockwise	

Figure 15-10: Rotary encoder outputs.

The sequence of levels you get from the sensor as it's rotated is also shown in Figure 15-10. Notice how, as the rotation proceeds, only one bit will change at a time. This property in a code makes the code what is known as a *Gray code*, named after its inventor, Frank Gray. To a certain extent, it's self-correcting against contact bounce by having some forbidden transitions. If you see one of these transitions, you know it's an error and it's a simple matter to ignore in software.

To condition these signals into a form suitable for input to the Raspberry Pi's GPIO pins, a comparator or Schmitt trigger circuit is normally used. The LM339 has four comparators in one package and also has an open collector output, which means it can be simply pulled up to the 3V3 logic supply of the Raspberry Pi with a resistor. The schematic of this buffer circuit is shown in Figure 15-11.

This circuit can handle the rotation outputs for two motors. Each output is connected through a 10K resistor to the positive comparator input to provide some protection against interference pickup. All the comparator's negative inputs are connected together and set to a voltage that is halfway between the two extremes of the signal. The sensor circuit in the motor is powered by not 5V but 4.3V. We're sure it would work fine with 5V, but it's easy enough to provide the correct voltage by simply passing it through a diode. Any rectifying diode will do fine.

Constructing the motor control system

Building both aspects of the motor control system on one circuit board is best, so we've have combined the two schematics (Figures 15-9 and 15-11). Here are the parts you need:

- Four 10K resistors (R1–R4)
- Five 3K3 resistors (R5–R9)
- One 4K7 resistor (R10)
- Four 0.1uF ceramic capacitors (C1–C4)
- A 1N4001 or similar rectifying diode (D1)
- A 74HC00 quad two-input NAND gate (IC1)
- An SN754410 quad half H-bridge (IC2)
- An LM399 quad comparator (IC3)
- Two RJ12 six-way sockets with offset latches (S1–S2)
- Stripboard

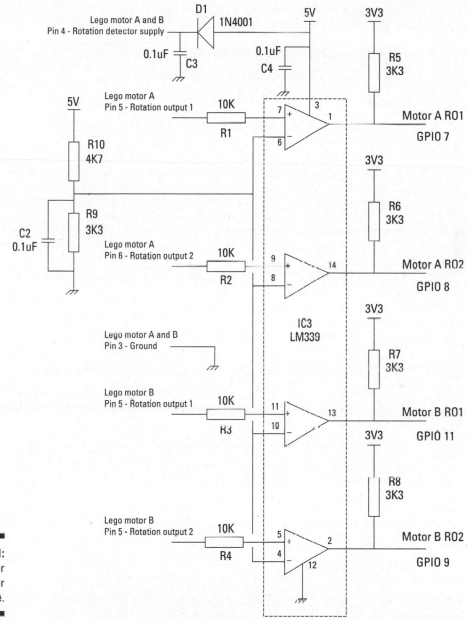

Figure 15-11:
The motor
sensor
interface.

> ✔ Connecting wire
>
> ✔ Two 14-pin DIL IC sockets (optional)
>
> ✔ A 16-pin DIL IC socket (optional)
>
> ✔ A 12-way screw terminal strip, 0.2-inch pitch
>
> ✔ A 4-way screw terminal strip, 0.1-inch pitch

The last two items can be combined as a 16-way 0.2-inch screw terminal strip at the expense of having a larger stripboard.

The only component you may have trouble getting ahold of is the RJ12 socket; you can get them from the same supplier you get the RJ12 plugs from. You can dispense with them altogether if you cut a cable in half and solder the wires directly onto the stripboard. If you do get a socket, you have the problem of mounting it on the stripboard. The trouble is that the socket is not on a 0.1-inch grid, so there is a bit of work to mount it. Just follow these steps:

1. **Drill two 2.5mm mounting holes for the fixing lugs four and a half holes apart.**

   Drilling the half-space hole can be tricky.

2. **Run two rows of three holes together by putting a small router bit in your drill.**

3. **Remove the copper between the two slots with a scalpel.**

4. **Before you push the socket into the board, smear a small spot of Gorilla Glue to the base of each socket in order to provide a good mechanical joint.**

5. **Wrap thin wire around the protruding socket connectors.**

   The pin out of this socket as viewed from the underside is shown in Figure 15-9. A photograph of the slots we cut in the stripboard are shown in Figure 15-12.

Figure 15-12:
Stripboard preparation for mounting the RJ12 socket.

The wires connecting this board to the Raspberry Pi's GPIO pins are connected on our board through screw connectors. In order to fit them onto the board size we chose, we used two sizes of screw connectors, but for economy you can eliminate these altogether and solder wires directly to the stripboard.

A photograph of our board is shown in Figure 15-13. There is little point showing the wiring because the stripboard isn't used to make any connections — it's all wired up on the underside of the board.

Figure 15-13:
The motor
interface
board.

Writing the software

Having built the interface board, you need some software to run it. This software needs to have access to the GPIO pins. There are a few libraries to choose from, but we chose WiringPi2 for Python. This is a port of Gordon Henderson's C library. It uses a syntax that will be familiar to any Arduino user. If you aren't an Arduino user, it takes just as much learning as any other library syntax.

So, the first thing to do is install it. From a command line, type the following:

```
sudo apt-get update
sudo apt get install python-dev python-pip
```

When that has finished, type the following:

```
sudo pip install wiringpi2
```

That's it. However, Linux now throws you a curveball in that you have to run as root before it will allow you access to the GPIO pins. If you use IDLE to do your Python development, you can run this as root. From the desktop, open a command window and type the following:

```
gksudo idle
```

The IDLE package opens and you can use it as normal.

The non-real-time aspects of Linux makes controlling a motor not as precise as you may like, but you can still do a lot. You can apply the same PWM signal to both motors, which comes out on GPIO 18. The other signals can be connected to any GPIO pin, but keep the serial port pins (GPIO 14 and 15) free for communicating with the sensors. We connected the board as shown in Figure 15-14. The motors can be driven by the Python software shown in Listing 15-1.

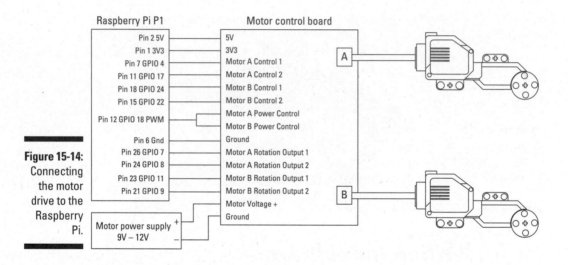

Figure 15-14:
Connecting
the motor
drive to the
Raspberry
Pi.

Listing 15-1:   Driving LEGO Motors

```
#!/usr/bin/env python
"""
Lego Motor Driver test 1 by Mike Cook June 2014
power (PWM) on GPIO 18 (12)
"""

import wiringpi2 as io
import time


mp = 18   # motor power pin    (12)
a1 = 4    # motor A control 1 (7)
a2 = 17   # motor A control 2 (11)
b1 = 24   # motor B control 1 (18)
b2 = 22   # motor B control 2 (15)
ar1 = 7   # motor A rotational sensor 1 (26)
ar2 = 8   # motor A rotational sensor 2 (24)
br1 = 11  # motor B rotational sensor 1 (23)
br2 = 9   # motor B rotational sensor 2 (21)
```

```python
motorControl = [(a1, a2), (b1,b2)]
print "Board Revision",io.piBoardRev()
print "If the program quits here start IDLE with 'gksudo idle' from the
            command line"

def main() :
   pinInit() # define inputs and outputs
   print "Python motor control test"
   print "Ctrl C to quit"
   while True:
      allOff()
      motor ="q"
      motorToMove = 0
      while not(motor == "A" or motor == "B") :
         motor = raw_input("Motor to move A or B ")
         motor = motor.upper()
      if motor == "B" :
         motorToMove = 1
      turn = "s"
      directionToMove = 0
      while not(turn == "C" or turn == "A") :
         turn = raw_input("Clock wise (c) or anti clock wise (a) ")
         turn = turn.upper()
      if turn == "A" :
         directionToMove = 1
      power = -1
      while power < 0 or power > 100 :
         power = input("Power 0 to 100 ")
      pwm = 1024* (power / 100.0)
      io.pwmWrite(18,int(pwm))
      duration = -1
      while duration < 0 :
         duration = input("Time in seconds for motor to move ")
      print "Turning on motor", motor, "for",duration,"seconds"
      io.digitalWrite(motorControl[motorToMove][directionToMove],1)
      time.sleep(duration)
      io.digitalWrite(motorControl[motorToMove][directionToMove],0)
      print "Turning off motor", motor
      print

def allOff():
   io.digitalWrite(a1,0)
   io.digitalWrite(a2,0)
   io.digitalWrite(b1,0)
   io.digitalWrite(b2,0)
   io.pwmWrite(mp,0) # motor off

def pinInit():
   io.wiringPiSetupGpio()
   io.pinMode(ar1,0) # input
```

(Continued)

Listing 15-1 *(continued)*

```
    io.pinMode(ar2,0)   # input
    io.pinMode(br1,0)   # input
    io.pinMode(br2,0)   # input
    io.pinMode(a1,1)    # output
    io.pinMode(a2,1)    # output
    io.pinMode(b1,1)    # output
    io.pinMode(b2,1)    # output
    io.pinMode(mp,2)    # PWM mode
    io.pwmWrite(mp,0)   # off to begin with

if __name__ == '__main__':
    main()
```

The code is reasonably straightforward. It starts by giving variable names to pin numbers, which means you can change things around by simply changing one line per pin. We've also defined the input pins here although they aren't used in this program. We do this so the pins are set in a known state for the hardware in case they have been set to something else.

The `pinInit` function sets the library to use the GPIO numbering system to address the pins and sets them up as inputs, outputs, and a PWM output. Next, the code follows a series of user inputs to get the motor's direction, the power, and the length of time it should be on. Each one of these is in a `while` loop that won't exit until the user has made a valid choice. With the power input, a percentage value (0 to 100) is converted into the 0 to 1,024 value needed by the PWM signal. Note that unlike some other systems, full PWM is achieved at a value of 1,024 and not 1,023.

What pins to write to for the motor control are defined in a tuple list called `motorControl`. This is the clever part of the code. The `motorToMove` variable picks the first or second tuple in the list, and the `directionToMove` variable picks the first or second number in the tuple. So, the pin to set to high to get the correct motor turning in the correct direction is returned by the following:

```
motorControl[motorToMove][directionToMove]
```

This makes the actual setting of the correct pin much simpler than any long-winded collection of `if` statements.

We tested this with both our EV3 motors and NXT motors. Both would move at 13 percent power but no lower, which is to be expected. We noticed that, for a given power, the EV3 motor moved faster and made more noise than the NXT motor.

The motor's sensors can be read as well. We used a simple sketch to try this out, as shown in Listing 15-2.

Listing 15-2:   Reading the Motor's Position Sensors

```python
#!/usr/bin/env python
#!/usr/bin/env python
"""
Lego Motor Encoder input test
encoder 1 wired to GPIO 7 (pin 26) & 8 (pin 25)
encoder 2 wired to GPIO 11 (pin 23) & 9 (pin 21)
"""
import wiringpi2 as io
import time

motorId = ["A", "B"]
ar1 = 7  # motor A rotational sensor 1 (26)
ar2 = 8  # motor A rotational sensor 2 (24)
br1 = 11 # motor B rotational sensor 1 (23)
br2 = 9  # motor B rotational sensor 2 (21)

print "Board Revision",io.piBoardRev()
print "if the program quits here start IDLE with 'gksudo idle' from the
              command line"
io.wiringPiSetupGpio()
io.pinMode(ar1,0) # input
io.pinMode(ar2,0) # input
io.pinMode(br1,0) # input
io.pinMode(br2,0) # input
print "Hi from Python"
lastEncoder = [-1,-1]
count = [0,0]
upCode = 2
downCode = 1
while True:
        port = [io.digitalRead(ar1)<<1 | io.digitalRead(ar2),
              io.digitalRead(br1)<<1 | io.digitalRead(br2)]
        for e in range (0,2) :
            encoder = port[e]
            if lastEncoder[e] != encoder and lastEncoder[e] == 0:
                if encoder == upCode:
                    count[e] +=1
                elif encoder == downCode :
                    count[e] -=1
                print "Motor",motorId[e]," moved ",count[0], count[1]
            lastEncoder[e] = encoder
```

This follows the same convention as before in defining the input pins. You can move the motors by hand to make the encoders respond.

The endless loop combines the two sensors from each motor into a number that ranges from 0 to 3, by using the shift operator (<<) and logical ORing it with the other sensor using the bitwise OR operator (|) to get a two-bit number. This is put into a list called port. Then the current value of the sensor number is compared to the last one, and if the last one was 0, a count is incremented or decremented depending on whether the current sensor number is 2 or 1. If the current sensor number is 3, this indicates that a transition has been missed and you can't be sure what direction it has moved in, so you do nothing with the count. This is part of the self-correcting nature of the Gray code. If the count has changed, then the new value of both counts is printed out.

In Python, printing takes a comparatively long time, so if you can avoid printing, you can cope with faster movement of the sensors.

Listening to Sensors

Communicating directly with LEGO sensors is not quite as easy as you may hope. The EV3 sensors use two methods: one for the simple touch sensor and the other for color, ultrasonic, Gyro, and IR sensors.

Touch sensors

The simplest sensor is the touch sensor. These are annoyingly different for the NXT and EV3 kits. Basically, they both consist of a switch and 2K2 series resistor. In the NXT version, the resistor is connected between pins 1 and 2 — sensor to ground. In the EV3, the resistor is connected between pins 6 and 4 — sensor and positive power rail. What's annoying is that early NXT touch sensors didn't have pins 2 and 3 connected together, so they won't work with the EV3 brick unless you modify either the sensor or the cable to short these two wires. Figure 15-15 shows how to wire up a LEGO touch sensor to the Raspberry Pi for both types of sensors.

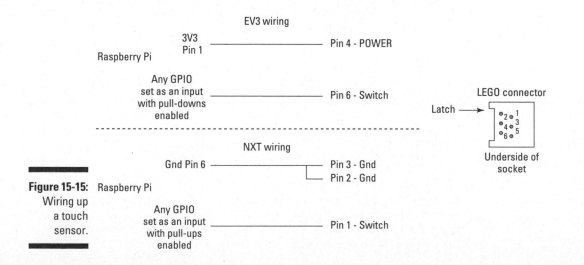

Figure 15-15:
Wiring up
a touch
sensor.

All you need to do to read the touch sensor is to set a GPIO pin as an input and enable its pull-down resistor for an EV3 touch sensor, or enable the pull-up resistor for an NXT touch sensor. Note that the I2C lines have strong external pull-up resistors on the Raspberry Pi board, which will override any settings of the internal resistors. These are pins GPIO 0 and 1 on issue 1 boards and GPIO 2 and 3 on issue 2 boards. The code needed for reading this sensor is shown in Listing 15-3, which is essentially a simple switch input.

Listing 15-3:   Reading a Touch Sensor

```
#!/usr/bin/env python
"""
Lego touch sensor test
"""
import wiringpi2 as io
import time

EV3touch = 10
NXTtouch = 25
print "if the program quits here start IDLE with 'gksudo idle' from the
                command line"
io.wiringPiSetupGpio()
io.pinMode(EV3touch,0) # input
io.pinMode(NXTtouch,0) # input
io.pullUpDnControl(EV3touch,1) # pull down activated
io.pullUpDnControl(NXTtouch,2) # pull up activated
lastEV3state = -1
lastNXTstate = 1
print"Lego touch sensor reading"
while 1 :
    EV3state = io.digitalRead(EV3touch)
    NXTstate = io.digitalRead(NXTtouch)
    if EV3state != lastEV3state :
        print "EV3 sensor now at",EV3state
    if NXTstate != lastNXTstate :
        print "NXT sensor now at",NXTstate
    lastEV3state = EV3state
    lastNXTstate = NXTstate
    time.sleep(0.4)
```

The code will only print out the state of a sensor when it changes, which prevents lots of the same numbers from scrolling up the screen.

Advanced sensors

The advanced sensors that come with the EV3 kit are the color sensor, the IR sensor, the EV3 Ultrasonic sensor, and the Gyro sensor. The last two are supplied only in the Education Edition of the MINDSTORMS EV3 and not in the Home Edition. Fortunately, you can buy the sensors separately and download the "blocks" to use them with the Home EV3 software.

WARNING!

There is an NXT Ultrasonic sensor that will also work with the EV3 software, but they're very different inside and what we're about to show you won't work with the NXT sensors.

The four advanced EV3 sensors communicate with the EV3 brick by serial communications using standard 5V logic levels. This is slightly odd because the EV3 brick is a 3V3 device, so there are buffers in the brick to cut down the 5V signal to a suitable level. However, there are no buffers that boost the 3V3 serial signal from the brick to the sensor. That means the sensors can cope with this voltage, so that simplifies things somewhat. The reason it works is because the Raspberry Pi is also a 3V3 system, so following LEGO's example, there is no need to boost the transmit signal — you just have to cut down the 5V incoming signal.

There is quite a lot of complication involved in the protocol of the brick talking to a sensor, but a lot of this is taken up by the LEGO brick auto-identifying a sensor when it's plugged in. This has to also accommodate the older NXT sensors, as well as third-party sensors and sensors that haven't even been thought of yet. If you know what sensor you're using, you can greatly simplify the software needed to talk to the sensor.

The sensor sends out a list of information about itself, which identifies its type, the modes it can operate in, the range of readings for each mode, and even the baud rate it wants to communicate in. All this happens at the slow rate of 2,400 bauds. When the brick has this information, it sends an acknowledgement and the sensor then switches to its preferred baud rate. Then the sensor sends data back continuously, with the brick sending an acknowledgement byte at least every 300 mS. If the brick fails to do this, the sensor reverts to the slow speed and starts sending its identification data again. This little dance is summed up in Figure 15-16.

The sensor starts working in its default mode, which is Mode 0, the last one to have its information sent to the brick. Any time the sensor is sending information, the brick can command it to use another mode by sending it a command write message. The sensor continues in this mode until commanded into another mode, or it resets due to a power down or not receiving a NACK byte for 300 mS.

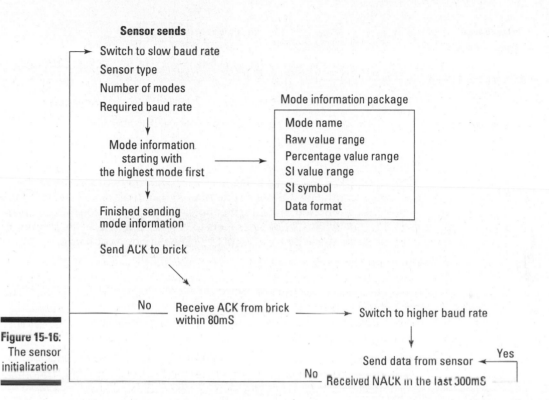

Sensor sends

Switch to slow baud rate

Sensor type

Number of modes

Required baud rate

Mode information starting with the highest mode first

Mode information package

Mode name
Raw value range
Percentage value range
SI value range
SI symbol
Data format

Finished sending mode information

Send ACK to brick

No   Receive ACK from brick within 80mS   Switch to higher baud rate

Send data from sensor   Yes

No   Received NACK in the last 300mS

Figure 15-16: The sensor initialization

There is a further complication: The brick can tweak its own baud rate to match the sensor's, which can be required because the sensor has no accurate crystal clock. Unfortunately, there is no way to do this on the Raspberry Pi because the baud rate is governed by dividing the fundamental clock frequency of the processor, so there is little point in describing that process, because there is nothing that can be done. We found that the sensors we have work correctly with the Pi without any adjustment, despite their baud rates being slightly off.

This information is sent back and forth in one of two ways: as a single byte or as a data packet. When the information is a single byte, this byte has its top two bits as zero, so they're easily identifiable, whereas the start of packages have one or both of these bits set.

A package consists of three parts: a message type, a payload, and a single-byte check sum (see Figure 15-17).

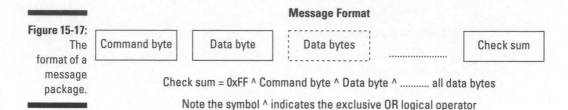

Figure 15-17:
The
format of a
message
package.

Message Format

Check sum = 0xFF ^ Command byte ^ Data byte ^ .... all data bytes

Note the symbol ^ indicates the exclusive OR logical operator

- ✔ **Message type:** The message type byte is complex and is split up into a number of fields, as shown in Figure 15-18. The top two bits define the message type, the next three define the payload length, and the last three define the action. Note how the meaning of these last three bits changes depending on what sort of message is being sent. When this is an info or data message, these bits are simply the sensor's current mode.

- ✔ **Payload:** The payload length indicates how long the body of the message is going to be. This is not a simple number like the mode number; instead, it's an encoded value with the values shown in the diagram. The other twist to this is that an info message byte will be followed immediately by a command byte, making these sorts of messages a byte longer than any other message.

- ✔ **Check sum:** The check sum is calculated by performing an exclusive OR operation with all the previous bytes and with the number 0xFF (or 255 in decimal). When the data arrives, you can calculate the value of the check sum and see if it matches the value that is sent. If it doesn't match, you know there is an error; if it does match, there is much less chance of there being an error. A simple check sum like this is not foolproof; you can get two or more errors that cancel out and give a false good. Other more complex check sum algorithms do exist, but something simple like this is good enough most of the time.

To talk to the sensor with a Raspberry Pi instead of the EV3 brick, you need to understand this message structure and be able to replicate it. But first you have to connect the sensor and Pi together. The circuit to do this is shown in Figure 15-19, and it's pretty straightforward. The GPIO pins brought out to the Raspberry Pi's connector include two whose alternative functions include a serial port; these two pins are GPIO 14 and 15. The transmit pin (TX) can be connected directly to the sensor's receive pin, but the 5V output from the sensor needs to be cut down with a potential divider to bring it into the 3V3 range.

First byte in message

Message type	Payload length	Message action

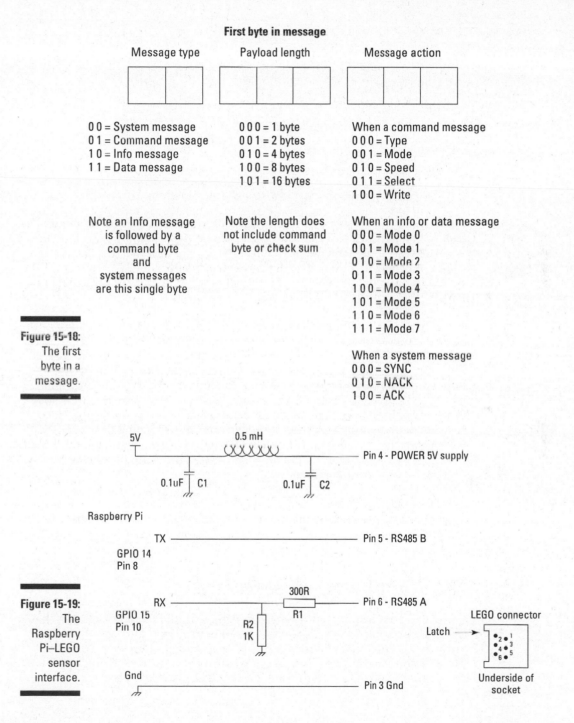

0 0 = System message
0 1 = Command message
1 0 = Info message
1 1 = Data message

0 0 0 = 1 byte
0 0 1 = 2 bytes
0 1 0 = 4 bytes
1 0 0 = 8 bytes
1 0 1 = 16 bytes

When a command message
0 0 0 = Type
0 0 1 = Mode
0 1 0 = Speed
0 1 1 = Select
1 0 0 = Write

Note an Info message
is followed by a
command byte
and
system messages
are this single byte

Note the length does
not include command
byte or check sum

When an info or data message
0 0 0 = Mode 0
0 0 1 = Mode 1
0 1 0 = Mode 2
0 1 1 = Mode 3
1 0 0 = Mode 4
1 0 1 = Mode 5
1 1 0 = Mode 6
1 1 1 = Mode 7

When a system message
0 0 0 = SYNC
0 1 0 = NACK
1 0 0 = ACK

Figure 15-18:
The first
byte in a
message.

5V   0.5 mH   Pin 4 - POWER 5V supply

0.1uF C1   0.1uF C2

Raspberry Pi

TX   Pin 5 - RS485 B

GPIO 14
Pin 8

Figure 15-19:
The
Raspberry
Pi–LEGO
sensor
interface.

RX   300R   Pin 6 - RS485 A
R1

GPIO 15
Pin 10

R2
1K

LEGO connector

Latch →

Underside of
socket

Gnd   Pin 3 Gnd

The parts list for this circuit follows:

- ✔ One 300R resistor (R1)
- ✔ One 1K resistor (R2)
- ✔ One 0.5mH inductor (optional)
- ✔ Two 0.1uF ceramic capacitors (C1, C2)
- ✔ Stripboard, 1 x 2 inches
- ✔ LEGO connector socket
- ✔ Four-way 0.2-inch pitch screw connector

If you're eagle-eyed, you may say, "That 300R resistor is too low. It should be 510R to get 5V down to 3V3." And you would be right, if not for one hidden fact: The sensor itself includes a 220R resistor in series with this line already, so you only need to add another 300R to give, in effect, a 520R resistor for the top of the potential divider. So, this circuit is suitable only for LEGO sensors, not general-purpose 5V serial inputs.

The only other thing that may surprise you about this circuit is the inductor in the power line. In fact, you can do without it, but the Raspberry Pi will reset every time you plug a sensor in. This is because the sudden inrush of current to the sensor causes the 5V line on the Raspberry Pi to dip to a point where the reset is triggered. What the inductor does is limit the sudden inrush and prevent a reset. The actual value isn't critical, and it can be absolutely any value above that shown in the diagram. A series diode also does the trick of preventing reset, but it reduces the voltage going to the sensor and messes up the readings from the color sensor. Replace the inductor with a piece of wire if you don't mind the reset. We built this up on a small piece of stripboard, as shown in Figure 15-20.

If you're wondering where capacitors C1 and C2 are, they're surface mount capacitors mounted on the underside, but you can use a leaded capacitor if you prefer.

The Raspberry Pi software

In order to successfully use a sensor directly with the Raspberry Pi, you have to write a program to handle the initialization protocol. This mainly involves writing a function that will read the serial port and split up what comes out into individual messages. To start off, let's look at how to read and display the identification information coming from the sensor and display it.

Figure 15-20:
The built
Raspberry
Pi–LEGO
sensor
interface.

The Raspberry Pi's serial port is used during the boot-up process. So, to prevent the sensor from interfering with the boot up, you must disable getty. Here's how:

1. **Use the File Manager to navigate to the directory /etc/.**

2. **Choose Tools⇨Open Current Folder as Root.**

   A new window appears.

3. **Right-click the file inittab and choose Open with Leafpad.**

4. **Now find the line that says the following, and comment it out by putting a # in front of it:**

   ```
   T0:23:respawn:/sbin/getty -L ttyAMA0 115200 vt100
   ```

5. **Save the file.**

6. **To stop the Raspberry Pi from sending out data to the port, with the root view in the File Manager go to the /boot/ directory and open the cmdline.txt file.**

7. **Find the line that says the following and delete it:**

   ```
   console=ttyAMA0,115200 kgdboc=ttyAMA0,115200
   ```

8. **Save the file and reboot the Pi.**

9. **If you don't have the Python serial module, install it from a command-line window by typing the following:**

   ```
   sudo apt-get install python-serial
   ```

Now you're all set to go. You can type in the code shown in Listing 15-4, which will basically monitor the serial port until the sensor has finished sending all its data and then send a byte command to trigger the sensor into its high-speed mode. Then it will write to the sensor the required operating mode and milk the data by sending a NACK command every 230 mS and display the data package sent after that.

Listing 15-4:   Reading a Serial EV3 Sensor

```python
#!/usr/bin/env python

# Serial sensor by Mike Cook June 2014
# Raspberry Pi serial sensor tested with the EV3 color sensor and IR sensor
# It should also work with the EV Ultrasonic sensor (not the NXT one) and
#             the EV3 Gyro

import time
import serial

SYNC = 0x00   # Synchronization byte
ACK  = 0x04   # Acknowledge byte
NACK = 0x02   # Not acknowledge byte

payloadLookup = [1, 2, 4, 8, 16, 32, 0, 0]
messageLength = 0
# to fit max message plus command and checksum
message = [ n for n in range(0,34) ]

refreshTime = 0.230  # Rate to read data must be less than 300 mS
checkSumError = False
ser = serial.Serial('/dev/ttyAMA0', 2400, timeout =2 )

def main() :
  print "Sensor read"
  setup()
  mode = 0 # sensor mode to use
  changeMode(mode)
  print "running in sensor mode",mode
  lastRefresh = time.time()
  while True :
   if time.time() - lastRefresh > refreshTime : # send NACK and look at data
     ser.write(chr(NACK))
     lastRefresh = time.time()
     ser.flushInput() # remove old data
     getMessage() # get the data
     if not checkSumError :
        printMessage() # view data message

def setup():
   global ser
```

```
    print "initializing the sensor"
    while not(message[0] == 0x90 and message[1] == 0x80 and ⊃
            checkSumError == False) :
        getMessage()
    if ord(ser.read(1)) != ACK :
        print("not got an ACK");
    ser.write(chr(ACK)) # tell the sensor to go
    time.sleep(0.006) # give it time to finish sending the ACK
    ser.close()
    ser = serial.Serial('/dev/ttyAMA0', 57600, timeout =2 )

def getMessage() : # parse input stream into message
  global checkSumError, messageLength
  checkSum = 0xff
  command - ord(ser.read(1))
  if command == 0x00 or command == 0xff : # color sensor sometimes ⊃
                throws these
    return
  message[0] = command
  if (command & 0xC0) == 0 : # single byte
    pass
  else : # multibyte message
    checkSum ^= command;
    payloadLength = payloadLookup[(command >> 3) & 7] # number bytes ⊃
                in message
    if (command & 0xC0) == 0x80 :
        payloadLength += 1 # info message has command byte following
    for n in range(1, payloadLength + 1) : # read in the message up to the
            check sum
      message[n] = ord(ser.read(1))
      checkSum ^= message[n]
    # get check sum
    message[payloadLength + 1] = ord(ser.read(1))
    messageLength = payloadLength + 1
    if message[payloadLength + 1] != checkSum :
        checkSumError = True   # check sum error
    else :
        checkSumError = False # check sum fine

def printMessage() : # not the check sum
  for n in range(0,messageLength) :
    print hex(message[n]),
  print

def changeMode(newMode):
  if newMode <= 5 and newMode >= 0 :
    sendMessage(0x44, 0x11) # command write
    for n in range(0,3) :
        sendMessage(0x43, newMode & 0x7) # command mode
    ser.write(chr(NACK));
```

(continued)

Listing 15-4 *(continued)*

```
def sendMessage(cmd, data):
  cSum = 0xff ^ cmd ^ data;
  ser.write(chr(cmd))
  ser.write(chr(data))
  ser.write(chr(cSum))

if __name__ == '__main__':
  main()
```

The main function starts off by calling the setup function, which reads what the sensor is sending until the final message in the sequence. This is always the data format of the sensor's mode zero. Then the sensor should send an ACK byte to say it's ready to switch into sending the data. At this point, you have 80 mS to reply with an ACK byte or the sensor will start sending its data again. The setup function sends this and then sleeps for a short time to allow the byte to be sent. Then the serial port is closed and opened again using the faster speed before returning. Then the main function writes to the sensor the mode you want to operate it in. By default, this is mode 0, but if you want to change it, the code is provided to do so. Changing the mode is simply done by sending three bytes — the command, mode number, and check sum. We noticed that the LEGO brick sometimes sends this message a few times, so this code sends it three times, followed by a NACK byte. This is done in the functions changeMode and sendMessage. Notice that this last function also generates the check sum by using ^ the exclusive OR operator.

The while loop runs forever. Here, the system timer is used so that once every 230 mS (to give Linux a bit of slack when it steals time from you) the Raspberry Pi keeps the sensor alive by giving a NACK byte, flushing the serial buffer, and reading and printing out the next data message sent. This is done because the sensor sends data continuously and not every NACK, so the buffer will have old data in it. If you want to do something with data coming faster, you can simply read the message as often as you need to.

The heart of the program is the getMessage function. This reads data a byte at a time from the serial port and analyzes it to see how many bytes are in the message. Then it goes on to read those bytes and calculate and verify the check sum. This keeps the input data stream in sync. The result is a sequence of data messages like this:

```
0xc0 0x48
0xc0 0x4a
0xc0 0x4c
```

This is for an IR sensor running in mode 0 proximity and represents the distance to an object in front of it. Most of the time, the data is in the second byte, but in the case of reading the numbers from the IR remote, there are four bytes; the one populated with the key number depends on the channel the remote is set to. We didn't get much joy from the angle measurement seek mode, however, because the data returned seemed inconsistent.

It isn't possible to print out the information messages as you go because printing in Python takes a long time and you lose the synchronization between the data coming in and the need to respond to it. We wrote a much longer program that will print out and decode all the messages the sensor sends and then, in effect, does what this program does. You can find that program along with a text file of its output from the IR sensor on www.dummies.com/go/raspberrypiprojects.

A commercial alternative

The best way to control the LEGO components is not with a Raspberry Pi but with some other real-time microcontroller like the Arduino. The people at Dexter Industries have taken what's, in effect, two Arduino processors on one board and produced a controller specifically designed to run with the Raspberry Pi. It's called BrickPi.

The BrickPi fits completely over the top of the Raspberry Pi board and even includes a top and bottom plate with holes so that it can be fitted into a LEGO model. As of this writing, it can only talk to NXT sensors, but beta software containing EV3 capability has been released. It has example code for Java, Ruby, C, Python, Scratch, and BlockyTalky along with a support forum.

We had some slight difficulty installing the system on our Pi, but we were given prompt and helpful support from the administrators. If you're shy about using the soldering iron, we highly recommend the BrickPi as an alternative to the normal brick programming environment. Sadly the motor movement is not very accurate with the current software. Check the forum pages for the latest updates: www.dexterindustries.com/forum/?forum=brickpi.

Part V
Exploring RISC OS

In this part . . .

- ✔ Discover a great alternative to Linux.
- ✔ Write programs in the structured BBC BASIC.
- ✔ Make your own desktop applications with ease.
- ✔ Access the general-purpose input/output (GPIO) from within RISC OS.
- ✔ Build a transistor tester.
- ✔ Build your own accurate digital voltmeter (DVM).

Chapter 16

Introducing RISC OS

*O*ne of the great things about the Raspberry Pi is that it's so easy to change the operating system: Just change the SD card! Several different operating systems are available, but most of them are just another flavor of Linux. However, RISC OS is unique, forged in the depths of time from almost the start of personal computing in the 1980s and developed into the most advanced operating system of the 1990s. Many of the things you take for granted on a Linux, Windows, or Macintosh desktop first appeared in RISC OS and inspired the two personal computing giants. So, take a step back into the past and the future and explore the operating system made by the inventors of the ARM chip. And be prepared for a blisteringly fast Raspberry Pi!

Toto, we're not in Kansas anymore

Once upon a time, Mary Goldring, a British journalist, asked the head of Acorn Computers, "So, do you make the chips in the computer?"

"No", came the reply, "we only put them together."

That was one of those unsung moments when the world shifted on its axis without anybody noticing. It very possibly sparked the invention of the ARM chip, the most widely used processor on the planet. A very small group of people got the go-ahead to design an experimental microprocessor, one that ran using much simpler but smarter instruction. The machine code instructions used in hundreds of programs were analyzed to find out what programmers actually needed as opposed to what the chip designers gave them. Then a simpler and faster processor architecture was designed. It was sent off to the fabrication plant and almost forgotten as a financial crisis overwhelmed Acorn and threatened its existence.

(continued)

(continued)

When the chip arrived back, it sat unopened in its packaging for a few days while the demoralized engineers wondered if they would even get paid at the end of the week. Eventually, the chip was opened and tested and, miraculously, found to work, with only one minor change. This was totally unheard of! The first iteration of a new processor working? This chip was the first ARM chip, which initially stood for "Acorn RISC Machine" (where *RISC* stood for "Reduced Instruction Set Computer").

Although the hardware engineers made a few refinements to the chip, the software people looked at licensing a graphics-based operating system. The cheapest came with a fee larger than their telephone number, so someone said, "We could write one in a week," and a week later the first version was running. It was called Arthur.

Eventually, this grew into RISC OS. The latest version is available for download for free onto an SD card to run on the Raspberry Pi.

The RISC OS desktop, shown here, uses the now familiar desktop or wimp system (short for windows, icons, menus, and pointers) along with the Acorn innervations of an icon bar showing running programs and context-sensitive drop-down menus.

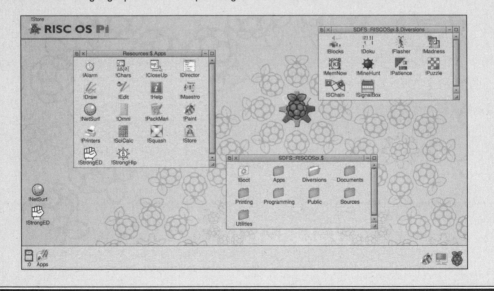

Knowing What Makes RISC OS Unique

The biggest difference between Linux and RISC OS is under the hood. Linux is a preemptive multitasking system, whereas RISC OS is a cooperative multi-tasking system.

When the Linux operating system decides what bit of code, or thread, is going to run, it also determines how long that code will run for. It doesn't matter if that code isn't quite in a state to pause. The rug is pulled out from underneath it, and control is passed back to Linux. The code has no control over this, nor does the programmer. There are things you can do about allocating thread priorities, but at the end of the day, the rug will be pulled.

RISC OS, on the other hand, has a cooperative approach. Control is passed over to the next thread, or program, in the list of tasks, and this thread continues to run until the code tells the operating system it's ready to be swapped out and the next task can be run. From our perspective, this is a much more civilized way of going about things and gives the programmer the choice over how much time to use before letting other tasks have a turn. So, if you want or need all the processing power, you can have it, which makes the operating system much more responsive.

Although the preemptive nature of Linux is fine in a multiuser system, in a single-user system like so many Raspberry Pis run in, it's just a bit too "Big Brother" for our liking. Debates run very passionately about this point, and a lot depends on whether you like the protection given by preemptive multitasking or you think it's treating you like a child who needs supervision.

Preparing for Action: Getting RISC OS

The simplest way of getting RISC OS is to buy it on an SD card. You can get it from www.riscosopen.org/content/sales along with some other RISC OS goodies.

However, if you have a spare SD card, making your own is simple: First, download the latest RISC OS image at www.raspberrypi.org/downloads. Unlike the gigantic Linux distributions, RISC OS weighs in at a very trim 113MB (zipped). Unzipped, it inflates to 2GB. Next, you have to get it onto an SD card. You can use any size SD card you like as long as it's at least 2GB. Note however, that anything over 2GB is no advantage because this is the maximum you can use. This might sound like a restriction, but 2GB is almost infinite in the world of RISC OS.

Installing RISC OS is the same as installing any other operating system on the Raspberry Pi. There are lots of methods — the one that's best for you depends on the computer you have available. Your best bet is to go to www.elinux.org/RPi_Easy_SD_Card_Setup and choose the option that suits you. Alternatively, www.pilearn.com/Pages/Page1001.html gives you a step-by-step guide for using the Mac to set up an SD card, with links to information for a PC. (A word of warning: On that page, you find instructions for using a Raspberry Pi for making a card, but we haven't been able to get those instructions to work.)

If you need to set the over scan parameters in the `config.txt` file to make the desktop fit your TV, use the same number for the left over scan as you do for the right over scan. Similarly use the same number for the top over scan as you do for the bottom over scan. Version 12a (the latest one as of this writing) has a small bug that gives you an offset mouse pointer if you use asymmetric stretches side to side or up and down.

The mouse

The mouse is somewhat unusual. It has three buttons:

- **Left (select) button:** The select button is used for the normal operation of dragging and double-clicking to run or open a file like all the other operating systems.

- **Right (adjust) button:** The adjust button normally performs some sort of variation on the select button operations. For example, dragging a window with the adjust button doesn't bring it to the front; you can drag a window behind another one with the adjust button. With the adjust button, you can select several files at once. Clicking the adjust button adds an icon to the group selected. It also deselects selected files without deselecting all of them.

- **Middle (menu) button:** The menu button brings up a drop-down menu. The menu that's brought up is dependent on where the pointer is when the middle button is clicked; it's known as *context sensitive*. The middle button is the biggest hurdle for a newcomer to get over; other operating systems don't reinforce the menu button mindset so beginners can trip up over this. When in doubt, try the menu button.

RISC OS is best used with a mouse equipped with a center scroll knob that doubles as a button. If you don't have this kind of mouse, there is a program you can install that simulates the middle mouse button when you press the Windows key on the keyboard. It's in the `Utilities` folder and is called !WinMenu.

The keyboard

A wide variety of keyboards can be used with the Raspberry Pi, and not all of them are the standard PC type. When you first power up RISC OS, the system is set for the default British keyboard, which isn't too dissimilar from the U.S. keyboard — the only real difference is that Shift+3 gives you £ instead of #. (You can change this later if you want.)

It's best if your keyboard has a row of function keys from F1 to F12. These are used a lot more on RISC OS than on other systems. Many keyboards don't have that many function keys, but the keys F12 and F10 are important in RISC OS. F10 is the break key. F12 is involved in a lot of tasks: By itself, pressing F12 takes you into the command-line mode; Pressing Ctrl+F12 brings up a task window; and pressing Ctrl+Shift+F12 shuts down the system (although you can do this from the desktop if you prefer).

The network

The network connection used to be disabled by default, but on the latest release (which as of this writing was version 12a), the network connection is enabled. It requires a network to be connected into the Ethernet socket; unfortunately, there is no support for a wireless interface (as of this writing).

The network connection is described as "Ethernet over USB," but it's actually the Ethernet socket. In our setup, we connected the Ethernet port to a Mac laptop. Then we opened System Preferences, clicked Sharing, and enabled Internet Sharing to share our Wi-Fi connection with our Thunderbolt Ethernet. This will also work on non-Thunderbolt-enabled systems. You can do the same sort of thing with a PC or have a direct cable connection to your router if you prefer.

All Systems Go: Starting Up RISC OS

Insert the RISC OS SD card into your Raspberry Pi and power up the Pi. Unlike with Linux, you'll be at the desktop in about 15 seconds — be prepared for that kind of speed up! The first time only, you get a progress bar as the fonts are scanned, and then a web browser window from NetSurf pops up with a "Welcome to RISC OS" page held in an internal file.

Now just look at the window. Along the bottom runs what is called the *icon bar,* a familiar thing on desktops (but remember that RISC OS had them first!). On the left are icons concerned with storage; on the right are icons indicating which programs are running. At startup, there are just two icons, and those are always there: One is an icon of a monitor and is used to set the monitor resolution; the other is a raspberry (in the old days, it was an acorn), which is used to control the system. A left click brings up a task window showing how much memory is allocated to each task. You can drag the red bars and change the allocated memory.

Scroll to the bottom of the window. The sixth line from the bottom says "RAM disc." Click and drag out a red bar to something like 400K. As you release the mouse button, a new icon appears on the left side saying "RAM." This is a temporary fast storage area that uses some of the system's memory to look like a mass storage device. Anything put in it will disappear when the Pi is switched off, but it saves wear and tear on the SD memory (and in the old days was much faster than a floppy disk).

If you click the raspberry with the center button, a menu appears. One of the choices is to shut down. This is what you do before turning off the power. In sharp contrast to Linux, it's almost instantaneous. You see a window inviting you to restart, but you can just turn off the power knowing that all the files have been closed correctly.

Taking a look around

Click the Apps icon on the left of the icon bar. A window with some very basic applications in it appears. Double-click !SciCalc, and the icon of a calculator appear on the right side of the icon bar. Left-click that icon to see the calculator. On the top right of the calculator frame, you see a square. Click that square to see the calculator's other functions.

The anatomy of a window is shown in Figure 16-1. It has the close icon as a cross, as you may expect. However, there are some other things that you may not expect. For example, there is an Iconise button, which will turn the whole window into a small icon you can drag around the desktop, useful for quickly clearing some space on the desktop. You also have a Back button. Unlike most other operating systems (in which anywhere you click a window, it comes bounding up to the front like an overeager puppy), a RISC OS window only comes to the front when you click its title bar. The Back button puts it firmly in its place.

Try clicking the Back button and then drag the window by its title bar but hold down the right mouse button. The window gets dragged as you would expect, but when you encounter another window, it's dragged behind that. It looks odd if you aren't used to it.

Now move your mouse over the calculator window and press the middle mouse button. You see a drop-down menu. Move to the bottom entry, Help, and left-click. A document window appears, telling you all about the workings of the calculator. You can explore other options in this menu as well. For example, the View option allows you to toggle between the compact and expanded view of the calculator; the Edit option allows you to copy the calculator's results to the clipboard.

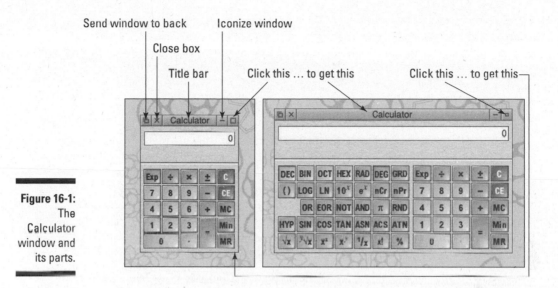

Send window to back Iconize window

Close box

Title bar Click this … to get this   Click this … to get this

Figure 16-1:
The
Calculator
window and
its parts.

Point at the calculator icon on the bottom icon bar and click the middle mouse button again. This time a menu pops up, and the top entry is Info. This is consistent in all applications; Info tells you a bit about the program. (You can also access the Help here exactly as you could with the application window menu.)

The Choices entry brings up another window (shown in Figure 16-2). The choices are self-explanatory, but look at the icon to the right of where it says Base Decimal. This is a drop-down list icon. Click it for a list of available number bases. Note that there are radio buttons for choosing from a number of options and check boxes for selecting many options.

Double-click the !Help icon in the Apps window. Now every time you hover your pointer over some aspect of the window, a pop-up contextual help message appears. This is very useful when you're first learning RISC OS. You'll know when you've learned the basics because this pop-up help message becomes really annoying.

This is the basic way of interacting with a RISC OS application. You may get a bit muddled at first because you're used to another OS, but it quickly becomes second nature.

Making your own space

In this section, you create some folders of your own. This will illustrate the unique way RISC OS has of handling saving.

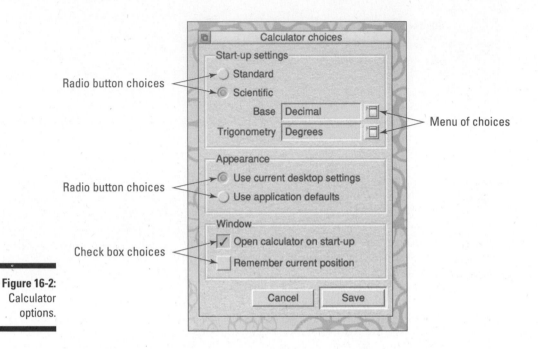

Radio button choices

Menu of choices

Radio button choices

Check box choices

Figure 16-2:
Calculator
options.

At the bottom left of the icon bar, you see the icon of an SD card. This is the SD card from which you're running RISC OS. Left-click the icon and you see the basic root window of the filing system. Its path name is displayed as the window's title: SDFS::RISCOSpi.$. SDFS stands for "SD card filing system"; RISCOSpi is the name of the SD card; $ is the top level. Note the double colons (::) separate the filing system type from the name of the volume it's currently using. The dot (.) is used to separate folders.

Unlike in Linux, there is no root user, super user, or any other form of user — there is just you. If you double-click the Apps folder, you open the same window you did when you clicked Apps in the icon bar. In fact, they're one and the same thing, except the one from the icon bar is protected (you can't add or delete anything from it). The Apps folder you opened from the root window has the path name in the window's title.

It's time to make some space for your own work. Middle-click the root window and scroll down to New Directory. Move to the right and in the text box, type the name of your new directory folder. We used the name Mike, but you probably want to pick something a bit more personal. When you've finished, press Return or click OK, and that directory will appear in the root window. Double-click it to open your blank window and keep it open while you work through the next section.

Saving and loading by dragging and dropping

Saving and loading files are the operations that may be most different from all the other computer desktops that came after RISC OS. Most computers use a mini filing system list to identify files. Some systems allow you to load a file by dragging its icon onto the application icon, but RISC OS takes this a whole step further.

Follow these steps for saving a file:

1. **In the Apps window, double-click !Edit.**

   The !Edit icon appears on the icon bar.

2. **Left-click the !Edit icon.**

   A blank text window pops up.

3. **Click inside the window.**

   You see the red "focus" cursor.

4. **Type a few words.**

   The title bar will say <untitled> *. The asterisk informs you that the file's contents have not been saved. You're now going to save the file in your own folder that you created in the preceding section.

5. **Click the menu button and choose Save or press F3.**

   A window appears like the one you saw when you created your folder, except this window has a default name already in it.

6. **Press the backspace key until you clear the default name and type Text_test but do not press the Return key.**

7. **Drag the text file icon above the name Text_test and drop the icon into your folder.**

   A text icon appears and your text window has the file's path name in it.

8. **Type a few more characters.**

   You see the asterisk (*) in the title bar again, indicating you have unsaved data. Updating your file now is very easy.

9. **Click the menu button, choose Save, and click OK.**

   The filename has the full path name of the file in it, without an asterisk.

If you want to create a new file with the updates you've made, just add characters to the filename. If you want to save the file somewhere else, simply drag and drop the icon in the save box into the folder you want to keep it in.

These actions are summarized in Figure 16-3.

Unsaved title bar

Title bar showing path name, file name, and * unsaved update

Figure 16-3:
Saving a
file.

First save: Name file and drag and drop into a folder

Subsequent saves: Just click OK

Here's a unique trick: Type in and save another text file. Then drag that file's icon into the text window of the first file. Bingo! The contents of the new file are added to the old file! You can imagine how easy this makes adding standard paragraphs to things you type. Many applications work like this — merging data directly into a file you're working on by drag and drop. Some applications do this with images or other types of data. Of course, the addition has to make sense — for example, dragging a JPG image into a text file won't work (well, other than dumping the bytes of that file and looking at it as a text file, which you might want to do).

Focusing on file types

Most operating systems identify the type of file by an explicit extension to the filename. Typically, a text file would have the extension `.txt`. In RISC OS, things are slightly different. Here's how:

✔ Each file has a type, but the file type is hidden inside the file.

✔ The file type determines what sort of icon is shown for the file.

✔ The file type is a three-digit hexadecimal number, but many file types are enumerated — that is, they have an associated word with the file type.

What the !

In RISC OS, you see many icons whose names begin with an exclamation point (pronounced *pling*). These are applications or programs you can run with a simple double-click. However, like most superheroes, they have a secret identity: They're just folders. In your folder, click the menu button and create a folder called noApp. It appears with the normal folder icon. Now menu-click the folder and choose Dir. "noApp"⇨Rename and press the backspace key to put an exclamation point (!) at the start of the name. The icon changes to the default application icon. If you double-click it, you get — not surprisingly — an error box saying it has failed to find a file called !Run.

So, how do you reveal an application's secret identity as a folder? Simply hold down the Shift key while you double-click the icon, and it opens like a folder. You can do this to see inside

!Edit or !SciCalc. This tip makes it easy to build your own desktop clickable applications by gathering together all the files you need under one folder.

Hold down the Shift key and double-click your noApp icon, and the empty folder opens. Now use the text editor to type **This file is no help** and save the file in the open folder under the name !Help. Now close the folder and close the folder containing the noApp application. Open the folder containing the noApp application again, menu-click it, go to the second item (App "!noApp") and then choose Help. Your unhelpful Help file will be shown.

Simple, understandable structures like this make RISC OS refreshing. Other operating systems require you to have access to special tools to do things like this. But not RISC OS!

If you menu-click the Text_test file you created in the preceding section, and move your pointer onto File "Text_test" and then move it down to Set Type and then move it along to the text box, you see the file type shown as "Text." Press the backspace key here and type the word **BASIC** and press Return. Immediately, you see the icon change. It's the same file, but now the computer treats it differently if you click it. Don't click it now; instead, go back and set the file type to FFF, and it's a text icon again. The file type Text is represented by FFF; you can type either to set the file type.

You can reload the file into an edit window by dragging it onto the !Edit icon or by double-clicking it.

Handling Graphics with !Paint and !Draw

Two of the staples of any computer system, !Paint and !Draw have been in the RISC OS since the beginning. !Paint handles bitmap graphics; !Draw handles vector graphics. Although they may seem a bit clunky by today's standards, they have the great advantage of being understood formats by most RISC OS applications. In fact, !Paint plays a vital part in the whole construction of the desktop world.

!Paint

A !Paint file is called a sprite file, and it can hold one or several images or sprites. The most common use for sprites is making desktop icons. There are a number of different types of sprites, mainly differentiated by the number of colors they contain. The majority of desktop icons have only 16 colors, reflecting their early origins, but you can have sprites with 2, 4, 16, 256, 32,000, and 16 million colors. The color selection window changes to reflect the color choice. The higher color depths are suitable for photographs, although a passable photograph can be rendered in 256 colors.

The drawing tools are as you would expect: single pixels (pencil), spray can, brushstrokes, camera (copy block), scissors (move block), hand (shift whole sprite), as well as a selection of solid and line shapes. One thing you may not find in other packages is the way the colors are applied — they can be simply set, or they can be the result of a logic operation between the working color and the color already in the background.

As a quick example, follow these steps:

1. **Double-click the !Paint icon in the Resources apps window.**

   The !Paint icon appears on the icon bar.

2. **Open the Diversions folder.**

3. **Hold down the Shift key and double-click the !Patience icon.**

4. **Drag the !Sprites22 file onto the !Paint icon in the icon bar.**

   You see a window with two sprites: a large sprite and a small sprite. The larger one is only 34 pixels square, and the smaller one is 18 pixels square.

5. **Double-click the larger sprite.**

   You see a colors palette and the sprite along with the paint tools.

6. **Menu-click this sprite and select the zoom option. Repeatedly click the up arrow next to the first box to get an enlarged view.**

   These windows are shown in Figure 16-4.

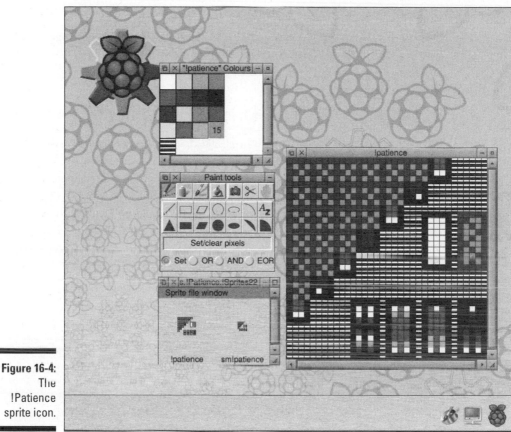

Figure 16-4:
The
!Patience
sprite icon.

Create your own sprite by left-clicking the !Paint icon on the icon bar. The Create New Sprite window appears with an invitation to set the parameters, including the size. The window defaults to a sprite the size of the whole screen, but you can use the arrows or type directly in the boxes to get any size you want. The sprite shown in Figure 16-5 is a high-resolution sprite we made to show the effects of various logic operations on filled circles. Notice how the color selection is controlled by three sliders. It has the option of control by RGB (that is additive color — red, green, and blue). It can also use the subtractive color model of CMYK (cyan, magenta, yellow, and black) or the HSV (hue, saturation, and value) color space.

!Draw

Whereas !Paint uses individual pixels, !Draw is a vector drawing tool. Here a drawing is made up of lines, and all that's stored are the parameters of those lines. This makes !Draw files very small compared with the larger bitmaps. !Draw files are very good with splines (curves), allowing you to enter a spline by clicking and dragging. Then you can edit the control points of the curve by first selecting the curve with a right-click to show all the control points. Then you can drag the control points around again with the right (adjust) mouse button.

Producing a good vector drawing takes some skill, but one of !Draw's major uses is collating sprite, text, and line drawings. To add a text file or sprite image, simply drag the icon into the drawing or save the object by dragging the save box into the !Draw window. They can then be manipulated and composed.

There are some comprehensive online tutorials on these packages. For how to use the basic tools in !Draw, check out www.riscos.com/support/users/userguide6/draw/chap02.htm. For some interesting ways to design patterns, look at http://homepages.nildram.co.uk/~riscos/tutorial/pattern_tut. And for a rundown of the tools you get in !Paint, check out www.riscos.com/support/users/userguide6/paint/chap02.htm.

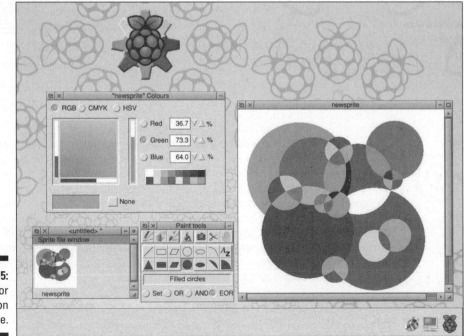

Figure 16-5:
A high color resolution sprite.

Connecting to the Outside World

If your network is not configured, double-click the !Configure icon on the desktop. A folder with lots of applications in it opens. You should notice something strange: These applications don't start with an exclamation point — they're presented differently.

To configure your network connection, follow these steps:

1. **Single-click the Network icon.**

   The Network Configuration window appears.

2. **Click the Internet icon.**

   The Internet Configuration window appears.

3. **Click the Enable TCP box and then click the Interfaces icon.**

   The Interfaces window appears.

4. **Click the Ethernet over USB check box and then click the Configure button next to it.**

   The USB 0:Ethernet over USB window appears.

5. **Click the Via DHCP radio button and click Set.**

6. **Click Save in the Network Configuration window and agree to the restart request.**

   If you couldn't before, you should now be able to browse the web using !NetSurf.

When we tested this out, an entire web page loaded in about 5 seconds, whereas the best that Midori could do under Linux, loading the same page, was 15 seconds.

When you're online, there are a number of interesting things you can download. !Store is already installed on the desktop; it takes you to a source of applications, both paid for and free. There are a number of utilities and games worth looking at. Open the application details window and click an application for a description of it. Some names used can be quite cryptic or require a knowledge of RISC OS history in order for it to make sense. For example, Hatari is an Atari emulator, whereas Rise of the Triad is a first person shoot-'em-up game, a bit like Doom. For Rise of the Tria, you need !UnixHome to be run first; you can find it at `www.riscos.info/packages/SupportDetails.html`.

When you download something, make sure that you have a window open where you want to store the application so you can drag it in.

Most online software comes in a compressed format. The format of choice is called Spark. Double-clicking the file opens the archive just like a normal window. You can run many applications directly from this compressed archive window. However, if the application needs to write anything back to the application's folder, this will fail, so it's best to drag the icons you need out of the archive into your own folder before you run them.

Identifying the Resources That Are Already Installed

Many resources come already installed on the SD image, many of which would've cost you quite a bit of money when RISC OS was in its heyday. The highlight of these resources is the Programmers Reference Manual (PRM), in the Documents.Books folder. This five-volume set cost more than a hundred bucks in the '90s, but here you get them as a set of PDFs for free. The books cover all the operating system calls for all sections of the machine; they aren't exactly light reading, but they do contain all sorts of vital information. (Although you can get PDF readers for the Raspberry Pi, you may want to transfer the PDFs to your computer because there you'll be able to search the PDFs much more efficiently.)

Many authors have released their work under Creative Commons licenses. We recommend you look at PipeDream, a fully integrated office suite of word processor, database, spreadsheet, and charting package all in the same window. The application itself is in the Apps folder, and a full set of tutorials is in the Documents folder.

Check out the high-quality vector graphics examples in the Documents. Images folder and the games in the Diversions folder. These aren't the most exciting things you'll ever see, but the Tetris clone !Blocks is as addictive as it ever was, and !Meteors was retro when the OS was new. Perhaps the oddest diversion is !Madness — it slowly nudges all the open windows around the screen and is meant as a demonstration of interapplication messaging. (Just make sure you read the Help file to find out how to stop it before running.) Finally, we have to mention !SignalBox, a graphically spectacular simulation of the Exeter West train station, shown in Figure 16-6.

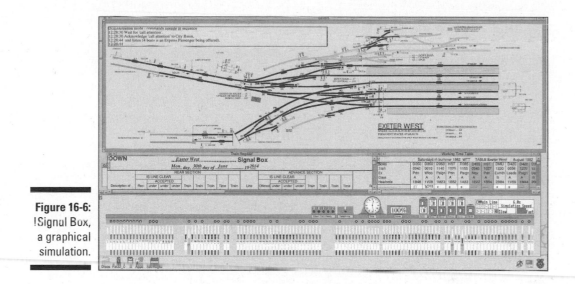

Figure 16-6:
!Signal Box,
a graphical
simulation.

The Utilities folder contains !ChangeFSI, which is a great way to convert images between JPG and sprite formats. However, it isn't just limited to JPGs — it also handles a wide variety of input graphics file formats (see the Formats file, located inside the application, inside the Documents folder). The application is also capable of a number of image processing functions like histogram equalization, gamma correction, and sharpening.

Shift+click to open an application.

The FSI part of the name !ChangeFSI comes from the Floyd-Stenberg method of dithering, a way of showing high-resolution images on a lower-resolution screen by using an error diffusion technique.

There are many other delights to explore in the RISC OS distribution. You may not understand them all — we don't ourselves — but over time you can get to know them. People who explore all that RISC OS has to offer tend to grow to love this operating system.

Chapter 17

RISC OS Coding

A RISC OS system is easy to program. Not only can you run simple programs, but you can also build complete desktop applications without too much bother. Unlike Linux, the operating system is almost static — it doesn't change very often and code you write tends to have a remarkable shelf life. This is because most of the changes in the operating system maintain an unprecedented degree of backward compatibility.

In this chapter, we show you how to go about writing code, starting off with the simple "Hello world!" program. Then we move on to a desktop insulting machine and graphics modes, and end up mangling bits of images by symmetric reflections. Along the way, we point you toward some great simple demos as you see how to bend this operating system to do what you want to do.

In the Beginning Was BASIC

Once upon a time, all home computers came with a built-in language. In the vast majority of cases, this language was some version of BASIC. These days, BASIC has developed a reputation for being unstructured and producing *spaghetti code* (code that jumps all over the place using the infamous GOTO instruction, making it almost impossible to follow).

Acorn BASIC, or BBC BASIC as it's known, is different. Yes, it still has the GOTO command (as does the C language), but just like the C language, you never need to use it. The latest version of BBC BASIC, called BASIC V, is different. It's structured. In fact, it contains most of the same sort of control structures as languages like C and Python. There is error handling, and it even uses pointers and indirection in a much simpler way than C. Although it has retained the subroutines of traditional versions of BASIC, those subroutines are rarely used; instead, it has functions or procedures just like Python and C.

BASIC V also has a few tricks up its sleeve. It has error handling, something that no other version of BASIC has. Also, you can drop into machine code any time you want in a program. This means that you can write the majority of your program in a high-level language and drop into machine code when you need the speed for a certain section. (However, there is little need for that with the blistering speed you get from the Raspberry Pi.) You can also fully interact with the machine's operating system using a process known as software interrupt (SWI), which allows you to write any desktop application entirely in BASIC. Code written in BASIC tends not to become obsolete under new revisions of the operating system or the hardware. Programs we wrote in 1982 on a BBC Model B work just as well on the Raspberry Pi — the only difference is that they run at lightning speed now.

The BASIC language was once the first exposure most people got to a computer language, but you may be arriving here from another route. You could've started on Scratch, learned C or Python, and now find yourself learning BASIC. If so, you've gotten a good start — you already know about programming structures and flow. Inevitably, there are differences among the languages, but most of them are cosmetic. In this section, we provide a quick rundown of the major differences you see.

Uppercase letters

Most modern computer languages are case sensitive and this version of BASIC is no exception. However, in the early days of computing, everything was done in uppercase characters mainly because the mechanical teleprinters used for computer terminals didn't have lowercase characters. So, BASIC was designed with uppercase commands. Nowadays, a program written in all uppercase seems like it's shouting at you. Variables and function names can still be in lowercase, but it's common to see them in uppercase, too.

Variable types

In C, each variable is declared with a *type* (the sort of data it holds). In Python, this is still true, but the language does backward somersaults to hide this fact from you, which is a pity because often you need to know what type you're dealing with.

With this version of BASIC, the variable type is built into the name. If you just have a name, you have a floating point variable. If the name ends in a percent symbol (%), it's an integer variable. If the name ends in a dollar sign ($), it's a string variable.

Incidentally BASIC has some of the simplest-to-use and most-comprehensive string handling routines of any language we've come across.

Line numbers

Line numbers are absent in languages like Python and C, but most BASIC programs are written with line numbers. Most of the time, you don't have to use line numbers if you don't want to. Not having line numbers prevents you from actually using the dreaded GOTO command anyway. There are only two occasions when you may want to legitimately use line numbers: in error handling and when restoring the pointer for reading DATA statements.

Indentation

In Python, indentation is the hidden builder of structure. (You and your friends can debate whether this is a good thing or a bad thing.) In C, indentation is mainly decorative (although there is some debate about its use and the style you write the language in). C is a lot more relaxed than Python.

With BASIC, indentation is almost unheard of. Most of the code is written from the first column, which can be a shame because indentation can make things much easer to follow. You can use indentation just as you do in C, to aid the readability of the code, although indentation isn't used nearly as much as it should be.

Only one equal sign

Most languages use a single equal sign for an assignment operator and a double equal sign for a comparison operator (used in an if statement). This causes all sorts of problems for beginners and causes if statements to apparently not work.

With BASIC, there is only one equal sign used for both sorts of operations, so it's much simpler to learn (although if you're used to other languages, you may be a little confused at first).

Scope

In C, variables are valid only when they're used in the function they're defined in. If they're defined outside of any function, then they're global and accessible by all functions. In Python, it's roughly the same except if you want to alter a global variable in a function, you have to declare it as global at the start of the function.

In traditional BASIC, there is no scope to variables at all, but in this current version there is. Variables can be declared as local in a function, but by default they're all global. This is the opposite of what other languages do as a default, but it's better than nothing.

Indirection

C is strong on pointers, but this version of BASIC has indirection operators, which essentially are the same thing. Suppose you have a variable called P%. As noted earlier, the % means it's an integer. If you just use P% in a statement, you get the value stored in that variable, as it should be. However, each variable is stored in the computer's memory, and you can access the contents of the memory byte-by-byte using the indirection operator question mark (?). This is most useful when dealing with arrays, which can then be treated as arbitrary memory allocations.

Check out the following operation:

```
A% = P%?2
```

This operation will assign to the variable A% the contents of the memory byte two bytes along from the memory pointed at by P%. The ! operator does the same thing, but it deals with four-byte chunks of memory.

Note that this works on both sides of an equal sign. So, to clear the byte one address away from the memory pointed by P%, you would use the following:

```
P%?1 = 0
```

This is much easer to use than the pointer system used by C. And it's a much more flexible arrangement that the PEEK and POKE instructions used in other implementations of BASIC.

Operating system calls

There are several ways that a BASIC program can interact with the operating system, but the main one is the SYS command, which transfers a string to the operating system interpreter. Many of these commands are in the form of SWI calls, instructions that cause a subroutine to be executed in exactly the same way as an interrupt service routine is evoked by a hardware signal. So an SWI call causes the SWI handler routine to be called, and in RISC OS, it causes specific operating system functions to be called depending on the word that follows the SWI. So, it acts as a sort of pseudo machine code instruction.

The upshot of this is that you can easily invoke a myriad of operating system calls. These are detailed in the Programmers Reference Manual (PRM), along with the other ways of affecting the system.

Most things to do with the display can be manipulated by visual display unit (VDU) commands, which send bytes to the display engine to display onscreen as ASCII characters. However, the nonprinting ASCII characters control various aspects of the display, like the screen origin or the color. The other two system calls are OS_Byte and OS_Word; these take in either a single byte or word to perform operations. There is nearly always an SWI equivalent of these calls.

Hello World

When computers were first appearing in retail outlets, they would sit on display showing nothing but the BASIC prompt. A popular pastime for kids was to type in some sort of variation of this and then run away:

```
10 PRINT "Hello World"
20 GOTO 10
```

The hapless sales clerk had no clue what to do as the message filled the screen. (The message often contained some sort of expletive, and the sales clerk hadn't a clue how to stop it.)

The past revisited

You can re-create this world very simply on your fancy desktop operating system. Simply follow these steps:

1. **Press F12.**

   The whole screen scrolls up and an asterisk (*) appears at the bottom of the screen. This is the command-line prompt.

2. **Type BASIC and press Return.**

   You see the BASIC prompt of >.

3. **Type the following two lines.**

   ```
   10 PRINT "Hello World"
   20 GOTO 10
   ```

4. **Type RUN and press Return.**

   Your message fills the screen so fast that it looks like it has stopped.

5. **Press the Escape key to restore the BASIC prompt.**

   At this point, you can type **LIST** to see a listing of the program or **NEW** to wipe the old code so you can type in another one. If you type **SAVE** *name*, that saves the code (where *name* is the name you want to call the file containing the program). Type **LOAD** *name* to load code from the current directory. Finally, type **QUIT** to leave BASIC and go back to the operating system prompt.

Operating system modes

In RISC OS, there are basically three different modes the computer can operate in:

- ✔ **Command mode:** The asterisk (*) prompt; the computer boots up into this mode.
- ✔ **BASIC mode:** The old BASIC mode with a > prompt.
- ✔ **Desktop mode:** The familiar desktop.

You can switch between these modes quite simply. Figure 17-1 shows how these modes operate. Basically, you can swap modes in either a desktop window or the full screen. The keys needed to enter and exit these modes are shown next to the connecting lines. The modes are hierarchical in the sense that they "remember" the mode that called them, so when a mode is exited, the mode before the call is restored.

This quick transfer into and out of the desktop is in stark contrast with Linux, where when the desktop is exited, the whole thing restarts afresh when you return. With RISC OS, when you go back to the desktop, everything is where you left it.

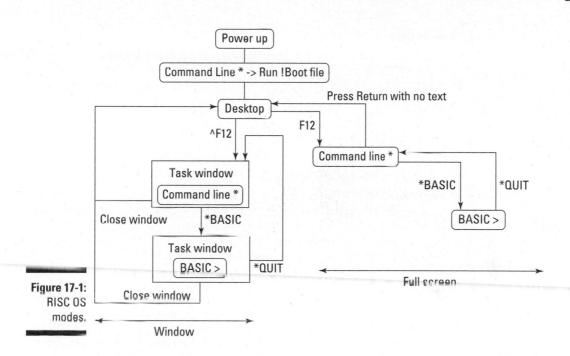

Figure 17-1:
RISC OS
modes.

When you close a task window, you're given the opportunity to save it. This allows you to look again at your session or incorporate things like a list of modules in other texts.

BASIC mode

This is how the very first Acorn computers booted up. The idea is that there is a single BASIC program you're working on and the commands deal with that. Most of the commands have a shortcut ending in a full stop to save you typing, and they're all in uppercase. These commands are the most useful:

- ✔ **RUN:** Runs the current program.
- ✔ **LIST:** Prints the current program. (You can use the shortcut L instead of typing LIST.)
- ✔ **LIST 40:** Prints just line 40. (You can use any other number here or even a range of numbers separated by a comma.)
- ✔ **PRINT variableName:** Prints the value of the variable.
- ✔ **RENUMBER:** Renumbers the program in increments of ten.
- ✔ **HELP:** Takes you to Help documentation on all the commands. Just type **HELP** and it tells you about the current program. Type **HELP A**, and you get a list of all BASIC commands starting with the letter *A*. Type **HELP ABS** and you get a description of that particular command.
- ✔ **QUIT:** Exits BASIC.

Command mode

There are many commands, but the most useful are the following:

- ✔ ***CAT:** Catalogue or list the current directory. In Linux, this is ls.
- ✔ ***DIR:** Change the current directory. In Linux, this is cd.
- ✔ ***DESKTOP:** Go back to the desktop.
- ✔ ***QUIT:** Go back to the calling program.
- ✔ ***BASIC:** Enter BASIC mode.
- ✔ ***HELP:** Get help with commands. Help will give you a hierarchical help. Typing ***help** along with one or more keywords will bring different levels of help. For example, typing ***help modules** gives you a list of modules, typing ***help FileSwitch** gives you a list of file switch commands, and ***help** *any command* will give more information on the command. This is a handy function when you're stuck.

Directory path names are similar to those in Linux except directories are separated by a dot (.) not the slash (/) that Linux uses. Note that when you're at the command-line prompt, you don't have to use the asterisk (*) in front of the command, but in other environments like BASIC, prefixing a command with an asterisk marks it out for sending to the operating system command line.

There are many more commands — the PRM tells you what most of them are. However, this system is extensible, and there are ways to add your own commands with relocatable modules.

Desktop mode

In desktop mode, you can write code in a desktop editor like !Edit. There are other editors that you can use, like !StrongED and our favorite, !Zap. These often have enhancements when writing BASIC, like automatic coloration of keywords and renumbering facilities.

The modern way of doing things

The command line BASIC is not used very much these days. Life is so much easier when you use a graphics editor. It has all the functions you may expect and quite a few more. However, copy and paste don't work like other functions — they're menu options.

The RISC OS distribution comes with two editors, the simple !Edit (covered in Chapter 16) and the very powerful !StrongED. We've never really liked !StrongED — there was a bit too much to do in order to get it to work the way we wanted. Our favorite editor is !Zap, and it's still available through !Store for free. Installation is slightly more complex than normal. Just follow these steps:

1. **With an Internet connection, double-click the !Store application.**

2. **Click the Catalogue icon.**

3. **Locate !Zap in the PlingStore applications window.**

   It's the last one in the list at the moment. Select it by clicking the name.

4. **Click the download icon.**

   A box appears telling you that you aren't logged in. You can ignore this. If you log in, the !Store application records what you've downloaded so you don't download anything twice.

5. **Double-click the !Configure icon on the desktop.**

   A configuration window appears.

6. **Click the Boot icon in the configuration window.**

   The Boot sequence window appears

7. **Choose the Install option by clicking it and then dragging the !Boot file from the zap archive window into the BootMerge window.**

8. **Click Merge to start the process.**

   It takes a few minutes.

9. **Drag the !Zap fie into the Apps folder at the top level.**

   You're done.

Now double-click the !Zap icon to run the program and put it on the icon bar. Menu-click it and choose Create⇨New File⇨&FFB Basic, and a new window appears. In that window, type the code in Listing 17-1.

Note: There is no need to type the line numbers or the colon — these will appear as soon as you start typing. If the line number increments are not 10, don't worry — after you've typed it in, choose Mode⇨BASIC⇨Renumber.

Listing 17-1:   Hello Again

```
10 : A%=0
20 : PRINT "Hello for the ";A%;" time"
30 : A% += 1
40 : GOTO 20
```

Now you need to run it. You can do this from !Zap by choosing Mode⇨BASIC⇨Run Program⇨Run Then Quit. A window opens and the program is run in it. Press Escape to end, and then press any other key to get back to the desktop. You see that the program prints about 300 lines a second. (Eat your heart out, Linux Python!) We did a quick test and timed the number of lines printed out over 30 seconds. BASIC produced 293.7 lines per second and Python printed 6.2 lines per second.

From !Zap's Mode menu, you can get all sorts of useful things to happen. There is a renumber function and numerous run options. One of the most useful is the simple Drop into BASIC. Here, a window opens and you have the BASIC prompt (>). If you then type **RUN**, the program will run as you might expect. However, any syntax error is accompanied by a line number. Suppose an error message says there is an unknown variable at line 250 and you type **LIST 250** to see the line. What do you do if that line contains many variables? How do you know which one is wrong? Just print them out one at a time. Type **P** and then use the cursor keys to maneuver up to the line, and use the copy key (on the keyboard, it says End) to copy the variable name. Then press Return, and the value of the variable will be printed out. However, if it says "Error Unknown Variable," then you know that's the one that's wrong.

Use the cursor method of copying to avoid making a mistake in typing what you think is the name of the variable rather than what really is the name.

You can also use the same technique for editing a line. Move the cursor up to the line you want to change and use the copy key to copy part of it. Then use the normal keys to type in the bit you want to change. Finally, press Return to put that line back into the text. This is often faster than returning to the desktop, although you need to save the file if you want those changes to be permanent.

Although BASIC and Python are both interpreted languages, BASIC has a few tricks up its sleeve. A Python program is just a simple text file whereas in BASIC it's a tokenized file. This means that all the BASIC instructions, like PRINT and WHILE, are compressed into a single byte or token, making it much quicker for the interpreter to know what instruction needs to be performed. Then the BASIC interpreter itself is so small that it fits inside the high-speed on-chip memory or cache of the ARM processor, making it much faster to run. The cache is special on-chip memory that runs as fast as the processor, something that doesn't happen with all kinds of memory.

So when you save a BASIC file, you aren't saving a text file — you're saving a file where all the BASIC instructions are compressed. If you want to see what this looks like, in !Zap choose the Mode⇨BASTXT. You see the strings you typed in, and your variable names, as well as some other strange symbols. To convert your BASIC program into real text, choose File➪Dump to Text, and a new copy of the file in text form will be produced.

The Insult Generator

The insult generator is one step up from "Hello World." It isn't a difficult concept to grasp, but it shows you more of the fundamentals involved with writing and arranging code in a system. The idea is simple: The program generates insults by simply choosing a random word or phrase from two files. One contains nouns and the other contains adjectives. It prints out:

> You *random adjective random noun*

And then repeats on any key press. To set this up, create a new directory and call it Insult. Then menu-click the !Zap icon and choose Create➪New File➪&FEB Obey.

Into that file, type the following:

```
| Boot file for Insulter
Set Insult1$Dir <Obey$Dir>
IconSprites <Obey$Dir>.!Sprites
```

Save the file under the name !Boot in your Insult directory. The first line starts with a | and is treated as a comment. The second line sets a system variable, with the path name to where the file currently is when it's run. The final line tells the desktop to look at a file called !Sprites to find what icons to use. This file is not present at the moment, so nothing will happen, but you may get an error message, so just ignore it for the moment. Now double-click this !Boot file; again, nothing will appear to happen, but the path name will be set.

Looking at the main program

Now for the meat of the program, this is shown in Listing 17-2 and is the BASIC program that actually does stuff. When you've typed it in, save it in a file called Insult1.

There is no need to type the line numbers or the colon — the editor will put those in for you.

Listing 17-2: The Insult Generator

```
10 : REM Insulter plain BASIC version
20 : REM Version 0.5 By Mike Cook
30 : REM Freeware
40 :
50 : MxL%=300
60 : MxI%=200
70 : MxN%=100
80 : DIM Ins$(MxI%),Inn$(MxN%)
90 : PRINT"Insult Generator - Escape to quit"
100 :
110 : PROCreadInsults
120 : PRINT"Any key for an insult":PRINT
130 : REPEAT
140 : A% = RND(100)
150 : B% = ADVAL(-1)
160 : UNTIL B%<>0
170 : A$=GET$ : REM dummy read
180 : WHILE(TRUE)
190 : PROC_Insult
200 : PRINT:PRINT"More?"
210 : A$=GET$
220 : PRINT
230 : ENDWHILE
240 : END
250 :
260 : DEF FNread
270 : LOCAL x$,A%
280 : x$=""
290 : REPEAT
300 : A%=BGET#F%
310 : IF A%>&1F THEN x$=x$+CHR$(A%)
320 : UNTIL A%<&20 OR LEN(x$)>250
330 : =x$
340 :
350 : DEF PROCreadInsults
360 : Insults%=0
370 : F%=OPENIN("<Insult1$Dir>.adjective")
380 : REPEAT
390 : Ins$(Insults%)=FNread
400 : Insults%+=1
410 : UNTIL Insults%=MxI% OR EOF#F%
420 : Insults%-=1
430 : CLOSE #F%
440 :
450 : F%=OPENIN("<Insult1$Dir>.nouns")
460 : names%=0
470 : REPEAT
480 : Inn$(names%)=FNread
490 : names%+=1
```

```
500 : UNTIL names%=MxN% OR EOF#F%
510 : CLOSE #F%
520 : names%-=1
530 : ENDPROC
540 :
550 : DEF PROC_Insult
560 : PRINT "You "+Ins$(RND(Insults%))+", "+Ins$(RND(Insults%))+
      ", "+Inn$(RND(names%))+"."
570 : ENDPROC
```

The main program runs until line 240. The rest of the listing consists of function and procedure definitions. Line 80 has the dimension statement that defines two string arrays. You're going to fill them up by reading the words out of a text file. This is done with the PROCreadInsults procedure.

This is a bit more complex than it could be, but the way we've done it here makes the text files containing the insult words a lot more simple to prepare. In effect, the insulting words file consists of plain text, with a new, selectable insult on every line, so it could be one word or a few. This means that the program has to read individual bytes out of the file and build up the words to put into the insult arrays. This is done by the function FNread, which returns a string comprising one line of the text file.

The colon (:) operator is used to mean a new line, despite it not being on a physical new line. It's often used to shorten listings or group commands together.

The files are opened using the path name given by the system variable, which was set when you double-clicked the !Boot file, plus the actual file name (adjective or nouns). This then reads in all the word files. The final procedure (PROCinsult) prints out the random words that make up the insult.

Lines 130 to 160 need a bit of explanation. This is a crafty way of initializing the random number generator. By constantly generating random numbers in the random time it takes for the user to hit the first key, you're assured of a new starting point every time for the random number generator.

All we need now before we can test this is to generate the two text files of words. So, on the !Zap icon, choose Menu⇨Create⇨New File⇨&FFF Text and enter some adjectives shown in Listing 17-3 and save the file as adjective. Then repeat this using Listing 17-4 and save the file as nouns.

Listing 17-3: Adjective File Contents

```
artless
bawdy
beslubbering
bootless
brutish
churlish
cockered
clouted
craven
currish
dankish
dissembling
droning
errant
fawning
```

Listing 17-4: Noun File Contents

```
baggage
barnacle
bladder
boar pig
bugbear
bum bailey
canker blossom
clack dish
clotpole
coxcomb
codpiece
death token
dewberry
flap dragon
flax wench
flirt gill
foot licker
fustilarian
giglet
gudgeon
haggard
harpy
```

You need to press Return after the last word in each of these files. There are much longer versions of the files at www.dummies.com/go/raspberrypiprojects.

Having everything in place, you can now run the insult generator by double-clicking the Insult1 BASIC icon. If you get errors, go back into the editor and correct them. Make sure that it's running correctly before proceeding to the next stage.

Smartening it up

You can't do much about the actual output, but you can present a better view of this program to the desktop. You had to double-click the !Boot file before you ran the program. These next steps will give you a program-like icon to double-click.

First, you have to create an icon to represent your program. We made a representation of a well-known cartoon character who is known for his insults:

1. **Load up !Paint and click the icon bar icon of !Paint.**

   A new window invites you to create a new sprite.

2. **Choose the 256 color mode, set the size as 32 x 32 pixels, set the name as !Insult, and click OK.**

3. **Menu-click over the now blank icon in the window with the !Insult title, and select a zoom of 11 to 1 in the magnify window.**

4. **Again, menu-click and choose Paint⇨Show Tools and Paint⇨Show Colors.**

5. **Now use the pencil tool to input your artwork.**

   Figure 17-2 shows you an enlarged view of what we have. We're sure you can work out the colors of this yellow-skinned blue-shirt-wearing fellow, from the grayscale picture.

6. **Save this sprite file under the name of !Sprites in the Insult directory.**

   Now you need a file to direct operations when the folder is double-clicked.

7. **Create an Obey file from !Zap (choose Create⇨New File⇨&FEB Obey), type the following into the file, and save it as !Run:**

```
| Run file for Insult1
WimpSlot -min 32k -max 32k
Set Insult1$Dir <Obey$Dir>
Run <Insult1$Dir>.Insult1 %*0
```

This is the sequence of commands that are needed for running the program. The first line is a comment you used in the !Boot file and could be omitted. The next line allocates some memory for the program to run it — in this case, no less than 32K and no more than 32K. Next, there is the setting of the path name, just like the !Boot file. This is done again just in case this system variable has been overridden by some other program. Finally, the last line runs the basic program.

8. **Rename the** `Insult` **directory** `!Insult`**.**

9. **Close the directory that contains it, and open it again.**

You should have your new icon ready to double-click. It isn't a true desktop application, but it has all the outward appearances of such. You may like to include a `!Help` text file in the directory (see Chapter 16).

Figure 17-2:
The insult
icon.

The insults themselves have a rather 17th-century restoration comedy sound to them. You may want to have more colloquial words in your lists. The longer the lists, the more varied the results. Lines 50 to 70 define the maximum number of each type of word, and those are easily changed.

Understanding Full Desktop Applications

At www.dummies.com/go/raspberrypiprojects, you can find not only the finished code for !Insult but also a "real" desktop version called !Insulter. !Insulter's icon appears on the icon bar, the output is in a movable window that you can iconize, and it happily multitasks with the rest of the desktop. It uses exactly the same function as this example, but there is a lot more "wimp stuff" hung round it. (Wimp is short for "windows, icons, menus, pointers." Wimp stuff is the fundamentals of any desktop-type application, no matter what the operating system.)

Any desktop application is written in what is known as an *event-driven style*. Events are things that happen. For example, a user clicks a box, a window control, or a scroll bar, or performs a menu click. This event is notified to the program, and the program deals with it as appropriate to the application. An event could also be that some other program wants to send your program a message, or you want to send another program a message.

On the other hand, you could get a null event — nothing has happened. That doesn't necessarily mean there is nothing to do. You could advance an animation, do a bit more of a long calculation, or check input/output ports for any activity.

The act of asking the operating system for an event is the way that the whole cooperative multitasking thing works. If you ask for an event, the operating system takes the opportunity to switch to other tasks because, after all, your program has nothing to do at the moment or it's your program's choice, at this point, to relinquish control for another task. If you never ask for an event, nothing else gets a look in, just like the way the simple !Insult program ran — while that was running, nothing else on the desktop would work.

This may look complex, but this "wimp stuff" is virtually the same from program to program so you can reuse a lot of it, at least the structure. The heart of it is the wimp poll system, a loop that's in lines 510 to 610 of !Insulter. The program calls `Wimp_Poll` and, in doing so, informs the operating system of any events it isn't interested in. When this call is returned, the program gets back a number that indicates what, if any, events have occurred. A case statement then decides what has occurred and responds to those events of interest. Table 17-1 shows all the results you can get back from `Wimp_Poll`.

This whole wimp business is covered in Volume 3 of the PRM.

Other things can help you with window definitions. Instead of specifying every element of a window, you can read them off a file. The files can be created by a graphics program so you can build up each window from the desktop by clicking, dragging, and using tick boxes. The original program that did this was called !ResEdit, but it won't work with the new OS, so now there is one called !TemplEd and another called !WinEdit. These are both found ready to be installed at the path `Programming/DrWimp/Utils` of the RISC OS installation.

Table 17-1	Wimp Poll Codes
Code	*Reason*
0	Null_Reason_Code
1	Redraw_Window_Request
2	Open_Window_Request
3	Close_Window_Request
4	Pointer_Leaving_Window
5	Pointer_Entering_Window
6	Mouse_Click
7	User_Drag_Box
8	Key_Pressed
9	Menu_Selection
10	Scroll_Request
11	Lose_Caret
12	Gain_Caret
13	Poll word non-zero
14–16	reserved
17	User_Message
18	User_Message_Recorded
19	User_Message_Acknowledge

Many of the windows can even be copied from other applications and then customized with these programs. In fact, many elements of the wimp system can originate from other applications, like the sprites.

The other thing that needs to be set up is the memory that defines the menu structure. This is done in PROCsetupmenu and consists of simply filling memory with numbers. These numbers are interpreted as menu items. Again, the PRM tells you which numbers mean what. In this example, there are only two menu items: one that opens the information window, a standard part of any application, and another to quit the application.

You can see the process of "wimpifying" an application in Figure 17-3. It shows you the basic steps and flow of an event-driven desktop application.

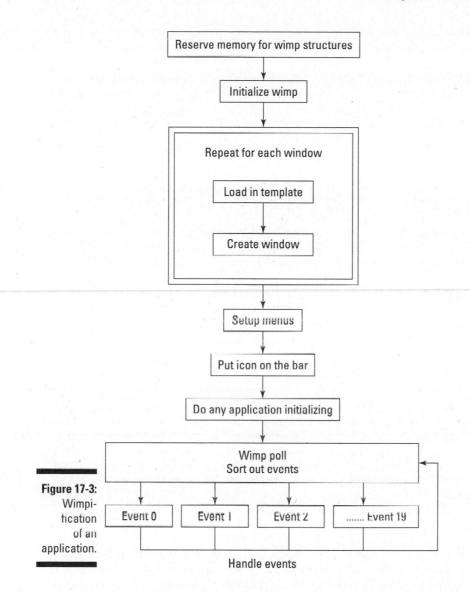

Figure 17-3:
Wimpi-
fication
of an
application.

Reserve memory for wimp structures

Initialize wimp

Repeat for each window

Load in template

Create window

Setup menus

Put icon on the bar

Do any application initializing

Wimp poll
Sort out events

Event 0   Event 1   Event 2   .... Event 19

Handle events

You see a lot of use of the word indirection operator (!) in the !Insulter example. It's mainly used to fill and read blocks of memory that are used to pass
information back and forth between BASIC and the operating system. So,
when Wimp_Poll is called, a pointer to a memory space is passed to it — in
this case, by the variable q%. Notice how earlier this had been dimensioned
as an array, with a DIM statement. This is filled in by the operating system in

a manner that depends on what event occurred. For more information about wimp programming, see the `Documents/Books` directory.

 DrWimp is a tool that attempts to automate this process. It's included in the distribution and is found in the programming directory. There are blank applications for you to customize and plenty of examples to look at in the `Examples` directory; there are also tutorials online. There are other such tools online that do this as well.

Working with Graphics in RISC OS

When it comes to graphics, RISC OS has a lot of legacy to cope with. Early machines had very limited amounts of memory and there were various compromises that could be made regarding resolution, the number of pixels, and *pixel depth* (the number of colors each pixel could be). This was done by defining graphics modes, a preset set of compromises. Although that memory restriction no long applies, the use of modes are still around and are often still convenient to use, in a non–desktop application context.

Modes and resolution

Although different modes had different resolutions, an attempt was made to have some sort of mode independency in the software. Things were arranged so that the drawing coordinates were larger than the actual resolution so that drawings look approximately the same no matter what mode you were in. It was just that some modes looked much more chunky than others, but the chunky modes had more colors. Basically, the range of coordinates the software worked on was 0 to 1,279 for the x-axis and 0 to 1,023 for the y-axis. This has been now overtaken by the new hardware, and you can get real pixel resolution much greater than this.

As more advanced Acorn machines were introduced, the number of modes multiplied. Eventually, the mode became not a single number but a string of parameters. These give the x and y resolution, the color mode, the relationship between pixels and screen coordinates, and the frame rate. If you menuclick the display icon in the bottom-right corner of the icon bar, you see what mode your desktop is set to. On the Raspberry Pi, all the named modes default to a 64-color display of various resolutions.

You can get an idea of this if you type in the program in Listing 17-5. This draws a fan of lines in each mode up to mode 53.

Listing 17-5: Mode Tester

```
 10 : REM Mode tester by Mike Cook
 20 : FOR M% - 0 TO 53
 30 : MODE M%
 40 : PROC_Size
 50 : FOR N% = 0 TO 90
 60 : GCOL N%
 70 : MOVE 0,0
 80 : Th = RAD(N%)
 90 : X% = Xmax%*COS(Th)
100 : Y% = Ymax%*SIN(Th)
110 : DRAW X%,Y%
120 : NEXT N%
130 : GCOL 255, 255, 255
140 : PRINT TAB(0,20); "Mode ";M%;" Resolution ";XLim%;" by ";YLim%
150 : PRINT "Coordinates ";Xmax%;" by ";Ymax%
160 : A$ = GET$
170 : NEXT M%
180 : END
190 :
200 : DEF PROC_Size : REM get the screen size
210 : SYS"OS_ReadModeVariable",-1,4 TO ,,Xfact%
220 : SYS"OS_ReadModeVariable",-1,5 TO ,,Yfact%
230 : SYS"OS_ReadModeVariable",-1,11 TO ,,XLim%
240 : SYS"OS_ReadModeVariable",-1,12 TO ,,YLim%
250 : Xmax%-XLim%<<Xfact%
260 : Ymax%-YLim%<<Yfact%
270 : VDU 5
280 : ENDPROC
```

If you run this program, you see that most of the modes look the same on the screen. The program uses a system call to read data about the screen mode. The lim% variables are the actual number of pixels, and the fact% variables are the multiplication factor between the drawing coordinates and actual pixels, expressed as a power of two. So, by shifting the number of pixels on the screen to the left by the multiplication factor, you get the maximum coordinate size for each axis.

To get a taste of what it used to look like, download an application called GraphTask from www.armclub.org.uk/free. This application emulates the old modes in a graphics task window. If you double-click it to get its icon on the icon bar and then drag the mode tester file into it, you see the modes as they used to look. Note, however, that the system calls that read the screen mode variables apply to the whole screen, so the values for resolution and coordinates will not reflect the mode. Despite this, GraphTask can be a very handy utility to have around, and it comes with lots of interesting examples. One of the examples in this package is called Rope. We used this as a starting point to illustrate something rather interesting that you can do. Our more readable version of Rope is shown in Listing 17-6.

Listing 17-6: Rope

```
 10 : REM >Rope
 20 : MODE 0
 30 : CLG:CLS
 40 : OFF : REM Turn off flashing text cursor
 50 : OSCLI "POINTER 1"
 60 : N=10: L=700: E=0.7: g=0.2: D=L/N
 70 : DIM V(N),W(N),P(N),Q(N)
 80 : REPEAT
 90 : MOUSE X,Y,B:MOVE X,Y
100 : FOR I=1 TO N
110 : x=P(I)-X+V(I)*E:y=Q(I)-Y+W(I)*E
120 : d=D/SQR(x*x+y*y+.4)
130 : X+=x*d:P(I)=X:Y+=y*d
140 : Q(I)=Y:d=d/2-.5:V(I)+=x*d
150 : W(I)+=y*d-g:V(I-1)-=x*d:W(I-1)-=y*d+g
160 : NEXT
170 : WAIT
180 : CLG
190 : FOR I=1 TO N
200 : DRAW P(I),Q(I)
210 : NEXT
220 : UNTIL 0
```

Run this program and you see a rope dangling off the end of the mouse pointer. Move your mouse and see how it dangles and moves. This is an example of Mode 0 graphics. Try also dragging the program file into GraphTask and see how the movement is not quite so free.

Next remove the MODE command in line 20, either by deleting the line or by putting a REM at the start of the line. (This is known as *commenting out* a line.) Now run it again. Note that the line is finer and the movement is more fluid. This is because you're now using the native screen graphics mode. Finally, as a piece of magic, you're going to break the illusion of a desktop. Remove or comment out lines 30 and 180. These clear the screen between drawing each iteration of the rope's movement. Double-click the program file and twirl the rope around the whole desktop. Figure 17-4 is what it looked like when we did it.

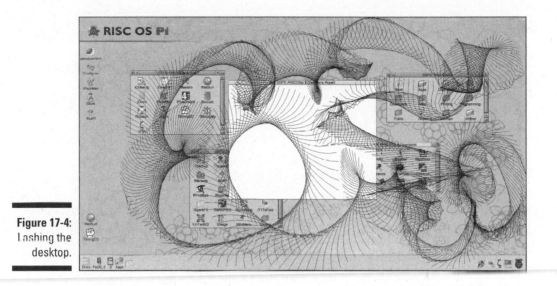

This sort of thing is not supposed to happen. Other operating systems go to great lengths to prevent it. RISC OS is much freer, and if you want this to happen you can do it very easily. You have to go to a bit more trouble to restrain the graphics and restore the illusion.

Lines and shapes

As you can see in the last couple of listings BASIC has MOVE and DRAW functions to create a line. You just move to the starting point and draw to the ending point to produce a line. There is also a single pixel plot instruction called PLOT. With these fundamental actions, you can draw everything. The MOVE and DRAW functions are combined in the LINE function, where you specify the start and the end of the line you want to draw.

Shapes come in two varieties — outlined and filled — and allow you to draw rectangles, circles, and ellipses.

However, all these drawing commands are just special cases of the general-purpose PLOT command, confusingly the same name as the single-pixel plot function. This one takes in three numbers: a plotting mode and x- and y-coordinates. Where the shape being plotted needs more than a single pair of coordinates, PLOT uses the previous positions of the graphics cursor to fill in the missing values. The plotting mode number is quite complex — it consists of a single byte, where the top five bits define the drawing operation and the bottom three bits define how it will be drawn. Basically, these different ways of drawing are how the coordinates are interpreted, absolute on the screen or relative to the last coordinates. Also, it defines if the operation is a draw or a move, and if it uses the current foreground color, background color, or logical inverse of the color already on the screen.

TIP

For a full list of plot commands see www.bbcbasic.co.uk/bbcbasic/manual. This is a good place to see all the commands BASIC can offer. There are also downloadable documents with these BASIC commands explained.

Images

BASIC is capable of plotting images. There are two main formats that are handled directly: sprites and JPGs. The &E8 to &EF PLOT commands handle the drawing and plotting of sprite formatted images or bitmaps. However, all image handling is also included in the "Sprite Extended Modules" covered in Section 107 in Volume 5 of the PRM.

At www.dummies.com/go/raspberrypiprojects, you can find an application we've written called !Tiler, which takes an image in the form of a sprite and reflects it in a number of ways in a kaleidoscope-like manner. The result is an image that is a 4 x 4 copy of the original image, so four times larger in each dimension. Each 2 x 2 block is a reflection of the original sprite. However, in a bit of a mind-boggling stretch, the original image may be reflected along a diagonal in a number of different ways. Figure 17-5 shows the way that the sprites can be reflected.

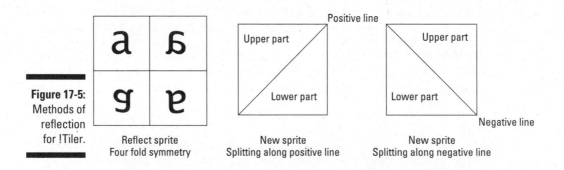

Figure 17-5:
Methods of
reflection
for !Tiler.

Reflect sprite
Four fold symmetry

New sprite
Splitting along positive line

New sprite
Splitting along negative line

Basically, you can split a rectangle along one of two diagonal lines. Reflections can be made on a diagonal from bottom left to upper right, known as a *positive line* (or P for short). The part of the sprite reflected can be above this line (known as U for upper part or L for lower part).

The reflection could also occur on the opposite diagonal — from the upper right to lower left of the sprite. This is known as a *negative line* (or N for short). Again, the part of the sprite above or below this can be used for the reflection.

Thus, this gives four extra modes, as well as the simple reflection mode:

- **8 Fold PU:** Positive slope, use above the line, or upper, part of the image
- **8 Fold NU:** Negative slope, use above the line, or upper, part of the image
- **8 Fold NL:** Negative slope, use below the line, or lower, part of the image
- **8 Fold PL:** Positive slope, use below the line, or lower, part of the image
- **4 Fold:** Just the original sprite reflected

When you've created an image you like, you can save it or try it out as a background image on your desktop. If you want to make it permanent feature of your desktop, menu-click anywhere on the desktop and choose Save and click OK. Figure 17-6 shows an example of what it produces. The original image was a part of the Midget drawing in the `Documents/Images/Artworks` directory.

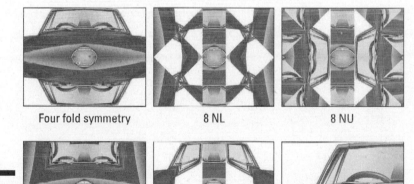

Four fold symmetry   8 NL   8 NU

Figure 17-6:
!Tiler
output.

8 PL   8 PU   Original image

Chapter 18

Transistor Tester

• •

In This Chapter

▶ Understanding how a transistor works

▶ Finding out about NPN and PNP transistors

▶ Discovering how to control I2C devices from RISC OS

▶ Building a fully functional, small-signal transistor tester

▶ Writing software to control and analyze the measurement made on the transistor

▶ Getting a desktop application version of the software

• •

*T*his project is perhaps one of the most useful things we've ever made (if we do say so ourselves). Not only does it test to see if a transistor is working, but it tells you its gain and even what the pin out is. This is great not only for trawling through transistors recovered from recycled boards, but also for saving you the time of looking through data sheets and trying to identify the specific packaging version of any transistor that you have. This is a valuable working tool that we come back to again and again during the course of constructing electronic equipment. It also serves as a good example of using the I2C bus to construct a stand-alone piece of equipment.

The transistor tester project consists of four basic aspects:

✔ You need to understand what you're going to measure and why.

✔ You need a means of configuring the transistor's wiring to achieve a test circuit.

✔ You need a way of taking measurements on the transistor and getting them back into the computer.

✔ You need software to take the measurements, analyze them, and display the results.

We cover all these subjects in this chapter.

Getting Acquainted with Transistors

Transistors are the foundation of modern electronics. All devices contain transistors in one form or another. Although patented as early as 1925, the first working transistor was not made until 1947. In the 1950s, transistors became commercially available, and the word *transistor* was synonymous with the word *radio*. In fact, radios were described by the number of transistors they contained. A five-transistor radio was a common standard. Today, a microprocessor chip like the one in the Raspberry Pi contains billions of transistors, all fabricated on a single chip.

But what *is* a transistor? A better name for it would be a *valve* (except the thermionic vacuum valve was in common use almost 50 years before the first transistor, so that name was already taken) because it does accurately describe what a transistor does. With a valve of any type, a large flow of something is controlled by a small amount of something else. So, you can control the water flow into your house with a few turns of a screw. Similarly, a transistor uses a small flow of electricity to control a much larger flow of electricity. We call the flow of electricity *current*.

In essence, a transistor consists of a three-layer sandwich of two different types of material — N-type and P-type semiconductors. The semiconductor bit means that the material is partway between an insulator and a conductor. What makes these two types of semiconductor different is the way electricity is carried in them. In N-type material, electrical conduction is mainly by means of negative charge carriers; in P-type material, it's mainly by means of positive charge carriers.

At this point, beginners are often confused and ask, "What direction does current flow?" The answers to that question, while all true, depend on the substance through which the electricity is flowing, and have different levels of complexity:

- **It doesn't matter.** This answer is the simplest. It simply doesn't matter in which direction the current flows. Often, a question of direction arises because beginners think that direction matters. "But what if the current flows through this resistor first?" they say. Flow is taken as a whole, through a whole circuit. The current flowing into a simple resistor is the same as the current flowing out of it. A resistor by itself does not "use up" current or reduce voltage.

- **From positive to negative.** Positive-to-negative flow is called *conventional current flow*. It helps to *think* of a flow direction even though the direction doesn't matter, so this direction is what we use in this book and what all electrical and electronics books use.

✔ **From negative to positive.** Flow from negative to positive is sometimes wrongly considered to be the correct direction. This is because, in most solid materials, the majority of charge carriers are negative electrons and they do flow in that direction. The "conventional" explanation for this is that earlier experimenters didn't know which way current flowed, so they guessed (and guessed wrong). Actually, early experimenters *did* know which way current flowed, but they were studying current flow in liquids where most charge is carried by positive ions. In other words, they were studying a P-type material, although such a term was not known at the time.

There are two types of transistors, defined by what types of material make up the "filling" and "bread" of the "sandwich": NPN transistors and PNP transistors.

✔ **NPN transistors:** NPN transistors (see Figure 18-1) are the most common type of transistor today. As the name implies, there are two layers of N-type material with a "filling" of P-type material. Each layer is brought out to a separate wire to give the three connections of a transistor — the collector, emitter, and base. If we make a small current flow through the base/emitter junction, a larger current will be forced to flow from the collector to the emitter.

The ratio of the two currents — that is, the collector-to-emitter current, over the base-to-emitter current — defines the gain of the transistor. This is sometimes called the *amplification factor,* but it's important to understand that the input current itself does not get amplified. Instead, the input current causes a much larger current to flow in the output. As the input current increases, the output current increases by the same factor. It's a bit like a mechanical pantograph where one action causes a much larger secondary action. Note that you can only get an output current up to what your power supply can provide.

The symbol of a transistor is shown in Figure 18-1. An important thing to note is the arrow on the emitter. Here, it points out of the symbol, which means it's an NPN transistor. A diagram with that arrow pointing the other way means it's a PNP transistor.

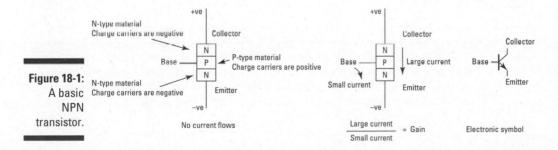

Figure 18-1:
A basic
NPN
transistor.

✔ **PNP transistors:** When transistors first became available, they were nearly all PNP transistors because they were easier to make using the technology available at the time. A PNP transistor is sometimes known as an "upside-down transistor" because it's used just like an NPN transistor, but the supply voltages are inverted when compared to an NPN transistor. Figure 18-2 shows the two types of transistors in action.

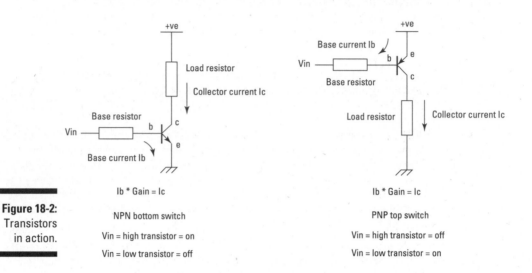

Figure 18-2:
Transistors
in action.

There are three ways of connecting a transistor. Here we look at just the most common way of using a transistor, called a *common emitter circuit.* In a common emitter circuit, the emitter is connected to the common point between input and output (that is, both the input and the output have a common point, and that's the emitter). The less often used configurations are the common collector circuit (sometimes called an emitter follower circuit) and the common base circuit.

Note that because the transistor is a symmetrical three-layer sandwich, you should be able to swap the collector and emitter and have the same sandwich. A transistor wired up with its emitter and base swapped over will still function as a transistor.

Resistors are used to limit the current flow over a wide range of voltages. In the circuit on the left in Figure 18-2, the NPN transistor conducts more collector-to-emitter current as the input voltage increases. However, if you look at the voltage on the collector, the more current that flows, the lower that voltage will be. It has to be that way because, in order to make more current flow through the resistor, it has to, in effect, reduce the resistance between the collector and the emitter. Sometimes we say that this circuit is a signal inverter because a high voltage in at the base results in a low voltage out at the collector.

On the right side of Figure 18-2 is a PNP transistor. Note that the emitter here is connected to the positive rail. So, in order to get a current to flow between the emitter and the base, the base has to be a lower voltage than the emitter. Therefore, to turn off the transistor, the base needs to be up to the rail; to turn it on, it has to be a low voltage. There is still the signal inversion — a low voltage on Vin still gives a high voltage on the collector. The transistor works just the same, only upside down.

If you think of the transistor as a switch, it's between the collector and emitter, controlled by a voltage on the base. Then you can think of the NPN as a bottom switch — it turns on the load (puts current through the load resistor) by connecting it to ground. On the other hand, the PNP transistor is a top switch — it turns on the load by connecting it to the positive supply rail.

Configuring Transistors

In this project, I use a simple but effective means of testing a transistor: First, with no base current applied, measure the collector current. Then apply a voltage to the base resistor and measure the collector current again. If the collector current increases in the second reading, it's a good transistor and you can calculate the gain from the ratio of collector current to base current.

Measurement circuit

Measuring current involves measuring the voltage across a known resistor value. Then, by making a calculation using Ohm's law, you can work out the current. This is how most current measurements work. Therefore, you have to wire up the transistor under test in a way that you can measure the two currents (see Figure 18-3).

The base resistor and the collector resistor have been split into two resistors in order to measure the current. This has been done to keep the voltages produced within the limits of the chip we're going to use for the measurements. The collector and base resistors are very different: One is 220R (ohms) and the other is 220K (thousand ohms). Note that the transistor is tested under very small currents, the base resistor and a 5V supply means the base current is only 10uA. Small currents are where transistors are at their best. The gain will tend to drop off as the base current increases.

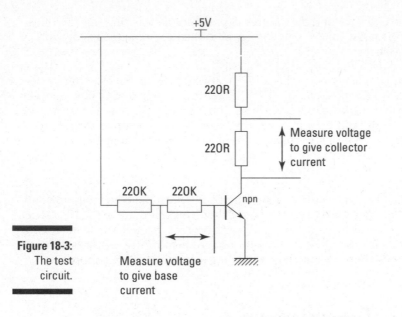

Figure 18-3:
The test
circuit.

Switching configurations

If you just implemented the circuit in Figure 18-3, it would be simple enough to make the tester, but we wanted to find out not only the gain but also the pin-out of the transistor. In order to do that, you must measure the gain with every combination of wiring for the transistor pins. That means each of the inputs connectors, which hold the transistor under test, must be capable of being switched to be a collector, an emitter, or a base, in a common emitter mode for both PNP and NPN transistors.

That's quite a lot to get your head around in one go, especially if you look ahead at the schematics for this project shown later in this chapter. So we'll break it down into steps.

The 74HC4066 (which you use in the circuit shown in Figure 18-9) is a quad bilateral switch. The "quad" bit means there are four in one package, and the "bilateral" bit means current can flow in both directions. So, in effect, this looks like a simple on/off switch that can be controlled by a logic-level input. This is exactly what you need to switch the input pins of the transistor under test to the four basic positions in the circuit — base, collector, 5V, and ground.

Figure 18-4 shows what that switching arrangement should look like. We've labeled each switch with an *S* prefix number and the transistor's input connector with a simple number.

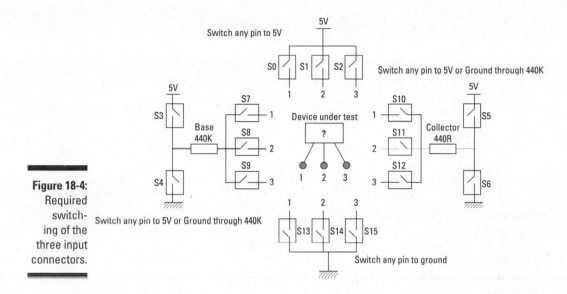

Figure 18-4:
Required switching of the three input connectors.

Switches S0 to S2 connect 5V to either of the three input connectors, and S13 to S15 do the same for the ground. To the left, S7 to S9 connect any of the three transistor connectors to a resistor; likewise, the switches S10 to S12 do the same, albeit a different value of resistor. The other end of these resistors must be capable of being switched to either 5V or ground to cope with the possibility of having an NPN or a PNP transistor.

This scheme does carry a bit of danger in that, for example, if switches S1 and S14 were to be closed at the same time, there would be a short circuit across the supply and things might melt. Likewise, S3 and S4 should never be on at the same time, nor should switches S5 and S6, S0 and S13, or S2 and S15. You have to make sure that only certain combinations of switches are on at any one time.

For an NPN transistor with the base on connector 1, the emitter on connector 2, and the collector on connector 3, in order to have this transistor configured correctly for a gain measurement, switches S3, S5, S7, S12, and S14 must be turned on while all the other switches are off. This is shown in Figure 18-5.

If you set the switches like this and measure the currents, and you see a gain, then you have an idea that you have a working NPN transistor with the "base, emitter, collector" configuration. What you have to do is go through each valid configuration and write down the states of the switches. We've done this, and the result is shown in Figure 18-6.

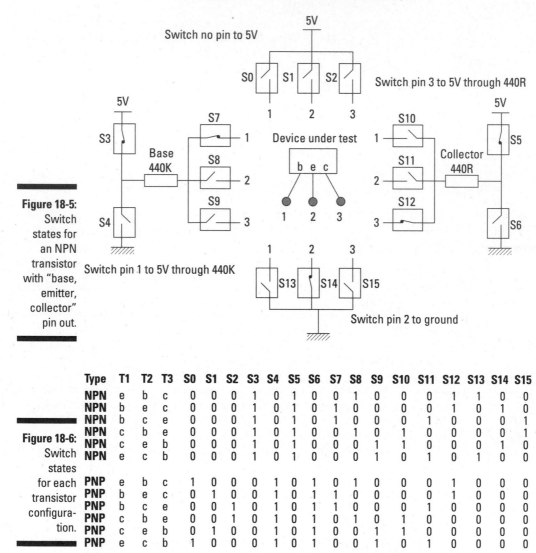

Figure 18-5:
Switch
states for
an NPN
transistor
with "base,
emitter,
collector"
pin out.

Figure 18-6:
Switch
states
for each
transistor
configura-
tion.

Type	T1	T2	T3	S0	S1	S2	S3	S4	S5	S6	S7	S8	S9	S10	S11	S12	S13	S14	S15
NPN	e	b	c	0	0	0	1	0	1	0	0	1	0	0	0	1	1	0	0
NPN	b	e	c	0	0	0	1	0	1	0	1	0	0	0	1	0	1	0
NPN	b	c	e	0	0	0	1	0	1	0	1	0	0	1	0	0	0	1
NPN	c	b	e	0	0	0	1	0	1	0	0	1	0	1	0	0	0	1
NPN	c	e	b	0	0	0	1	0	1	0	0	0	1	1	0	0	0	1	0
NPN	e	c	b	0	0	0	1	0	1	0	0	0	1	0	1	0	1	0	0
PNP	e	b	c	1	0	0	0	1	0	1	0	1	0	0	0	1	0	0	0
PNP	b	e	c	0	1	0	0	1	0	1	1	0	0	0	1	0	0	0
PNP	b	c	e	0	0	1	0	1	0	1	1	0	0	1	0	0	0	0
PNP	c	b	e	0	0	1	0	1	0	1	0	1	0	1	0	0	0	0
PNP	c	e	b	0	1	0	0	1	0	1	0	0	1	1	0	0	0	0
PNP	e	c	b	1	0	0	0	1	0	1	0	0	1	0	1	0	0	0

There are six different combinations of input pins for each of the two types
of transistor, giving 12 combinations in all. Each switch is either a 0 for off or
a 1 for on. Note how switches S3 and S5 are on for every combination of NPN
transistor and off for every combination of PNP transistor. Also, note how S5
is always the opposite of S6 and likewise for S3 and S4; to do otherwise would
cause a short as we mention earlier. These then are the set of combinations
for the switches for each measurement. The combination whose measurements makes sense tells you the pin out of the transistor.

Designing the Circuit

When designing a circuit, it's always best to start with a block diagram, one that shows the broad functions and how they interrelate. The transistor tester's block diagram is shown in Figure 18-7.

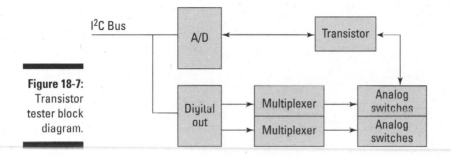

I²C Bus

On the left, there is the I2C connecting both the analog-to-digital (A/D) converter and the digital outputs to the Raspberry Pi. The A/D converter is then connected to the resistors in the test circuit, and the test circuit itself is connected to the analog switches. Because there are only 8 output lines from the I2C digital chip we used, these lines are expanded up to 16 by means of a multiplexer (an addressable latch, to be precise).

The I2C bus is a simple system of connecting many devices to the same pins. Each device has a unique address to use for communication. In theory, up to 128 can be used on the one bus. In practice, this is normally fewer than ten or so devices. There has to be a pull-up resistor on each of the two lines of the bus. It's built into the hardware design of the Raspberry Pi, so there is no need to add them to anything you attach to this bus. It also copes with the 3V3-to-5V conversion. Devices can be powered with 5V, but the data signals themselves can be 3V3, forming a neat interface.

Raspberry Pi interface circuit

The circuit of the transistor tester is simpler to understand if it's split into two parts. The first part is the I2C interface from the Raspberry Pi and is shown in Figure 18-8.

The interface circuit consists of two chips: PCF8591 (the A/D converter) and PCF8574A (the digital input/output). If you've read *Raspberry Pi For Dummies,* you know we used the PCF8591 for some projects in that book as well. It's a versatile chip offering a four-input A/D converter and a single D/A output.

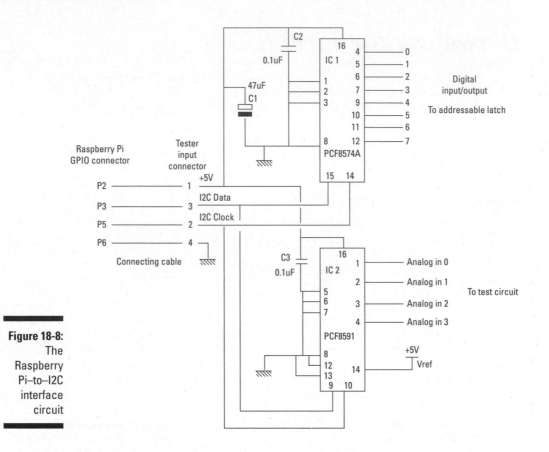

Figure 18-8:
The
Raspberry
Pi–to–I2C
interface
circuit

We won't be using the D/A output in this project, but we will be using all four analog inputs. There is a mode that this chip can operate in, in which you can configure the inputs into two differential pairs of inputs. A differential A/D converter is one that measures the difference in voltage between two inputs. If input 0 is a higher voltage than input 1, the difference has a positive value; if it's the other way around, it has a negative value. The same applies for inputs 2 and 3: If 2 is higher, it's positive; otherwise, it reads negative. This is exactly what you need to measure the current in the base and collector circuits because when they're configured for a PNP transistor, these currents are negative; they're positive for an NPN transistor.

All the external address lines on these two chips are connected to ground, which makes the actual I2C address of each device their base, or lowest address. Note that there are two types of the digital input/output chip — the PCF8574 and the PCF8574A. They're identical chips, but they have a different base address. If you use a PCF8574, you have to alter the software; this change is just one line, though.

The capacitors C1 to C3 are decoupling capacitors and should be fitted as close to the chips as possible. The value of C1 isn't critical, but C2 and C3 must be of the ceramic type.

Test circuit

The test circuit part of the project is shown in Figure 18-9; the component numbering leads on from the previous schematic. There are two 74LS259 addressable latch chips, and four 74HC4066 bilateral switches. Each chip should have a 0.1uF capacitor soldered across the power and ground as close to the chip as possible. (These are omitted from the schematic to make the wiring look less cluttered, which is a standard practice for some schematics.)

Note that output 3 (pin 7 of IC1 in Figure 18-6) is not used and so does not appear in Figure 18-9.

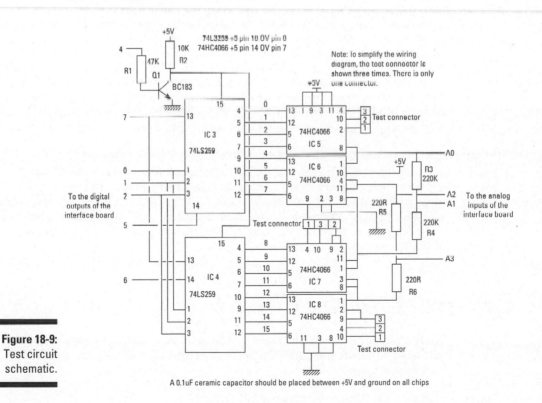

Figure 18-9:
Test circuit
schematic.

A 0.1uF ceramic capacitor should be placed between +5V and ground on all chips

The other thing to note is that the test connector is shown three times, again to keep the wiring from being cluttered. There is only one connector, and pin 1 on the real connector should be connected to the three instances of pin 1 shown in the schematic. This sort of thing in a schematic is known as *intersheet connections,* and it's often used to make wiring less cluttered, although some people take it too far and have hardly any connecting wires shown at all.

The idea of the 74LS259 addressable latch is that the number of the output you want to change is placed on the select lines — pins 1, 2, and 3 — as a binary number. The logic level you want to set that output to is placed on pin 13, the data input. Then that value is transferred to the addressed output when pin 14, the enable line, is taken low and then high again. You see that the input pins to both latches are wired together apart from the enable, pin 14. This is so we can trigger the two latches independently.

There could be a problem if the wrong switches are turned on, so we've made use of pin 15, the clear input. This sets all the output latches to 0 and turns all the switches off. However, on powering up, the outputs of the 74LS259 could be at any state, so it would be good if you could arrange the clear input to be low on power up, because it may be some time before the software has a chance to do anything. Although you don't know the state of the 74LS259 outputs, you do know the power-up state of the PCF8574A's outputs — they're high. There is no magic about this — it's just that it says so in the data sheet. Unfortunately, this is opposite of what you want. Therefore, we've put in a transistor, Q1, to invert the power-up state of the PCF8574A's, ensuring that all the switches power up in a state of being turned off.

The 74HC4066 can be replaced with other chips of the same type, like the CD4066. It's the 4066 part that defines the function. There are subtle differences between these different chips, but they mainly concern the *on resistance* of the switch. For this application, it's very small compared to the other resistances in the circuit. IC5 handles switches S0 to S4, IC6 handles switches S5 to S8, and so on. Resistors R3 to R6 are the series resistors used to measure the currents in the base and collector.

Constructing the Circuit

We built the circuit on stripboard in a small plastic box. Before you start you need to gather the parts. Component reference numbers are shown in parentheses.

- One 47uF electrolytic capacitor (C1)
- Eight 0.1uF ceramic capacitors (C2–C9)
- One 47K resistor, ¼ or ⅛ watt (R1)

- One 10K resistor, ¼ or ⅛ watt (R2)
- Two 220K resistors, ¼ or ⅛ watt (R3–R4)
- Two 220R resistors, ¼ or ⅛ watt (R5–R6)
- One PCF8574A–I2C digital I/O (IC1)
- One PCF8591–I2C A/D (IC2)
- Two 74LS259–octal addressable latches (IC3–IC4)
- Four 74HC4066–quad bilateral switches (IC5–IC8)
- One BC183 or similar general-purpose NPN transistor (Q1)
- Three miniature crocodile/alligator clips (test connector)
- One 0.1-inch pitch stripboard, with 4-x-2-inch strips running vertically
- Ten M2 10mm screws, washers, and nuts
- One plastic box measuring at least 2¼ x 4⅜ inches
- One 8-pin two-row 0.1-inch header socket
- One 4-pin single-row 0.1-inch header socket
- One 4-pin single-row header pins plug
- One 6-inch four-core cable
- Four 14-pin DIL sockets (optional)
- Four 16-pin DIL sockets (optional)

We always use IC sockets in our projects. They're very handy for fault finding, and the ICs are reusable on other projects. They also make the testing easy in that you can plug in the chips one at a time for testing the circuit, as we describe later in this chapter. However, you can save a bit of money if you solder them directly onto the stripboard.

We found a 2¼-x-4⅜-inch plastic box and trimmed our stripboard to suit. Then we drilled four holes in the corners of the stripboard and the box to fasten the two together. We fitted the sockets and cut the tracks between the pins on each side of the IC and also on the tracks between ICs. Most of the wiring was done on the underside of the board. This is just about the minimum space you can use. You may want to use a bigger box and piece of stripboard to give yourself a bit more room. The finished project is shown in Figure 18-10.

To allow hot plugging, you need to first connect the ground and positive supply and then finally the signals. If you look at something like an SD card or a USB memory stick, you'll see some connections longer than the others. As you plug it in, the longer connections get made first.

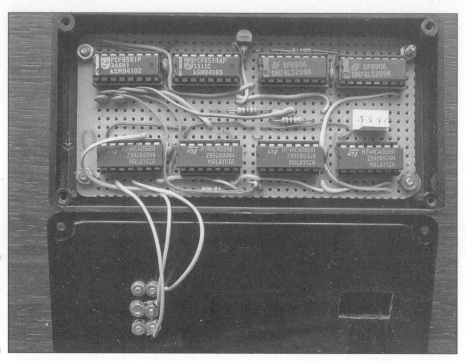

Figure 18-10:
The
transistor
tester circuit
board.

The I2C connector back to the Raspberry Pi is in the center-right of the board. We cut a small square hole in the top of the lid to get access to the pins.

The test connector is made up of three miniature alligator/crocodile clips. These are just about an inch long. We drilled two M2 holes in the back end of each one, and mounted them on the box lid as close together as we could without their touching. You can see the connections to the back of these screws in Figure 18-10. In Figure 18-11, you can see them from the top; this shows how you can connect a transistor to them. The most vital thing is that you label each clip 1 to 3, because the software is going to tell you what number clip is what connection on the transistor.

We used a polarized pin header for the lead back to the Raspberry Pi. You may want to solder a lead straight in. At the Pi end, we used a twin row socket just four connectors long on each side (eight connectors in all) and fitted them over the end of the Pi's P1 plug. Because we need only four connections, there isn't much point in getting a full-width connector, but you have to be careful to get the pins aligned.

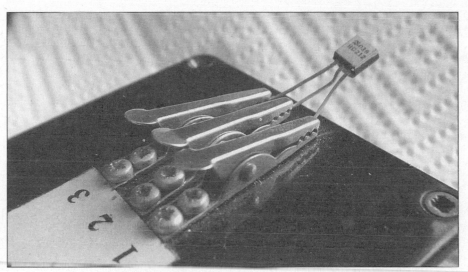

Figure 18-11:
The test transistor clips.

Writing the Software

Having built the hardware, it's now time to look at the software to drive it and perform the analysis of the results. Get the interface working one bit at a time. This is where sockets come in. Just plug in IC1, connect to the Pi, and power up.

Never plug something into the Raspberry Pi when it's powered up unless the thing you're plugging in is designed for hot plugging, like a USB connector.

Testing the digital interface

Now, if you have a system with just IC1 fitted, type Listing 18-1 to test out the digital interface.

Listing 18-1:   Testing the I2C Interface

```
10 : REM> I2C Test digital out
20 : PRINT"I2C BUS OUTPUT"
30 : PRINT"Binary count to device at &70"
40 : PRINT"By Mike Cook"
50 : DIM PBK% 3
60 : REPEAT
70 : FOR A%=0 TO 255
```

(continued)

Listing 18-1 *(continued)*

```
 80 : ?PBK%=A%
 90 : SYS "IIC_Control",&70,PBK%,1
100 : TIME = 0: REPEAT : UNTIL TIME > 1
110 : NEXT
120 : UNTIL FALSE
```

This sends a binary count to the digital output pins of IC1. To test that it's getting there, wire up an LED and a 1K resistor, put the positive end to 5V, and touch the negative end on each of the outputs in turn. At output 0, you should see the LED blink rapidly. As you touch the higher outputs, the LED will blink increasingly slowly.

The line that actually outputs data to the I2C lines is line 90 (page 977 in Volume 1 of the PRM tells you all about it). Note that it's called IIC, which is an alternate name for the I2C bus that was more popular at the time the operating system was written.

The first parameter passed to it is the address. This is a full 8-bit address with the least significant bit determining if it's a read (=1) or a write (=0) operation. The next points to a block of memory (4 bytes) that contains the data to transfer. In our case, we dimensioned the variable PBK% to point to 4 bytes of memory. Line 50 says three, but that's the highest byte number to use and we start at zero. The final parameter is the length of the block in bytes. This is one, because we only want to send the one byte. The block is set up with the loop variable in line 80, using the indirection operation question mark (?).

Line 100 is a 10mS delay. Try removing this line and you see that most of the outputs are flashing so fast that they look like they're on all the time.

Now if you have sockets on your circuit, you can test the analog input, power down, fit IC2, power back up, and run the program in Listing 18-2.

Listing 18-2:   Analog Input Test

```
 10 : REM> I2C Test analogue input
 20 : PRINT"I2C BUS Analogue Input"
 30 : PRINT"Read an A/D device at &90"
 40 : PRINT"By Mike Cook"
 50 : DIM PBK% 3
 60 : ?PBK% = 0
 70 : SYS "IIC_Control",&90,PBK%,1
 80 : REPEAT
 90 : SYS "IIC_Control",&91,PBK%,1
100 : PRINT "Reading ";?PBK%
110 : TIME = 0:REPEAT : UNTIL TIME >50
120 : UNTIL FALSE
```

The program sets up the PCF8591 to just read analog input 0, which is done by writing 0 to the control register (line 70). Then there is an endless loop that reads the value from the analog results register (line 90), which prints it out and then has a half-second delay before repeating. In line 90, note that the least significant bit of the address is set to 1, meaning it is a read operation. The memory block PBK% is reused so that it receives the data from the I2C bus, with the indirection operator (?) being used to fetch the actual byte at this address for the print statement.

When you run this, you see numbers being printed out. If you touch a ground wire onto pin 1 of IC2, you should see this number go to 0. If you touch the pin with your finger, you should see the numbers change randomly, and if you touch a wire between pin 1 and the 5V line (pin 16), the number should go to 255, the maximum.

Setting the switches

Having tested the two I2C devices, it's time to plug in the rest of the ICs and consider what we need to do to test a transistor. Figure 18-6 showed what states you need to set each switch to in order to get the correct configurations. This showed the switches from left to right. But in order to turn those switches into numbers, we need to reverse that order so that bit 0 of the number controls switch 0 and bit 15 of the number controls switch 15. So we simply reverse the bit pattern and turn it into a number. Using hex makes things so much simpler, as shown in Figure 18-12.

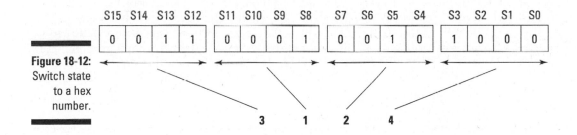

Figure 18-12: Switch state to a hex number.

This is for the first line, where the transistor is an NPN with a pin out of emitter, base, collector, and yields a hexadecimal value of &3124. This process needs to be repeated for each line in the table and transferred into an array.

Now BBC BASIC has a neat way of handling sets of numbers like this, one that we think is far better than C or Python: the DATA statement. This is a line that contains a sequence of numbers or strings. To get that into an array, there is a READ statement that takes the next value and puts it into the variable that accompanies the READ statement. This is way more efficient and flexible than assigning each array element individually, which is what you have to do in other languages if you want to redefine the contents of an array.

The configuration list along with switch states to test for that configuration are shown in Listing 18-3.

Listing 18-3: Initializing the Configuration and Switch Arrays

```
REM Initialise switch pattern
DEF PROC_SPinit
LOCAL A%
FOR A%=0 TO 11
  READ Lead$(A%),Config%(A%)
NEXT
DATA ebc,&3128,cbe,&8528,ecb,&2A28,ceb,&4628,bce,&88A8,bec,&50A8
DATA ebc,&1151,cbe,&0554,ecb,&0A51,ceb,&0652,bce,&08D4,bec,&10D2
ENDPROC
```

Notice how the READ statement has two array variables: a string for the pin out and a number for the switching configuration. It's in a FOR loop, and the loop variable is used as the array index. When data is exhausted from one DATA statement, the program automatically looks to the next DATA statement.

Having acquired the number that defines the switch configuration, you have to use it to set the switches. That means driving the two addressable latches to have the switch states on their outputs correspond to this number. Figure 18-9 showed you what the schematic of the latches is, it does not help a programmer very much to know what to do. So, in Figure 18-13 you can see a programmer's view of the addressable latches.

This gives the view of the individual bits of the I2C digital interface and how they drive the addressable latch. Bit 4 is the clear input. When it's high, all the bits in the latch are cleared — that is, set to zero. This is very handy for quickly turning off all the switches when you're changing configurations. You need to do this so that in moving from one configuration to another you don't accidentally turn on a forbidden combination of switches that would cause a short circuit.

Analog readings

When it comes to making the voltage measurements that allow you to determine the currents in base and collector, you need to set the PCF8591's configuration register to be two differential inputs. This is done by setting bits 4 and 5 in the control register. The channel number in this mode is set by just bit 0. So, to read the collector current, first write the hex value &30 into the control register and then read the value, and for the base current write &31 into the control register and read the results.

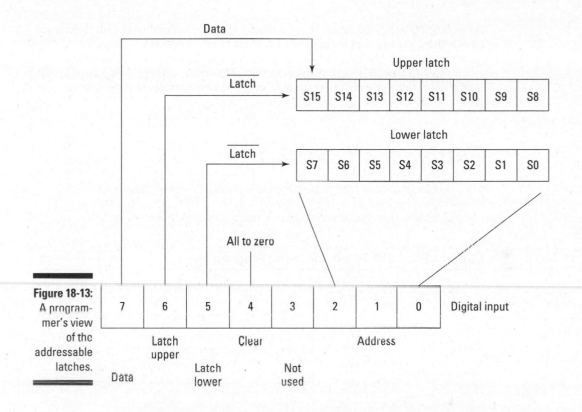

Figure 18-13:
A program-mer's view
of the
addressable
latches.

So, to set up any one switch, you have to set bits 0 to 2 to the least significant three bits of the address you want to write to. Put the data you want to write onto bit 7. Then pulse bit 6 if the most significant bit of the address you want to write to is 1; otherwise, pulse bit 5 if it is a 0. This involves you in a little piece of numeric gymnastics using bit shifts.

Transistor testing methodology

As we mention earlier, a transistor will work with its emitter and collector swapped over — the difference being that when it's wrong, the gain is smaller. Therefore, when testing a transistor, you need to make a note of the gain for each configuration. You must also guard against the case where the transistor has a short between collector and emitter. That initially may look like it has a high gain, so for a good transistor, you need to see that you don't have this high gain when you remove any base current. If you do this, and you still have a high gain, you know you have a faulty transistor. Similarly, a current reading of 0 in the collector when you do have base current also indicates that the transistor is faulty.

As you test each configuration, you need to keep a record of the configuration if the gain you just measured is greater than any gain you previously measured. So, at the end of looking at all the combinations, you have the combination that gives the maximum gain. However, if the maximum gain is less than two or you reached the end of the combinations with no maximum gain set, then you know it's a faulty transistor.

Putting it all together

Let's see how all this comes together and produce a program to test our transistor. The listing for this is shown in Listing 18-4. Note that this is just a simple BASIC program at the moment, not a desktop application.

Listing 18-4: **The Transistor Tester Program**

```
 10 : REM>IICtt
 20 : PRINT"IIC Transistor Tester"
 30 : PRINT"By Mike Cook"
 40 : DIM PBS% 4,PBK% 8,Lead$(12),Config%(12)
 50 : AA%=&90 : REM Analogue Chip Address
 60 : DA%=&70 : REM Digital Chip Address for 8594A - &40 for 8574
 70 : PRINT"8574 chip at ";~DA%;" and 8591 chip at ";~AA%
 80 : PROC_SPinit
 90 :
100 : REPEAT
110 : MGain%=0
120 : LC%=12
130 : PRINT
140 : PRINT SPC(15);"Ic        Ib        Gain"
150 : FOR A%=0 TO 11
160 : IF A%<6 THEN Type$="NPN" ELSE Type$="PNP"
170 : Gain%=0
180 : REM First test with no base current
190 : PROC_Mulout(Config%(A%) EOR &18)
200 : IF DeviceD%=FALSE THEN PRINT"IIC Digital chip not responding":END
210 : PRINT Type$;" ";Lead$(A%);"  ";
220 : PROC_AIN
230 : IF DeviceA%=FALSE THEN PRINT"IIC Analogue chip not responding":END
240 : IF ABS(col%)<5 THEN
250 : PROC_Mulout(Config%(A%))
260 : PROC_Analyse
270 : ELSE
280 : PRINT"Not Valid"
290 : ENDIF
300 : IF Gain%>MGain% THEN MGain%=Gain%:LC%=A%:Atype$=Type$
310 : NEXT
320 : REM Disconnect transistor
```

```
330 : PROC_Rsm
340 : PRINT
350 : IF LC%=12 OR MGain%<2 THEN
360 : PRINT"Faulty transistor"
370 : ELSE
380 : PRINT"This is a ";Atype$;" transistor, pinout "Lead$(LC%);" Gain
        ";MGain%
390 : ENDIF
400 : PRINT"Press any key for another test"
410 : A$=GET$
420 : UNTIL FALSE
430 :
440 : DEF PROC_Analyse
450 : PROC_AIN
460 : Ic=((5*col%)/256)/220
470 : Ib=((5*bas%)/256)/220000
480 : IF Ib<>0 AND Ic<>0 THEN Gain%=Ic/Ib
490 : PRINT ;Ic;" ";Ib;" ";Gain%
500 : ENDPROC
510 :
520 : DEF FNtc(N%)
530 : IF N%>&7F THEN N%=&FFFFFF00 OR N%
540 : =N%
550 :
560 : DEF PROC_Rsm
570 : ?PBK%=&FF
580 : SYS "XIIC_Control",DA%,PBK%,1 TO ;Fl
590 : ENDPROC
600 :
610 : DEF PROC_Mulout(N%)
620 : LOCAL A%,B%,C%,M%
630 : PROC_Rsm
640 : FOR A%=0 TO 15
650 : B%=N% AND 1
660 : N%=N%>>1
670 : M%=B%<<7 OR A% OR &60
680 : ?PBK%=M%
690 : SYS "XIIC_Control",DA%,PBK%,1 TO ;Fl
700 : C%=M%
710 : IF A%>7 THEN C%=C% AND &BF ELSE C%=C% AND &DF
720 : ?PBK%=C%
730 : SYS "XIIC_Control",DA%,PBK%,1 TO ;Fl
740 : ?PBK%=M%
750 : SYS "XIIC_Control",DA%,PBK%,1 TO ;Fl
760 : NEXT
770 : IF (Fl AND 1) =1 THEN DeviceD%=FALSE ELSE DeviceD%=TRUE
780 : ENDPROC
790 :
800 : DEF PROC_AIN
```

(continued)

Listing 18-4 *(continued)*

```
 810 : LOCAL Fl,B%
 820 : ?PBS%=&30
 830 : REM Set up the control register
 840 : SYS "XIIC_Control",AA%,PBS%,1 TO ;Fl
 850 : SYS "XIIC_Control",AA% OR 1,PBK%,2 TO ;Fl
 860 : bas%=PBK%?1
 870 : ?PBS%=&31
 880 : SYS "XIIC_Control",AA%,PBS%,1 TO ;Fl
 890 : SYS "XIIC_Control",AA% OR 1,PBK%,2 TO ;Fl
 900 : IF (Fl AND 1) =1 THEN DeviceA%=FALSE ELSE DeviceA%=TRUE
 910 : col%=PBK%?1
 920 : col%=FNtc(col%)
 930 : bas%=FNtc(bas%)
 940 : ENDPROC
 950 :
 960 : REM Initialise switch pattern
 970 : DEF PROC_SPinit
 980 : LOCAL A%
 990 : FOR A%=0 TO 11
1000 : READ Lead$(A%),Config%(A%)
1010 : NEXT
1020 : DATA ebc,&3128,cbe,&8528,ecb,&2A28,ceb,&4628,bce,&88A8,bec,&50A8
1030 : DATA ebc,&1151,cbe,&0554,ecb,&0A51,ceb,&0652,bce,&08D4,bec,&10D2
1040 : ENDPROC
```

This will test a transistor attached to the hardware and print out the results in terms of transistor type, pin out, and gain. Lines 50 and 60 define the addresses of the two I2C devices. If you set the external address lines or get a PCF8574 instead of a PCF8574A, then you only have to change the address here.

The infinite loop of the main program goes from line 100 to line 420. It prints out the result of testing each configuration as it goes and finally comes up with a result. Because the first six configurations are for NPN transistors, the current transistor type is easily set; this is done in line 160.

Next, the transistor is tested for the current configuration, but with the base resistor switched to the common line. This is the test without any base current. This is done by simply exclusive ORing the configuration number with &18, which controls the two base switches, S3 and S4. It inverts the state of those bits so that where it would normally be set for a current source (high for PNP or low for NPN), it's switched to the same potential as the emitter. This is done in line 160.

Then, at line 250, the normal configuration is set and the transistor's readings are made and analyzed. This is repeated for all 12 configurations, and the transistor is disconnected. Then the conclusions are printed, and the program waits on a user pressing a key before doing it all again. To quit this program, press the Escape key.

Let's look more closely at some of the procedures that do the hard work. Line 560 is the start of the very short procedure Rsm (reset switch matrix). Its job is to write all 1s to the digital interface, thus triggering the latch's clear line. Notice that the SYS call has an X in front of it. This is a trick you can use in programming for the desktop. It means, "Don't throw an error if something goes wrong." This is to allow the calling program to handle any error, the TO;F1 at the end of the call is telling the computer to put the error byte into a variable F1. It isn't used in this procedure, but it's in the multiplex output procedure (Mulout).

This procedure takes in a number and outputs it to the multiplexed addressable latch. This is the numeric gymnastics we mention earlier. It writes the number passed to it one bit at a time in a FOR loop starting at line 640. The least significant bit of the number is put into the variable B%, and then the number is shifted one place to the right to move the next bit into the least significant bit for next time around the loop.

The variable M% in line 670 is used to gather the bits you need to write to the digital output. First, the bit you want to write is shifted up seven places to the left. To put it into bit 7, this is the logically ORed with the loop counter (which is the latch address), as well as the number &60, which sets the two data latches high. This is then written to the digital output. Then the appropriate data latch is set to low and again this is sent out to the device. Finally, the first number is written to the output again. This ensures that the data and address is stable on the latch inputs before the enable line is sent low and then high. The procedure also used the error flag F1 to set a variable that tells if the analog device is actually present.

The procedure AIN (analog in) sets the channel to read and then reads it. Note that when reading the data back, the byte we're interested in is the second byte. Hence, line 860 uses the ?1 indirection operator (meaning one byte away from that pointed to by the variable).

The function tc may look odd. It just takes in a number and converts it from the 8-bit signed value received from the A/D converter into a 32-bit signed value that BASIC uses.

When this code is run, it produces an output like the following:

```
IIC Transistor Tester
By Mike Cook
8574 chip at 70 and 8591 chip at 90
              Ic          Ib        Gain
NPN ebc  0 0 0
```

(continued)

```
NPN cbe  Not Valid
NPN ecb  0 0 0
NPN ceb  Not Valid
NPN bce  0 0 0
NPN bec  Not Valid
PNP ebc  -2.752130682E-3 -9.232954547E-6 298
PNP cbe  -1.775568182E-4 -9.854403409E-6 18
PNP ecb  Not Valid
PNP ceb  0 0 0
PNP bce  Not Valid
PNP bec  0 0 0

This is a PNP transistor, pinout ebc Gain 298
```

Note the two lines with a gain are configurations where the collector and emitter are swapped over. However, you can see the drastic reduction in gain for the "wrong" pin out.

Out to the desktop

Now that listing is all well and good, but it isn't a desktop multitasking application. The code for that is too long to print here, but it's downloadable at www.dummies.com/go/raspberrypiprojects. Just like the example in the last chapter, the listing shown here is the working part of the code. All the rest is wimp stuff.

Figure 18-14 shows a portion of the screen while it's running. You just need to click the Test box to run a new test, and the window displays the gain, transistor type, and pin out. Happy testing!

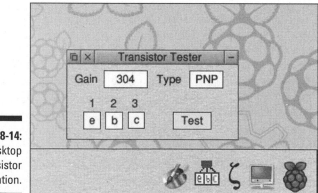

Figure 18-14: The desktop transistor application.

Chapter 19

The General-Purpose Input/Output Port in RISC OS

***

In This Chapter

▶ Seeing how to access the GPIO pins under RISC OS

▶ Making an LED blink

▶ Mixing BASIC and machine code

***

*I*n this chapter, we show you how to use the GPIO pins under RISC OS. We present the obligatory flashing LED, a sort of "Hello world!" for hardware. We also tell you how to speed up output using machine code embedded into the BASIC program. Finally, we show you how to read a GPIO input.

When you know the fundamentals of using the GPIO from RISC OS, you can handle any interfacing project. After reading this chapter, you may want to try to write the programs for the projects in Chapters 5 and 6 in BBC BASIC instead of the Python we used. Have fun using this hidden side of the Raspberry Pi!

Using the GPIO Pins in RISC OS

In the last chapter, we look at using the I2C bus, which occupies just two of the pins of the GPIO connector. Both the Raspberry Pi Model A and the Raspberry Pi Model B have 17 pins available to control or monitor things, whereas the Raspberry Pi Model B+ and Raspberry Pi 2 Model B+ have 28 pins. However, in order to talk to these pins under RISC OS, you have to resort to a little trickery.

The GPIO port is described on page 89 of the Broadcom BCM2835 ARM Peripherals reference manual (www.raspberrypi.org/wp-content/uploads/2012/02/BCM2835-ARM-Peripherals.pdf), which may seem overwhelming at first, but when you break it down isn't so difficult.

To read or write physical logic levels on those pins you read or write to memory locations within the chip. These special memory locations are connected to logic circuits that eventually appear as signals on the GPIO lines. The Raspberry Pi is made from an advanced chip, so there are many options and modes that the GPIO pins can operate in, which can be very confusing at first.

Each GPIO pin is capable of being switched between various hardware peripherals inside the chip. Each pin can be switched to being an input or an output, but there are six other alternative options for each pin, although not all the options are actually connected to anything. GPIO pin 18 is one pin with more alternate functions than most. A diagram of how the GPIO pins are switched, and GPIO 18 in particular, is shown in Figure 19-1.

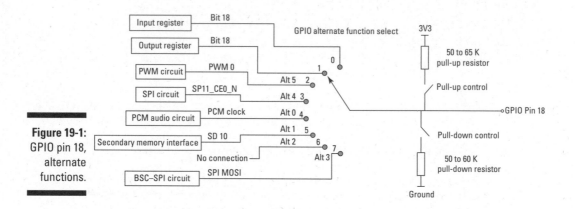

Figure 19-1:
GPIO pin 18, alternate functions.

This diagram may look complex, but it's a simplification of how every pin is wired up. The only difference between this pin and the others is what extra circuitry, associated with the ALT (alternative) functions, it's connected to. In a move whose reason is perhaps known only to the chip designers, the switch positions and the alternative function numbers do not match up. So, when the switch is in, say, position 4, as defined by the alternate function register bits for that pin, it is said to be in the ALT 0 position.

On the end of each pin are two switches allowing the pin to be pulled up, pulled down, or not connected to either resistor. Pulling a pin gives a default input level, if needed, for the pin. Note that the resistor values are not very precisely defined, because it's difficult to fabricate accurate resistor values in a silicon integrated circuit (IC). All input pins must be driven to one logic level or the other, and using an internal pull-up or pull-down resistor is the simplest way to do this.

Most of the time, someone is kind enough to provide a library to sort these registers and functions into manageable proportions. There are several libraries for GPIO manipulation under Linux; each language has a choice of more than one. Things are slightly more complex under RISC OS for two reasons:

- ✔ The operating system remaps the address of these registers.

- ✔ The area of memory allocated to these registers is accessible only when the processor is running in supervisor mode, and you can only enter that from machine code. Fortunately, using machine code is easy to do from BASIC.

There is a GPIO library, implemented as a relocatable module (RM), from a user who goes by the name of Tank, at www.tankstage.co.uk/software. html. RMs are the way RISC OS extends its operating system. Over the years, the number of modules has grown, and most of the operating system updates are now performed by adding RMs. This is the equivalent of libraries or drivers in Linux. You can see what modules are already loaded by opening a task window (menu-click the raspberry icon) and type **modules**. You can save this window or scroll up and down.

Getting an LED to Blink

Time to get practical. Here, we start off by blinking an LED. Every project we've worked on that uses a microcontroller starts off by blinking an LED. At the same time, you can control the speed of the blinking by a GPIO input. Follow these steps:

1. **Attach the cathode (negative end) of an LED to a ground pin, connect the anode to a 220R resistor, and connect the other end of the resistor to a GPIO pin.**

   A photograph and diagram of this are shown in Figure 19-2. Although the pin out labels in this figure are for a revision 2 or later board, the only pins used are unchanged on any board revision. We used single-pin header sockets to connect to the pins, and we soldered the LED and resistor between two of them. We used GPIO 17 for the LED output and a single wire connected between GPIO 4 and ground for the speed control input.

2. **Download and unpack the GPIO module from** www.tankstage. co.uk/software.html.

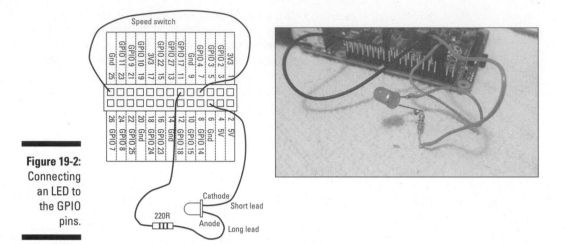

Figure 19-2:
Connecting
an LED to
the GPIO
pins.

3. **Double-click the file called GPIO.**

   This loads in the RM and adds extra software interrupt (SWI) calls to the operating system. You only need to do this once per boot-up. If you fail to do it, an error window will appear, telling you that there is an unknown SWI in any program in which you try to use the GPIO calls. Correctly loading this module results in no visible feedback.

4. **Now create a BASIC file and enter the program shown in Listing 19-1.**

Listing 19-1:   LED Blinking

```
 10 : REM GPIO blink
 20 : PRINT"Blink an LED"
 30 : PRINT"By Mike Cook"
 40 : PinOut%=17
 50 : PinIn%=4
 60 : SYS "GPIO_WriteMode", PinOut%,1 :REM Make output
 70 : SYS "GPIO_WriteMode", PinIn%,&18 :REM Make input with pull up
 80 : PRINT "Using GPIO ";PinOut%;" for the LED and ";PinIn%;" for speed
         control"
 90 : PRINT:PRINT"Escape to end"
100 : REPEAT
110 :    SYS "GPIO_WriteData", PinOut%,1
120 :    PROC_Delay
130 :    SYS "GPIO_WriteData", PinOut%,0
140 :    PROC_Delay
150 : UNTIL FALSE
160 :
170 : DEF PROC_Delay
180 : T% = TIME + 10
190 : SYS"GPIO_ReadData",PinIn% TO A%
```

```
200 : IF A% = 0 THEN T% = T% + 30
210 : REPEAT: UNTIL TIME>T%
220 : ENDPROC
```

Lines 40 and 50 define what GPIO pins to use for the LED and speed control. The operating system call in line 60 then sets the output, and line 70 sets the speed control as an input. Note that the first three bits of the number set the alternate mode switch, and the next two bits define if there is a pull-up resistor switched in and if it's a pull-up or pull-down.

It's much easier to define bit patterns like this in hexadecimal, because you can see the bit pattern almost directly. The number we used here is the hexadecimal value 18, which corresponds to the binary bit pattern 11000.

Finally, an infinite loop is entered that sets the output pin first to a 1 and then to a 0. This is called *toggling*. In between each of those operations, a delay procedure is called. This slows down the program so that you can actually see the blink. Otherwise, it blinks too fast and you think the LED is on all the time. The delay procedure sets the variable T% to a time 0.1 second ahead of the current time (line 180). Then line 190 reads the value on the input pin and puts it into the variable A%. If this pin is at 0 (that is, it's grounded), then an extra 0.3 second (or 30 centiseconds) is added to T%. The rest of the procedure then keeps checking the current time until it exceeds the variable T% when it will return.

5. **Save the file and then double-click it to run.**

   You should now have a happily blinking LED. Connect a wire between GPIO pin 4 and ground, and note how the blink rate slows down. Press the Escape key to stop it and try altering the numbers in the delay function.

6. **If you have access to an oscilloscope or a frequency counter, remove lines 120 and 140 and run the code again.**

   Look at the frequency, and you see that you can change the state of the LED every 48 microseconds (uS) or so. Although that is by no means the fastest it can go, this is an interpreted language and there is quite a lot of instruction needed to change just a single GPIO line.

   Note that this pulse train is not totally steady. This is because of interrupts going off to do things like updating the system TIME variable and looking at the keyboard input. But it's much steadier than the equivalent program running under Linux.

Mixing Languages

One of the biggest advantages of the RISC OS version of BASIC is that you can drop into machine code any time you need to make something go faster. Machine code is the raw language of the processor, so it executes at maximum speed. It isn't difficult to learn, but it is different.

The processor has 16 registers — R0 through R15 — or internal memory locations, to play about with. R15 is used as the program counter, so generally you don't use that. Registers R14 and R13 also have special uses with this operating system, as the return address storage and stack pointer, respectively, so you should avoid them. All the others are up for general use. You can also load and store registers in memory, but many of the machine code functions you may be writing don't involve that.

A good introduction to machine code programming is given in Appendix A of Volume 4 of the Programmers Reference Manual (PRM), which is already in the documentation directory of the RISC OS distribution. Alternatively, an up-to-date version is online at www.riscos.com/support/developers/prm/asm.html.

You use machine code from BASIC a bit like an assembler. You program in mnemonics, and when you run the program, BASIC turns this into machine code and places it into memory. For *forward referencing* (referring to memory location labels the assembler has not seen yet), you need the assembler to make two passes. This is done with a FOR loop and suppressing the errors during the first pass with the OPT call. You can save that memory block the machine code has been assembled into and load it into future programs if you like. But by far the simplest method is to run it in the same program because assembly is very quick and happens one time only.

As an example of using machine code, we've taken the LED blinking code, with no delays, and turned it into machine code version shown in Listing 19-2.

Listing 19-2:   Simple Machine Code Blink

```
10 : REM GPIO Speed Test
20 : PRINT"GPIO Speed Test"
30 : PRINT"By Mike Cook"
40 : PRINT"How fast can machine code flash an LED:-"
50 : Pin%=17
60 : SYS "GPIO_WriteMode", Pin%,1 :REM Make output
70 : PRINT"Using GPIO ";Pin%
80 : DIM CODE% 255
90 : FOR A%=0 TO 3 STEP 3
```

```
100 : P% = CODE%
110 : [
120 : OPT A%
130 : .entry
140 :     MOV R8,#&300000 :REM Change for longer time
150 : .loop
160 :     MOV R0,#Pin%
170 :     MOV R1,#1
180 :     SWI "GPIO_WriteData"
190 :     MOV R0,#Pin%
200 :     MOV R1,#0
210 :     SWI "GPIO_WriteData"
220 :   SUBS R8,R8,#1
230 :   BNE loop
240 :   MOVS PC,R14 : REM return to BASIC
250 : ]
260 : NEXT
270 : REPEAT
280 : PRINT "This will flash for 5 seconds"
290 : PRINT "Any key to continue - escape to quit now"
300 : A$ = GET$
310 : CALL entry
320 : UNTIL FALSE
```

This is still using the system calls that the GPIO module gives, but this time they're called from machine code. This means that they aren't interpreted by the BASIC language. You can't stop a machine code loop with the Escape key. We've written this program so that it loops for a fixed number of cycles before returning to BASIC. This takes about five seconds.

When calling an SWI from machine code, the parameters are passed and returned in the registers, using R0 for the first parameters, R1 for the next, and so on. When the SWI returns, R0 will contain the first returned value, R1 the second, and so on. Most calls have only one or two parameters. This explains why R0 needs to be loaded with the pin number to write to just before every call, because the value in R0 is overridden by the call itself when it exits.

Note that you can use variables set up in BASIC in your machine code, so the pin number to output to is what has been set up before. However, once the code is assembled, any further changes in that variable will not be recognized. Register R8 has a big number in it — it is the number of cycles to flash the LED before ending. After each flash, line 220 decrements this number and if it hasn't reached 0, it jumps back to the "loop" label.

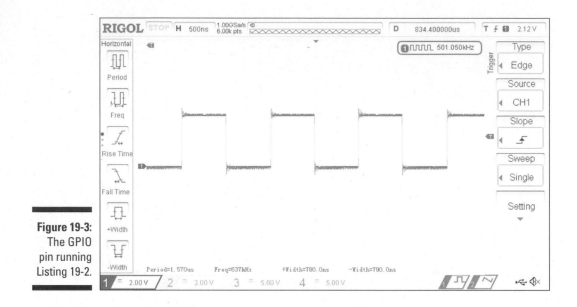

Figure 19-3:
The GPIO pin running Listing 19-2.

When you run this, you see that the LED looks like it's permanently on, but a bit dimmer than before. If you look at this pin with an oscilloscope, you see that it's rapidly turning on and off. Figure 19-3 shows a screenshot from our oscilloscope.

Basically, an oscilloscope gives you a graph of voltage against time. You can see that the pin is spending 780 nS high and then going low for about the same amount of time, which gives a frequency of 673kHz. The SWI is still doing a lot of work behind the scenes, and the absolute maximum speed you could toggle that pin is about 20MHz with the right software. Of course, at that speed, there is no time to do anything else.

In Tank's download, there is an application called !GPIOconfig. If you click that application, you get a graphic representation of the GPIO connector, which will change depending on whether you're using a Model B or a Model B+. Pins are shown outlined in red for inputs or green for outputs, and, rather cleverly, the center of the pin is filled in for a logic 1 and gray for a logic 0. The GPIO pins are already set up after running the last program, so you can see the link being connected and disconnected on pin 4 and, by clicking pin 17, you can make the LED turn on and off. A menu-click on any pin will bring up a small menu allowing you to select the mode of operation for the pin. Figure 19-4 shows this application for a Model B+.

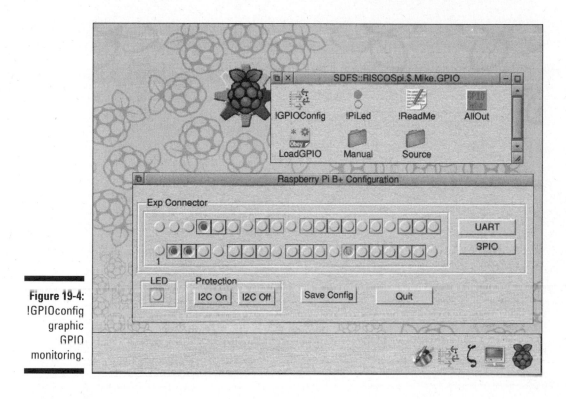

Figure 19-4:
!GPIOconfig
graphic
GPIO
monitoring.

Part VI
The Part of Tens

In this part . . .

- ✔ Find ten great LEGO Raspberry Pi projects from around the Internet.

- ✔ Find out about ten reliable suppliers of tools and components and learn about different classes of suppliers.

Chapter 20

Ten Great LEGO Pi Projects

In This Chapter

▶ Uncovering useful and interesting LEGO contraptions

▶ Using LEGO bricks with commercial software

▶ Bringing your old RXC brick back to life

*L*EGO bricks are great mechanical prototyping tools. They allow you to explore mechanical design with the minimum of tooling and construction. Although some people see them as nothing more than children's toys, those who know better see working with LEGO bricks as an exciting and quick way to give a physical side to your electronic projects.

Panobot

Created by Andrew Mulholland, the Panobot (http://pi.gbaman.info/?p=174) allows the Raspberry Pi to take a series of pictures using the Raspberry Pi camera. These pictures can then be stitched together to produce spectacular panoramic pictures. The Panobot works by moving the camera both up and down and left and right. It's run by a Python script, which allows you to set how wide the panorama should be and how many elevation pictures to take. After the images are taken, you download them to a laptop and stitch them together into one image using the application Hugin (http://hugin.sourceforge.net).

Andrew is a teacher in Northern Island who formed a robotics club at his school. The club won the FLL Northern Ireland Technical Design Award in 2012 and came in first in the category in the UK-wide PA Consulting Raspberry Pi competition. A photograph taken with the Panobot won the 2014 Adafruit Raspberry Pi photograph competition for Andrew as well.

MATLAB and Simulink

Not so much a single project but a whole bunch of projects using the Simulink package of the MATLAB language, this is a two-wheel balancing, edge-following, and obstacle-avoiding robot (`http://makerzone.mathworks.com/lego`). It can even balance on a ball, all from LEGO. MATLAB isn't free — a home license costs $149 as of this writing.

Raspberry Pi LEGO Case

There are lots of takes on producing a case for your Raspberry Pi using LEGO bricks. This may not be the most high-tech project you'll come across, but it's simple, fun, and practical! You can be creative and make your own unique case, or you can copy a case someone else has made — just search the web for images using the keywords "Raspberry Pi case." We particularly like the one at `www.raspberrypi-spy.co.uk/2012/06/my-raspberry-pi-lego-case`.

Book Reader

With a handful of LEGO bricks, a Raspberry Pi, and a Raspberry Pi camera, you can make a book reader. The camera takes photographs of the pages of the book and, using optical character recognition software, converts it into a text file. A LEGO contraption turns the pages of the book, and you can even use some free text-to-speech software to read the book out loud. This project requires a BrickPi (`www.dexterindustries.com/BrickPi`) for the control. Find out more at `http://makezine.com/projects/lego-bookreader-digitize-books-with-mindstorms-and-raspberry-pi`.

A Stop-Motion LEGO Movie

Be the next Nick Parker — make your own LEGO movie using the Raspberry Pi! You can create your own original film, or re-create a popular film or sporting event. During the FIFA World Cup 2014, England's goals were successfully reproduced by stop-motion LEGO (`http://gu.com/p/3q643/stw`). Matches involving the United States have also been reproduced in LEGO. You can find the project code and worksheets at `www.raspberrypi.org/learning/push-button-stop-motion`.

SriShooter

Using your mouse, a BrickPi, and the Raspberry Pi, you can control a ball-shooting robot to freak out your family. You can find the materials you need at www.dexterindustries.com/BrickPi/projects/shooter.

browserBot

browserBot is a web-browser-controlled robot using the BrickPi. You can control it from any computer, phone, or tablet connected to the same network, with only a few lines of code. This is a great beginner's project using the dedicated Raspberry Pi extension controller board. Find out more at www.dexterindustries.com/BrickPi/projects/browserbot.

BrickPi Remote Sentry Cannon

Using the Raspberry Pi camera with a gun sight overlay, this project employs a Python program to aim and fire a LEGO cannon via a network connection. Jasper Hayler-Goodall put this together using a BrickPi interface and the SriShooter to locate a target and fire. This just uses one axis of rotation to steer the robot and has a Pygame interface, which introduces a bit of lag into the video feedback. It isn't a perfect project, which means that it's ripe for improvement! Check it out along with Jasper's camera-feed remote-control vehicle, at http://topshed.tumblr.com.

LEGO Digital Clock

Hans Anderson designed a digital clock where the numbers are displayed on the face of Rubik's Cube–like blocks. Then blogger dwalton76 took it and wrote a version to use with the Raspberry Pi using Python and the BrickPi. The results are quite stunning. You can find out more at http://programmablebrick.blogspot.co.uk/2014/06/lego-digital-clock.html.

The Original LEGO MINDSTORMS

The original LEGO MINDSTORMS RCX kit has not been forgotten! This project shows you how to program it using your Raspberry Pi and a language called NQC. NQC stands for Not Quite C. It's a simple C-like language that you can use to program the original LEGO control brick using the USB IR tower of the 2.0 version of the kit or the serial IR interface of the earlier ones. There are still lots of projects online for the older system. Go to http:// minordiscoveries.wordpress.com/2014/01/20/using-nqc-on-a-raspberry-pi-to-program-a-lego-mindstorms-rcx-brick to find out how to recompile the NQC compiler, as well as how to get the base software on the brick. This project may be a bit involved, but it's worth it to bring your old controller back to life with the Raspberry Pi!

Chapter 21

Ten Suppliers of Components and Tools

*N*o matter what project you undertake, you need the right components, the right tools, and the idea. Most of this book is about the idea, but components and tools are vital for any project's success, and that's where this chapter comes in.

Farnell/Newark

Farnell (known as Newark in the United States) is a major distributor and partner of the Raspberry Pi Foundation. It has a vast range of parts, but it does tend to charge top price, and some one-off delivery charges on some items are high. You can start shopping at www.farnell.com or www.newark.com. A subsidiary of Farnell, called CPC, handles most hobby orders. Next-day delivery ensures minimum disruption to your projects.

Farnell also runs element14, a forum for developers and hobbyists, with web events, video tutorials, and webinars. You can find out more at www.element14.com.

RS Components

RS Components is the other major UK distributor. It used to be known as Radio Spares (not to be confused with Radio Shack in the United States). RS Components is hobbyist friendly and carries a great range of stock. Along with Farnell, it oversees the production and distribution of the Raspberry Pi. Find out more at www.rs-online.com.

Rapid Electronics

Rapid (www.rapidonline.com) tends to have some parts that are a lot cheaper than Farnell/Newark and RS Components, and it also has a specialized education section. Rapid's website is more hobbyist friendly, and although it doesn't have as wide a range as some distributors, it's worth looking at.

Mouser Electronics

Mouser (www.mouser.com) is another major distributor, bigger in the United States than in the UK, but still accessible worldwide. It has a wide range of items in stock and offers free shipping in the UK on orders over £50.

Digi-Key

The last of the big five major distributors, Digi-Key (www.digikey.com) ships product to more than 170 countries worldwide from a single location in Thief River Falls, Minnesota. It has a wide range of products and easily accessible data sheets, along with a good search section.

Proxxon

Proxxon (www.proxxon.com) is a German manufacturer of small, high-precision tools. Its tools aren't the cheapest, but they're the best we've come across. Often, small tools are just cut-down versions of larger ones, but Proxxon understand that, as you go smaller, you have to push up the precision of the tool. One of this book's authors, Mike Cook, couldn't be without his bench drill press, bench circular saw, and disc sander. They're made for light work and are ideal for model making and prototyping.

Adafruit

Adafruit (www.adafruit.com), founded by the now legendary Limor Fried (one of the founders of the open-source movement), is a strange hybrid of supplier and designer of hobbyist-friendly boards and sub systems. It supplies its own designs, taking advantage of whatever interesting components come on the market. Adafruit has produced a number of Raspberry Pi expansion boards, which it calls *plates*. It also organizes competitions and has regular live podcasts with a strong learning/teaching bias. Adafruit is based in the United States but has distributors in many countries.

SparkFun

SparkFun (www.sparkfun.com) is another hybrid supplier/designer like Adafruit, with its own manufacturing facility. As its name implies, SparkFun is enthusiastic and puts the fun into the subject. It offers a great many breakout boards, which are small PCB boards with a surface-mounted IC with easy soldered or breadboard access to the chips. Mainly a U.S.-based company, SparkFun has some worldwide distributors.

Electronic Goldmine

Electronic Goldmine (www.goldmine-elec-products.com) specializes in surplus components and equipment and is a veritable treasure trove of electronic delights. This is the sort of place you don't so much go looking for something specific, but instead look through its catalog and think, "Ooh, I could use that for. . . ."

E.M.A. Model Supplies

Electronic components are important, but so is the enclosure you put them in. Companies like E.M.A. (www.ema-models.co.uk) supply parts for making the mechanical components of a project, from sheet plastic to plastic beams, screws to glue, as well as a few tools.

Straight talk about pricing

The main problem with components and tools is that consumer electronics have given people the wrong idea about cost. In the past, it was always cheaper to make something yourself. Unfortunately, electronics doesn't work like that today. The process needed to make integrated circuits is, by and large, the same no matter how complex the circuit is; but when you go to buy one, you'll see a vast range of prices. This range of prices is mainly due to how new a device is, where the manufacturers are trying to cover their development cost, what the yield is (how many actually work off the end of the line), and last but no means least, the number you want to buy. When buying parts, quantity is everything.

Now, we're not talking about the quantities that the average hobbyist may buy. We're talking about industrial quantities that are measured in the millions of parts. Sure, there are small price breaks (sometimes for 10 or 100 of a single part), but most manufacturers won't get out of bed for anything less than half a million. This is where

distributors come in. They buy in bulk and sell to smaller buyers, taking a cut.

The last in the chain are the suppliers, which are different from distributors in that they're specifically geared toward hobbyists. By and large, suppliers sell you quality parts. But the new players on the block are the many suppliers on sites like eBay. They may have prices that look too good to be true — and in some cases, they are. A lot of these suppliers have limited quantities of end-of-line stock picked up for next to nothing, or even access to the reject bin of manufacturers, so you don't always get what you think, or the supply is limited. You can get some bargains, but you can also end up with junk. You can even find yourself with some fakes, where the chip actually looks fine but nothing is inside. Buying from less-than-reputable sites is a gamble, and there is little chance of getting your money back if anything goes wrong. You can't go wrong with the suppliers we mention in this chapter, but when you start shopping elsewhere, do your research and be prepared to get what you paid for it.

Index

● *G* ●

• H •

• I •

Notes

Notes

Notes

About the Authors

Mike Cook: Mike has been making electronic things since he was at school. Former Lecturer in Physics at Manchester Metropolitan University, he wrote more than 300 computing and electronics articles in the pages of computer magazines for 20 years starting in the 1980s. Leaving the university after 21 years when the Physics Department closed down, he got a series of proper jobs where he designed digital TV set-top boxes and access control systems. Now retired and freelancing, he spends his days surrounded by wires, exhibiting at maker fairs, and patrolling the forums as Grumpy Mike.

Jonathan Evans: Jonathan has a lifelong interest in computers and electronics. Captivated by the microcomputer age in the 1980s, he taught himself how to program a computer and quickly learned the marriage between computers and electronics. He has gone on to become a distinguished IT professional with more than 20 years of experience. His passion for creation and innovation combines perfectly with the Raspberry Pi phenomenon. In his spare time, he enjoys exploring projects to make the Raspberry Pi relevant to everyday life. He enjoys sharing his ideas at http://projects.privateeyepi.com, where he continues to explore the endless possibilities of this computing platform.

Brock Craft: Brock is a lecturer in creative coding in the Department of Computing at Goldsmiths, University of London, and a senior tutor at the Royal College of Art. He is a specialist in physical computing, data visualization, and the Internet of Things. Brock's background is in the field of human–computer interaction; he has more than a decade of experience making interactive things that people can use, explore, and play with. When he isn't teaching and learning, Brock likes to make interactive stuff and digital art.

Dedication

To my sons, Alec and Graham. I am very proud of them both. As different as chalk and cheese while being the same as peas in a pod.

—Mike Cook

For Joann, Gabriella, and Jemma.

—Jonathan Evans

For Barbara and Eleanor.

—Brock Craft

Authors' Acknowledgments

I would like to thank Brock Craft and Jonathan Evans for their contributions to this book. I would also like to thank the staff at John Wiley & Sons for all their help, encouragement, cajoling, and cooperation, especially Craig Smith, Katie Mohr, Linda Morris, and Elizabeth Kuball.

—Mike Cook

Thanks to my wonderful family for allowing me the space to dedicate time to this book. Thanks also to the talented staff at Wiley, in particular Craig Smith, who spotted me and converted me from blogger to writer. Full credit to my two co-authors, especially Mike, who provided technical assistance with Chapter 9: Advanced Interfaces and whose idea spawned the Connect Four section in Chapter 11: Webcam and Computer Vision.

—Jonathan Evans

Putting this book together has been a long and rewarding process. It would not have been possible without the support of my family, colleagues, and friends, to whom I owe a tremendous debt of gratitude. I also thank my many students, whose questions have inspired me to come up with all kinds of new projects and ideas. Finally, I acknowledge the tireless work of my co-authors, with whom I've had the great pleasure to collaborate.

—Brock Craft

Publisher's Acknowledgments

Senior Acquisitions Editor: Katie Mohr

Project Editor: Elizabeth Kuball

Copy Editor: Elizabeth Kuball

Technical Editor: Daniel Soltis

Production Editor: Vinitha Vikraman

Cover Image: © Mike Cook

Apple & Mac

iPad For Dummies,
6th Edition
978-1-118-72306-7

iPhone For Dummies,
7th Edition
978-1-118-69083-3

Macs All-in-One
For Dummies, 4th Edition
978-1-118-82210-4

OS X Mavericks
For Dummies
978-1-118-69188-5

Blogging & Social Media

Facebook For Dummies,
5th Edition
978-1-118-63312-0

Social Media Engagement
For Dummies
978-1-118-53019-1

WordPress For Dummies,
6th Edition
978-1-118-79161-5

Business

Stock Investing
For Dummies, 4th Edition
978-1-118-37678-2

Investing For Dummies,
6th Edition
978-0-470-90545-6

Personal Finance
For Dummies, 7th Edition
978-1-118-11785-9

QuickBooks 2014
For Dummies
978-1-118-72005-9

Small Business Marketing
Kit For Dummies,
3rd Edition
978-1-118-31183-7

Careers

Job Interviews
For Dummies, 4th Edition
978-1-118-11290-8

Job Searching with Social
Media For Dummies,
2nd Edition
978-1-118-67856-5

Personal Branding
For Dummies
978-1-118-11792-7

Resumes For Dummies,
6th Edition
978-0-470-87361-8

Starting an Etsy Business
For Dummies, 2nd Edition
978-1-118-59024-9

Diet & Nutrition

Belly Fat Diet For Dummies
978-1-118-34585-6

Mediterranean Diet
For Dummies
978-1-118-71525-3

Nutrition For Dummies,
5th Edition
978-0-470-93231-5

Digital Photography

Digital SLR Photography
All in One For Dummies,
2nd Edition
978-1-118-59082-9

Digital SLR Video &
Filmmaking For Dummies
978-1-118-36598-4

Photoshop Elements 12
For Dummies
978-1-118-72714-0

Gardening

Herb Gardening
For Dummies, 2nd Edition
978-0-470-61778-6

Gardening with Free-Range
Chickens For Dummies
978-1-118-54754-0

Health

Boosting Your Immunity
For Dummies
978-1-118-40200-9

Diabetes For Dummies,
4th Edition
978-1-118-29447-5

Living Paleo For Dummies
978-1-118-29405-5

Big Data

Big Data For Dummies
978-1-118-50422-2

Data Visualization
For Dummies
978-1-118-50289-1

Hadoop For Dummies
978-1-118-60755-8

Language & Foreign Language

500 Spanish Verbs
For Dummies
978-1-118-02382-2

English Grammar
For Dummies, 2nd Edition
978-0-470-54664-2

French All-in-One
For Dummies
978-1-118-22815-9

German Essentials
For Dummies
978-1-118-18422-6

Italian For Dummies,
2nd Edition
978-1-118-00465-4

Ⓔ **Available in print and e-book formats.**

Available wherever books are sold. **For more information or to order direct visit www.dummies.com**

Math & Science

Algebra I For Dummies,
2nd Edition
978-0-470-55964-2

Anatomy and Physiology
For Dummies, 2nd Edition
978-0-470-92326-9

Astronomy For Dummies,
3rd Edition
978-1-118-37697-3

Biology For Dummies,
2nd Edition
978-0-470-59875-7

Chemistry For Dummies,
2nd Edition
978-1-118-00730-3

1001 Algebra II Practice
Problems For Dummies
978-1-118-44662-1

Microsoft Office

Excel 2013 For Dummies
978-1-118-51012-4

Office 2013 All-in-One
For Dummies
978-1-118-51636-2

PowerPoint 2013
For Dummies
978-1-118-50253-2

Word 2013 For Dummies
978-1-118-49123-2

Music

Blues Harmonica
For Dummies
978-1-118-25269-7

Guitar For Dummies,
3rd Edition
978-1-118-11554-1

iPod & iTunes
For Dummies, 10th Edition
978-1-118-50864-0

Programming

Beginning Programming
with C For Dummies
978-1-118-73763-7

Excel VBA Programming
For Dummies, 3rd Edition
978-1-118-49037-2

Java For Dummies,
6th Edition
978-1-118-40780-6

Religion & Inspiration

The Bible For Dummies
978-0-7645-5296-0

Buddhism For Dummies,
2nd Edition
978-1-118-02379-2

Catholicism For Dummies,
2nd Edition
978-1-118-07778-8

Self-Help & Relationships

Beating Sugar Addiction
For Dummies
978-1-118-54645-1

Meditation For Dummies,
3rd Edition
978-1-118-29144-3

Seniors

Laptops For Seniors
For Dummies, 3rd Edition
978-1-118-71105-7

Computers For Seniors
For Dummies, 3rd Edition
978-1-118-11553-4

iPad For Seniors
For Dummies, 6th Edition
978-1-118-72826-0

Social Security
For Dummies
978-1-118-20573-0

Smartphones & Tablets

Android Phones
For Dummies, 2nd Edition
978-1-118-72030-1

Nexus Tablets
For Dummies
978-1-118-77243-0

Samsung Galaxy S 4
For Dummies
978-1-118-64222-1

Samsung Galaxy Tabs

For Dummies
978-1-118-77294-2

Test Prep

ACT For Dummies,
5th Edition
978-1-118-01259-8

ASVAB For Dummies,
3rd Edition
978-0-470-63760-9

GRE For Dummies,
7th Edition
978-0-470-88921-3

Officer Candidate Tests
For Dummies
978-0-470-59876-4

Physician's Assistant Exam
For Dummies
978-1-118-11556-5

Series 7 Exam For Dummies
978-0-470-09932-2

Windows 8

Windows 8.1 All-in-One
For Dummies
978-1-118-82087-2

Windows 8.1 For Dummies
978-1-118-82121-3

Windows 8.1 For Dummies,
Book + DVD Bundle
978-1-118-82107-7

e Available in print and e-book formats.

Available wherever books are sold. **For more information or to order direct visit www.dummies.com**

Take Dummies with you everywhere you go!

Whether you are excited about e-books, want more from the web, must have your mobile apps, or are swept up in social media, Dummies makes everything easier.

Leverage the Power

For Dummies is the global leader in the reference category and one of the most trusted and highly regarded brands in the world. No longer just focused on books, customers now have access to the For Dummies content they need in the format they want. Let us help you develop a solution that will fit your brand and help you connect with your customers.

Advertising & Sponsorships

Connect with an engaged audience on a powerful multimedia site, and position your message alongside expert how-to content.

Targeted ads · Video · Email marketing · Microsites · Sweepstakes sponsorship

21 Million Monthly Page Views & 13 Million Unique Visitors

# of For Dummies

Custom Publishing

Reach a global audience in any language by creating a solution that will differentiate you from competitors, amplify your message, and encourage customers to make a buying decision.

Apps • Books • eBooks • Video • Audio • Webinars

Brand Licensing & Content

Leverage the strength of the world's most popular reference brand to reach new audiences and channels of distribution.

For more information, visit www.Dummies.com/biz

A Wiley Brand